ALSO BY TIMOTHY M. GAY

Tris Speaker: The Rough-and-Tumble Life of a Baseball Legend

Satch, Dizzy & Rapid Robert

THE WILD SAGA OF INTERRACIAL BASEBALL BEFORE JACKIE ROBINSON

Timothy M. Gay

Simon & Schuster
NEW YORK   LONDON   TORONTO   SYDNEY

Photo credits: 2–4,6–8, 10, 17, 18, 23–28 courtesy of the
Baseball Hall of Fame; 9 courtesy of the North Dakota Historical Society;
5, 11–14, 16, 20–22, 29 courtesy of the Ben and Alma Jones Archives;
1, 15 courtesy of Transcendental Graphics; 19 by Jim Hansen, photographer,
Look Magazine Collection, Library of Congress, Prints & Photographs Division
(Reproduction Number 55-6347)

Simon & Schuster
1230 Avenue of the Americas
New York, NY 10020

First Simon & Schuster hardcover edition March 2010

SIMON & SCHUSTER and colophon are registered trademarks
of Simon & Schuster, Inc.

For information about special discounts for bulk purchases,
please contact Simon & Schuster Special Sales at
1-866-506-1949 or business@simonandschuster.com.

The Simon & Schuster Speakers Bureau can bring authors
to your live event. For more information or to book an event,
contact the Simon & Schuster Speakers Bureau at
1-866-248-3049 or visit our website at www.simonspeakers.com.

Designed by Paul Dippolito

Manufactured in the United States of America

1   3   5   7   9   10   8   6   4   2

Library of Congress Cataloging-in-Publication Data

Gay, Timothy M.
Satch, Dizzy & Rapid Robert : the wild saga of interracial baseball before Jackie
Robinson / Timothy M. Gay.
p.   cm.
1. Baseball—United States—History. 2. Discrimination in sports—
United States. 3. African American baseball players—History.
4. Negro leagues—History. 5. Paige, Satchel, 1906–1982.
6. Dean, Dizzy, 1910–1974 7. Feller, Bob, 1918– I. Title.
GV863.A1G398 2010
796.357' 640973—dc22   2009027132

ISBN 978-1-4165-4798-3
ISBN 978-1-4391-7631-3 (ebook)

To the Beautiful Life of Patrick Ryan Gay
1985–2007
My Nephew and Hero

The past is a long and twisty road.
—LEROY "SATCHEL" PAIGE

Contents

Author's Note

I began researching this book in October 2006 by covering the Pop Lloyd conference outside Atlantic City, New Jersey, an annual gathering that celebrates the glories of the old black baseball leagues. That weekend was the first time I'd had the pleasure of interviewing distinguished Negro Leaguers. Among others, I spent an enlivening couple of hours in the company of Stanley "Doc" Glenn, the president of the Negro League Baseball Players Association's board of directors.

Doc is a trim, soft-spoken man now in his eighties. A former catcher for the Philadelphia Stars of the Negro National League, he carries himself with a bearing almost military in its correctness. When Doc reminisces about the thrill of catching Satchel Paige, though, his eyes twinkle and an impish grin appears.

Glenn is blessed with looks that belie his age. "Good black don't crack," the late Buck O'Neil liked to joke when people complimented Buck's appearance. Doc Glenn doesn't waste a word; every phrase is measured, at least when a tape recorder is running.

Doc was a keynoter that evening at the Lloyd banquet. "You have a long time to be dead and a short time on this earth to do some good," he told the audience, drawing warm applause. "There is no time to be bitter."

He left such an impression that I bought a copy of his memoirs, *Don't Let Anyone Take Your Joy Away: An Inside Look at Negro League Baseball and Its Legacy.* Doc's book is full of much gentle wisdom; it should be required reading for young people of every race.

During our first interview, Doc had been reluctant to discuss his exposure to bigotry as a young man; he deftly sidestepped several questions. But when we met a second time that night, he shared a chilling story. In 1951, after seven years in the Negro Leagues, Doc was signed by the Boston Braves organization. That spring, the Braves' minor leaguers trained for a time in Meridian, Mississippi.

The Meridian hotel where the Braves' prospects were staying would not allow Doc, the team's lone African American, to bunk there. Nor was he allowed to dine with white teammates in the hotel restaurant. Clerks insisted that Doc take his meals outside, on a patio next to the pool. Sensing an opportunity for sweet mischief, after each meal Doc would jump in and thrash around for a minute or two. And following each dip, the hotel staff would drain the pool—for fear that no white guest would deign to swim in water tainted by a black man.

Doc never made it to the big leagues. After leaving the Braves organization and spending a couple of years playing integrated ball in Canada, he returned to Philadelphia and expanded his wholesale electrical supplies business. Now, to his credit, he's determined to help other former Negro Leaguers live their twilight years in dignity—and to ensure that their contributions to the pastime and society are not forgotten.

After I bade Doc good night, I drove to my motel a few minutes across town. From its decaying exterior, it was clear that the place had at one time been a Howard Johnson's. Weeds now sprouted in a parking lot that hadn't been paved in years.

Before checking in, I pulled into a gas station around the corner. Since this was New Jersey, where pumping your own gas is tantamount to a capital offense, an attendant trudged out.

He glanced at my out-of-state plates and asked, "Where ya headed?"

"Next door," I gestured. "I'm spending the night there."

He winced, then looked around in a conspiratorial way. "Be careful," he hissed. "It's all nig—" he caught himself—"All black back there, you know."

Less than twenty minutes had passed since Doc had told me the Meridian story. Yet here was disheartening evidence that all these years later, ethnic fear continues to divide us. Even with an African-American in the White House, racial issues make many Americans uncomfortable, especially if we come from upbringings as cloistered as mine.

My childhood was spent in Warren, Pennsylvania, a stately Allegheny River town that struck it rich in the old oil days. The intervening decades haven't always been kind; the specialty steel plants that kept the place humming were all but shuttered years ago. Like a lot of towns in the Rust Belt, Warren is hurting. But Victorian homes still grace boulevards lined with oak, maple, and birch.

A few of those manses were around in 1895, when a twenty-one-year-old infielder from outside Pittsburgh came upriver to play for Warren's entry in the Iron and Oil League. Honus Wagner batted .377 that summer, presaging his greatness to come. Pop Lloyd, a nimble shortstop, was often called the "black Honus Wagner." After Hans watched Lloyd in action, Wagner said he was flattered by the comparison.

Warren was lily-white in Hans's day; the town's ethnicity has changed little in the past century. It also happens to have been the hometown of Robert Peterson, the late journalist and historian whose 1970 book *Only the Ball Was White* spawned renewed interest in the Negro Leagues. Young Bob was a good enough catcher to have played against the Homestead Grays and other black teams as they barnstormed through Warren. He was behind the plate at Russell Field one afternoon when the Grays' Josh Gibson hit a shot over the trees in left center that caused jaws to drop, Bob's included. The indelible image of Josh's blast never left Bob—nor did the specter of black men trying to get by in a segregated America.

"The arrival of black ballplayers was a signal event in Warren," Bob wrote years later. "They were viewed as exotic figures from another world, which, in a sense, they were. I believe townspeople were more oblivious to race than racist. Still, the black men could not lodge in Warren's two hotels, and no doubt they had to take their food at the back door of restaurants."

I wish my recollections of Warren's racial attitudes were as benign as Bob's—but they're not. One of my early basketball coaches loved to toss around the "n" word when appraising black players from Franklin or Meadville. The coach was also fond of derogatory labels such as "coon" and "chocolate drop," as in "Dammit, don't let those little chocolate drops beat you!" Despite his stirring oratory, teams with black players routinely stomped us.

Doc Glenn would be the first to tell you that he was a journeyman catcher. He'll never be confused with Josh Gibson or Biz Mackey or Ted "Double Duty" Radcliffe or Joe "Pig" Greene or Quincy Trouppe or other iconic Negro League receivers.

But Doc's book helped me grasp the sad nobility of blackball, a term that encompasses the Negro Leagues, both "major" and "minor," as well as the full gamut of barnstorming outfits. As Bob Peterson put it, "Negro baseball was at once heroic and tawdry, a gladsome thing and a blot on America's conscience." The same can be said of the interracial exhibitions played against the backdrop of Jim Crow America. It took no small amount of heroism back then to stage certain black-white games—but the whole exercise was shamefully tawdry.

Interracial contests had been part of the pastime's fabric for a half century before Satchel Paige, Dizzy Dean, and Bobby Feller came on the scene. Almost every luminary from baseball's early days—black and white—played in these exhibitions. Interracial games were no different than other barnstorming affairs: they were fueled by club owners, players, and promoters out to grab extra cash. Black-white exhibitions evolved willy-nilly, usually at the tail end of the major leagues' regular season. Still, they proved enormously popular. By the 1920s, interracial ball was so big among fans on the West Coast that it often eclipsed interest in the World Series, infuriating Commissioner Kenesaw Mountain Landis.

A few years later, when Paige, Dean, and Feller were on the marquee, black-white games became even bigger box office. Think how Bill Cosby and Robert Culp stirred the cultural *zeitgeist* in television's *I Spy*—and that was *after* passage of the 1960s civil and voting rights acts. Paige, Dean, and Feller were out on baseball's hustings before Cosby was born—and long before bigotry became a societal epithet.

Historian Bruce Chadwick limned the beautiful grit of black baseball in *When the Game Was Black and White*. "All the [separate] seating sections in ballparks," Chadwick wrote, "the angry orders that 'niggers can't dress here,' the segregated restaurants, run-down black-only hotels, dirty laundry, 'redneck' cops, bigotry, and racism, all those things meant something. The Negro Leaguers didn't just change baseball, they changed their country, forever."

So, in a small but indispensable way, did the games that Paige and fellow blackballers played against Dean, Feller, and other white big leaguers in the years before integration. To be sure, these men were out to make a buck, not make history. Nevertheless, history was made. In their short time on this earth, they did some good.

—*Timothy M. Gay*
Vienna, Virginia, 2009

Satch, Dizzy & Rapid Robert

May 1942

It takes both black and white keys of a piano to
play the "Star-Spangled Banner."

—CHESTER L. WASHINGTON, COLUMNIST,
PITTSBURGH COURIER

The crowd surging into Wrigley Field that late May afternoon was loud and raucous, looking for a good time. Chicagoans needed to smile: five months earlier, their lives had been upended by an abrupt bulletin from a navy base in Hawaii. The latest news from the Pacific Theater was bleak: after a bloody siege, Corregidor, the Allies' last lifeline in the Philippines, had finally fallen. In all, some ninety thousand weary American and Filipino troops—many wounded or already suffering from disease and malnutrition—were now prisoners of the Imperial Japanese Army.[1]

This day, though, promised something of a respite from the travails against Tojo and Hitler. Baseball's most flamboyant pitchers, longtime barnstorming rivals Dizzy Dean and Satchel Paige, were squaring off.

Promoted by black-sports impresario Abe Saperstein and billed as a fund raiser for wartime charities, the exhibition had been hyped hard in the Chicago papers. Ol' Diz and his makeshift squad of white "all-stars" were taking on Ol' Satch and his Kansas City Monarchs, perennial champions of the Negro American League (NAL).

Since first joining forces in 1933, the two consummate showmen had barnstormed together all over the country. A Diz-Satch game was almost as much vaudeville as baseball, often featuring dueling impersonations, pantomimed trash talk, feigned (and sometimes real) outrage at umpiring decisions, crazy-legged baserunning, and other

1

goofball antics. The old troupers loved to put on a show—and the big crowd streaming into Wrigley knew it.

Dean and Paige were such surefire box office lures that Saperstein snagged them to meet in two other "war charity" exhibitions that spring, one at Griffith Stadium in Washington, D.C., the other at Victory Field in Indianapolis. Paige was so beholden to the cocksure promoter that Satch dubbed him "Abraham Lincoln-stein."[2]

It was a Sunday, a few minutes before three o'clock. Many of the thirty thousand patrons pouring out of cabs and streetcars and pounding down the steps of the Addison Street L stop were dressed in go-to-meeting finery. In that era's urban black culture, Sunday baseball was practically an extension of church service—"Amen!" and "Hallelujah!" giving way to "Attaboy!" and "Hum, babe!"

Most fans that afternoon were dark-skinned, an unheard-of happenstance at Wrigley, which had always been off-limits to black baseball. The Negro Leagues' annual East-West Classic (all-star game) and other big blackball match-ups were traditionally played at Comiskey Park on the city's South Side, home to a teeming ghetto known as the Black Belt.

In the early '40s, though, the North Side still represented alien territory for Black Belt denizens. Many shops and taverns in the Lakeview neighborhood surrounding Wrigley refused service to people of color; those that admitted minority customers kept them a healthy distance from whites. African Americans were welcome to spend their money at Marshall Field's and other State Street department stores—but only if they steered clear of dressing rooms, lest white shoppers take offense.[3]

Somewhere around twenty thousand full-throated Black Belters—fully two-thirds of the crowd—made it inside Wrigley that afternoon. As they bustled toward unfamiliar seats, many were craning their necks to glimpse the mythic Paige, the lanky Alabamian whom black columnist Wendell Smith had christened "The Million Dollar Stringbean."[4] In keeping with their customary Sunday ritual, the Stringbean, first baseman John "Buck" O'Neil, and other Monarchs were scoping the stands for fetchingly attired females. Women decked out in high heels and stylish frocks gave Sunday black baseball the patina of a fashion parade.

"My goodness," Negro Leaguer Doc Glenn remembered. "It could be 90 degrees out, and a woman would be sitting there with her back just as straight as could be, and the men were the same. They'd come to the ballpark in shirts and ties, shoes shined, looking for women to woo."[5] Pictures snapped at the ballpark often dominated the society pages of African-American newspapers.

Milling around Wrigley that afternoon were hundreds of servicemen of both races. Their khaki and navy blue uniforms stood in stark contrast to the silk and sharkskin, the gray flannel and gabardine.

Bleacher seats that afternoon could be had for fifty-five cents; reserved tickets went for a pricey $1.10. Wrigley was buzzing with almost the same excitement it exuded during the '32, '35, and '38 World Series—all, alas, disappointments for its Cubs.

Even the game-time announcement that Cleveland Indians fireballer Bobby Feller would not appear failed to dampen the crowd's enthusiasm. It had been heavily publicized that Feller, a chief petty officer then studying gunnery tactics at the Naval War College in Newport, Rhode Island, would be granted a weekend pass and fly to Chicago to toe the same rubber as his barnstorming cronies.

Although a tender twenty-three, Feller was already a veteran of a dozen or more black-white exhibitions played from St. Louis to San Diego—many of them against Paige. Eight months earlier, Bobby had outdueled Satch at Sportsman's Park in St. Louis, 4-1, wowing a racially mixed albeit still segregated crowd.[6]

For the Wrigley game, Rapid Robert had promised to donate his thousand-dollar appearance fee to the Navy Relief Fund. Saperstein worked overtime to ensure that Feller's gesture was applauded in the *Daily Tribune*, the *Daily News*, the *Daily Times*, the *Sun*, the *Herald-American*, and the black community's *Chicago Defender*. Indeed, press accounts left the impression that proceeds would go to other service charities, when in fact the biggest chunks were being pocketed by Saperstein and his business partners, Monarchs owners J. L. Wilkinson and Tom Baird, not to mention the two headliners.

At the last minute, Feller's superiors determined that the CPO couldn't be spared; Feller's leave was suddenly canceled. Black columnists, including the *Defender*'s Eddie Gant, accused baseball commissioner Kenesaw Mountain Landis of backroom machinations in keeping Feller billeted at Newport.[7]

Landis loathed barnstorming, especially of the interracial variety. In two decades as commissioner, Judge Landis had gone out of his way to discourage white stars from "demeaning" the majors by competing against blacks. Moreover, despite increasing pressure from politicians and the press, Landis cynically thwarted any effort to hasten integration of the big leagues. Within a year, Landis purportedly quashed Bill Veeck's attempt to acquire the Philadelphia Phillies and stock the team with Negro Leagues stars.

Even with Feller a no-show, there were plenty of other players—black and white—at whom the Wrigley crowd could marvel. The '42 Monarchs club, Buck O'Neil always said, was one of blackball's most luminous.[8] Five of the men on the diamond that day, four of them African-American, would be enshrined in Cooperstown: the two headliners plus Hilton Smith, Willard Brown, and Frank Duncan. "You've been wanting to see our [black] boys against [white] big league stars and here is your chance," the *Defender* reminded readers the day before the game.[9]

The Monarchs were led by charismatic catcher-manager Duncan, a two-decade veteran of blackball. Besides Paige, the Monarchs' staff boasted curveballer Hilton Lee Smith, a barrel-chested righty. Smith's curve dropped so demonically that Mexican fans nicknamed it *El Diablo*.[10] In interracial exhibitions, Smith's usual role was to relieve Paige after Satchel had handcuffed the big leaguers for a few innings. More often than not, Hilton proved as stingy as Satch.

Kansas City's centerfielder was Willard "Home Run" Brown, a slugger of such prolific power that when he played in Puerto Rico, awed locals called him *Ese Hombré*—"That Man." One winter, Ese Hombré reportedly won the Puerto Rican league's triple crown with a .432 batting average, 27 home runs, and 86 RBIs—all in just sixty contests.[11] Venerable Negro Leagues umpire Bob Motley thought that Brown's intuitive genius for the game rivaled Willie Mays's.[12]

With the exception of thirty-one-year-old Dizzy, who'd served (unmemorably) in the army as a teenager, members of the white team were drawn entirely from men on active military duty. The Wrigley exhibition, in fact, had originally been conceived as a way for the Chicago chapter of the Italo-American National Union to pay tribute to army private Henry "Zeke" Bonura.[13] Big Zeke was a popular, if slightly screwball, former first sacker for both the White Sox and the Cubbies.

Bonura was usually ranked among league leaders in fielding percentage, but only because his range was so limited. He waved at nearby ground balls with what one wag called "the Mussolini salute."[14]

Affectionately nicknamed "Banana Nose" or "Spaghetti Zeke," Bonura often had trouble following signs flashed his way. One afternoon when Zeke was in the batter's box, White Sox manager Jimmy Dykes kept signaling, to no avail, for Bonura to move a runner over by bunting. Finally, Dykes got so fed up he bellowed, "Bunt, you meathead! Bunt! Bunt! B-U-N-T!"[15] Jimmy's pleadings went unheeded: Zeke still swung away.

In 1938, after Sox owner J. Louis Comiskey, the son of franchise patriarch Charles, got wind of rumors that a romance was budding between his daughter and Spaghetti Zeke, Bonura was shipped off to the Washington Senators. Following Bonura's banishment, manager Dykes didn't bother to change the club's hand signals, since Zeke had never learned them in the first place.[16]

The one genuine all-star on Dean's roster was Cecil Travis, the sweet-swinging third baseman and shortstop of the Washington Senators. In 1941, Cecil's .359 batting average finished second in the American League, behind only Ted Williams's otherworldly .406. Even with Williams and Joe DiMaggio (Joltin' Joe's 56-game hitting streak occurred that same season) having big years, Travis was the only major leaguer in '41 to collect more than 200 hits.

Most of Diz's squad was made up of minor leaguers or major-league castoffs. It was this motley group that Saperstein had the temerity to bill as "all-star." Abe, who generally collected a hefty 35 percent of the take, operated no differently from other promoters back then; he had journalists of both races, including the *Chicago Defender*'s sports editor, Frank "Fay" Young, on his payroll.[17] Saperstein's largesse paid off when the *Defender* described pedestrian hurler John Grodzicki as a "sensation" at Columbus in the American Association.[18] Private Grodzicki had one job that day: to ready himself in the bullpen. Given the frailty of Diz's arm, Grodzicki knew he would pitch the bulk of the game before yielding to the other pitcher in Dean's bullpen, former Yankee farmhand Aloysius Piechota.

The bleacher bums jostling for tickets along Sheffield Avenue, though, had come to watch the two mound icons go mano a mano, if only briefly. Leroy "Satchel" Paige and Jay Hanna "Dizzy" Dean may have been of indeterminate age, but their impact on baseball and American culture was indisputable.

Paige and Dean first hit the barnstorming circuit together in the teeth of the Great Depression. At a time when baseball and other institutions were hemorrhaging, these incorrigible southerners helped stanch wounds. Before a 1931 game in Los Angeles, a promoter urged Paige to "put on a good exhibition." To which catcher Larry Brown snorted, "Goddamn! That's all Satchel's *got* is a good exhibition!"[19] Industrialist Henry Ford said in 1934 that Dizzy Dean had "done more to bring the world out of its doldrums than any other man alive."[20]

Ol' Diz and Ol' Satch were, simultaneously, heroes and antiheroes of the Dirty Thirties, a brutish decade of breadlines, "Brother, Can You Spare a Dime?," and bank heists. "Them banks that weren't closin' was gettin' robbed," Dean liked to joke in later years.[21]

In the fall of '34, the day after the FBI gunned down Pretty Boy Floyd in an Ohio cornfield, Diz was asked if he'd ever met Floyd's family back in Oklahoma. "No," Dean allowed, "but I heard they was nice folks, and Pretty Boy's mama said he never did nuthin' they say he did."[22]

A couple of months later, newsreel cameras were getting footage of Dean relaxing at home in Bradenton, Florida, when word surfaced that the feds had Ma Barker and her son Freddie trapped in Oklawaha, two hours north. The crews frantically tossed their tripods into car trunks and sped off. They got there in time to photograph a grisly scene; after a six-hour shootout, some fifteen hundred bullet holes were found in the Barkers' blood-spattered hideout, along with the lifeless bodies of Ma and Freddie. The next day, the cameramen returned to Bradenton (Diz modestly referred to the town as "Deanville") to film America's favorite pitcher grilling steaks and snoozing in a chaise longue.[23]

Even the gruesome Dust Bowl didn't stop Paige and other black barnstormers from scouring the heartland in search of a few bucks. One of Satch's mates remembered scenes that could have been penned by John Steinbeck. "It wasn't a pretty sight. Everything was burnt up. Hot weather had people packing up and moving west. Every day you'd see people with stuff on the top of their cars [and] trucks."[24] It was not uncommon in the '30s for black ballplayers to share a roadside meal with desperate Okies heading to California.[25]

The striking similarities between the two hurlers weren't lost on contemporaries. "[Satch] is to colored baseball what Dizzy Dean is to the majors," black columnist Chester L. "Ches" Washington of the *Pittsburgh Courier* opined in 1936, "with many debates developing as to which player is the 'dizzier' at times."[26]

Neither was the Boy Scout type, which only heightened their public appeal. Paige was "not the kind of guy you'd want to introduce your sister to,"[27] one of Satch's teammates cracked. "Oh, old Satch could be a pain in the butt," his barnstorming buddy Monte Irvin recalled in 2007. "[Paige] liked to party, and there were times he'd be partying when he should have been at the ballpark. If he saw a pretty girl, he might go wherever she was going."[28]

Young Diz, too, knew how to slink from saloon to cathouse. While in their twenties, both reportedly contracted venereal diseases. Paige once mused that "Diz and me were about as alike as two tadpoles."[29] Larry Tye, Paige's biographer, posits that their "fractured aphorisms were so alike it seemed that Satch and Diz were writing one another's lines—or perhaps stealing them."[30]

Many white men of that era would have been mortified to compete against a black man, for fear of public humiliation. Dean, a native Arkansan, not only embraced Paige and other black ballplayers but, to his enduring credit, praised them at every turn. "It's too bad these colored boys don't play in the big league, because they sure got some great players,"[31] Diz said at a time when it was heresy for a white southerner to advocate integration. During their '34 tour, Dean told Paige that if Satch were to join the Cardinals, between them they'd win sixty games. "Hell, Diz, I'd win sixty by myself," Satch supposedly retorted. The Monarchs' Newt Allen, a revered figure in blackball, called Dean "a prince of a guy."[32]

Baseball's clown prince began his reign just as radio was becoming the country's dominant medium. His goober charm and proclivity for on-air howlers turned Dizzy into one of America's first pop culture stars.

Satch and Diz reveled in the limelight. They knew the power they wielded and exploited it to the hilt. In an era when few ballplayers had much business savvy or the brass to pursue big-money endorsements, Diz finagled deals that must have made Babe Ruth's head spin. Satch, for his part, pocketed appearance fees and gate percentages that caused fellow black players to shake their heads—and more than a few to shake their fists. When a blackball owner in the '30s offered Paige $450 a month, Satch sneered, "I wouldn't throw ice cubes for that kind of money."[33]

They were straight out of Mark Twain: scheming rapscallions never beneath a scam, grubbing and squandering cash, yet living their lives with something approaching dignity, and—most of the time, anyway—leaving laughter in their wake.

Baseball's Huck and Jim shared much in common: dirt-poor upbringings; dysfunctional childhoods; sketchy school attendance; scrapes with authorities; renegade reputations; a yen for shameless self-promotion; running gags about their birth dates; disdain for contracts and the executives who proffered them; an endearing gift for loopy language; wild windups that saw their arms and legs churn every which way; and sinew in their right arms that must have been blessed by Providence.

Even their vagabond ways evoked the restlessness of Huck and Jim. "I stopped [barnstorming] twice, but I had the misery with me," Paige said in his twilight years. "You stay out a month and you get that itch on you."[34] Satch and Diz—together—scratched that itch so often they became America's first black-and-white buddy act, trading playful gibes in the press.

Almost lost in all the folderol is their brilliance. At the time of the Wrigley exhibition, Paige had been a blackball legend for sixteen years—"Paul Bunyan in Technicolor," as sportswriter Tom Meany put it.[35] Thanks to his peripatetic travels, Paige's star shone: he baffled hitters on two continents, various Caribbean islands, nearly a dozen countries, and every state in the union—except, Satch said, "Maine and Boston."[36] As hurler-for-hire he pitched before huge crowds in Yankee Stadium and on rocky sandlots from San Juan to Saskatchewan—and back again.

It's been documented that in 1935 and again in 1941, Paige took the mound every day for a solid month.[37] Another year he claimed to have appeared in 153 games and—who knows?—maybe he did.[38]

For years Satch had been only a rumor to most white fans. But early '40s profiles in *Time* (which branded him "large, dark Leroy"), *Life,* and the *Saturday Evening Post* changed all that. "For the first time," wrote black columnist Ric Roberts in '42, "the white media [has] burned incense at the foot of a black man outside the prize ring."[39] Betraying the era's casual bigotry, the teaser for the *Saturday Evening Post*'s article described Paige as "Chocolate," then asked, "Is Colored Boy Leroy (Satchelfoot) Paige Baseball's Best Pitcher?"[40]

By insinuating—incorrectly, by the way—that Paige owed his nickname to oversized feet, the white press was playing to wink-wink innuendo about the sexual potency of black men. In truth, given his six-foot-four frame, Satch's feet were not so big. But by photographing his cleats close-up, journalists played to white readers'—and their own—prurient appetites.

Life's photo spread in '41 hailed Paige as a pitching machine who, in interracial matchups, nonchalantly shut down such white stars as Joe DiMaggio. Its pictures depicted Paige as a shiftless street punk—an image Satch was only too happy to perpetuate.

Almost everything about Paige's on-field persona, from his stoop-shouldered shuffle to his what-me-worry? mien on the mound, reinforced racial stereotypes. "Remember the comedian 'Stepin Fetchit'?," Newt Allen once asked, referring to black actor Lincoln Perry, who depicted one servile character after another in Hollywood's early talkies. "[Satchel] sounds just like him."[41] Almost overnight in the early '40s, Paige became a household name in white America.

Dean had been a household name from the instant he first buttoned up a major-league jersey. *Saturday Review* essayist Norman Cousins once compared Dizzy to a "human sound track";[42] Dean arrived in St. Louis with a blare in 1931 and continued to screech with every appearance as a Cardinal and, later, as a Chicago Cub. Even before Dean threw a pitch in the big leagues, his mouthy exploits had been heralded by the likes of the *New York Times*'s John Kieran.[43] By mid-decade, Dean had become baseball's "new gate god, [Babe Ruth's] successor to the throne of public appreciation and idolatry," as Dick Farrington asserted in the *Sporting News.*[44]

Sportswriters of that generation had cut their teeth on Ring Lardner's *You Know Me, Al*, his uproarious tales about the misadventures of a pitcher from the sticks. The real-life Dean was dizzier than any "busher" invented by Lardner. Dean captured Depression America's heart almost as thoroughly as that other '30s symbol, the racehorse Seabiscuit.[45]

Dizzy's performance in the '34 Fall Classic against the Detroit Tigers, where he won two games (including a shutout in the Series clincher), exchanged wisecracks with humorist Will Rogers, hobnobbed with Hollywood hotshots Joe E. Brown and George Raft, canoodled with screen seductress Mae West, chitchatted on the wireless with Antarctic explorer Richard Byrd, earned round-the-clock security protection after a feared kidnapping attempt, shook off a blow to the skull that sent him to a hospital, hectored opposing pitchers, mugged before dozens of cameras, and woofed into every notebook and microphone thrust in his direction, was the stuff of legend.

Paige and Dean fanned so many myths about themselves that, decades after their deaths, baseball scholars are still struggling to establish reality. "There shouldn't be criticism of Dizzy if some of his narratives depart from the strict truth," St. Louis columnist (and Dean ghostwriter) J. Roy Stockton wrote in the '30s. "[Dean has] told so many whoppers so frequently and with such fancy embellishments that for the life of him, no doubt, he can't differentiate between fact and fiction."[46]

This much is certain: Dean and Paige were in on the joke. Both deliberately played the bumpkin; their "Bubba" images helped them cash in big-time. Paige mastered what baseball historian Jules Tygiel called "minstrel show one-liners."[47] Diz's métier was the country boy yarn. Both knew how to mangle a quip to their advantage.

Reporters played along; Dean and Paige never tired of providing their pals with good copy. "How did I manage to stay in there pitchin'?" Diz rhetorically asked in a 1955 bylined article for the *Los Angeles Times*. "Not by bein' no shrinkin' violet!"[48]

The biggest difference between them was, of course, skin pigmentation. Paige was a street urchin who'd grown up in Mobile, Alabama. One of perhaps eleven children of a derelict father and an overwhelmed mother, he ran wild when not lugging bags at Mobile's Louisville & Nashville Railroad depot. At age twelve, Paige was caught shoplifting cheap jewelry and, as a multiple offender, sent to a juvenile penitentiary.

Dean's mother died of tuberculosis when he was still a boy. Two older Dean siblings failed to survive infancy. Dizzy's father was a down-on-his-luck sharecropper who bounced from state to state trying to keep sow belly and cornmeal mush on the table for his three sons, the oldest of whom, Elmer, was mentally impaired. The Deans' saga was so grim it could have been chronicled by Depression-era photographer Walker Evans. Dean senior even had the gaunt stare of the Dust Bowl refugees so poignantly captured in Evans and James Agee's *Let Us Now Praise Famous Men.*

Another difference between Paige and Dean was durability. As young men, both threw an ungodly number of pitches in regular-season, postseason, and barnstorming play. They injured themselves at more or less the same time. Satch's arm mysteriously gave out in the summer of '38. For more than a year he was reduced to pitching for the "Baby Monarchs," the franchise's B team, throwing slop curves because his arm couldn't withstand the stress of a fastball. Somehow Paige's pitching arm recovered its former strength.

Diz wasn't as fortunate. A line drive off the bat of the Indians' Earl Averill in the 1937 All-Star Game at Griffith Stadium ripped into Diz's left shoe, fracturing his big toe. Despite searing pain, Dean was determined to finish his three-inning stint; after all, his hero, President Franklin D. Roosevelt, was watching from a box seat. In the clubhouse afterward, Diz was in such agony that his cleat had to be removed with scissors.

At the insistence of Cards' general manager Branch Rickey, who wanted his meal ticket back on the mound, Dizzy tried to come back too quickly. By the early '40s, Diz was washed up as a big-league pitcher, ending his career with "just" 150 wins.

Dean still made a good living. Ten months before the Wrigley exhibition he had become a popular if unlikely broadcaster; on the side, he turned himself into a carnival attraction. Diz would show up at exhibitions like the one at Wrigley and make a few ceremonial tosses, all the while raking in a substantial "p-c"—barnstorming slang for a "percentage" of ticket sales.

"Ten years ago," the *Chicago Daily News* observed the day before the '42 Wrigley contest, "a mound duel between Dean and Paige would have been an epochal occurrence, but today 'Dizzy' is just a part-time pitcher while Paige threatens Cy Young's record for longevity on the mound."[49]

Adorned in ceremonial sashes, representatives of the Italo-American National Union presented Private Zeke Bonura with a radio and a basket of flowers that had bananas conspicuously hanging off its sides.[50] Minutes earlier, Banana Nose had thrilled a group of soldiers and sailors by leaning across a railing and signing autographs, a scene splashed across the next day's papers.

Once the pregame ceremonies were complete, the Wrigley crowd gave Bonura and other servicemen a warm ovation; then Dizzy, Zeke, Cecil, and their ragtag squad took the field. Dean, a Cubbie from '38 to '40, curiously chose to wear his old Cardinals' uniform. The next day, a tsk-tsking *Herald-American* chided him for showing up in enemy colors, reminding Dean that his bum arm had cost the Cubs a painful $185,000.[51]

No matter: Chicagoans cheered as Ol' Diz emerged from the dugout. Even Dean's gait was countrified. He didn't walk so much as waddle, his head bobbing as if heading off to a favorite fishing hole. Joshing with newspapermen before the game, Dean had said: "My only pitch now is my 'hope pitch.' I throw it and hope nobody behind me gets killed."[52]

By then Diz was no longer an emaciated escapee from the Arkansas flatlands. Years of gluttony had fattened his six-foot-two frame; he was already heading well over two hundred pounds. Writer Paul Gallico once observed that Dean was "a strange looking fellow. He has high Slavonic cheek bones and a large, big-lipped mouth that is never quite closed."

A sore arm didn't preclude Dizzy from doing a whirling dervish windup, punctuated by a trademark leg kick, which sent his left cleat soaring head-high.

Diz and his hope ball set down the Monarchs 1-2-3, inducing outs from outfielder Bill Simms, third baseman Herb Souell, and outfielder Teddy Strong. Hilton Smith later conceded that the Monarchs had colluded not to embarrass Diz. Dean "wasn't too good; we kind of carried him along."[53] Diz found a seat on the bench to concentrate on his managerial duties, which he was supposedly sharing with honoree Bonura. So Dean had an excellent vantage point from which to witness Paige's grand entrance.

With twenty thousand or more black voices cheering each step, Satch sauntered out of his dugout. "Just the sight of [Paige] strolling languorously toward the mound," historian Robert Peterson wrote, "was enough to send waves of excitement coming through the ballpark."[54] Paige walked something like a penguin, with feet jutting outward. He was so bony, Satch liked to joke, that "if I stood sideways, you couldn't see me."[55] Paige's skin was smooth and almost jet black; his hair at that point betrayed only a fleck or two of gray. His dark brown eyes had seen much sadness; only occasionally when photographers were around would Satch let them twinkle. Paige's on-field theatrics belied his wariness around people—a lack of trust that he never quite got over.

But on the mound, Paige was pure entertainer. *Washington Post* columnist Shirley Povich called Paige's pitching style "a one-man melee."[56] His languid leg kick made his ferocious pitches—each of which Satch nicknamed—seem even faster.

His high, hard one he called "Long Tom." What sounds like a cut fastball was labeled "the Bat Dodger," while his change-up was coined the "Four-Day" (or "Midnight") "Creeper." Satch's old reliable was affectionately known as the "Bee Ball"—because, he said, "it be's just where I want it to be." Then there was his "Hesitation" or "Hiccup" pitch, where he dramatically paused in middelivery, his right arm frozen before it suddenly whipsawed the ball toward the plate. The great catcher-pitcher Ted "Double Duty" Radcliffe once said that handling Satch was "like trying to catch a freight train barreling at you with the brakes gone bad."[57]

Long Tom and all the rest dizzied Dean's doughboys. Satch, in the words of *Defender* columnist Young, "was 'in his sins' that afternoon."[58]

Paige walked only one and gave up just two scratch hits in six innings. He fanned three hitters, a modest figure by his standards.

"Paige was smart," the *Defender* commented. "He went in there to pitch to the batters' weaknesses."[59]

Both of the safeties that Paige allowed came in the bottom of the third. One of Dean's servicemen beat out a grounder—then advanced to third when the Monarchs' second baseman, Bonnie Serrell, failed to cover first on a sacrifice bunt back to the mound and Paige's throw toward first glanced off the back of the runner. An infield grounder plated the run. It was the only tally Diz's squad would score all day.

When Willard Brown drove in the tying run in the top of the fourth, black fans went "into hysterics," said the *Defender*.[60] Grodzicki lived up to Saperstein's hype, yielding seven hits but only one run in five clutch innings of relief. Zeke Bonura, the Associated Press observed, "showed nice form at first base, but failed to get the ball much past his waistline at the plate." In three at-bats, Bonura grounded out twice and went down swinging. Cecil Travis also went zero-for-three.

Through six innings, the score remained 1-1. Al Piechota, with two lifetime big-league wins, took over for Grodzicki in the top of seventh and was greeted by Brown's second sharp single.

Brown showed off his all-around game by swiping second for the second time that afternoon. When catcher Joe Greene "dumped a hump-backed line drive"[61] into left center, Willard raced around third with the go-ahead run. The Wrigley crowd, wrote the *Defender*, went "wild with enthusiasm."[62] Satch's mates pushed an insurance run across in the top of the ninth. The Monarchs ended up with eleven hits and three steals but scored just three runs—yet made them hold up.

Hilton Smith's hook fanned three and shut down Diz's men over the last three innings. The curveballer gave up only one hit, a line-drive single to lead off the bottom of the ninth; one out later, Cecil Travis came to the plate. Years later, Smith recalled that second baseman Serrell hollered over, "Make him [Travis] hit it on the ground!"[63]

Serrell proved prophetic. Fay Young described the game's final moment: "Dangerous Cecil Travis, late of the Washington Senators, slammed one at [shortstop Jesse] Williams who came up with it, tossed to it Serrell to kill [Claude] Corbitt going into second and then Serrell's rifle peg to O'Neil at first completed a lighting double play when [Buck] scooped the ball up with one hand."[64]

The final margin was 3-1, Monarchs. Smith got credit for the win since the score was knotted when he took over for Paige. The losing pitcher was Piechota, who gave up two runs while working the last three frames.[65] In the clubhouse afterward, Fay Young asked Dean to size up Satch's performance. Without missing a beat, Diz declared, "Paige is the greatest pitcher I've ever seen."[66]

That afternoon, Dean and Saperstein pleased fans by announcing that the Navy Relief Fund would still get the thousand dollars intended for the grounded Feller.[67] Left unaddressed was how much other game revenue would be donated to service charities. Subsequent stories in the *Defender* suggested that no additional philanthropic contributions were made and blamed white reporters for misconstruing Saperstein's pregame remarks.[68] Three days after the Dean-Paige contest, Wrigley Field hosted a bona fide fund-raiser for wartime charities. A crowd only one-third the size of the Dean-Paige turnout showed up to see the Cubs take on the Cincinnati Reds.[69]

After Landis issued an edict that June barring major-league parks from being used for wartime exhibitions, *Defender* columnist Eddie Gant smirked that the judge's crackdown on interracial games "serves to convince us beyond a reasonable doubt" that the commissioner always "disliked colored players and colored baseball."[70]

Landis gave detractors more ammunition when he pulled levers to scrub the June 7 exhibition in Indianapolis. The commissioner again acted out of pique, angered that the Paige-Dean game in Washington, D.C., on May 31 had attracted an additional 22,000 customers, on top of the 30,000 who had paid their way into Wrigley on May 24. Landis was not only steamed that somebody else besides his club owners was making money on baseball; he was mortified that Satch, this time teamed with the Homestead Grays, had again dominated Dean and his white pros. In his five-inning stint at Griffith Stadium, Satch fanned seven in winning, 8-1.[71] When Paige struck out the Washington Senators' own Cecil Travis that afternoon, the crowd erupted, occasioning this account from the leading daily in the nation's capital, the *Washington Evening Star*: "Negro blades in zoot suits stood and filled the air with 'yippe,' 'yay,' and 'yea boy, yo' got 'im!' Darkies did flip-flops."[72]

The *Defender's* Fay Young had been so stirred by the Monarchs' performance in Chicago that his May 30 column did somersaults, too: "White and black baseball fans were out to see Satchel Paige—and they got what they came to see. They wanted to see Paige win because of the color prejudice in organized baseball—and although Paige left the game after six innings with the score tied, the fans were well pleased—and since the Monarchs won, everything was hotsy-totsy."[73]

If only race relations in baseball—and society generally—were as hotsy-totsy as on that near-idyllic afternoon on the North Side of Chicago. In the middle of the Allies' fight against fascism, whites and blacks peacefully gathered to celebrate the pastime. Blacks that day applauded the sacrifice of white servicemen. Whites saluted the brilliance of black men excelling at our national game. For a few brief hours, Wrigley's residents set aside worries about their countrymen of all races being held at bayonetpoint on the Bataan peninsula.

Sadly, though, the Wrigley exhibition was the exception, not the rule. Jim Crow had America's pastime by the throat. As the *Los Angeles Times*'s Jim Murray put it in a 1982 reminiscence, "Baseball, in those days, was as segregated as an Alabama rest room."[74]

So was most of society, especially Chicago, notorious for decades as one of the North's most racially divided cities. Just days before the Wrigley exhibition, the U.S. Navy announced that, despite yawning manpower shortages, it would delay induction of black sailors until segregated barracks at Chicago's Great Lakes Naval Training Station could be completed.[75] Maintaining Jim Crow, in other words, took precedence over mobilizing for a world war.

Until Eleanor Roosevelt personally intervened, African-American nurses were allowed to treat only black soldiers and wounded prisoners, not white GIs. The *Defender* ran an editorial cartoon that spring that showed a *Wehrmacht* officer with a swastika armband surveying race prejudice in the United States and gleefully rubbing his hands. Its caption read, "Every little bit helps."[76] By midwar, Hilton Smith, Willard Brown, and other Monarchs—more than half the team in all—would be pressed into military duty. Like all African-American servicemen, they served in segregated units.

Dark-skinned ballplayers back then were often treated as vagrants— or worse. Buck O'Neil recalled showing up for a game in Macon, Georgia, only to discover a Ku Klux Klan leader. "You boys aren't going to play here tonight," proclaimed the wizard. "We're going to march."[77]

Between the harsh realities of Jim Crow and the hostility of local cops, it was tough for black ballplayers to find a decent meal or lodging, let alone walk through a town square in the middle of the day. "Negro baseball truly mirrored the America of its time," Bob Peterson wrote.[78]

Witting or not, the interracial forays of Satchel Paige, Dizzy Dean, and Bob Feller—games that fostered goodwill in communities across the country—helped "put a little dent in Jim Crow," as Satch put it. Sadly, more than a few black-white contests—even those played as late as the '40s—have disappeared into ether. In all, Paige appeared in some two dozen games against squads led by Dean and roughly double that against clubs captained by Feller. In addition, Satch hurled scores of exhibitions against teams headlined by other white stars. Dean and Feller, moreover, faced black clubs anchored by someone other than Paige about two dozen times each.

In the '30s and '40s, it was exceedingly rare for whites to share public venues with dark-skinned people—and vice versa. The allure of these famed flamethrowers, however, packed fans of both races into ball yards from Seattle to the Bronx. Often, blacks and whites sat or stood shoulder to shoulder. The quality of ball they witnessed was often inspired. Bob Feller called black-white games "real grudge matches."[79] Feller's touring mate Washington Senators' first baseman Mickey Vernon remembered that interracial games played in front of large black crowds were particularly intense, complete with the occasional knockdown pitch. "But in the small towns, they'd be more casual, because there were no colored fans in the stands."[80]

When Dizzy Dean and his crazed pal from the Cardinals' Gas House Gang Pepper Martin barnstormed through a small town, they liked to stir things up by standing on opposite sides of the main drag, noisily exchanging insults and bragging about what they were going to do in that day's game.[81] Their sidewalk smack worked: they usually packed 'em in—especially when Satch was involved.

Paige, Dean, and Feller spent much of their lives combing America's back roads—part of the last gasp before television, mass marketing, and interstate highways forever dulled our culture. They were, in some ways, baseball's first free agents: flinty entrepreneurs hell-bent on earning something akin to what they were worth.

The vast majority of their interracial contests took place before Jackie Robinson broke the color barrier. Paige, Dean, and Feller attracted hundreds of thousands of enthusiastic and, in the main, accepting Americans of both races. The caricatures that have evolved around them—Paige as blackball's Stepin Fetchit, Dean as hapless hillbilly, and Feller as crass money-grubber—do a disservice to their legacy. Such labels fail to take into account the remarkable role all three played in helping America become a better place. Their exhibitions helped puncture baseball apartheid; they went a long way toward making the game a *national* pastime.

"When you talk about the giants of civil rights in this country, you begin with Lincoln and Jefferson, Harriet Beecher Stowe, Dred Scott and John Brown's body and F.D.R. and the Warren Court—and, of course, Dizzy Dean and Bob Feller," argued Jim Murray in that '82 column. Some of Diz's and Bob's greatest pitching duels, the Pulitzer Prize–winning Murray wrote, were "against a superannuated, gangly black who had to wear four pairs of socks so his legs would be visible and gripped a baseball with spidery fingers and skinny wrists no bigger than a rubber band."[82]

Buck O'Neil played in dozens of interracial games. As O'Neil delivered his graveside eulogy to his gangly friend Satchel Paige in June 1982, he was surrounded by fellow Negro Leaguers. "Our lives have been beautiful," Buck affirmed, "but it could have been better. I was cheated. Yeah, all of these men were cheated. This is America, and that shouldn't have happened. [But] I do think that our baseball did so much toward changing [our country]."[83]

ONE

Interracial Barnstorming Before Satch

Over the years, a rich store of baseball lore accumulated around barnstorming experiences. . . . Such scenes were a measure of the depth and spread of baseball's roots.

—HAROLD SEYMOUR, *BASEBALL: THE GOLDEN AGE*

Herman Wouk once wrote that the past of immigrant America is like a fog: "Clutch at it and it wisps through your fingers."[1] Much of interracial baseball's saga before Paige, Dean, and Feller came along is similarly elusive. Yet games between all-black and all-white squads had long been a staple of barnstorming. Indeed, virtually all of early baseball's demigods—from pitcher Walter Johnson and outfielder Ty Cobb to blackball ace Cyclone Joe Williams and peerless shortstop Pop Lloyd—played in interracial exhibitions.

These black-white games "revealed a fundamental irony about baseball in the Jim Crow era," historian Jules Tygiel observed. "While organized baseball rigidly enforced its ban on black players within the major and minor leagues, opportunities abounded for black athletes to prove themselves against white competition along the unpoliced boundaries of the national pastime."[2]

No baseball boundary was as unpoliced as barnstorming's. The term is a vestige from a bygone age. Many nineteenth-century farm communities lacked halls or theaters, so itinerant entertainers— early vaudevillians, black-faced musical minstrels, even actors doing abridged versions of Shakespeare—would perform in barns, packing them to the rafters. As William Safire's *New Political Dictionary* explains, politicians eager to cultivate the farm vote began "storming" barns, too.[3]

Later the phrase was adopted by stunt pilots, who charged fairgoers a few bucks for the thrill of buzzing barns in a biplane. The *Oxford English Dictionary,* as Thomas Barthel's *Baseball Barnstorming and Exhibition Games, 1901–1962* points out, defines *barnstorming* as being applied "deprecatively to a strolling player."[4]

The reception to early baseball barnstorming, however, was anything but deprecatory. Fans turned out in droves. How else could folks in the hinterlands see their heroes up close? When a barnstorming team came barreling through, local leaders declared a holiday. Schools and businesses often closed early.[5]

Hitting the road helped black teams and white teams fill their coffers. It also provided entrepreneurial players with a chance to earn extra cash if their clubs didn't do the organizing.

Until the 1940s, paychecks for white big-leaguers arrived only during the season. Barnstorming, then, became an important way to fatten money clips during the fall and winter. But for black players, barnstorming was a life preserver that kept them afloat since their "regular" pay was so meager. Kent State University historian Leslie Heaphy argues that the majority of games played by black teams during the course of a typical season were exhibitions of one kind or another—not "official" league contests.[6] Barnstorming became such a profitable enterprise for white professionals that some autumns during the Roaring Twenties, a dozen or more squads were out on the circuit, many of them competing against black teams.[7]

America's first recorded game between an all-black squad and an all-white team took place in 1869, four years after the Confederate surrender at Appomattox, Virginia. The contestants were the black Pythians of Philadelphia and a Caucasian nine comprised mainly of Philly newspapermen known as the City Items. Angered that the National Association of Base Ball Players had rejected their application for membership on racial grounds, the Pythians pummeled the Items, 27-17.[8]

This inauspicious meeting was the genesis of hundreds of interracial games over the next three-quarters of a century. Certain exhibitions were products of choreographed tours, where a white "all-star" team would take on a black unit (often an aggregation playing under the banner of the "Colored All-Stars" or the "Colored Elite Giants" or some other convenient label) several times over the course of a week or so.

Most black-white games, however, mirrored other postseason barnstorming. They tended to be hastily arranged affairs thrown together by players and promoters as the regular season was winding down. Interracial "barnstorming" covers the full swath of contests, from nationwide cavalcades to onetime exhibitions; from games in the Caribbean and other remote places to marquee matchups before massive crowds in New York, Chicago, and Los Angeles.

The first known encounter between black and white "professional" teams took place in 1885 when the Cuban Giants, an outfit founded by black waiters at Long Island's Argyle Hotel, met the New York Metropolitans of the American Association. Gotham's original Mets triumphed, 11-3.[9] The black players attempted to disguise their identities by jabbering in Spanglish, hoping to pass themselves off as real Cubans so they could join a white circuit. The ploy didn't work, although it foreshadowed similar fakeries to come.[10]

At that time, blacks had not yet been barred from white professional leagues. In 1883, Moses Fleetwood Walker, an alumnus of Oberlin College and the University of Michigan Law School, was signed as a catcher for the Toledo Blue Sox of the Northwest League. When the Northwest loop transformed itself into the American Association, it became in the eyes of baseball officialdom a "major" league. Two years later, the Toledo franchise collapsed; Fleet Walker returned to the "minors" by joining Cleveland's Western League club. It would be another six decades before someone of black African descent played in the big leagues.

The first black baseball association, the League of Colored Baseball Clubs, lasted all of two weeks before disintegrating in the spring of 1887. On July 14 that season, white baseball's most forbidding figure threatened to boycott an exhibition against the Newark minor league club because it employed a black pitcher. Adrian "Cap" Anson was the revered player-manager of Albert Spalding's Chicago White Stockings of the National League. Anson was also an unalloyed bigot who had long made noises about refusing to play against blacks.[11]

In all likelihood, Anson's 1887 walkout was staged—probably in collusion with Spalding and other owners, who were convinced that blacks on the field meant poison at the box office. That same day, perhaps not coincidentally, International League owners adopted a prohibition against black players.

New York Giants manager John "Muggsy" McGraw enjoyed wintering in Cuba so much in the early 1900s that he opened a casino there. Muggsy's Havana nightclub soon became an off-season hangout for his Runyonesque pals, including Damon Runyon himself.

White players loved the quick buck they could make in Cuba. Black players, for their part, felt welcomed in the racially tolerant Caribbean, which they weren't in the States. Many black stars joined Cuban winter league teams in the early twentieth century, staying for weeks or months at a time. In other years, entire U.S. black teams would descend on the island to play a slate of games against local squads.

In 1910, American League president Ban Johnson, embarrassed that members of the world champion Philadelphia Athletics had been cuffed around by Cuban clubs, tried to decree the island off-limits to AL teams.[12] A year later, McGraw brought his National League Giants—including Big Six himself, pitcher Christy Mathewson—to Cuba in late November. Although McGraw's men won nine of twelve games against a team known as the Blues, there were some ragged moments in Havana. In her memoir *The Real McGraw*, Muggsy's widow recalled that after the Giants lost two of their first three games, McGraw roared: "Take the next boat home! I didn't come down here to let a lot of coffee-colored Cubans show me up!"[13]

In game four, Matty hooked up with José Méndez, a brilliant all-around Cuban player whose dark skin consigned him to blackball. Méndez gave up just five hits, but Matty allowed only three in a 4-0 Giants win. McGraw's joint must have been jumping that night. Before the first pitch, the Giants scared up eight hundred bucks, found a pliant Havana bookie, and wagered the bundle on themselves.[14]

For years, Muggsy kept a diary of the black players he would sign if he lived long enough to see the fall of the big-league color barrier.[15] He didn't. Toward the end of his life, McGraw turned against integration, apparently believing that society would never accept it.[16]

One noteworthy black-white series took place the year after the Chicago Cubs won their last world championship. In October 1909, the second-place Cubbies, who'd won 104 times that season but lost the chance to defend their Series crown to Honus Wagner's Pirates, played a three-gamer at Gunther Park against submarine screwballer Rube Foster and his Leland Giants, as they were then known. Some thirty thousand fans of both races packed Gunther for the series.[17]

The second game ended in a blaze of catcalls and recrimination. Foster, recovering from a broken leg suffered three months earlier, was protecting a 5-2 lead in the ninth when the Cubs rallied for three scores. With the winning run—in the person of Frank "Wildfire" Schulte—camped at third, Foster called time-out to discuss his team's options with colleagues on the beach.

Columnist Ring Lardner, a devotee of blackball, was there to describe the bizarre goings-on. "As [Foster] left the field, the Cubs rushed onto the field protesting that Foster had no right to delay the game. . . . Amid the arguing, Schulte suddenly dashed for home. Foster whirled and fired the ball to catcher Pete Booker, but the ump ruled Schulte safe on a very close play, whereupon the exuberant Cubs fans swarmed on the field. Foster was fit to be tied, but the ump ruled the Cubs winners."[18] Rube's team also narrowly lost the other two games of the series.

The rotund Foster was not only among the best hurlers of his generation (Rogers Hornsby, never noted for effusive praise of blackballers, called Rube "the smoothest pitcher I've ever seen"[19]), but he would become the key figure in founding the Negro National League. As a field manager, Foster forged blackball's pedal-to-the-metal style of play: stealing bases, slapping bunts, and hitting-and-running with abandon.[20] Eventually known as the Chicago American Giants, Rube's team became a template for other black franchises. Watching the American Giants take the field in their Old English–script "CAG" jerseys, the young Buck O'Neil remembered, was "like seeing the gods come down from heaven."[21]

Foster and his CAGs would take on anyone, anywhere. In 1910, his squad integrated the California Winter League, establishing an interracial tradition in West Coast off-season ball that endured for four decades.[22] In 1920, Foster realized his dream of organizing a black baseball association. Rube's Negro National League—the first black baseball circuit truly professional in scope—lasted ten years before being snuffed out by the Depression.

Foster died young in 1930 after a crippling bout with mental illness. His body lay in state for three days. Three thousand mourners braved Chicago's winter chill to pay their respects.[23]

Early interracial ball's most unsettling episode took place in the fall of 1915. The Indianapolis ABCs, a black team led by flinty twenty-one-year-old center fielder Oscar Charleston, played at home against a makeshift squad that included a pair of Detroit Tigers, shortstop Donie Bush and outfielder Bobby Veach.[24] The white team was leading 1-0 in the fourth inning when Bush was called safe on a disputed play at second. Second baseman Bingo DeMoss, who'd applied the tag, howled in protest. Charleston, a native of Indiana whose temper was almost as prodigious as his talent, charged in from center and punched the white ump in the jaw. "In an instant," blackball historian John Holway writes, "players and fans were mixing it up on the field in what was called a 'near race riot' before police broke it up with billy clubs."[25]

Charleston and DeMoss were carted off in a paddy wagon. After the ABCs' owner put up bail, Charleston apologized and the two brawlers were released. They promptly lit out for winter ball in Cuba.

Dizzy Dean once said that Charleston "could hit that ball a mile—he didn't have a weakness" at the plate.[26] "The Hoosier Comet" also didn't lack for toughness, having run away from home at age fourteen to join the army. He served in the Philippines, helping to quell a guerrilla uprising that turned savage on both sides. Monte Irvin relates in *Few and Chosen: Defining Negro Leagues Greatness* that Charleston once confronted a robed Klansman, ripped off his hood, commanded him to speak—and lived to tell the tale.[27]

Few social experiments in the early twentieth century were carried out with the panache of James Leslie Wilkinson's All-Nations team. The All-Nations were inveterate barnstormers, precursors to the Kansas City Monarchs, and the only truly integrated club of its era.

J.L., the son of the president of Iowa's Algona Normal College, became smitten with baseball as a youngster. To escape the wrath of a disapproving father, J.L. took to pitching under an assumed name.

In his teens, much like Rogers Hornsby and Joe Wood at comparable ages, J.L. signed on with one of the traveling Bloomer Girl baseball teams—typically, an actual girl or two surrounded by crudely disguised young men. After sporting a wig for a few weeks, Wilkinson was promoted to the group's manager. He showed promotional savvy by adding a marching band and a professional wrestler.

Weary of baseball in drag, Wilkinson decided that a racially integrated club might draw even bigger crowds than his "girls." His initial sponsor was a Des Moines sporting goods store. When one of the proprietors ran off with the team's cashbox, J.L. took over as owner.[28]

The composition of his artfully branded "All-Nations" team was breathtaking for 1912: Wilkinson, who was white, employed African Americans, Native Americans, Cubans, Asians, Polynesians, Italian immigrants, even a woman he christened "Carrie Nation"—although she had no connection to the ax-wielding antisaloon zealot. Never beneath a little hucksterism, J.L. had his charges do plenty of clowning. Still, he insisted that his All-Nations travel first class; he acquired a $25,000 Pullman coach and transported portable bleachers and a canvas fence.[29] Wherever his rail car was sidetracked, folks got their money's worth: after games, he often staged wrestling matches and dances.[30]

In 1915, the year D. W. Griffith's film *The Birth of a Nation* was released, Wilkinson moved his All-Nations club to Kansas City to take advantage of the city's superior rail connections and burgeoning black population.[31] By then he had enlisted some first-rate African-American ballplayers, among them John Donaldson, a southpaw often compared to Rube Waddell; future Satchel Paige mentor and beanball artist William "Plunk" Drake; and infielder extraordinaire Newt Joseph.

The All-Nations barnstormed all over. In '15 and again the following year, they thumped Rube Foster's Chicago American Giants, earning a favorable review in *Sporting Life*. Wilkinson had assembled "an outfit that baseball sharps claim is strong enough to give any major league club a nip-and-tuck battle, and prove that it is possible for blacks and whites to play on one team"[32]—rare praise in an America where people were flocking to see Griffith's "heroic" Klansmen rescue Southern belles from buck-toothed black soldiers.

In 1920, Wilkinson renamed his club the Monarchs, reviving the moniker of an old Kansas City blackball squad, and converted it into an all-African-American outfit. The Kansas City Monarchs became bulwarks of the original Negro National League; over time Wilkie became Rube Foster's great ally and one of the game's biggest benefactors. J.L. also became the driving force behind many of the interracial barnstorming tours of Satchel Paige, Dizzy Dean, and Bob Feller— serving as the linchpin of a syndicate that often included Wilkie's pal Abe Saperstein (later to achieve fame as the founder and coach of the basketball's all-black Harlem Globetrotters), promoter Ray Doan, and a cabal of blackball booking agents. Wilkie and his compadres carved up spheres of influence like nineteenth-century European potentates. Sometimes blackball agents were at war—but most of the time they behaved like a cartel.

Throughout the Depression years, J.L. gave his Monarchs humane salaries when he could have gotten away with paying less.[33] He also pioneered the use of portable lights for night baseball, beating the big leagues by a half decade. His gasoline-powered engine made a deafening racket, belched blue smoke, and cast such a shallow arc that fielders had trouble following pop-ups. But it thrilled fans and effectively doubled the games his barnstormers could play.[34] To pay for his contraption, Wilkie enlisted Kansas City pool hall magnate Tom Baird, who became his partner in the Monarchs.

Saperstein, whom *Newsweek* later dubbed the "Little Big Man of Hoops,"[35] was a key Wilkinson ally. Abe opened the Chicago market to big-money blackball; his baby, the late summer East-West game at Comiskey Park, became the Negro Leagues' biggest stage. At key moments, Saperstein also served as Satchel Paige's booking agent, spokesperson, and public relations consigliere.

By the mid-'30s, Wilkie's Monarchs had become America's most popular traveling club—in no small measure because they frequently played white teams.[36] The Michigan-based Old Testament fundamentalist sect House of David also turned to Wilkinson to promote its touring clubs of bearded ballplayers; eventually, Wilkie acquired ownership of the hirsute wonders. Under his leadership, the various squads playing under the aegis of the House of David stumped all over the country. "[Wilkinson] not only invested his money, but his very heart and soul" in baseball, black columnist Wendell Smith wrote.[37]

Barnstorming was so big it enticed even baseball's highest-salaried players. George Herman "Babe" Ruth, by far baseball's biggest attraction of the '20s and early '30s, loved the extra spending cash that barnstorming brought him. Most falls, the Babe was out on the road.

In his misspent youth, Ruth had run the mean streets of Baltimore with kids of every ethnic stripe. Babe respected opponents regardless of skin color; he relished the chance to compete against black players.

Jealous peers, in fact, looked at Ruth's flat nose and thick lips and accused him of a mixed racial heritage.[38] His reform school chums called Ruth some variation of "Nigger Lips" a hundred times a day, Leigh Montville wrote in *The Big Bam*.[39] The "part nigger" innuendo dogged Ruth all his life.

According to research conducted by Ruth biographer Bill Jenkinson, the Babe's barnstorming itinerary included games against black teams in 1918 (when he was still a member of the Red Sox), then again in some seven of the off-seasons between 1920 and 1935 (after he'd left the Yankees and joined the Boston Braves).[40] Ruth's black-white contests ran the gamut from spirited competition with and against top-notch players to glorified pickup games, where he was the sole white attraction surrounded by local stiffs.

With the Great War still raging, the '18 major league season ended in early September. The September 15, 1918, *Hartford Courant* reported that Babe, fresh off the Red Sox's controversial World Series triumph over the Chicago Cubs, had played the previous day in New Haven with a Connecticut outfit called the Colonials. Ruth's homer accounted for the Colonials' only tally in a 5-1 loss to the black Cuban Stars.

Two years later, a crowd of ten thousand in Philadelphia's Shibe Park saw the African-American Atlantic City Bacharach Giants beat "Bustin' Babe," as the *Philadelphia North American* called him, and his all-stars, 9-4. Among the major leaguers touring with Ruth that fall were veteran catcher-outfielder Wally Schang (who'd hit .305 in '20 for the Red Sox), young outfielder Lefty O'Doul (who'd appeared in just thirteen games that year for the Yankees), and Carl Mays (who went 26-11 that season), the Yankee whose submarine pitch had killed Cleveland's Ray Chapman a few weeks before, major league baseball's only on-field fatality.

The *North American* scolded Ruth's boys for sloppy play, saying they "booted and kicked chances galore." Atlantic City's "dusky skinned athletes" got to Mays and his "sieve defense" for eight runs over the first five innings, most of them unearned. The Bacharachs' ace, Hall of Fame right-hander Dick "Cannonball" Redding, gave up only one run—a Bambino homer, naturally—through the first eight innings. In the ninth, though, Cannonball misfired, giving up three tallies after Ruth led off with a single.[41]

Cannonball was a pivotal figure in early blackball and had become the Bacharach Giants' player-manager. Redding could neither read nor write but the 225-pounder could throw the ball as hard as anyone. In 1919, the native Georgian reportedly threw a no-hitter at his archrival, the equally powerful part-Indian black player Cyclone Joe Williams, only to lose the game. Two years later, Redding was said to have beaten Carl Mays in a fifteen-inning marathon, 2-1.[42] The *Chicago Defender* claimed that in an early '20s exhibition, Cannonball struck out nineteen big leaguers.[43] Redding's career eventually stretched twenty-seven years. A veteran of the front lines in France during World War I, he died in a mental hospital at age forty-nine.

Later on the 1920 tour, Mays and Ruth were joined in Buffalo by former New York Giants hurler Jeff Tesreau and Yankees catcher Truck Hannah for a pair of games benefiting Canisius College. The big-leaguers hooked up with a local semipro nine known as the "Polish Nationals."[44] On consecutive days they faced a black squad operating under the name "Pittsburgh Colored Stars." The black club included sidearm flinger John Emery and, it's believed, eventual Hall of Fame third baseman William "Judy" Johnson, who would have been twenty-one that fall and playing in Pittsburgh.

Babe, a converted Catholic, put on quite a show for Canisius's Jesuit fathers, playing first base, right field, and pitcher, even turning in a one-inning stint as a left-handed catcher. He also crushed two homers, eliciting "deafening screeches from the kiddies," the *New*

York Times reported.[45] Ruth and the Polish contingent won, 10-0, that afternoon, then beat Emery and the Colored Stars again the following day before another overflow crowd.

Ruth's enthusiastic embrace of black-white games helped pave the way for Paige, Dean, and Feller. One of Ruth's last interracial contests came in October 1935 against Luis Tiant Sr., the Cuban southpaw. Twelve thousand New Yorkers at the Dyckman Oval, the Washington Heights diamond that served as the home of the New York Cubans, saw "Lefty" Tiant hold the Babe to just one hit.

In 1946, *Chicago Defender* columnist Fay Young wrote a nostalgia piece that recalled Ruth's performance against the Hilldale Club twenty-six years before. Young maintained that in October 1920, Philadelphia's famed black squad blanked a Ruth all-star team, 5-0. The Babe struck out three times against Hilldale pitcher "Pud" Flournoy, Young claimed.

Historian Jenkinson, who has compiled a day-by-day record of the Bambino's barnstorming, confirms that Flournoy did whiff Ruth twice (not three times) in a game that fall. By the '20s black teams were proving their mettle against whites.

Indeed, during that same week in 1920, Young said, black teams scored three other victories over white major leaguers.

- The St. Louis (Colored) Giants defeated their crosstown rivals, the Cardinals, 5-4, in a game that drew the ire of the Spink family, publishers of the hometown *Sporting News*;
- St. Louis's black squad then vanquished the "Phillies," an all-star troupe led by Bob Meusel of the New York Yankees, 7-1; and
- The Hilldale Club, days after its triumph over the Babe, defeated a squad organized by Philadelphia Athletics's owner-manager Connie Mack, 2-1.[46]

Former federal judge Kenesaw Mountain Landis was just taking the reins of organized baseball in the fall of '20. Named after the Civil War battle where his father was wounded, Landis got the commissionership for two reasons: First, because he had a reputation—much of it exaggerated—as a foe of corruption. And second, because with his stern visage and shock of white hair, he looked the part. If Fay Young's account of black-white game is accurate, no wonder the judge developed such scorn toward interracial ball.

As with much of black history, however, reliable records either never existed or have disappeared. Even in the salad days of the Negro Leagues, game accounts and box scores often didn't appear in newspapers. Thanks to well-heeled promoters, black contests tended to be hyped in advance, but few were covered in much depth afterward. Team executives, caught up in blood feuds where players routinely jumped contracts, were loath to release too much information. Moreover, since African-American papers were weeklies, it was impossible for undermanned sports departments to report on events that happened days before, often in places hundreds of miles away.[47]

Historian Neil Lanctot, author of *Negro League Baseball: The Rise and Ruin of a Black Institution*, regards almost all Negro Leagues statistics—even such rudimentary records as year-by-year team standings and individual batting and pitching numbers—with a jaundiced eye.[48] Erratic record keeping, however, should not diminish the stature of the Negro Leagues, especially the all-star squads that took on white major leaguers. Lanctot and other scholars believe that when the likes of Satchel Paige or Cyclone Joe Williams were on the mound, Negro Leaguers could compete with major leaguers. When a first-rate pitcher wasn't going, blackball was roughly the equivalent of organized baseball's high minor leagues. Some thirty blackballers have now been enshrined in the Hall of Fame, thanks to an expert panel.

Hall of Famer Monte Irvin, who played a decade in blackball before signing with the New York Giants in 1949, says that Negro Leaguers, many of whom came up as raw teenagers, were not necessarily grounded in the game's fundamentals. But after seeing a properly executed play, blackballers quickly adapted.[49]

Negro League stalwarts such as David "Cap" Malarcher, the long-time manager of the Chicago American Giants, liked to claim "we [black players] always beat 'em," but that's hyperbole. As historian Holway maintained in Ken Burns's PBS series *Baseball*, of the 432 interracial exhibitions that he has been able to document, black teams won 266—a hair more than 60 percent.[50] Jim Reisler cites comparable statistics in his *Black Writers/Black Baseball*: of 445 known interracial games, black teams won 269, lost 172, and tied 4.[51] It wasn't always a fair fight: in many instances, the African-American team was composed of the best that blackball had to offer, whereas white teams often consisted of a big leaguer or two accompanied by minor leaguers, retirees, or semipros.

Still, black players savored the chance to demonstrate that they belonged on the same field. Almost every dominant white pitcher from the early decades of the twentieth century—from Rube Waddell, Grover Cleveland Alexander, and Rube Marquard to Lefty Grove, Schoolboy Rowe, and Lefty Gomez—lost games to black opponents.[52]

Doubts remain about certain statistics, but what is beyond doubt is that so many fans of both races swarmed to these exhibitions that promoters and players cashed in big. So big that white players fought back hard when their bosses tried to take barnstorming away from them.

Commissioner Landis was officially installed in the winter of 1920–21, in the wake of jarring revelations that members of the Chicago White Sox had thrown the 1919 World Series. After pretending he had cleansed the game by banning for life the eight indicted (but never convicted) "Black Sox," Landis turned his attention to barnstorming. The owners to whom Landis owed his fifty thousand dollars per annum empowered him to rein in off-season ball.[53]

Landis's opening shot was to announce plans to enforce the owners' 1914 edict restricting barnstorming. Among other directives, the rule forbade World Series participants from barnstorming after the postseason ended. It also proscribed games against "ineligibles," which clearly included players of black African descent, as well as convicts and ex-cons.

The new sheriff in town wasn't going to be pushed around. In the fall of '21, Landis slapped Babe Ruth and Bob Meusel with big fines for violating the Series-participant barnstorming ban. The judge took away their Series earnings and suspended them without pay for the first month of the '22 season. Landis eventually declared that only three players per franchise could barnstorm together at a given time.[54] Organized baseball's crackdown, the *Sporting News* harrumphed, ought to "make some ball players with Bolshevik tendencies to hesitate."[55]

The next season American League owners, sensitive to criticism that Ruth's and Meusel's punishment had been too severe, voted to allow their charges—including World Series players—to barnstorm until October 31 each season.

But owners became increasingly shrill about anything that smacked of interracial ball. Yankee co-owner Colonel Tillinghast L'Hommedieu "Cap" Huston told the *New York Times*'s John Kieran:

> I agree with the gentlemen who think this barnstorming business is getting past a joke. First, I was all for the boys. I couldn't see why they should be deprived of earning the extra money in the fall, but, gee whillikers, some of the happenings in these barnstorming trips have made me sit up and take notice. Think of several teams of major leaguers losing farcical contests to colored teams. Either they ought to quit playing or at least draw the color line.[56]

Throughout his tenure, Landis made ominous noises about drawing a sharper line on barnstorming. In 1933, American League president Will Harridge, fretting over injuries sustained by Jimmie Foxx while the star slugger was touring, urged a complete prohibition. Predictably, Yankee co-owner Jacob Ruppert and the *Sporting News* embraced Harridge's call. But big leaguers continued to thumb their noses, especially after Landis sought to limit barnstorming to the ten days immediately following the end of the World Series.[57]

Players also defied Landis's attempts to curtail off-season exhibitions on the West Coast, particularly the California Winter League. It annoyed Landis that the CWL had become a lucrative gig for major leaguers, not to mention an unacknowledged testing ground for racial integration.[58] Despite harsh economic times and white owners' disdain for integrated games, black-white exhibitions continued to draw sizable crowds—particularly when baseball's most charismatic figures began hitting the circuit.

CHAPTER TWO

Satch Hits the Chitlin' Circuit

No man can avoid being born average, but there ain't no man got to be common.

—SATCHEL PAIGE

In the 1930s, certain areas north of the Mason-Dixon Line were almost as perilous for black people as Satchel Paige's native Alabama. African-American ballplayers barnstorming through South Jersey saw crude signs that read, "We don't take colored trade" or warning minorities to avoid particular towns.[1] Outfielder Jimmy Crutchfield remembered that Philadelphia cops could be as hostile as any down South.[2] Heads got busted if undesirables wandered into Philly's stretch of tony shops between Market and Chestnut.[3]

Venturing into a racially charged community was "miserable," recalls Philadelphia Stars middle infielder Mahlon Duckett, now in his late eighties. "[There was] no place for us to stay. . . . The restaurants were closed by the time the ballgames ended. [It was] go to the back of some store, get some lunchmeat, eat on the bus."[4]

Blackballers called their nomadic lifestyle "hittin' the chitlin' circuit." The circuit could be dangerous: one night in Indianapolis, a white cop happened upon the Stars eating dinner in a hotel restaurant, didn't care for the way they looked, and threw them into jail without bothering to charge them with an offense.[5] Monte Irvin remembers that, without provocation, a white woman once began screaming epithets at the Newark Eagles. How can she hate us? Irvin recalled thinking, She didn't even know us.[6] Jim Crow didn't spare anyone—no matter how gifted.

Economic conditions were so ghastly by the mid-'30s that, in some cities, the unemployment rate among African-American men was 75 percent—three times the national average of white workers.[7] Judy ("Juice") Johnson, the Pittsburgh Crawfords' third baseman, whose defensive genius evoked comparisons to Pie Traynor, barnstormed all over the hemisphere in the '20s and '30s. "We would get tired from the riding, we would fuss like a bunch of chickens, but when you got the suit on it was different," Johnson said late in life. "We just knew that was your job, and you'd just do it. We used to have a lot of fun, and then there were some sad days, too, but there was always sun shining someplace."[8]

The sun shone plenty on Satchel Paige, Dizzy Dean, and Bob Feller in the 1930s. At a time when dire circumstances cast a cloud over baseball, they gave the pastime a ray of light. Professional baseball, black and white, was in dismal shape during the Depression. "The early '30s brought sparse crowds, deficits, a dramatic contraction in minor-league operations, and relentless retrenchment throughout the baseball business," historian Charles Alexander wrote in *Breaking the Slump*.[9]

In a symptomatic sign of the age, the Negro National League came back from extinction only because the Pittsburgh Crawfords' strongman, Gus Greenlee, persuaded underworld bosses to bankroll it.[10] Black baseball, then, took on the same taint as the early white major leagues. Too many owners, coaches, and players consorted with disreputable characters in the first three decades of the twentieth century, casting a pall over the game's integrity.[11]

With salaries being cut in the '30s, barnstorming became a sorely needed source of revenue for cash-strapped ballplayers. Blackball's sketchy finances, moreover, made promoters and booking agents doubly important during the Depression years. Given scarce dollars, there were fewer barnstorming tours in the '30s than in the previous decade, but Satchel Paige—black baseball's irrepressible force and soon interracial ball's top dog—was constantly on the road.

After Paige had skipped out on teams in almost every corner of the Americas, ditching with equal impunity signed contracts and handshake deals, bosses and teammates must have wondered what lay behind his compulsive need to pull up stakes. "I don't own Satchel Paige," Abe Manley, the exasperated head of the Newark Eagles, confessed to the *Chicago Defender* in 1939 after Satch failed to honor a commitment. "He owns himself."[12] Paige liked money—but it was more than greed that fueled his wanderlust.

As a child, Paige had known little but tumult. Satch's frenetic traveling may have given him a sense of security that he never had in Mobile or anyplace else he called home. Maybe the only time he felt at ease was hurtling from game to game in a big sedan, usually a Cadillac, which he drove at breakneck speed.

Sometimes the Lean One, as the *Courier*'s Ches Washington liked to call him, lashed a canoe on top of his car, so he would be ready in case the Caddy passed an inviting pond. The Lean One's fishing habit caused chronic tardiness. Satch also loved to hunt—but even with expensive hunting rifles couldn't hit anything, his pal Newt Allen chuckled.[13] Paige's car trunk was always crammed: he rarely toured without gear and tackle, hunting equipment, a portable typewriter, a record player, several cameras, various musical instruments, an assortment of silk suits, and a bag full of medicinal remedies for his balky arm and queasy stomach.[14]

Satch was frequently pulled over by state troopers suspicious about a "boy" driving such a fancy car. He was hassled so often in Alabama that, at one point, Paige swore he'd never go back.[15]

"[Paige] never had a home—other than his car," the *Saturday Evening Post*'s Ted Shane wrote in 1941.[16] Most years, Paige's car logged upward of thirty thousand miles. Since Satch's auto was his home, he was careful to protect it. Whenever Paige hit the highway, he packed heat, he confided to his onetime ghostwriter, Hal Lebovitz, then with the *Cleveland News*.

Paige's pistol-packing worried Larry Doby, his roommate in 1948 with the Cleveland Indians. When Lebovitz, under orders to get Paige's life story, first knocked on Paige and Doby's hotel room door, Satch wasn't there. But Doby warned the reporter never to startle Satch, for fear that Paige might reach for his revolver.[17]

Around teammates, Paige was the "soul of ease and friendliness,"

Richard Donovan of *Collier's* wrote in his 1953 series on Satch. "[But] with reporters, people after him for public appearances, promoters of one kind and another, he [was] wary, abrupt or sullen."[18]

After he joined the major leagues in 1948, at the age of forty-two, Paige rode the same train as the rest of his teammates (at least in theory), usually arriving at the station at the last possible instant. As Satch ambled down the platform, African-American cooks and porters would hang out the windows, hooting and hollering for their hero. "All right, brothers," Paige would declare with a big smile as he finally climbed aboard, "let us ramble."[19]

According to legend, a cop once arrested Paige as his car sped past the bus carrying his teammates, who happened that day to be the Indianapolis Clowns. As Satch forked over the money, he doubled his own fine, saying, "Keep the change. I'm comin' in the same way I'm goin' out."[20] After Satch's death, his friend and Indians teammate Bob Feller remarked, "No ad agency or writer could have created a character like Satchel Paige. Only the good Lord can be that creative."[21]

Fans of both races heard stories about Satchel calling in his fielders while on the mound, or his braggadocio about striking out the first six or nine batters, or the fanciful names he gave his pitches, and concluded he was nothing but a clown. They misread him. Satchel Paige loved to play the fool, but underneath that façade lay a brooding soul and a calculating intellect.

His great friend and benefactor Bill Veeck, who out of respect always called Paige by his given name, liked to say that Leroy was "unlettered but not unlearned."[22] Satch was a renaissance man, with passions for music (he loved harmonizing in a quartet and could play a passable piano, guitar, banjo, ukulele, and harmonica), boogie-woogie dancing (he wowed nightclub patrons by busting moves taught him by Bojangles Robinson and the Mills Brothers),[23] mimicry (his imitation of a ranting Huey Long was said to be hilarious),[24] photography (he owned dozens of cameras), birds (he collected books on ornithology), automotive repair (he claimed that he could listen to a motor and predict within fifty miles when it would need an overhaul),[25] rare firearms (he prided himself on his cache of antique rifles),[26] and hobnobbing (he palled around with the likes of jazz artists Billie Holiday,

Louis Armstrong, Count Basie, and Jelly Roll Morton, not to mention boxers Henry Armstrong and John Henry Lewis).[27]

Satch could also recite biblical passages from memory, often impressing teammates with Old Testament allegories that fit the moment. "Satch is an expert on every subject from engineering to mule-skinning," Veeck said in the '60s.[28]

Above all, Paige was a genius at throwing a baseball. Like most geniuses, he knew it—and wanted to make sure others knew it, too. If that meant stretching the truth from time to time, so be it. Paige was, in the words of one contemporary, a "raconteur—what we called a damn good liar."[29] Satch loved to tell friends that his momma liked to counsel her children to rehearse a lie—and if it didn't sound believable to their ears, to keep the deception to themselves. Paige must have done a lot of rehearsing; he became expert at twisting things to his advantage.

Monte Irvin remembered that Satch could never keep names straight. Paige had a stable of generic nicknames that he called teammates: Irvin's was "Young 'Un."[30]

Catcher Quincy Trouppe roamed all over the Great Plains and Canada with Paige in the '30s and '40s. "I got to know Satch pretty well," Trouppe wrote in his memoirs. "I soon learned [Paige] could clown one moment and become deadly serious the next. His complex personality made him immensely interesting."[31]

Paige once took his Monarchs mate Buck O'Neil to Drum Island, the infamous port off Charleston, South Carolina, where centuries earlier hundreds of thousands of chained Africans had been herded off ships and auctioned into slavery. Satch and Buck stood there for a long while, neither one saying anything. Finally, Paige broke the silence by whispering, "Seems like I been here before."[32]

Satch enjoyed gags about his age so much he had one memorialized on his gravestone; instead of a birth year, question marks are etched into his headstone. But all the jokes masked the heartache of a profoundly disjointed childhood.

Paige grew up, by his own estimation, a "nigger kid" in a virulently segregated world.[33] Like almost all blacks in Mobile in the early twentieth century, the Paiges lived in squalor on the south side of town near the bay. Their shack was called a "shotgun house" because its four tiny rooms formed a straight shot from front to back. "Satch came from nothing, even less than most black people did back then," O'Neil said, "and he had a burning desire to prove himself."[34]

His father was a constantly out-of-work landscaper. "I only remember pieces and snatches about him," Satchel wrote. "He wasn't hardly a part of my life."[35] Lula, his mother, earned fifty cents a day cleaning the homes of rich white people.

The Paiges couldn't afford to keep their kids in school. When her boy turned seven, Lula insisted that young Leroy emulate his older siblings by toting suitcases at the Louisville & Nashville depot. After his first day on the job netted only a dime, disappointing his mother, the enterprising youngster claimed to have rigged a pole that allowed him to haul three or four satchels at the same time. Another young redcap took a look at the contraption and proclaimed that Paige looked like "a walking satchel tree."[36] Young Leroy had a nickname that lasted a lifetime.

Paige's first exposure to baseball came when he got a job sweeping out Eureka Gardens, home of the semipro black Mobile Tigers. Watching the Tigers throw the ball around the park fascinated Leroy. Since his family couldn't afford a baseball, he began chucking rocks.

Satch earned a spot on the W. H. Council School's team—a remarkable feat since he rarely passed through the school's door.[37] Paige's rock-throwing skills came in handy whenever bullies from a nearby white academy or north side toughs challenged Satch and his friends.

"That's where I learned my Hesitation pitch," Satch told Ed Storin of the *Miami Herald* five decades later, perhaps not facetiously. "If a man was throwing at you, you wouldn't just stand there, you'd duck," Satch claimed. "But if a man started to throw, and you ducked, and then he stopped, where would you be? You'd be standing there ducking—with your bare face ready to be plunked big as you please."[38]

In July 1918, when he was twelve, Satch was nabbed by a store security guard as he tried to rip off costume jewelry. It wasn't the first time that Leroy's mother had been dragged down to the police station to bail out her wayward boy. This time, though, truant officers insisted that Leroy be sent to a juvenile penitentiary—over Lula's tearful protests.[39]

Satchel spent nearly six years at the Industrial School for Negro Children at Mount Miegs, Alabama. As he later acknowledged, the barbed-wire jail turned out to be the best thing that ever happened to him. "When you grow up as poor as me, a place like Mount Miegs can be mighty warm and good," Satch said.[40]

His baseball coach at Mount Miegs, Edward Byrd, appears to have played the same role for Paige that Brother Mathias had a decade earlier for Babe Ruth at St. Mary's reform school in Baltimore: part surrogate dad, part parole officer.[41] Coach Byrd taught Paige to kick his left foot high, concealing the ball until the last possible instant. Byrd also told Satch to observe a batter's knees for weakness, much as a matador studies a bull's legs.[42]

In later years, Paige enjoyed baiting batters by bellowing, "I'm gonna throw a pea at yo' knee!" In the fall of '47, Paige gave Pirates slugger Ralph Kiner his "pea at yo' knee" harangue (although in Kiner's telling it was a "*bee* at yo' knee, a taste at yo' waist, and better at yo' letters!"), and struck him out on three pitches.[43]

Satch was released from Mount Miegs in December 1923, six months shy of his eighteenth birthday, all skin and bones but still growing. He soon became the ace of the Mobile Tigers. His big break occurred in the spring of '26 when fellow Mobile sandlot star Alex Herman was hired as player-manager of the Chattanooga White Sox (soon to be the Black Lookouts) of the Negro Southern League. Herman watched Satch dominate hitters one afternoon and offered the youngster fifty bucks a month.

Founded by black entrepreneur (and racketeer) Tom Wilson of Nashville, the Negro Southern League in the '20s was regarded as the high minors of blackball. A decrepit bus that apparently rattled over every pothole in Tennessee took Paige on his first road trip.

When the bus finally arrived in Memphis in the middle of the night and pulled up next to the ballpark, a gullible Paige asked Herman to have the driver take him to "wherever we're staying." Herman stared at his young charge. "Staying? This is where we're staying, Satch. You think we can afford staying in a hotel?"[44]

Using their grips as pillows, the players bunked on the outfield grass. Breakfast consisted of a campfire hot dog, washed down with warm orange soda. Yet Chattanooga managed to beat Memphis that afternoon.

Satch surmised that the only way to avoid sleeping alfresco was to increase the club's take at the box office. After word got out about the kid pitching sensation, turnstiles all over the Negro Southern League started clicking. Chattanooga, at least on occasion, could afford to stay in fleabag hotels and boardinghouses that catered to blacks.[45]

Paige's celebrity was based almost exclusively on word of mouth. There were no radio stations to applaud his shutouts, no big marketing campaigns to trumpet his next game. The few newspapers that served the African-American community were hard-pressed to keep up with blackball happenings in remote places like Chattanooga. So the legend of Satchel Paige began to spread, slowly but surely, in bleachers, churches, speakeasies, and barbershops.

In early '27, without Herman's knowledge, Satch dickered with several Negro National League teams, finally jumping at a $275 per month offer from the Birmingham Black Barons.[46] Birmingham gave Paige more than a bigger stage. The Black Barons provided him with a manager, Big Bill Gatewood, who appreciated Paige's skill but was determined to improve on it; and catchers who knew when and where to deploy Paige's arsenal.

At that point, Paige was throwing two kinds of blazers: his Bee Ball, which was released from the smooth side of the ball and more or less maintained a level path to the plate; and his Jump Ball, which, Paige claimed, rose four to six inches after he flung it with fingers placed across the seams. "It got so I could nip frosting off a cake with my fastball," historian Larry Lester quotes Satch as saying.[47] Indeed, it was during warm-up sessions in that period where Paige honed one of his favorite routines: putting a chewing gum wrapper or a matchbox on the plate and amazing teammates and hangers-on by throwing pitch after pitch directly over the minuscule object.

Another trick, perfected later, was to have two batters hover over the left- and right-hand sides of the plate a few inches apart—sometimes, for effect, with cigars or cigarettes dangling from their lips—and whiz fastballs through the tiny opening. He also birthed his most notorious pitch while a Black Baron. Old-time blackballer Plunk Drake, a veteran of Wilkinson's All-Nations squad, taught Satch the Hesitation move.[48] Paige got so adept at the Hiccup, one fan remembered, that sandlot hitters sometimes swung before Satch released the ball.[49]

He became a huge gate attraction. Longtime Negro Leaguer Jimmy Crutchfield recalled that when Satch pitched, eight thousand or more fans would pack Birmingham's Rickwood Field—double or triple the usual crowd.[50]

To gild his own pocketbook and help other black squads at the box office, Barons' owner R. T. Jackson rented Satch, for a hefty fee, to teams large and small. It got to the point, his teammates recalled, where the only time they'd see Satch was for big Sunday games. One weekday afternoon in Albany, Georgia, Paige got into a tiff with a white umpire who ruled that Satch had missed second base while legging out a triple. Unfortunately for Satchel, the arbiter doubled as the local sheriff. As Paige's complaints turned nasty, the off-duty cop threatened to arrest him.[51]

At some point during the 1930 season, Jackson worked a deal to have Satch pitch with the Baltimore Black Sox on a semiregular basis. For the remainder of that summer, Paige seesawed between the Black Barons and the Black Sox, plus cashed in his usual share of one-off games.

It was in the fall of '30 as a member of a Black Sox all-star contingent that Satchel played against white major leaguers, including an outfit headed by Babe Ruth. Alas, it does not appear that Satch and the Bambino had any head-to-head showdowns. But Hall of Famers Hack Wilson and Babe Herman did face Paige—and Satch whiffed both. Paige always claimed that Wilson was the first white big leaguer he ever struck out.

Buck O'Neil went to his grave swearing that he witnessed Ruth hitting a meteoric home run against Satch in a Chicago exhibition, followed by good-natured woofing as the Bambino circled the bags. But beyond Buck's usually reliable memory, there's no box score or game account to verify the claim. Satch himself told the *Sporting News* in December 1964 that "I never got to face [Ruth]. He was always bench managin' the day I was moundin'." Arthur Daley of the *New York Times*[52] and Fay Young of the *Defender* were among the many chroniclers who believed Paige's boast that he'd once struck out twenty-two

Ruth all-stars in a single game; again, no documentation has been found.

Satch also hurled in October 1930 with a Chicago American Giants club that played a four-game series against a white squad that included Lefty O'Doul (.383, 97 RBIs in that year of the rabbit ball) of the Philadelphia Phillies, as well as Harry Heilmann (.331, 91 RBIs) of the Cincinnati Reds, and the hitter who would become Paige's personal nemesis, Charlie Gehringer (.330, 98 RBIs) of the Detroit Tigers. Paige liked to pitch to batters by "reading" their feet and legs; Gehringer stood in the box flat-footed, which flummoxed Satch.

On October 6 in Chicago, Satch got schooled late in the game by Gehringer and company, but with relief help the CAGs held on to win, 7–6. The American Giants reportedly took three out of four that autumn from the white all-stars.[53]

In the early '30s, Paige became the biggest star on the most storied team in blackball history. Gus Greenlee's Pittsburgh Crawfords were as dynastic in their own way as the Yankees and Athletics of the same era. The Craws' outfielders were so quick, Satch once quipped, that "not even a raindrop would fall" between them.[54]

Unlike the Yanks or the A's, the Craws' dominance is not easily quantified. The Craws clobbered opponents, but much of the time they were playing mediocre black clubs or pedestrian road teams.

Nevertheless, the Craws' lineup—consisting at various times of left fielder Cool Papa Bell, catcher Josh Gibson, aging first baseman–manager Oscar Charleston, catcher-pitcher Double Duty Radcliffe, third baseman Judy Johnson, and outfielders Jud Wilson, Jimmy Crutchfield, and Rap Dixon—was as potent as any "Murderers' Row" the Yanks or A's could muster. The least celebrated players in that group—Wilson, Crutchfield, and Dixon—all had multiple tools. Blackball historian James A. Riley says that "no outfielder had better hands or better eyes in judging a ball" than Crutchfield.[55] Among those legendary Craws, all but Dixon have been enshrined in Cooperstown.

In the fall of '32, the Craws played a seven-game series against a white all-star team organized by Casey Stengel, by then long retired as a player but not yet the celebrated manager that he would become. The "Ole Perfesser" loved to put on a show. Casey enjoyed disguising himself as a farmer and taking a seat in the stands, loudly braying that he could hit better than the guys in uniform. When, on cue, the players would begin yipping back, Stengel the Hayseed would vault the railing, grab a bat, dig in at the plate, and—much to the crowd's delight—begin walloping the ball.[56]

Joining Stengel's "stars" that October were outfielders Hack Wilson (he hit .297 with 23 homers in '32) and Johnny Frederick (.299) of the Dodgers, Chick Fullis (.298) of the Giants, plus shortstop–third baseman Woody English (.272) of the Cubs, and rookie catcher Tom Padden (.263 in 47 games) of the Pirates.[57]

The series started in York, Pennsylvania, a favorite barnstorming venue because it was roughly equidistant from Baltimore and Philadelphia; the tour then crossed the mountains to Pittsburgh, Altoona, and Cleveland.[58] Paige, in his only appearance in the Stengel set, won the fourth game, 10-2. Satch outpitched Roy "Tarzan" Parmelee of the Giants, a beefy right-hander whose career big-league record was 59-52. Satch went the distance in Cleveland and struck out 15.[59]

Greenlee's squad reportedly took five out of seven against Casey's club. Stengel's only wins came against forty-five-year-old Joe Williams and Duty Radcliffe, who got bopped around in the Cleveland nightcap after Satch's radiant performance in the opener.

The following year, 1933, Greenlee, abetted by gambling cronies, tried to resuscitate the Negro National League—with mixed results. In truth, despite the efforts of Greenlee and his sometime ally, J. L. Wilkinson, the Negro Leagues were never restored to blackball's pre-Depression golden age. But by the late '30s two reasonably stable "major league" circuits had taken shape: the western-based Negro American League, with Wilkie's Kansas City Monarchs, plus the Memphis Red Sox, the Atlanta Black Crackers, the Chicago American Giants, the Indianapolis ABCs, and the Birmingham Black Barons; and the eastern-based Negro National League, with Greenlee's Pittsburgh Crawfords, Cum Posey's Homestead Grays, the Baltimore Elite Giants, the Newark Eagles, the Philadelphia Stars, and the New York Black Yankees. So long as everyone got a taste of the action, club owners in the two Negro Leagues were able to put aside their differences to stage the East-West game every year. But a postseason "colored World Series" remained elusive.

All that was years off, however, as Greenlee struggled in the early

'30s to keep his empire (his numbers racket, his Crawford Grille restaurant/nightclub, and the Craws) afloat. Satch bristled when Greenlee not only cut back on salaries but skimmed a larger take from Paige's one-off exhibitions. Trouble was brewing, even though Satch was romantically tied to one of the waitresses at Gus's restaurant.

By '33, "Satchel [had] learned that he could make more money as a showman than he could ever hope to draw as a brilliant flinger," observed Sam Lacy, the revered sports editor of the *Baltimore Afro-American*. "The result was [that] the redoubtable [Paige] turned his slab assignments into a combination vaudeville act and pitching performance."[60] The vaudevillian was about to take his act to a stage he'd never imagined.

In August 1933, a couple of months before his first duel with Dizzy Dean, Paige was pried away from the Craws by cash, a late-model roadster, and the prospect of playing with and against white "professionals." The cash was a doubling of his monthly salary. The car was a '29 Buick sedan off the lot of a dealer in Bismarck, North Dakota, named Neil Orr Churchill.[61] The pros were the Bismarck Capital Citians, the Jamestown Red Sox (or "Jimmies"), and other clubs that plied the Dakotas in the early '30s.

Paige's journey to the north country in 1933 and again two summers later may not have grabbed the press's fancy back then, but the exploits of Paige and other blackballers in the Great Plains of the Depression era remain one of interracial baseball's sweetest legacies. Satch's trips to and through the Dakotas, moreover, proved almost as lucrative as his stumping with Dean and Feller.

Neil Churchill had, his players remembered, a prickly personality and an ego to match. A self-made man born on the wrong side of the tracks, Churchill had been a fair country outfielder in his day. He played against black barnstorming squads and watched as town nines across the border in Minnesota hired such African-American stars as John "Lefty" Donaldson and Webster "Submarine" McDonald to pitch big-money matches. Churchill also got friendly with Abe Saperstein when Abe's Globetrotters came to play Bismarck's basketball team.[62] It was a relationship destined to pay dividends for both.

The black player migration to the Dakotas began in midsummer

'33 when a rival team in Jamestown, a hundred miles east of Bismarck, convinced pitcher-catcher Ted Radcliffe to leave Greenlee's Crawfords. Double Duty became, remarkably enough, player-manager of James-town's integrated squad—believed to be the first black manager of a racially mixed professional team. At Saperstein's urging, Radcliffe served as a conduit for other black players to come north.[63]

Why would town teams in far-off North Dakota hire black mer-cenaries? As Churchill knew better than anyone, prairie ball was a blood sport. Competition among towns was so fierce—and wagering so intense—that fans demanded ringers. Since racial attitudes were less rigid in the Dakotas than elsewhere, communities began vying for some of blackball's biggest names.

Soon after Saperstein and Radcliffe came calling, Red Haley, an infielder with the Memphis Red Sox, Roosevelt Davis, a right-handed pitcher with the Pittsburgh Crawfords, and Quincy Trouppe, a twenty-year-old switch-hitting catcher with the Chicago American Giants, all headed to the plains. When his frequent batterymate Radcliffe tried to recruit Paige, Satchel demurred, joking that he wasn't sure North Dakota was part of "Uncle Sam."[64] But Paige's reaction was different a few weeks later when, at Saperstein's urging, Churchill sent Satch a series of telegrams. When Greenlee, known as "Mister Big" in Pitts-burgh's underworld, learned that his meal ticket had been ripped away, he supposedly threatened Churchill with bodily harm.[65]

Paige claimed that it wasn't until after he accepted Churchill's offer that it dawned on him that he'd not only be playing *against* white players but *with* them. "For the first time since I started throw-ing," Satch wrote in his autobiography, "I was going to have some of them [white players] on my side. It seemed real funny. It looked like they couldn't hold out against me all the way after all."[66]

By the summer of '33, windstorms were tearing topsoil from farms all over the region. How people in the northern plains could afford a buck or two to attend ballgames remains unclear—but somehow they managed.

The *Bismarck Tribune* buzzed at the prospect of one of the Negro Leagues' most vaunted pitchers joining the local boys in time for another Sunday afternoon match-up with nemesis Jamestown. A special Northern Pacific express whisked a thousand Jimmies fans to Bismarck. Churchill supposedly wagered a Jamestown official a grand that Satch would beat the Jimmies' black hurler, left-hander Barney Brown.[67]

Hundreds of cars and wagons ringed Bismarck Ball Park, crammed to double its capacity. Early in the game, Satch tickled spectators by spearing a hot comebacker and making a big show out of grabbing the resin bag to "dry" his right hand before firing on to first. He also drew howls by liberally using his Hiccup.[68]

Barney didn't have a hesitation move, but his pitching was as sparing as Satch's. Neither team scored until Paige gave up three hits and a walk in the top of the sixth. Two of the Jimmies came home. The game remained 2-0 until the bottom of the eighth, when Haley walked; Trouppe and a fellow Capital Citian then bagged back-to-back triples, knotting the score.

"They get no mo' runs," Satch supposedly vowed as he took the rubber in the top of the ninth.[69] Sure enough, the *Tribune* reported that he struck out the side on ten pitches. In the bottom of the ninth, with a runner camped on first, Jamestown's left fielder attempted a shoestring catch and came up empty. Bismarck's winning run scored, sending the crowd into delirium and sweetening Churchill's wallet. Ecstatic Bismarckians raced onto the field, practically tearing the jersey off Satchel's skinny frame. Paige whiffed eighteen, giving up five hits. Barney struck out five fewer but also allowed only five safeties.[70]

Jamestown demanded and got a rematch the following weekend, this time on home turf. Churchill arranged for a discounted round-trip train fare of $1.10 for Bismarck's faithful. At least eight thousand people were shoehorned into a park designed to seat a quarter that number. After twelve innings, darkness set in and the game was called a 1-1 tie. Satch again jacked eighteen Jimmies.

Churchill immediately scheduled a three-game set with the Jimmies in Bismarck over Labor Day weekend. To ensure that the press hyped the series even harder, he unilaterally declared it "The North Dakota State Baseball Championship."

Huge throngs turned out. Surprisingly, game one became a slugfest as neither Barney nor Satch had his best stuff in a 7-7 game again called for darkness.

For game two, Jamestown brought in the ultimate ringer: Willie

Foster, the left-handed star of the Chicago American Giants, one of blackball's premier hurlers. Among fans, Foster's stature was such that he was voted the West's starting pitcher in the Negro Leagues' first-ever East-West Classic, which took place the following week at Chicago's Comiskey Park.[71] Paige, by contrast, finished third in the public's balloting for the East's starting pitcher. Still agitated at Greenlee for stiffing him and miffed at what he perceived as a slight from the fans, Satch would skip the first East-West game.[72]

So many Dakotans showed up for the Paige-Foster face-off in Bismarck that hundreds of ticketless fans climbed an elevated train track next door. Foster, a future Hall of Famer, was wild that Sunday, walking ten and allowing six hits. Paige, on no rest, struck out fifteen and won the game, 3-2; he even drove in the winning run with a heart-thumping single in the bottom of the ninth. Once again, Satch was mobbed by delirious (and now slightly wealthier) Bismarckians. The final game in the series also went to Bismarck as Roosevelt Davis shut down the Jimmies.

Trouppe recalled that Satchel started thirteen games for Bismarck in the late summer and early fall of '33, winning twelve. An examination of the *Tribune*'s box scores and game accounts, however, suggests that Satch pitched in nine games, winning seven against no losses and averaging about fifteen strikeouts per outing.[73]

Satch was a sensation in Bismarck, at least at the outset. In his autobiography, Paige remembered getting into an argument with a white teammate who called him a "dirty nigger." Satch replied, "I'm sure clean enough to be playing with your kind. Where would you high and mighty boys be without me?"[74]

Paige also recalled an episode where his outfielders sulked after Satch blistered their fielding.[75] They were so put out, in fact, that they refused to take the field for the next half inning, so Satch had one of his favorite tricks—emptying the outfield—turned on him. "The fans loved it," Satch recalled. "They thought it was a stunt. I'd pulled plenty of stunts like that before, but this time it was serious business."[76]

Once Paige apologized, the chastened Capital Citians took the field. After that, Satch wrote, he got along with his new mates.

The local newspaper was delighted with the team's new acquisition, labeling Satch "the Dizzy Dean of the Negro Pitching World."[77]

Reflecting the ethos of the day, the *Tribune* had no shortage of racially tinged descriptions of Paige, from "dusky speedball sensation" to "ebony stalwart."[78]

At first, Bismarck took Satch to its bosom—with perhaps a few distaff townies taking the task too literally. Churchill grabbed Trouppe one day and said, "Quincy, I don't know how to put what I'm going to say to you, but it's about Satchel. You know the fans are really wild about his performance, and so am I, but there is one thing I'd like for you to talk to him about on my behalf. I understand a man has got to go out with a woman, but there is a way to do it in any walk of life. Just tell him to be careful about riding white girls around in broad daylight."[79]

Trouppe doesn't reveal in his autobiography whether Satch curtailed his rumble-seat romancing. Churchill tried to find Paige a decent place to live—but townspeople weren't keen on having a black neighbor, especially one with an active libido. Satch's lodging turned out to be a converted railroad freight car that had, until recently, been home to prison work gangs.[80] The convicts' rolling jail cell was still perched on a side rail, in a seedy section of town near the stockyards.

His fiancée, Janet Howard, the feisty waitress at the Crawford Grille, was—at least at first—all in favor of the move to North Dakota and bigger dollars. Satch had been infatuated with Howard from the first time he spotted her. "From the minute she first set a plate of asparagus down in front of me, I began to feel paralyzed," he joked years later.[81] But once Janet arrived in Bismarck, Paige encountered "mean folks [that] didn't want colored people around."[82]

After Janet returned to Pittsburgh, Satch turned the railcar into such a busy bachelor pad that, this time, more than Churchill noticed. The town fathers, apparently worried about the deflowering of their daughters, asked Churchill to corral Satch.

One of Satch's favorite haunts in Bismarck was the Mandan Sioux reservation outside town. A young lass allegedly known as "Dorothy Deer" caught Satch's eye. Dorothy and the Sioux nicknamed Satch "Long Rifle"—or so Paige claimed in what, no doubt, was an apocryphal tale told two decades later to *Collier's*. During one visit with Dorothy, Satch complained of a sore arm, so they sought out a medicine man, who applied snake oil onto Satch's shoulder and elbow. After a few minutes, Satch said his arm felt like it was going to explode. For the rest of his career, Satch swore he kept a jar of the Sioux balm in his medicine chest and would occasionally break it out on the road.

With cold weather descending in the fall of '33, the man with the exploding arm left Bismarck to chase big money back east and out to the West Coast. "The Dizzy Dean of the Negro Pitching World" was about to meet the real thing.

CHAPTER THREE

The Lean One Meets the Dizzy One

Ol' Diz was the one boy I wanted to run up against.

—SATCHEL PAIGE

J. L. Wilkinson could make only so much money having his Kansas City Monarchs play sandlotters or itinerant House of David clubs. Wilkie was eager to use his mobile lights apparatus to hawk games with big leaguers—especially when those exhibitions involved gate magnet Dizzy Dean of the St. Louis Cardinals, fast becoming America's favorite ballplayer. In the fall of '33, Wilkie got his wish.

The first recorded meeting between a Dizzy Dean–led barnstorming team and a professional black troupe could not have happened in a less likely place. Oxford, Nebraska, was miles from anywhere, a farming hamlet of a few hundred people just north of the Kansas border. But Oxford was proud of its baseball heritage. Its ballyard had long been a stop on Wilkinson's midwestern circuit.

It was there on the evening of October 4, 1933, that Wilkie arranged for a company of Monarchs to play a Dean-led group of big leaguers. Besides Dean (20-18 with a 3.04 earned run average in his second year in the big leagues) and his pal Pepper Martin (.316 with a league-leading 122 runs scored) from the Cardinals, pitcher Larry French and outfielders Paul Waner (.309 with 101 runs scored) and Forrest "Woody" Jensen (.296 in 70 games) of the Pittsburgh Pirates, plus over-the-hill shortstop Glenn "Buckshot" Wright (a career .294 hitter) of the Brooklyn Dodgers, all signed up for J.L.'s junket.

Waner, a sturdy barnstormer, was the older and stronger of the

Pirates' "Big Poison–Little Poison" combo with brother Lloyd. Three times the native of Harrah, Oklahoma, led the National League in hitting, finishing his career with a .333 average, while younger sibling Lloyd, a fellow Hall of Famer, hit a lifetime .316.

J.L.'s real coup, however, was to work a deal—through the still-smoldering Gus Greenlee, no less—to secure the services of Satchel Paige for at least part of Satch's busy October. Besides two stops in Nebraska, Wilkie's tour included visits to Kansas and Missouri—the heart of Cardinals Nation.[1]

A crowd estimated at 6,800 swarmed Oxford's diamond—not only the largest gathering in the history of Furnas County but the biggest crowd ever assembled in southwestern Nebraska, guessed the next day's *Oxford Standard*. "The admission charge of 60 cents was thought by many local fans to be excessive, but the expression was heard many times during the game, that had the charge been a dollar the same crowd would have been there, for they came from a long distance," enthused the paper.[2]

Dizzy thrilled the farm crowd by starting the game on the hill. But in the third inning he was conked on the left elbow by Monarchs' ace Chet Brewer, whose wicked emery ball had almost the same dip as a curve. Diz took himself out of the game to nurse his arm but returned an inning later to play left field.[3]

Dean pitched two-plus scoreless innings against a Monarchs team that featured Newt Allen and Newt Joseph in the infield, along with catcher T. J. Young, second sacker George Giles, and a first baseman believed to be future New York Black Yankee Jimmy Starks. Shortstop Allen bruised his thumb handling a low throw in the fourth inning and was replaced by Carroll Mothel, who subbed for Allen the rest of the series. Frank Duncan (usually a catcher and the Monarchs' future manager) and Eddie "Pee Wee" Dwight manned the outfield, along with Joe Rogan, normally a pitcher. Hall of Famer Rogan could play the outfield, Jimmy Crutchfield later told Bob Peterson, better than half the fly chasers in the major leagues.[4]

Charles Wilber "Bullet Joe" Rogan was the rugged type. The native Oklahoman spent ten years in the army, serving in such exotic locales as the Philippines and Hawaii, and didn't join the Monarchs until age thirty. Legend has it that Rogan was "discovered" by Casey Stengel when the Ole Perfesser was barnstorming against military teams out West.[5] At five-foot-seven and 180 pounds, Bullet Joe was built like a fireplug. He not only had an agitatin' fastball, as Dizzy Dean was fond of saying, but threw a mean spitter to go along with a backbreaking curve, a palmball, and a forkball.[6] "[Rogan] could do anything," Bob Feller told former MLB commissioner Fay Vincent seven decades later. "He was one of the best black ballplayers I ever saw."[7]

"Jeepers," Chet Brewer said years later of his mentor, "[Rogan] could throw the curve ball faster than most pitchers could throw a fastball."[8] Dean said that Rogan was "one of those cute guys. He never wanted to give you a ball to hit."[9] Rogan was such an accomplished hitter that even when the Monarchs' lineup was loaded, Rogan batted fifth or sixth. Bullet Joe played in the Negro Leagues until he was nearly fifty.

Satchel Paige, it appears, was not in Oxford, despite Wilkinson's promotional hoopla to the contrary. But Brewer pitched okay in Satch's stead, hurling a complete-game nine-hitter in a 5-4 victory by Dizzy's team. Tellingly, the *Standard*'s front-page headline read "K.C. Monarchs Bow to the Inevitable," as if it were preordained that the white squad would win.[10]

Brewer was familiar with the Farm Belt. Weary of racial intimidation, his family had left Kansas and moved to Des Moines, Iowa, when Chet was a youngster. Young Brewer attended integrated schools and, as a teenager in the early '20s, became a fan of Bullet Joe and the Monarchs. Chet quit school to join a team known as Brown's Tennessee Rats, which combined ballplaying with minstrel show antics.

At age seventeen, Chet was signed by Wilkinson. Brewer soon became one of blackball's toughest—and worldliest—right-handers, eventually pitching in the Caribbean, the Philippines, and China.[11] Seventy years later, Feller told Vincent that his fellow Iowan was "an exact clone of Bob Gibson."[12]

Brewer was indebted to Dizzy Dean for insisting that black players get a decent cut of interracial exhibitions. "[Dean] raised cain if he thought they were cheating us on our share of the receipts," Brewer remembered. Diz once gave Brewer his bright red Cardinals warm-up, saying, "Here's a jacket from one good pitcher to another." In the twilight of life, Brewer chuckled, "[Dizzy] was one good ol' boy from the South."[13]

George Giles, a fine all-around player, altered his hitting style when facing Dean, but Giles still couldn't get around on Diz's fastball. "That ball was by me before I could make my mind up to swing," Giles once admitted to Brewer after Dean overpowered him.[14] "I will never forget Dizzy," Giles recalled in the early '70s. "[Dean] was something else. He was a lot of fun. He never did take anything serious."[15]

The *Oxford Standard* couldn't get enough of the contest. "This was by far the most interesting session of the national sport ever held in this section of Nebraska and one that will be remembered by everyone in the huge crowd of observers," the paper applauded.[16] When Dizzy showed up someplace—even for a brief couple of hours—he left behind a lot of smiles.

Years later, after broadcaster Dizzy's mangled on-air syntax began stirring complaints, a guest on Dean's radio show admonished him, "Don't you know the King's English?"

"Ol' Diz knows the King's English," he replied. "And not only that, I also know the Queen's English."[17]

Maybe the exchange was real—and maybe it was contrived to embellish Dizzy's legend. Like so many anecdotes that have gotten attached to Dean, it's almost impossible to separate myth from reality.

After the Cardinals brought him to the big club for the first time in the fall of 1930, Dean demanded a meeting to discuss salary with St. Louis general manager Branch Rickey. After pitching all of one game in the big leagues, Diz was, naturally, comparing himself to Babe Ruth as a box office draw and demanding big bucks.

Rickey and Dean's parley went on for hours, noted a cub reporter for the *St. Louis Star* named Walter Wellesley Smith. The young scribe, who preferred the nickname Red, noted that Dean eventually slipped out a side door since Rickey knew that reporters were lurking out front. At long last, Red Smith recounted decades later, Rickey emerged from his office.

The Mahatma [Rickey's nickname] was coatless, his collar was unbuttoned and his necktie hung loose. His hair looked as though it had been slept in. He was sweating, and over the half-glasses on the end of his nose, his eyes were glassy. "By Judas Priest! If there were one more like him in baseball, just one, as God is my judge, I'd get out of the game!"[18]

Despite his lack of schooling, Dean possessed, *New York World-Telegram* columnist Joe Williams wrote, a "sort of red clay native cunning intelligence." Dizzy was such a showman, Williams chortled in '42, that "there wasn't any pose, no matter how ridiculous, [that Dean] wouldn't take for a photographer."[19]

Dean's compulsive braggadocio—uttering outrageous boasts, mugging for newsreel cameras, clowning on radio broadcasts—didn't happen by accident. They were all part of his calculated effort to create a public persona—the lovable "lunkhead," as the *New York Times*'s Gay Talese later called it—that Diz could take to the bank. It worked. Dizzy Dean became, in many ways, America's first multimedia superstar, a ballplayer who shrewdly leveraged his personality into a lucrative broadcasting and banquet-speaking career. Dizzy Dean made a pile of dough just being Dizzy Dean. "Fortunately for all of us, he never grew up," Jim Murray of the *Los Angeles Times* wrote.[20]

The perpetual boy's origins could not have been more humble. The Deans were a classic American archetype: pioneers constantly uprooting themselves in search of a better life.

Dizzy's great-great-grandfather, felicitously named Moses, abandoned Tennessee in the early nineteenth century because it got too crowded—or so family lore suggested. Moses moved his flock across the Ozarks to backwoods Missouri, not far from Rolla, a tiny timber town. The Deans stayed in Missouri for a couple of generations, long enough for Dizzy's paternal grandfather to serve two terms as Rolla's sheriff.[21]

According to a 1941 column written by the *Sporting News*'s J. G. Taylor Spink, at one point Sheriff Dean had custody over "a Negro in jail for a year, so he made a trustee of [the prisoner] and made him work the farm."[22] The Deans and their indentured sharecropper raised mainly corn.

Seven or eight years after Appomattox, Dizzy's father, Albert Monroe Dean, came into this world. "Ab" lived in Rolla until age fifteen, when his dad, the onetime constable, moved the family to the Indian Territories, as Oklahoma was then known. When the Depression of 1899 made jobs scarce, Ab, by then twenty-seven, moved to the scruffy flatlands of west-central Arkansas. He eventually found occasional work at a sawmill near the town of Lucas. The place was so backwoods that for most of the nineteenth century it was known as Crow Town. Besides the sawmill, the erstwhile Crow Town had a cotton gin, a blacksmith shop, and not much else.

In 1904, Ab married a local girl many years his junior named Alma Nelson. Everyone in town was fond of Alma; she was bright and vivacious and considered an exceptional athlete. Her husband, by contrast, was distant and dour; in a 2008 interview, his granddaughter remembered him as "stand-offish and not real warm."[23] Ab's disposition supposedly brightened only when playing third base for the Lucas town nine. Alma and Ab moved into a small tenant house, sharecropped to pay the rent, and set about starting a family—with heartbreaking consequences.

Their first two children, a boy and a girl, died in infancy. The third child, a boy named Elmer, was mentally retarded. Paul Dean's daughter remembers her uncle Elmer behaving "like a kid all the time."[24]

Hoping it would serve as a talisman, Ab and Alma named their next son after two titans of the Gilded Age: railroad tycoon Jay Gould, who at one time controlled the Union Pacific and a slew of smaller railroads; and steel magnate Mark Hanna, the Republican Party boss who took a rotund Ohio politician named William McKinley, parked him on his front porch, and made him president of the United States, twice over.

Young Jay Hanna wasn't destined to be a tycoon. In fact, Dean became an outspoken New Dealer—a political philosophy that would have horrified his namesakes. Dean was so taken with Franklin D. Roosevelt that Diz attended the 1936 Democratic convention in Philadelphia. Sporting a cowboy hat and screeching into a noisemaker, he led the Missouri delegation's demonstration after the president was officially renominated. Postmaster General James Farley, who was directing the convention, nixed the idea of bringing Dean onto the stage. Big Jim was worried that delegates would be so excited to see Dizzy that it might detract from FDR's moment.[25]

Elmer, Jay, and youngest son Paul were little boys when their mother contracted a fatal case of tuberculosis. Alma was buried next to her deceased children in a crude cemetery a few yards from their home.

Unable to make ends meet, Ab moved the family to Oklahoma, where the cotton crop was more reliable. The Deans picked cotton all over southeastern Oklahoma, in and around towns like Holdenville and Spaulding.

The boys' school attendance, never sterling when their mother was alive, became sporadic. Jay joked with the *Saturday Evening Post* in 1951 that he quit school after the second grade reader "only I didn't learn all of it."[26] Banquet audiences would roar when he'd say, "I didn't do too good in the first grade, neither."

The boys usually played ball barefoot since most of the time they couldn't afford shoes. While barely in his teens, Diz threw a shutout for Spaulding High School against the Oklahoma Teachers College. Mean college guys covered the mound with shards of broken glass that Diz had to sidestep—or so he told the *St. Louis Post-Dispatch* in 1934.[27]

Spaulding High and other schools were a luxury; Ab needed his boys working the fields. As they grew stronger, the brothers could pick several hundred pounds of cotton each day, earning a quarter for their labors. When reminiscing about his days as a field hand, Paul liked to tell his grandson Gary that there was a difference between "pickin' and pullin'." To get the best yield, Paul remembered, a field hand had to get both hands deep inside the plant and pull, which often left fingers bruised and bleeding.[28] "[Jay] never liked to pick cotton and never turned in as much as Paul did," Ab told the *Sporting News* in '41—a sentiment later echoed by Paul.[29]

Ab, Elmer, Jay, and Paul spent years in those fields, sweating shoulder-to-shoulder with people—white and black—whose desperate lot in life mirrored their own. Much of the racial superiority of white southerners came from a belief that downscale labor was not for white folks. But young Jay saw firsthand the dignity and pathos of itinerant pickers; surely it shaped his political views and his open mind on racial matters.

The Deans essentially lived off the land, Ab told writers years later. They stayed in shacks and ate what they called "plain grub"—sowbelly and cornmeal when there was a little money; sweet potatoes and peanuts when there wasn't.

Over the years, several versions of how "Jay Hanna" became "Jerome Herman" have found their way into print. The most commonly told account was described in the 1953 Cooperstown/Home Plate Press "Baseball's Immortals" series. When the Deans were still in Lucas, a boy named Jerome Herman lived next door. Young Jerome died after a long illness; Jay, then six or seven, went over to comfort the grieving father.

"Don't be sad," Dean told him. "I'll be Jerome Herman. My name's Jay Hanna and they're the same initials, anyway."[30] The confusion over Dean's name lasted for decades. When *Time* put Diz on its cover in 1940, it identified him as "Jerome Herman Dean."

When Jay was in his teens, Ab married a widow with three children of her own—a happenstance that further strained family finances. An older stepbrother told Jay that life in the army trumped cotton picking. So at age sixteen Jay had his father sign a document that stated he was two years older. "You got your shoes free and all the grub you wanted," Diz remembered about his army experience. "And the pay was $19 a month and that was more money than I'd ever seen or was gonna make on a farm somewhere."[31]

Off Dean went to Fort Sam Houston, on the outskirts of San Antonio. Much like Paige in juvenile jail, the three squares Diz got each day did him a world of good. So, at least in theory, did the discipline of army life. But Dean was, by his own admission, a miserable excuse for a soldier. "That boy couldn't pour piss out of a boot with directions on the heel," one of his drill sergeants growled.[32]

After stumbling at other chores, Dean was given full-time kitchen-patrol duty, where he peeled potatoes and mopped floors. But he got to play ball for the post laundry team. And on weekends, he snuck off base and hooked up with whatever local semipro club offered the most money and free barbecue.

A sergeant was drilling two platoons past the kitchen one afternoon when he happened to spot a potato hurtling toward a garbage pit in the back. He rushed over and discovered Dean chucking spuds from the back porch.

"You dizzy son of a bitch!" the sarge hollered, blistering Dean so loudly that the label stuck.[33]

In April 1928, the name "Dizzy Dean" appeared in print for the first time. Pitching for the 12th Field Artillery team, Private Dean struck out seventeen members of the St. Mary's University squad; he was saluted in the San Antonio paper as a "a star twirler."

Dean enjoyed hanging out with baseball-crazed twin brothers from San Antonio. The siblings had a rivalry that apparently revolved around Sunday afternoon money matches pitting one brother's squad against the other's. Diz, in a move Satchel Paige would have appreciated, would lease himself to the highest bidder, pitching for one brother one weekend, the other the next.[34]

One day in the spring of 1927, the Deans were on the side of an Austin highway fixing a flat tire on Ab's old truck. A fellow field hand apparently known to the family drove up, volunteering to lend a hand.

Exactly what happened next is the subject of dispute. One story is that Elmer was hungry, so Ab gave the boy a few cents and asked the Samaritan to drive his son somewhere to get food. Other accounts suggest that the worker was heading to the same fields as the Deans and offered to give Elmer a lift. Once the flat was fixed, the two cars somehow got detached. Paul told his children and grandchildren that the autos lost contact when a train came through.[35] Whatever happened, Elmer was separated from the rest of his family.

The Deans spent two days scouring Austin but Elmer never turned up. Since the family had neither a home address nor a telephone, it was impossible for the Samaritan to track them down. Inexplicably, Ab never went to the Austin police to report his impaired son's disappearance. It would be more than four years before Elmer resurfaced—and then only because he happened to spot his famous younger brother's picture in a newspaper.

By year two, army life was getting in the way of Dizzy's ball playing. When higher-ups suggested that Dean buy his way out of the final year of his hitch, Dizzy leaped. Somehow he came up with the requisite $120, either by Ab dipping into the family's savings or, more likely, through the good graces of a San Antonio semipro club interested in acquiring a star pitcher.

It didn't take long for a Houston Buffaloes scout named Don Curtis to begin bird-dogging Dean. After minimal dickering, Diz signed with the Buffs, a Texas League farm team of the St. Louis Cardinals, for three hundred dollars a month, effective the following spring, 1930. There was no signing bonus, despite Diz's later claims to the contrary.[36] For a time, at least, Diz tried to cop a "baseball age," claiming he was a year younger and feigning ignorance when the discrepancy was pointed out.

The Buffaloes thought Dean needed seasoning, so they sent him to a lower St. Louis affiliate, the St. Joseph (Mo.) Saints of the Western League. Along with other Cardinal farm clubs, St. Joe was conducting spring practice in Shawnee, Oklahoma. Houston officials gave Dean eight dollars and told him to buy a lower-berth train ticket. Dean either pocketed the cash or blew it gambling because he ended up hopping a freight.

When Diz arrived at the Shawnee hotel, he looked and smelled like a bum, teammates recalled. His face was so filthy that when he knocked on the door, one player thought Dean was "colored." Diz wasn't carrying a valise so they asked him the whereabouts of the rest of his clothes. His suitcases would be coming later, Diz fibbed. Within a day or two, it occurred to the Saints' manager that Diz was probably wearing the only clothes he owned, so he slipped Dean some money until payday.

St. Louis's general manager, Branch Rickey, wanted to check out the phenom for himself. Rickey puffed on a cigar while sitting behind the backstop in Shawnee one afternoon and never bothered to introduce himself. A few hours later, Dean happened to spot Rickey sitting in a hotel lobby reading the evening paper.

Diz sauntered up to Rickey, stuck out his hand, and announced, "Hello, Branch. I'm Dizzy Dean, the feller what struck out all them fellers today," recounted the *New York Times*'s Arthur Daley, perhaps a bit too colloquially, a quarter of a century later.[37]

At first Rickey greeted Dean's cheekiness with stony silence; after several more puffs on his cigar, he asked, "Are you a pitcher, Mister Dean?"

"Sure, Branch. Don't waste time sendin' me to St. Joe. Bring me right up with the Cardinals. Effen I kin strike 'em out in one league, I kin strike 'em out in the other. I kin win the pennant for you."[38]

It was an astonishing moment. Almost no one called "Mister Rickey" by his first name. Yet here was this bumpkin telling one of baseball's most respected architects how to construct his club. It didn't take long for the GM and his prodigy to develop a cantankerous relationship.[39]

Dizzy's boss never let on to Dean in that first meeting how highly the Cards valued him. Rickey later admitted his heart skipped a beat when he saw the pop on Dean's fastball and the snap on his curve. Dizzy's loose-limbed delivery, in fact, reminded Rickey of Christy Mathewson's.

Rickey wasn't alone. Years later, the *Saturday Review of Literature*'s Norman Cousins wrote that the first time he saw Dean, he pictured Matty, too. "You were attracted by the graceful rhythm of [Dean's] pitching motion: the long majestic sweep of his arm as he let the ball fly; the poised alertness after the pitch."[40]

By midseason, Rickey was saying, "I consider Dean the most promising rookie I have ever seen. He has blinding speed, a splendid curve, and marvelous control. Furthermore, he loves to pitch and would pitch every day if the opportunity afforded itself."[41]

It's true: Diz would have pitched every day. Eventually, egged on by Rickey, it would prove his undoing.

Dean pitched in thirty-two games for a St. Joe team mired in last place, striking out 125, and going 17-8. His earned run average was 3.69, which turned out to be the highest of his pre-broken-toe career.

His temper also ran high. Twice that year, his razzing led to bench-clearing brawls—both of which had to be broken up by the police. Dizzy's nocturnal carousing also caused problems. Without bothering to inform hotel clerks, he hopped from the St. Francis to the Robidoux—then holed up at St. Joe's YMCA. When confronted with overdue bills, he pleaded ignorance, claiming he didn't understand that he had to actually check out before sleeping someplace else. The Saints had to pay his outstanding tabs.

In early June, he was admitted to a local hospital, supposedly for an "ankle infection," although teammates believed it was a certain extremity north of his feet that had gotten infected. On days he wasn't pitching, Dizzy liked to bring girls to St. Joe's City Baseball Stadium. Sometimes he'd park his leased convertible out beyond right field and watch the game from there. Between innings, he and his date would neck.[42]

Since the Cardinals' top farm club in Houston was in the middle of a split-season pennant chase, Dean was transferred to the Buffaloes late in the year. He won eight games down the stretch for the Buffs, becoming an instant folk hero. Reporters for the *Houston Post-Dispatch* and the *Chronicle* knew good copy when they saw it. Dean was described as "cocky," "eccentric," and, in one memorable passage, "nuts."[43]

Dizzy wasn't shy about letting Houstonians know how fortunate they were to be in his presence. While cruising in taxicabs, he liked to stick his head out the window and holler at passersby, "I'm the Great Dean! Want me to sign somethin' for ya?" Since he blew through money faster than he could make it, much of the time he was broke.[44]

Satchel Paige craved attention and shirked responsibility, same as Diz. But Satch had too much dignity to stick his head out of a moving car and shout at people. Red Smith, who watched Dean become a demigod, wrote that Dizzy remained his entire life a "big, gangling gawk, appealing in his ungainliness."[45]

The gangling gawk's bravado was rewarded with a call-up to the Cards for the final days of their National League pennant-winning campaign in 1930. Manager Gabby Street did not want to entrust a rookie to pitch in a pennant chase, so he waited until the flag was clinched before letting Dean near a mound.

Just a few thousand fans were on hand at Sportsman's Park to see Dizzy's big-league debut against the Pittsburgh Pirates on September 28. The busher did not get off to an auspicious start. Dean walked two of the first three hitters, then gave up a run-scoring single to future Hall of Fame third baseman Pie Traynor.

But the youngster escaped without further damage—and settled down. The Bucs managed only two more hits and one more walk. Diz won a complete-game three-hitter, beating left-hander Larry French, 3-1.[46] Ironically, in the years to come, French became a fixture on the barnstorming circuit with Dean and Paige. Diz was ineligible for the postseason, so he was not part of the Cardinals' four-games-to-two loss to the Philadelphia Athletics in that fall's Series.

During the Cards' Bradenton spring training in '31, Dean underwent a tonsillectomy. John Kieran of the *New York Times* wrote that, a half hour after surgery, Diz was lounging in his hospital bed, smoking a cheap cigar and sucking on hard candy.[47]

Despite promises to clean up his act, Dizzy persisted in his reckless ways. The spendthrift needed more seasoning—and to be taught a lesson. Rickey and Street assigned Dean to Houston for the entire '31 campaign. As the Great Dean left camp, one of the Cards cracked, "This is the first time in baseball history that a team ever lost 30 games in one day."[48]

He didn't win thirty in Houston that season; he ended up winning a mere twenty-six. More important, though, he won the heart of perhaps the only woman willing to put up with him. Her name was Patricia Nash. Four years his senior, she was already a twice-divorced store clerk with a fondness for late hours and ballplayers. Rumors swirled about Patsy's past liaisons. When Rickey heard about Diz's whirlwind romance with a party gal, he used surrogates to try to talk Dean out of it. They couldn't: Diz was smitten. As Dizzy later told columnist Irv Kupcinet of the *Chicago Sun*, Diz knew that Pat wasn't chaste—but then, he wasn't, either.[49]

Pat forced him to put away a little money and curbed at least some of his bacchanalian ways. "She set the rudder," Roy Stockton wrote in the *Saturday Evening Post*. "She adored him, babied him, [and] bossed him."[50] Patsy could swear like a sailor and tell an off-color story with the best of them. They stayed together forty-three years.

Diz could still be the life of the party. At one point in Houston, he was out late bar-hopping when he bumped into Buffs owner Fred Ankenman. "So the ol' boy is out after curfew, eh?" Diz quipped. "Us presidents and stars must have our fun. But don't you worry none. . . . I won't tell nobody."[51] Riding his star's right arm, Ankenman's Buffaloes went all the way to the Texas League–Southern League "Dixie Series" that season, losing to the Birmingham Barons.

A troupe managed by Connie Mack's son Earle barnstormed through Houston that fall of '31. Diz pitched three innings against a squad that included right-hander George Earnshaw (21-7 that season) and out-fielder Al Simmons (an American League–leading .390) of the Philadelphia Athletics. Their teammate first baseman Jimmie Foxx (30 home runs and 120 RBIs) ended up playing with Diz and the Buffs. Foxx, Dean, and the Texas Leaguers beat Earle Mack's boys, 4-2. "I fanned Simmons and made him like it," Dean bragged to the *Sporting News*.[52]

A few days later, Diz joined his brother Paul, a Cardinals prospect then with Class D Springfield (Mo.) of the Western Association, in barnstorming small towns in Missouri and Arkansas.[53] In Joplin, Missouri, Diz demanded $150 up front, apparently prompting the game's cancellation when promoters couldn't come up with the cash.[54] There's no documentation that the Deans barnstormed against black clubs in the fall of '31 or '32.

Diz, his new bride, and Paul repaired to a little Arkansas town called Dardanelle, not far from the boys' birthplace. Later that autumn, they were surprised to receive a letter from a druggist in Plummerville, about a half hour east. A mentally challenged farmworker had been walking through the town's drugstore, spotted a newspaper picture of Dizzy in the Dixie Series, and told customers that he was the pitcher's brother. The day the letter arrived, Paul and Diz drove over. Sure enough, they found Elmer working on a nearby farm.[55]

After exchanging hugs, Diz and Paul quizzed their long-lost sibling about how he had gotten from central Texas to north-central Arkansas. The retarded man didn't know.

Years later, Paul remembered that it was tough persuading Elmer to leave the Plummerville farm. But finally they got Elmer and his pasteboard suitcase into the car. On the drive back to Dardanelle, Diz threw Elmer's flimsy valise out the window.

"Hellfire, Jay, them was my clothes. Them was all the clothes I got!" Elmer protested. But Elmer calmed down when they pulled into town; Dizzy treated his brother to some new overalls.[56]

Young Diz treated all of Cardinals Nation to yeoman pitching in '32 and '33. As a rookie in '32, he went 18-15 and led the league in innings (286) and strikeouts (191). The next year he improved those numbers to 20-18 and an NL-leading 26 complete games and 199 punch-outs. Despite Diz's gutty performance, the Cards both years finished in the middle of the pack. Their mediocre start in '33, in fact, impelled Rickey to fire manager Street and replace him with second baseman Frankie Frisch. The Fordham Flash, as New York's sportswriters were fond of calling college-boy Frisch, was destined to go down in history as skipper of baseball's motliest crew. Three members of that team—Diz, Pepper Martin, and their buddy Jimmy Wilson—briefly hit the barnstorming trail in the fall of '32, playing white town nines in downstate Illinois and backwoods Missouri.

In October of '33 it wasn't just southwestern Nebraskans who jammed ballparks to see the Monarchs take on Diz and Big Poison Waner. Crowds turned out in St. Joseph, Omaha, and Kansas City, too.

On October 5, the major leagues, buttressed by St. Joe sandlotters, defeated the Monarchs, 8-7, before fans who, according to the *St. Joseph's Gazette*, paid forty cents each to sit in City Stadium's grandstand seats. Carroll Mothel, George Giles, and Pee Wee Dwight each had two hits in a losing cause. Pitcher Andy Cooper held Paul Waner hitless but gave up eleven hits. Larry French and Sloppy Thurston shared pitching duties in St. Joe but, oddly, Diz didn't appear in his old stomping grounds.[57] He may still have been smarting from being hit by Chet Brewer's pitch the day before in Oxford.

The next night, before a predominantly black crowd at Western League Park in Omaha, the Monarchs won handily, 7-1, an outcome that earned a "Major Leaguers Pretty Punk" headline in, and stinging criticism from, the *Omaha World-Herald*. Charlie "Lefty" Beverly held the white all-stars to three hits and struck out twelve—a performance that was all but ignored by the paper. Again, Dizzy apparently didn't pitch in Omaha as the Monarchs jumped on left-hander Larry French for three quick runs.

The white team's bench was so thin that, as he had the night before in St. Joe,[58] Big Poison himself mopped up on the rubber, walking a batter, heaving a wild pitch, and allowing two runs—not altogether surprising, since in his twenty-year major-league career, the Hall of Famer never appeared on a mound. Nevertheless, Waner's bumpy outing drew the ire of the *World-Herald*.[59] "The exhibition pleased those present because they were mostly Negroes and ardent Monarch fans, but it was a lousy offering on the part of the major leaguers, barnstorming through what they call 'hoosier territory,'" dismissed reporter Robert Phipps. "The next time they're out this way we hope they skip Omaha and do us a favor."[60]

Phipps wasn't the only resident of Omaha who took exception to the specter of blacks playing in Nebraska's largest city. Three years later, local Klansmen allegedly torched the park after an appearance by Satchel Paige and the Monarchs, suggests evidence recently unearthed by University of Nebraska–Omaha historian Dennis Hoffman. The destruction of the Omaha park, Hoffman asserts, was "a perfect hate crime."[61] It took place in the midst of another perfect demonstration of hate: Adolf Hitler's 1936 Berlin Olympiad.

The big leaguers didn't fare any better on their next stop. When the tour hit Kansas City on the weekend of October 7 and 8, Wilkie made sure to spotlight Buckshot Wright, who a decade earlier had been a popular infielder for the local Blues of the American Association. Waner, perhaps sensitive to criticism that the white guys had rolled over in Omaha, assured Kansas Citians, "We're here to beat the Monarchs."[62]

It didn't happen. The Monarchs, led by Paige, dominated Dean and Larry French, 5-1, as Diz and Satch apparently pitched several innings each, although no box score has been found. Other Dean-Waner vs. Monarchs games may have occurred that weekend; the October 5 *Kansas City Star* reported that multiple local contests were in the offing.[63]

Alas, there was no wrap-up of the Sunday game(s) in Monday's *Star*. A year later, catcher T. J. Young told the Wichita newspaper that the Monarchs hit Diz hard that weekend at Muehlebach Field, their home ballpark.[64]

Dean was, by then, a seasoned barnstormer, having done brief off-season gigs against white sandlotters in '31 and '32. Diz was also sharp enough to recognize that, as the '33 caravan's biggest draw, he should have been pocketing more cash. Frustration with that fall's barnstorming experience, in fact, led Diz and Patricia, his money-conscious spouse, to control the purse strings of future trips.

The Deans not only knew how to count a crowd, they knew how to whip one up. They watched fans buzz with excitement as Diz and Satch strolled toward the mound in the fall of 1933 and decided there was a way they could cash in.

That October was the first time that Satchel Paige faced Pepper Martin, Diz's crazy-legged buddy on what was soon coined the Gas House Gang.

Paige's pals had warned Satch that Martin was a tough out. As Ted Shane related the moment six years later in his *Saturday Evening Post* article "Chocolate Rube Waddell," Satchel liked to "play dumb."

> As each batter faced [Paige] for the first time, he would ask lugubriously:
>
> "Is you Mr. Martin? . . . Is you?"
>
> Finally the real Mr. Martin faced him. "Is you Mr. Martin?"
>
> Mr. Martin grinned, swung a bat menacingly.
>
> "Mr. Pepper Martin?" Satchel persisted.
>
> Mr. Martin's grin broadened.
>
> "They tells me," Satchel drawled, "you kin hit!"
>
> Mr. Martin's bat danced over the plate.
>
> "Then hit this!" yelled Satchel, and flung a ball over as fast as a bullet.
>
> Pepper had barely time to blink before that same ball had fled past him again—and again, setting him down on strikes.

For his part, Martin admitted to Shane that he was bewildered by Satch's delivery. "You cain't see nuthin' but dat foot," Shane wrote in trying to capture the Oklahoman's argot. "It hides the ballpark and Satch, too. Sometimes you don't know the ball's been pitched till it plunks behind you."[65]

Ten days and fifteen hundred miles later, Pepper and Diz got to see Satch's Bee Ball plunk behind them plenty. The game took place in the Boyle Heights section of Los Angeles, at a field named after a local black semipro club that called itself the White Sox.

Satch's West Coast appearance against Martin and both Dean brothers was the brainchild of Joseph Pirrone (pronounced with a long "e"), a bon vivant nightclub owner who doubled as the godfather of the California Winter League, the only professional circuit back then that sanctioned the participation of black teams. The Martin-Dean exhibition was part of a slate of Pirrone-orchestrated games that fall pitting Paige against big league and Pacific Coast League players.[66]

The PCL of the '30s and '40s was a premier minor league, home to such iconic franchises as the Hollywood Stars, the Los Angeles Angels, the San Diego Padres, the San Francisco Seals, and the Oakland Oaks. Over the years it spawned stars including the DiMaggio brothers, Ted Williams, Ernie Lombardi, and Bobby Doerr. Many PCL players participated in the CWL during the off-season.

Nobody west of Abe Saperstein could flack a game like Pirrone. A crowd of both whites and blacks (the *Los Angeles Times* back then was fond of describing African Americans, already hemmed into a ghetto, as "Central Avenue types") turned out to see the first of what proved to be a slew of Diz vs. Satch matchups in Southern California.

Dean was playing with a creditable outfit that included Pepper Martin and Indians rookie shortstop Bill Knickerbocker (who hit .226 in 80 games that season), plus a collection of Pacific Coast Leaguers destined to have brief careers in the big leagues: catcher Hughie McMullen (.176 career hitter in just 108 big-league at-bats) of the Giants and Senators; infielder-pitcher Gene Lillard (.182, 44 at-bats) of the Cubs and Cards; and first sacker Jim Oglesby (.182 in 11 at-bats) of the Athletics.

Satch's teammates on Nashville-based entrepreneur Tom Wilson's "Royal Colored Giants" that fall were some of the most iconic names in blackball: sluggers Turkey Stearnes and Mule Suttles, magician shortstop Willie Wells, and speedster Cool Papa Bell—all future Hall of Famers. Tommy Dukes, whose heart made up for a lack of heft, played behind the plate.[67]

Norman Thomas "Turkey" Stearnes was a left-handed power hitter who contorted himself into a stance not unlike Stan Musial's, with his left cleat dug in close to the plate, his right cleat planted in the bucket, and his right heel ground into the dirt. Stearnes was a native Tennessean whose head bobbed up and down as he tracked balls in the outfield, hence the nickname. A mainstay of the Detroit Stars in the '20s, Turkey reportedly led the Negro National League in home runs seven times. Stearnes abandoned the Stars in '31 when the team couldn't meet payroll. He played for various squads for another decade; even well into his thirties, Turkey was considered one of blackball's quickest outfielders.[68]

George "Mule" Suttles was a strapping power hitter often called the "black Babe Ruth," although his beefy body and right-handed cut were more reminiscent of Jimmie Foxx. The Mule used a mammoth fifty-ounce bat. At Cuba's Tropicana Park one winter, Suttles supposedly hit a ball that soared over the sixty-foot-high center-field fence and splashed into Havana Harbor. "Don't worry about the Mule going blind," the Alabamian liked to say late in a close game, "just load the wagon and give me the lines."[69] Mule was twice credited with leading the NNL in homers.

Wells's range at short was so otherworldly that Mexican fans gave Willie the same appellation they later hung on Hilton Smith's curveball: *El Diablo*. Monte Irvin, who played with Wells on the Newark Eagles, remembers that he could chase pop-ups to shallow left and center better than anyone, black or white.[70] One historian credits Wells with a .364 batting average in interracial games.[71]

Even without Satchel's tall tales, Bell was one of the slickest base runners in history. With Paige's hyperbole, Cool Papa became mythic, the player who was so quick he could flip a light switch and be under the covers before the room went dark.

Diz and Satch didn't exactly go head-to-head that night in L.A., although the *Times* and the *Herald and Express* had billed it as a shootout. Both men had pitched the previous day: Dean in a semipro contest at Pasadena's Brookside Park; Satch in a CWL game at White Sox Park in which he gave up only three hits and fanned fifteen.

Egged on by Pirrone, Bob Ray of the *Times* wasn't subtle in pushing the confrontation. Dean, Ray wrote, was a "loud-mouthed hurler who can back up his remarks." Martin was tagged as the player "whose sensational exploits on the diamond practically single-handedly won the 1931 World Series." In the same article, Ray called Paige a "lean, colored fire-baller who has a fastball that sizzles on its way to the plate."[72]

In front of a capacity crowd at White Sox Park, Dizzy pitched the first three innings, giving up two hits—one of them a home run by catcher Dukes. Pepper's triple off Sammy Bankhead in the first set up the white team's initial run. The "Wild Hoss of the Osage" stampeded home on an infield dribbler, later swiped two bases, and made a couple of scintillating catches. Future Chicago White Sox and Cincinnati Reds right-hander Lee Stine (career big-league record 3-8), another Pacific Coast Leaguer, took over for Dean and "kept the colored stars' big guns effectively silenced," the *Times* reported.[73] The Giants mustered but four hits; Stearnes and Suttles were kept at bay.

Satch relieved Bankhead in the fourth and pitched the three middle innings, holding Pirrone's men scoreless. Hughie McMullen's eighth-inning homer off Jim "Cannonball" Willis proved to be the decisive blow, making a winner of Stine. Diz, Pepper, and company collected just seven hits, but they were enough to eke out a 2-1 win.[74]

As he had the previous two winters once he had finished his duties with the Craws, Paige spent much of the '33–'34 off-season in California, packing stadiums and, courtesy of Pirrone, picking up a generous p.c. Satch threw eighteen complete games in the CWL that season for the Royal Colored Giants, winning all but two. Along the way, Paige tossed seven shutouts and beat white major leaguer Sloppy Thurston (then wrapping up an 89-86 big league record) of the Brooklyn Dodgers, along with future Dodger Johnny Babich (career mark, 30-45) and future major leagues Bobo Newsom (career record 211-222), as well as Satch's midwestern barnstorming foil Larry French (who led the National League in '33 with 35 starts) of the Pirates.[75]

After his L.A. appearances in mid-October, Dean headed back east with wife Patsy. Before returning to Florida, however, the former Houston Buffalo stopped at the Buffs' park for another exhibition, this one to benefit a children's shoe charity. Joining him was younger brother Paul, who was coming off an impressive season with Columbus in the American Association. There was already much talk of Diz and Paul becoming a rugged one-two pitching combination for the Cards in '34.

While celebrating Dizzy's homecoming, the brothers went to a soiree honoring Galveston's own Gus Mancuso, a catcher with the newly crowned Series champs, the New York Giants. *Houston Post* sports editor Lloyd Gregory, who'd covered Diz in his Texas League days, reported that Dizzy's remarks at the Mancuso reception concluded with, "Well, gentlemen, I'm just about through with my speech. But my brother Paul here is a great pitcher and a great orator. I'm going to ask Paul to talk. I hope he tells you all about himself, and ALSO SAYS A FEW WORDS ABOUT ME" (emphasis Gregory's).[76]

Proud Poppa Dean was in the stands at Buffs Stadium, watching all three of his boys. Paul and Dizzy both started, with the younger Dean departing in the first frame, complaining of a sore hand. Dizzy's sandlot squad won, 9-1, over Paul's, but the highlight of the game was the "big wallop" bashed off Diz by none other than Elmer, who worked at the park as a peanut vendor.[77]

"Some of the fans thought Dizzy grooved one for Brother Elmer," wrote the *Post*'s Gregory, "but Brother Elmer smacked the pellet right smartly." Elmer's three-bagger led the Associated Press account of the game. Diz fanned six over three innings.

With that, the Deans retreated to Bradenton, Florida (a.k.a. "Deanville") for the winter. But the excitement that Satch and Diz had generated wasn't lost on the Deans. Nor was it lost on J. L. Wilkinson and the other moneymen who controlled interracial ball. Satch and Diz were just getting started—and Kenesaw Mountain Landis be damned.

CHAPTER FOUR

"Plenty Dizzy": Diz, Daffy, and Satch in 1934

[Dizzy] Dean was born with a natural and profound contempt for the laws of grammar, and had the added good fortune, as the years passed, to escape any enforced refinements in the way of classroom syntax.

—JOE WILLIAMS, COLUMNIST, *NEW YORK WORLD-TELEGRAM*

On October 6, 1934, the *Chicago Defender* ran an editorial cartoon. Titled "At the Knothole," it showed a forlorn black player goosing his neck to gaze inside a ballpark. Crumpled at the player's feet was a poster that reads "World Series Today."[1]

In the same edition of the *Defender,* columnist Al Monroe issued this rebuke: "Truly I cannot see how any team can call itself champion of the world that hasn't batted against Satchel Paige. . . . And I am wondering if 'Schoolboy' Rowe and the Dean brothers can gloat over their strikeout records and world's series wins over teams that failed to include Josh Gibson, Turkey Stearns [*sic*], Jud Wilson, Oscar Charleston and others in their lineup."[2]

Jim Crow may have precluded blacks from competing in major-league baseball and its fall classic, but the 1934 World Series certainly didn't lack for color.

After the seventh and deciding game—a lopsided St. Louis win—turned ugly, embittered fans began littering the field with garbage.

Extra security had to be summoned as several hundred Detroiters, many of them soused, gathered outside the visitors' clubhouse, cursing the Cardinals and making nasty threats against star Joe "Ducky" Medwick. With the Cardinals already leading 9-0 in the top of the sixth, Medwick had slid cleats-up into third, spiking Detroit third baseman Marv Owen and triggering a brief wrestling match. At the insistence of Commissioner Landis, who was attending the game, Medwick was removed from the field, ostensibly for his own protection. An hour or two later, as the giddy Cardinals readied themselves to depart the clubhouse, detectives insisted that Medwick disguise himself by yanking a civilian hat over his ears. So Ducky donned a fedora and wormed his way into the middle of the Cardinals pack. "Where's Ducky? Give us Medwick!" the Detroiters yelped. But the fedora did its job: Ducky went undetected in the phalanx of cops escorting the Cardinals.

As he left the ballpark, Dizzy Dean was sporting a pith helmet and an ear-to-ear grin. Dean repeatedly tipped his lid in mock acknowledgment of the crowd's jeers.[3] Diz had reason to smile: the next day, he was scheduled to embark on a barnstorming tour with black players that was guaranteed to swell his pocketbook.

Earlier that day, Diz had pitched a complete-game shutout, making good on his promise that "Me 'n' Paul"—his kid brother—would win the Series by beating Detroit four times. The Dean boys put up imposing numbers in the '34 Classic, appearing in five games and combining for an earned-run average of less than 1.50. Diz's dazzling postseason culminated his '34 campaign, when he led the National League with 30 wins, posted a 2.65 ERA, and pitched in relief a remarkable 17 times.

One of the first hands Diz had grabbed in the chaos of the Cards clubhouse belonged to Will Rogers. "We done it, didn't we, boy?" Diz told America's celebrity journalist. "I knew we'd whip them Tigers!"[4]

The pith helmet had been given to Dizzy before the Series started. It was a gag gift meant to help him "tame" the Tigers. His tiger-tamer act was just one of a bevy of attention-grabbing moments that Dean seized that October. The day before game one, Diz interrupted a Tigers practice session by insisting on taking cuts in the batting cage. Still decked out in street shoes and a three-piece suit, Diz shed his jacket, grabbed a fungo bat, and—with scores of photographers recording every antic and the Tigers pretending to be amused—sprayed line drives around Navin Field.

Sportswriter Paul Gallico, standing nearby, wrote, "Here was manna from heaven beyond [photographers'] wildest dreams. All you could hear was the snapping of shutters and the grinding of the movie cameras."[5] Gallico presciently noted that "The Cards look like winners. Dizzy Dean is all ice."[6]

Gallico's ice man didn't always stick to the same facts from interview to interview. Indeed, Diz gave wildly conflicting accounts of his birth date and birthplace. When his biographic anomalies were pointed out, Diz scoffed: "I was helpin' the writers out. Them ain't lies: them's scoops."[7]

The Series' tragicomic moment came in the bottom of the fourth inning of game four at Sportsman's Park. For some reason, Cards player-manager Frankie Frisch allowed Dizzy to pinch-run. With Dean treading off first, Pepper Martin hit a room service double-play grounder to Charlie Gehringer at second. After catching the toss from Gehringer and tagging second, shortstop Bill Rogell fired toward first.

"The speeding ball never found its target," Grantland Rice wrote that afternoon. "It struck Dean squarely on the head with such terrific force that it bounded 25 feet into the air. . . . The impact of ball and head sounded like the backfire of an automobile. . . . [T]he great Dizzy crumpled and fell like a marionette whose string had snapped."[8]

Knocked out for a moment or two, Dizzy was nonetheless chattering as he was carried off the field before a hushed crowd. Although he was taken to a hospital as a precaution, Diz's skull sustained no lasting damage. Nor did the next day's headlines say, "X-Rays of Dean's Head Reveal Nothing"—but Diz dined out on that bogus headline for years.

The '34 Series "was a rough, tough, rowdy, ripping, slashing, mauling, 'get-the-hell-out-of-my-way' exhibit," Rice wrote, "that brought baseball back to where it belongs."[9]

Among the fans at Sportsman's Park watching in rapt silence as Dean was carted off in game four was the Feller family of Van Meter, Iowa:

Bill, Lena, fifteen-year-old Bobby, and tiny Marguerite. Bill shut down the farm so his family could take their first real vacation.

Mrs. Feller spent days preparing for the trek, Bob remembered seventy-three years later. She packed lunch every day so they could save money. The Fellers saw all three games in St. Louis, spending their nights in a motor court that sounds like it came off the set of Frank Capra's *It Happened One Night,* which, that fall, was still delighting audiences at movie houses all over the country. (That week, in fact, when Poppa Dean arrived in St. Louis aboard a bus, a reporter facetiously asked if Ab had bumped into a "runaway heiress." Ab rarely had the spending cash to take in a movie; the old man did not understand the reference to Claudette Colbert's screen character.)[10]

Young Bobby had seen big leaguers barnstorm through Des Moines, but the '34 Series was one of the few times he had witnessed major-league competition in a major-league park. His next moment in a big-league setting would come twenty-one months later, after he signed with the Cleveland Indians. And it would again involve Dizzy Dean.

Satchel Paige's performance in the summer and fall of 1934 was as spectacular as Dizzy's, although the Lean One's exploits did not command attention from fawning white columnists. Nor were newsreel cameras recording Satch's every move. Paige was doing what he'd done since leaving the juvenile pen: pitching for any team willing to meet his price.

No matter what uniform he wore, Satch continued to turn in feats that boggle the mind. On July 4, 1934, Paige pitched a no-hitter against the Crawfords' crosstown rivals, the Homestead Grays, striking out seventeen in winning, 4-0.[11] Paige walked future Hall of Famer Buck Leonard in the first inning, then set down the Grays without a blemish. Long Tom was hopping so much that day that Leonard asked the home plate umpire to inspect the ball. "You may as well throw 'em all out," Satch supposedly barked from the hill. "'Cause they're all gonna jump like that!"[12]

Satch always claimed that later that same day he drove nonstop to Chicago and, without taking a break, threw a twelve-inning shutout for the American Giants.[13]

Five weeks later, Gus Greenlee bowed to the wishes of Monarchs owner J. L. Wilkinson and leased Satch to a House of David team that Wilkie and partner Ray Doan had cobbled together to compete in the prestigious *Denver Post* tournament. Known as the "Little World Series of the West," the *Post* tournament drew a huge following in the '30s.

J.L.'s Monarchs were also participating—the first time that Denver organizers had opened their tourney to an all-black team. Wilkinson arranged for a first-rate catcher, Bill "Cy" Perkins, one of Satch's batterymates on the Craws, to play for the House of David, as well. The bewhiskered boys were managed that summer by Grover Cleveland Alexander, the future Hall of Fame pitcher and a Doan client who, at that point in his life, rarely knew a sober moment.[14]

Slated to get a nice percentage of the Denver gate, since he controlled its two best entrants, J.L. smelled a big payday. Wilkie added to his Monarchs' roster such Negro Leagues titans as Turkey Stearnes, Sammy Bankhead, and the forty-two-year-old Lefty Donaldson.

A one-sided matchup against a team sponsored by a Denver bakery gave Satch a chance to pull a favorite bit of chicanery. As the crowd murmured, Paige positioned his outfielders just beyond the infield dirt—and didn't allow a ball to crease the outfield.[15] A bemused *Post* story referred to Paige as the "Chocolate Whizbang."[16]

The Whizbang annoyed his manager later in the week when Alexander spotted Paige "warming up" by whipping the ball while on his knees. An ugly exchange ensued, with Alexander threatening to suspend Satch; eventually, the two patched things up.[17]

Wilkinson and Doan had wired the brackets to perfection: the House of David and the Monarchs ended up meeting in the championship game. Paige, to satisfy the sect's sartorial requirements, either grew scraggly facial hair or donned a red costume beard, depending on whose story is to be believed.[18] Either way, "bearded" Satch beat Chet Brewer and the Monarchs on August 10 for the championship, 2-1, before an overflow crowd.[19]

Paige struck out 44 in 28 innings in Denver, running up 23 consecutive scoreless frames. Earning "Outstanding Pitcher," Satch was awarded a coffee percolator.[20] Turkey Stearnes won a watch as "Outstanding Player."[21] The winning team's share was $7,500; after Wilkinson took his cut, it turned out to be $406 per man, although Satch probably got a bonus.[22]

Paige's real bonus, though, came from the mainstream media exposure he earned in Denver. For perhaps the first time in Satch's career, his heroics were trumpeted in a big way on national wire services.

Sixteen days later, on August 26 in front of twenty thousand fired-up fans at Comiskey Park, Satchel pitched four scoreless innings in relief for the East in the Negro Leagues' second annual East-West Classic. Satch earned a 1-0 victory.

Somehow Paige found time in September 1934 to honor the pledge he'd made to Greenlee to pitch for Gus's Craws against Stuart "Slim" Jones and the Philadelphia Stars in a pair of much-ballyhooed match-ups at Yankee Stadium. A long-limbed lefty at six-foot-six and 180 pounds, Jones was a southpaw version of Paige, all arms and legs as he whipsawed the ball. Slim supposedly went 23-3 in league play that year, leading the Stars to the NNL pennant and shutting down the Chicago American Giants in the postseason clincher.

On September 9, a crowd of thirty-five thousand was transfixed as Satch and Slim threw bookend five-hitters. Slim had a perfect game going until Oscar Charleston broke it up with a single in the seventh inning. When the Craws finally coaxed a run across in the eighth against Slim, it knotted the score at one. The game ended a few minutes later, called on account of darkness while still tied.

Black newspapers instantly christened it "the greatest game ever played"—which was the phrase that Bojangles Robinson embossed on the travel bags that the tap dancer gave to Paige and Jones a week later when the rivalry was renewed. Another big Yankee Stadium throng saw Paige get the better of Jones this time, 3-1. Satch struck out eighteen and allowed just two hits. The score was tied at one when the Craws rallied for two runs in the eighth, the insurance run scoring on Satch's sacrifice fly.

Jones squandered what little money he had on the high life. Alcoholism derailed his career: the following year, Slim won only four games in league play. Three winters later, the twenty-five-year-old collapsed in the street in a drunken stupor and froze to death.[23]

J. L. Wilkinson and his partner on the Monarchs, Tom Baird, combined to organize "the Dizzy and Daffy Tour," a barnstorming series leveraging the Dean boys' popularity. On September 21 in St. Louis,

Ray Doan announced that he'd been hired to manage the excursion. Doan promised to procure other big-name ballplayers.[24]

The idea, Doan explained, was for the Deans to barnstorm from market to market, hooking up with local white semipros. Two-thirds of the time the Deans would be pitted against black teams—a proven crowd pleaser. When, two weeks later, the Dean brothers propelled the Cards to the Series triumph, becoming overnight the biggest sports celebrities in the country, Wilkinson, Baird, and Doan knew they'd cash in—and so would the blackball operatives with whom they'd partner. Ed McAuley of the *Cleveland News* spoke for sports-writers everywhere that fall when he observed that the Deans "have captured the imagination of the country's sportsmen as have no other athletic figures."[25]

For their part, Diz and Paul couldn't wait to get rolling. Dizzy had been frustrated by his earlier experiences with barnstorming; this time he was determined to make the cash register ring loud and long. Not everything went like clockwork, but the three-week hopscotch that Doan and the Dean boys engineered that October became a model for barnstorming tours to come.

Paul disliked being called "Daffy," the inevitable nickname given to him by the media. His teammates dubbed him "Harpo," after the mute Marx brother, because it fit his quiet but mischievous personality.

Besides barnstorming, Diz and Paul had a Broadway show and a movie deal with Warner Bros. in the works, plus Diz was lending his name to everything from Camel cigarettes (he actually preferred Lucky Strikes) and Grape Nuts cereal to Nunn-Bush shoes and M. Hohner harmonicas—an astounding forty thousand dollars' worth of endorsements, all told.[26] "This is one time in our lives to get the dough, and we're getting it while we can," Diz told the Associated Press.[27]

The promoter who helped Diz get the barnstorming dough was Raymond L. Doan, a small-town Iowa boy with big-city dreams. All through the '30s and '40s, Doan sported a stylish mustache à la Hollywood heartthrob Clark Gable. The *Sporting News*'s photographs always showed Doan impeccably turned out, with his arm around one luminary or another.

Doan was garrulous and earthy, never without a quip or a quick comeback. He proudly called himself the "father of donkey baseball." Fans in the hinterlands back then apparently couldn't get enough of players trying to navigate a baseball field while sitting atop mules. "I'm also the fellow who thought up playing softball with the infielders and outfielders tied to goats," Doan once claimed. "It's the funniest goddamned thing you ever saw."[28]

Doan had a remarkable facility for insinuating himself into celebrity ventures, whether it was running a popular Hot Springs, Arkansas, baseball academy with Rogers Hornsby, flacking the barnstorming adventures of the aging and often inebriated Grover Cleveland Alexander, handling some of Babe Ruth's commercial interests, or shilling for Olympic track star and professional golfer Mildred "Babe" Didrickson.[29]

Doan's All-Star Baseball Academy became a sad emblem of the Depression. Throughout the '30s, thousands of young men cadged rides or hopped freights to get to Hot Springs (and later the Doan camp in Jackson, Mississippi), desperately hoping to catch the eye of a professional scout. By mid-decade, Doan's school was luring four hundred "prospects" a year and attracting coverage from major media, including *Time*.[30]

For every kid who landed a Class D contract, scores left the Doan-Hornsby camp with hopes dashed and wallets lightened. Later in the '30s, Hornsby and Doan paid Dean, Gabby Street, Burleigh Grimes, Bobby Feller (who was younger than almost all the campers!), Rabbit Maranville (then in his midforties), Cy Young (then pushing seventy), and other big names some $250 a week to serve as "faculty members" in Hot Springs. A classic photo in the *Sporting News* showed "Professor Dean," in cap and gown, "lecturing" pupils, with the Rajah, Hornsby, sniggering in the foreground.

Early on, Doan, a native of Muscatine, cultivated a partnership with fellow Iowan Wilkinson. Wilkie and Doan worked out an arrangement on barnstorming ventures: J.L. would, in effect, serve as producer, providing resources and matériel; Ray, the director, would do the hard work. Ray did such an effective job promoting the House of David that the papers often called them "Doan's Davidites." At one point, Doan sued to protect the House of David "brand" from being bastardized by wannabes. For bigger markets, Wilkie and Doan worked in concert with such blackball moguls and booking agents as Abe Saperstein in Chicago, Ed Bolden (and eventually Eddie Gottlieb) in Philadelphia, Gus Greenlee in Pittsburgh, and Nat Strong (and eventually Alex Pompez) in New York—most of whom would factor in the Dizzy, Daffy, and Satch tour of '34.

Doan's brashness rubbed some people the wrong way. Nevertheless, Doan was the first and last word in profitable barnstorming—so even those who disliked him used his services.

Instead of hitting the cow town circuit in the fall of '34, Wilkie and Doan decided to concentrate on bigger metropolises with decent-sized facilities. Interracial games were scheduled in Oklahoma City, Wichita, Kansas City, Chicago, Milwaukee, Philadelphia, Brooklyn, Paterson, Cleveland, Columbus, and Pittsburgh, with a few contests against white sandlotters thrown in for good measure.

Wilkinson's Monarchs served as the Deans' foe for the midwestern part of the tour; Bolden's Philadelphia Stars took over in Philly; Strong's New York Black Yankees provided competition in New York and New Jersey; and Greenlee's Crawfords were the opposition in Ohio and western Pennsylvania. There were also plans for Diz and Satch again to cash in on California's lucrative winter circuit. If the stress of the '34 Series had gotten to Diz, he didn't let on. "Shucks, Paul and me are just getting warmed up," Dizzy told reporters after game seven. "I feel like I could throw baseballs all winter and then start right out on the 1935 season. So does Paul."[31]

Doan's initial deal with the Dean brothers called for the boys to receive seventy-five dollars each per outing, plus 50 percent of the gate receipts.[32] The pact lasted exactly one game—or as long as it took for Diz and Paul to count noses and demand an an additional 25 percent of the pot. As the tour got under way, the *Brooklyn Eagle* published an anonymous ditty titled "The Deans."

> *It's just a game that these kids once played.*
> *When they were in breeches frayed.*

It used to be for glory, though.
But now it's done for heavy dough.[33]

Even before the parade confetti stopped wafting through downtown St. Louis, Doan had arranged for the Deans and Pepper Martin to board a Central Airlines flight to Oklahoma City, where, on October 10, the trip's first leg was scheduled to start. At the last second, Martin demurred, claiming injury but promising to join the excursion later.

The Ford Tri-Motor touched down for ten minutes to refuel in Tulsa, which gave Diz time to tell local officials how bad he felt that Tulsa wasn't on the itinerary. There the plane picked up Oklahoma's junior U.S. senator, John W. "Elmer" Thomas, a populist firebrand and baseball buff, plus a couple of Thomas's cronies.[34] Senator Thomas and associates may have spent the hop to Oklahoma City discussing commercial opportunities in the Deans' erstwhile state of residence.

Tulsa had been the scene of a 1921 race riot that had left ten thousand people homeless. Ku Klux Klan–fueled arson tragically eviscerated what had been a surprisingly prosperous minority community.[35] The Klan was deeply rooted in Oklahoma culture; at least two governors in that period, asserts contemporary reporter Barry Lewis of the *Tulsa World*, were linked to the KKK.[36] In fact, two days before the Deans arrived, the *Daily Oklahoman* ran a front-page story about the local Klan's "secret investigation of radical and communistic operations." There was nothing furtive about the article's tone; it was written with a matter-of-factness that suggested that the Klan, an organization openly preaching racial genocide, was as mainstream as the Kiwanis Club.[37]

Wilkie, Doan, and the Deans had hoped Satchel Paige could join the tour right away. But Paige's commitments elsewhere forced Satch to miss the first seven stops—despite contrary claims in his *Maybe I'll Pitch Forever* and other sources.

A huge crowd greeted the Deans at the Oklahoma City airport. With baseballs and fountain pens in hand, autograph hounds oohed and aahed as the Deans plowed their way through the terminal. The *Daily Oklahoman* reporter kidded Senator Thomas that the Deans were overshadowing him.

Oklahoma City's population barely topped 150,000 in the mid-1930s. Texas League Park, the stadium named to honor the Oklahoma City Indians' minor league affiliation, held about seven thousand in its grandstand and bleachers.

October 10 turned out to be a gorgeous Wednesday evening. Maybe it was the thrill of seeing the two World Series idols up close, or the novelty of night baseball, or the prospect of watching white players test their mettle against blacks, but fans çame from far and wide.

Nearly twenty thousand people crammed into the tiny yard. Thousands more, most of them black, rubbernecked outside the fence. Reserved box seats went for a gaudy $1.90, eighty cents more than similar tickets fetched at the World Series. Kids and standing-room-only customers got in for a quarter.

The turnout was so immense that Doan and local officials had no choice but to cordon off additional SRO space along the outfield foul lines, which made for chaotic playing conditions. Many fans bought tickets under the impression that they'd be within arm's reach of Oklahoma's own Pepper Martin. But Doan, no fool, hadn't bothered to tell the local press that Martin wouldn't show.

Bus Ham, a reporter with the *Daily Oklahoman*, was there early and watched "a sea of humanity" overwhelm the park. "As someone remarked," Ham wrote the next day, "'any guy should be able to pitch with 7,000 outfielders.'"[38] At least a half-dozen fights—including one dustup in the press box—broke out as people elbowed one other to gain a better view.

The big crowd wreaked havoc with Jim Crow customs. It was virtually unheard-of in the Oklahoma of that era for massive numbers of blacks and whites to interact on common ground. But thousands did that night, scrambling for balls that were hit into the outfield's standing-room sections. In the grand tradition of barnstorming crowds, they refused to give the balls back.

Oklahoma City's police were called in—"all six of them,"[39] wrote the acerbic Ham—to exert crowd control. Players and overmatched cops urged fans perched in the outfield to back up, but "cash customers didn't budge an inch." It could not have been a comfortable evening for Doan and police chief Tom Webb.[40]

Among the Monarchs suiting up that night were the two Newts: Joseph played third and Newt Allen handed short. Bullet Joe Rogan wasn't scheduled to pitch that evening, so he manned left. Lefty Beverly, the "southpaw dazzler" who supposedly had struck out nineteen—including Lloyd and Paul Waner—in an Oklahoma City exhibition the previous year,[41] got the starting nod. At catcher was the solid T. J. Young.

Newt Allen later claimed that the Monarchs made $1,200 each for their share of the tour, which was no doubt an exaggeration. Still, even if the black players' take was less than half that, it was huge money.[42]

Diz and Paul were playing with local semipros whom Doan had shrewdly labeled the "Oklahoma All-Stars." The only other big leaguer whom Doan had arranged to join the Deans that night and for the next few games was Paul Derringer, a right-handed pitcher who'd gone 15-21 that season for the last-place Cincinnati Reds.

Paul Dean started for the white team. The Monarchs had plenty of base runners in the first three innings against Harpo, but none crossed the plate.

Diz, still pooped from the parade, the plane flight, and shutting out the Tigers the day before, came on in the fourth and allowed but one scratch hit over two innings. The elder Dean's performance was especially impressive because thousands of fans were threatening, at any instant, to stampede the mound.

"Every inning, [fans] would press closer to try to see Dizzy," recalled Newt Allen.[43] The competition to grab balls hit into the crowd (fair ones were called ground-rule doubles) became fierce. Under the circumstances, Lefty Beverly pitched well, but the white team pushed across four runs.

The game was called in the top of the sixth, ostensibly because they'd run out of baseballs—"sort of like running out of coconuts in the jungle," Ham cracked.[44] Maybe they truly ran short of baseballs, but surely organizers and the cops, eyeing the black-and-white sea heaving just beyond the infield dirt, must have been anxious to end the proceedings.

The final score was 4-0, Oklahoma All-Stars. There were only two throwaway references to the Negro Leaguers in Ham's account the next day—typical of the way white reporters treated blackball. As the Deans' tour continued, they competed for headlines with native Oklahoman Pretty Boy Floyd, who'd just shot his way out of an Iowa road trap and was last seen hurtling east.[45]

For the Deans and the Monarchs, it was more of the same on October 11 in Wichita, where the contest was sponsored by the local athletic club. The biggest crowd in the town's sporting history—an estimated 9,000 to 10,000 people—jammed into Lawrence Stadium. The black club, led by Kansan Young, was a familiar sight in Wichita. In hyping the Dean game, the *Eagle* claimed that the Monarchs had played in Wichita some thirty-three times the previous eleven years, losing only once.[46]

The Deans had taken the overnight train from Oklahoma City, while the Monarchs had piled into cars for the 150-mile jump, a breeze by blackball travel standards. Diz was still wearing a silk bathrobe that afternoon when the *Eagle* sent a photographer and reporter over to his suite at the Allis Hotel.

Pat Dean, Dizzy's wife, was described as a combination "secretary, manager and dietitian" in a story that ran with a big picture on page one. She and Dizzy had never had a major argument, she declared, but did admit that they'd "had a few little ones."[47]

Fighting a cold and a sore arm, Paul fended off autograph seekers as he and Diz arrived at Lawrence Stadium. Fans were packed ten-deep along both foul lines, posing a menace for fielders trying to snag foul balls.

The Deans were playing with an ad hoc group of local players, only one of whom—righty Ralph Winegarner—had sniffed the bigs.[48] Then the property of the Cleveland Indians, Winegarner (career major league record, 8-6) was slated to relieve the Deans.

Diz pitched gingerly during his three-inning stint, substituting "floaters" and change-ups for his usual fog ball. He gave up three hits and one run. *Eagle* reporter Pete Lighter noted that when Paul Dean came in for the fourth and fifth innings, his fastball had more zip than Diz's, sore arm and all. While at the plate, the younger Dean had trouble keeping hold of the bat; it kept slipping out of his hands, much to the crowd's amusement. For his part, Diz looked like a "washerwoman-style hitter" when swinging at curveballs but "played possum" by waiting for fastballs, slapping a double and a single to left field.[49]

Ted "Highpockets" Trent, a rangy right-hander on loan from the Chicago American Giants, started for the Monarchs and was done in by sloppy fielding; the black team was charged with five "boots," as the *Eagle* put it. The Dean squad scored four times in the bottom of the third. Lefty Donaldson, by then forty-two and in his last full year in the Negro Leagues, took over for Trent in midgame and saw the Dean team score four more tallies in the eighth.[50]

Highpockets Trent was rumored to enjoy the high life. Double Duty Radcliffe claimed that Trent had a habit of showing up for ballgames while still in his cups.[51]

"Big Florida," as he was also called, was an alumnus of Bethune-Cookman College. Despite his struggles with alcohol, Trent had a fifteen-year career that took him from St. Louis to Chicago to the Great Plains to Cuba to California. One statistican credits Highpockets with the twelfth-best career winning percentage among Negro League hurlers with fifty or more victories.[52]

Diz and Paul "packed up their duds and disappeared" in the sixth inning in Wichita, reported the *Eagle*. "All in all," the paper said, "the crowd seemed well satisfied and the Dean boys had nothing to crab about either." The paper estimated that the boys' share of the take would net them between $2,000 and $2,500.[53]

The press mania intensified as the caravan rolled on to Kansas City. "The whip which lashed the Detroit Tigers into submission . . . will be cracked by those effervescing Dean brothers in an exhibition at Muehlebach Field tonight," enthused the *Star*.[54]

But Diz and Paul were hardly effervescing. They were tapped out— and the stress was beginning to show. Nevertheless, the brothers tickled visiting youngsters from the National Scholastic Press Association by conducting an impromptu interview. The elder Dean did the talking; Paul, still not feeling up to snuff, stayed quiet.

Dizzy allowed that his arm felt all right and that he planned to return to the Cardinals in '35. When asked if he truly wrote "Poppin' Off!," the popular newspaper column that bore his name, Dizzy grinned and answered no, although he stopped short of identifying Roy Stockton as ghostwriter. Diz also volunteered that although a tobacco company was paying him to endorse its cigarettes, he had "never smoked one before in my life"[55]—which must have come as a startling revelation to his teammates, who used to say that Diz lived on root beer and Lucky Strikes. The Dean boys then signed every piece of paper thrust in their direction before ending the interview so they could grab lunch[56]—and probably a quick smoke.

Neither brother pitched well that night in their 7-0 defeat. The *Star*, as was its wont, chose not to run a box score and all but ignored the local black players. But the *Pittsburgh Courier* ran a detailed account with a complete box. "Fourteen thousand attended the thrilling exhibition game and watched [T. J.] Young, catcher and clean-up man of the Monarchs, steal the spotlight from the World Series heroes," the *Courier* wrote in its October 20 edition.

Paul started the game and was touched for a run in the second when Young tripled and scored on a sacrifice fly. Diz took over in the third and an inning later was also victimized by the black catcher. Young doubled, then scored when Bullet Rogan singled to center. The Monarchs' Andy Cooper frustrated Diz's boys all night, allowing only four hits in a complete-game shutout.

Things were almost as hectic the next day in Des Moines. The *Des Moines Register* picked up on Grantland Rice's alliterative description of the Dean brothers, "the Holdenville Horrors," which had its roots in one of the Oklahoma crossroads where the boys had picked cotton.[56] Diz and Paul were joined by local sandlotters, several of whom were attached to the 80th Field Artillery Team from Fort Des Moines.

A police escort delivered the boys to Western League Park. "You pitch tonight, Diz," the *Register* reported Paul as saying. "I'm tired—my arm is sore."[57]

Diz hurled the first three innings before some 3,500 fans, whiffing one Monarch in each frame and giving up a flared single to right in the second. He then joined Paul in the outfield for innings four and five. In the fourth, left fielder Diz stopped a run from scoring with a "beautiful peg" to the plate, noted the *Register*.

Two innings later, Paul took the mound, induced a groundout to second, and promptly left the game, complaining of soreness in his right shoulder. Earlier, he had slipped while warming up in the outfield, banging his right side. The cold and damp weather that plagued the latter part of the tour could not have helped his condition. It was the beginning of arm woes that would hasten the end of Paul's career at the too-young age of twenty-seven. Rogers Hornsby always said that Paul wrecked his arm by overtaxing himself on barnstorming tours.

When a couple of Des Moines semipros named Mule Brumley and R. C. Mack were pitching, the Monarchs went to town, scoring nine runs. Catcher Young had two hits, including a run-scoring double. Bullet Rogan, who played third that night, also had a pair of hits.

The star of the Des Moines game, though, was Lefty Beverly, who went the distance, striking out fifteen while giving up just five hits and no runs. Beverly has fallen into oblivion today, but he was a formidable left-hander for Wilkie's club in the early to mid-'30s. Lefty barnstormed all over North America, pitching against white opponents with consistent success.

Diz and Paul wanted to get a jump on their big payday in Chicago. In the middle of the sixth inning at Western League Field, they rushed off—police sirens again blaring—to grab a train to the Windy City.[58]

Ray Doan had done a superb—if misleading—job of promoting the game in the Chicago papers. The *Herald and Examiner* and *Defender* both excitedly reported that Satchel Paige would take the mound against the Deans at Mills Stadium, the ancient ballyard at Lake and Kilpatrick on Chicago's west side. But Satch didn't materialize. An estimated twenty thousand Chicagoans did, however. By far the biggest crowd in the history of the Mills semipro team saw a combined Mills-Dean team throttle the Monarchs, 13-3. Thousands of spectators who couldn't get into the park climbed atop nearby railroad tracks.

Sore arm and all, Paul started at Mills, going two innings and yielding three hits and a run when Monarchs first sacker George Giles, who couldn't get around on Diz's fastball but apparently could on Paul's, singled a run home in the first. Dizzy came on in the third and gave up three hits over two innings, striking out three. Two of the three runs scored off the brothers appear to be unearned. The Mills were "jittery," noted the *Daily Tribune*, committing seven errors. Diz had a single in two at-bats and scored a run.

The Monarch hurlers were knocked around hard. According to the *Tribune*'s box score, Chet Brewer started and gave up four hits in just two and a third innings. Burly southpaw Andy Cooper, whom Wilkie had acquired six years earlier in a trade with the Detroit Stars, then gave up two safeties in his one inning of work. Highpockets Trent, presumably clear-headed, gave up four hits in three innings and Raymond Brown (on loan from the Homestead Grays) mopped up, yielding two more in an inning and a third. Giles had two hits and two steals in a losing cause. Newt Joseph cracked a double.

Diz and Paul once again bid adieu, this time after the fifth. A retinue of cops escorted the brothers to the exit, triggering a "rousing cheer," noted the *Defender*'s Julius J. Adams. The police fought back fans who tried to intercept the Deans.[59]

The Chicago press, probably fueled by Doan, was less interested in what happened during the game than in what transpired at the turnstiles. "The pocketbook of Mrs. Jerome [Dizzy] Dean, treasurer for the firm of Dean and Dean," zinged the *Trib*, "was bulging with $5,000 more yesterday after the pair went through the motions of pitching a few innings each."[60] Other accounts suggested that Pat Dean had more than eight grand stuffed in her purse—an astonishing amount of greenbacks in Depression times. Surely, in a week when headlines about Pretty Boy Floyd and Lindbergh baby kidnapper Bruno Hauptmann were splashed all over front pages, it must have caused some unease to have the contents of Pat's pocketbook so openly discussed.

But that didn't deter Doan and the Deans from repairing to an office outside Mills to count their booty. Two hours earlier, a smiling Dizzy, surveying the stands, had inquired, "How many cash customers do you reckon this 'heah' place holds?"[61] The answer was, "plenty"—but the big payout created expectations for the remainder of the tour that could not be met.

"Twenty thousand fans went away well pleased," commented the *Defender*. "Reason: the fans didn't go to Mills Stadium to see a fine exhibition of baseball playing, they went to see Dizzy and Daffy Dean, heroes of the St. Louis Cardinals' outfit."[62]

The heroes' junket to Milwaukee the next day got off to a spirited start. At Doan's insistence, Diz paid a lunchtime visit to the Milwaukee Press Club. Dizzy packed the place, signed a pile of autographs, and elicited roars when he took the lectern. Paul, still ailing, stayed at the hotel.

Word about Paul's aching arm had reached Cardinals owner Sam

Breadon. The boss called the Deans that morning and demanded that Paul skip pitching for the rest of the tour.[63] Breadon also told the Deans to stop blabbing about their desire for new contracts. Naturally, Diz spent most of the day yakking about how he wasn't supposed to be yakking. At the press club, Dizzy dismissed reports of windfall barnstorming profits as "a lot of newspaper talk."[64]

When Ray Doan got wind of Breadon's call, he went into damage control mode, phoning the *St. Louis Post-Dispatch* to assure them that fears about Paul's arm were exaggerated. "There is absolutely no cause for alarm," Doan fibbed in a story that moved on the Associated Press wire.[65]

The colossal crowd in Chicago must have been on their minds as the Deans and their bulging pocketbooks pulled into Borchert Field, the boxlike home of the Milwaukee Brewers of the Western League. Some 3,300 fans had paid admission—not a bad turnout but small potatoes compared to Chicago.

Diz started and pitched the first two innings, giving up a run before repairing to left field for the next three frames. Paul started the game in right field and—perhaps with Breadon's ultimatum ringing in his ears—never set foot on the mound.

The Deans had been at Borchert Field for about ninety minutes when, in the middle of the sixth inning, their noisy motorcade split for the airport to catch an overnight flight to Philadelphia. When Milwaukee fans realized that the Deans had abandoned the premises, several hundred stormed the box office, demanding refunds. Police captain Arthur Luehman and nine other officers were called in to quell the mutiny.[66]

Local promoter Eddie Stumpf was so irate that he tracked down Doan and threatened to withhold the Deans' $1,700 purse. But Stumpf had no recourse: Doan's contract called for the Deans only to "make a personal appearance," not play or pitch a minimum number of innings.[67] Stumpf, branded the "goat" of the debacle by the *Milwaukee Journal*, vowed to take up the matter with Commissioner Landis. "I think Landis should know of the Dean runout [sic]," Stumpf fumed, "so that he can take some action against major leaguers who forget the public after tickets have been bought."[68]

The boys' abrupt departure to chase bigger bucks gave Landis, National League president John Heydler, and American League president Will Harridge plenty of ammunition to decry barnstorming. Harridge, in fact, began pushing an all-out ban that fall.[69]

The desultory affair at Borchert ended in an 8-8 tie. Despite Doaninduced press speculation that Satch would join the tour any day, Paige still hadn't shown. Satch and Janet Howard had plans to walk down the aisle two weeks later in Pittsburgh; maybe Paige was busy planning the big post-wedding bash at the Crawford Grille.

Diz and Paul had good reason to slip out of Milwaukee. Besides the next day's doubleheader at Shibe Park, they were scheduled to pocket a quick thousand bucks by merely showing up and waving to the crowd at a softball game in Atlantic City, New Jersey.[70]

The Deans' charter flew to Camden, just across the Delaware River from Philly. Photographers got shots of the boys climbing out of the Tri-Motor. "You don't get much sleep doing this jumping around the country," Diz told reporters. "I tried to sleep on the plane but my ears got all stopped up."[71]

First up that morning in Philadelphia was a visit to Dr. Van Bonk, a Philadelphia orthopedist, who examined Paul's arm and—to no one's shock—prescribed rest. Next up before the quick detour to South Jersey was a photo opportunity at the hoary Franklin Institute, which Doan had no doubt arranged knowing that the press would plumb its comedic irony. Sure enough, the Deans showed up for the museum tour in full baseball regalia. Upon greeting the institute's associate director, and with the specter of Atlantic City's thousand smackers looming in his brain, Dizzy stage-whispered, "We've only got five minutes to see this place."[72]

As they examined an exhibit or two, the guide volunteered that "it is very interesting that in a baseball bat there is a center of oscillation."

Dizzy put on his best dumb hick stare and stammered, "A center of . . . whaaat?" according to the Associated Press reporter who witnessed the exchange. The institute presented the two grade school dropouts with certificates supposedly reserved for "distinguished visitors only."[73]

The Shibe doubleheader pitted the distinguished visitors and a group of local semipros against a black squad put together by Eddie

Bolden, a onetime postal worker who'd made a mint running Philly's numbers racket. Bolden parlayed his gambling fortune into an ownership stake in the Hilldale Club, which was later transformed into the Philadelphia Stars.[74] Eddie's outfit for the Shibe twin bill was more or less the same squad that, a few days before, had dispatched the Chicago American Giants, four games to three, in the NNL postseason.

First-game starter Webster McDonald, the stocky submariner who reportedly went 12-4 for the Stars that season,[75] pitched a complete-game shutout against the Deans, winning 8-0. One statistician claims that McDonald went 14-2 lifetime in games against white big leaguers.

Slim Jones, three weeks after his storied Yankee Stadium matchups with Satchel Paige and less than a week removed from winning the Stars' postseason clincher, then limited the Dean team to seven hits and three runs. The second game was called on account of darkness after seven innings.

James Raleigh "Biz" Mackey, the switch-hitting Texan who for more than a decade had been a fixture on the Philadelphia black-ball scene, played first base in both games—collecting three hits and three RBIs. Earlier that month, Biz had hit a reported .368 in the Stars' seven-game postseason. Mackey normally played catcher and was noted for an exceptional arm. In the years to come, he earned acclaim for mentoring a young receiver named Roy Campanella. In 2006, Biz joined his protégé in the Hall of Fame, albeit posthumously.

Center fielder Ernest Judson "Boojum" Wilson, a member of the great Homestead Grays and Pittsburgh Crawfords teams of the early '30s, had four hits, including a homer in the second contest, and scored three times overall. Wilson got his onomatopoetic nickname from Satchel Paige, who heard one of Jud's wicked line drives whiz by his head and claimed it made a sound all its own. As Satch pronounced it, the sound was "Buh-Zhoom!" In Cuba, Boojum was known as Jorocon—"The Bull"—for his muscular hitting.[76] Boojum the Bull was inducted into Cooperstown the same day as his pal Biz Mackey—forty-three years after Wilson's death.

The Dean brothers' performance, wrote James C. Isaminger of the *Inquirer*," was nothing of which the Dean dynasty would be proud."[77] Dizzy pitched two scoreless innings in the second game—the only hurling either Dean did all day. Paul played an uneventful six innings of right field in the first game, went hitless in five at-bats—and then sat out the rest of the afternoon. Dizzy went zero for two at the plate in the first game, and had no official at-bat in the second. The boys weren't kidding when they said they were pooped.

A crowd of nine thousand applauded politely throughout the day. Even though the Deans had not broken a sweat, there was no repeat of the nasty scene in Milwaukee the night before. "Like a nut with a wormy kernel, the Dean brothers' trip around the provinces wasn't what it was cracked up to be," punned the *Philadelphia Record*'s Bill Dooly. Nevertheless, despite mental and physical exhaustion, Dizzy had proven to be a "born trouper," Dooly conceded.[78]

The troupers that night grabbed a train to New York, buoyed by news that Diz had just been named the Associated Press's most valuable player in the National League. The new MVP and his younger brother were playing at Dexter Park the next night with the legendary Bushwicks, the Brooklyn-based squad controlled by Nat Strong that was among the finest semipro teams in the country. Doan had arranged for World Series hero Joe Medwick, a New Jersey native, to join his Cardinals teammates as Bushwick-for-a-day.

After a series of interviews and photo opportunities at the Deans' Manhattan hotel, the New York press gave them the star treatment, with columns from Jimmy Powers in the *Daily News* and Dan Daniel in the *World-Telegram*, plus thumb-suckers in the *Herald Tribune* and the *Brooklyn Eagle*. "'Ah'm gittin' to shudder every time Ah see a camera,' said Diz as the flashlights flared," the AP reported. "'Ah'm so sore Ah can't bend.'" The *Eagle* even published a special Deans-hit-Gotham edition that sold like hotcakes at the ballpark.[79]

In his column "Daniel's Dope," Dan Daniel noted that Diz looked wan, claiming that he was a good twenty-five pounds underweight. Pat, on the other hand, was heading in the other direction: she couldn't stop munching cashews. Paul spent much of the session complaining about his arm. "Ray Doan, who is manager of the royal entourage," Daniel observed, "is on a carousel and thinks the whole world has gone daffy." As Diz reached for a cashew, a photographer snapped a picture and exclaimed, "'We'll label it 'Dizzy, Daffy, and Nuts!'

"'Label it anything you like, just as long as it keeps packing them into those ball parks,' yawned the pallid Dizzy. 'I wish this [tour] was over.'"[80]

In the *Daily News*, Diz pooh-poohed the money that he and Paul were supposedly raking in. "We average only $500 a night, split between us, and we both have sore arms and lean purses. We'll be lucky if we make $2,500 apiece."[81]

The pugnacious Powers wasn't buying it. "Correspondents in the tall celery," jabbed Jimmy, have calculated that "Jerome and Paul would shake down 35,000 coconuts from the trees during their barnstorming tour."

Still, Powers found himself charmed by the coconut shakers. "Now the amazing part of all this is the continued sportsmanship of the Deans. They are not money-hungry farmer boys. On the contrary, they are generous, happy-go-lucky fellows. Damn nice fellows, too."[82]

The Deans and their teammate Medwick were thrilled when they got to the ballyard in Woodhaven, just over Brooklyn's border with Queens. Despite chilly weather, Dexter Park was packed. Only about 5 percent of Brooklyn's population back then was black,[83] but a sizable number made it out to Dexter that night. Nearly twenty thousand working folks, "including women in housedresses, grocers in white aprons, [and] milk wagon drivers,"[84] were squeezed into the old yard, whose roots as a racetrack went back to the nineteenth century.

In consummate Brooklyn fashion, "the crowd amused itself by addressing its heroes, alternately applauding and censuring them as they performed."[85] The Bushwicks' competition that night was another team controlled by the omnipresent Strong, the New York Black Yankees. At that point in their history, the Black Yankees were a mediocre bunch.

Medwick was "none the worse for having gone into the fruit business on a minor scale recently," joshed the *Eagle* in a reference to the torrent of apples and oranges that had been thrown at Ducky by Detroit fans eight days earlier.[86] Nonetheless, Ducky-Wucky, as his bride called him, went hitless against lefty "Neck" Stanley and his wicked emery ball—a scuffed-up pitch that behaved like a spitter.

Paul didn't start but replaced his brother in right field in the fourth inning. The younger Dean's arm was in such rough shape that at no point that night did he throw overhand, noted the *Herald Tribune*.[87]

The black team's first-base coach, a professional comedian named

"Country Fair" Brown, kept everyone amused with pratfalls and pantomime routines.[88] The *World-Telegram* reporter watched Brown's burlesque act, Dizzy's hijinks, and the antics of other members of the Bushwicks' "dusky opposition" and chose to subhead his piece "Escaped from a Chain Gang."[89]

Once Diz left the mound that night, he slipped on his scarlet Cardinals jacket and went back to right field. There he traded jokes with kids draped over the "dilapidated fence," signed autographs, and "kissed a blonde baby girl that escaped its mother and ran out to greet him."[90]

An *Eagle* scribe overheard Diz's exchange with one of the Black Yankees who wandered over to the Bushwicks' dugout in midgame for an autograph. "Dizzy has all a native Oklahoman's love for the Negro," wrote the *Eagle* reporter, confused, as so many were, about the Deans' place of birth. "What Dizzy said to [the black ballplayer] is unprintable."[91] Dean biographer Robert Gregory claimed that Diz signed the program and then shooed away the black ballplayer with "Scat, you nigger, scat!"[92] If the autograph seeker took offense, it was not recorded. Like almost every southern white male of his generation, Dean used the n-word and epithets like *coon*—but not as maliciously as most in the redneck Cardinals dugout. Of the millions of words Dizzy Dean uttered for public consumption, only a few could be construed as racist.

One of the Black Yankees' eight hits that night was an RBI single by blackball icon John Beckwith. Big John, who cut his teeth playing third for Rube Foster's Chicago American Giants in the '20s, was a right-handed slugger who weighed more than 230 pounds. Double Duty Radcliffe swore, "Nobody hit the ball any farther than [Beckwith]—Josh Gibson or nobody else."[93] At age nineteen, Beckwith supposedly became the first person ever to hit a ball that cleared the roof of the laundry that sat beyond the left-field wall in Cincinnati's Crosley Field. The big guy was formidable off the field, too. "[Beckwith] didn't take any foolishness," Radcliffe remembered. "He would fight in a minute if somebody did something to him."[94] Beckwith's appearance against the Deans that week was among the last of his career. Big John purportedly took the few bucks he'd saved from baseball and put it into bootlegging booze and staging crap games.

As Diz, Paul, and Ducky Joe departed the field, Brooklyn fans gave them one last "great going over as they trooped to the dressing room," the *Eagle* reported. In the locker room, Dean did some razzing himself, accusing Brooklynites of not knowing their baseball. "The fans in this 'heah' town yell louder than anybody I ever did hear . . . but they know less," Diz snapped.[95]

Ray Doan managed to squeeze in another couple of paydays before the caravan was due in Cleveland two days later. Baltimore's city fathers were thrilled when Diz and Paul agreed to headline an October 18 exhibition to raise funds for a statue of Babe Ruth. The Baltimore native son's career was winding down and Doan—whose professional partnership with Ruth went back a ways—arranged for the Deans to hit the city for a quick p.c. against white sandlotters at Orioles Park, home of Baltimore's International League team.

That afternoon, the mayor asked Diz to pay a visit to Ruth's alma mater, St. Mary's Industrial School. Some seven hundred orphaned and wayward boys assembled to hear Dizzy's inspirational talk. Dean did not disappoint.[96]

"Until three weeks ago, Babe Ruth was the biggest figure in baseball," Diz declared. "Now you are looking at Dizzy, the man who is walking in Babe Ruth's shoes. And if you boys, each and every one of you, work hard and have determination, you can all become great men like me."[97]

Next up for the great man and his lesser sibling was a quick trip to New Jersey to play the Black Yankees again, this time in Paterson. Curiously, Jersey boy Medwick didn't show, despite press promises that he would entertain the home state folks. The game took place at three-year-old Hinchliffe Stadium, a tiny park built for Paterson's schoolboy league.

Diz and Paul hooked up with yet another Nat Strong–controlled semipro squad; this one went by the oxymoronic handle the "Brooklyn Farmers." As he had two nights before, Strong was probably making a three-way killing: getting a piece of Doan's action, skimming his usual percentage off the Black Yankees' take, and helping himself to a taste of what the Farmers netted, too. No wonder Strong tooled around New York in a chauffeur-driven limo.

Despite Strong and Doan's best efforts to hype the gate in the *Paterson Morning Call* and the *Evening News*, the weather did not cooperate. An icy night kept the crowd to fewer than three thousand. A majority of the fans, the morning paper noted, had "come to see the colored nine hammer the pitcher brothers into submission," which suggests a majority black audience. "[But] Dizzy made pitching to the slugging Black Yankee batsmen look easy."[98]

Diz toiled only two innings, the fourth and the fifth. Second baseman Walter "Rev" Cannady greeted Dizzy with a sharply hit drive down the left-field line that went for two bases. But that was it for the Black Yankees. Diz stranded Cannady by whiffing strongman John Beckwith and then coaxing a fly-out to Paul in right field. Diz got a measure of revenge against Clyde Spearman, the Black Yankees hero from two nights before, by striking him out on three pitches in the fifth. The fifth ended with Diz grabbing Hawk Thomas's one-hopper back to the box and pausing long enough to "read the signatures on the ball" before gunning out Hawk at first base. The Farmers won, 10-3.[99]

Amazingly enough, the Deans had a day off before they were due in Cleveland, so they enjoyed a leisurely train ride West. At long last, their pal Satchel Paige was to join the tour. It was worth the wait.

Before Paige headed to Cleveland, he had serious money to make pitching for the Crawfords in a set of exhibitions against the newly crowned Negro Leagues champion Philadelphia Stars.[100] Satch also delivered on his promise to Greenlee that he'd show for the Craws' big games against the Deans in Cleveland, Columbus, and back home in Pittsburgh. Cleveland was something of a homecoming for Satch, since he'd spent half a season there four years before with Tom Wilson's now-defunct Cubs.

Diz and Paul arrived in Cleveland the morning of the Craws' game to find that Don Palmer, a local cartoonist, had caricatured their mugs for the *Cleveland News*.[101] Palmer's page-one sketch was accompanied by a feature titled "These Incredible Deans," written by a twenty-four-year-old Associated Press reporter named James B. Reston. Scotty Reston was still five years removed from starting his Pulitzer Prize–

winning career as a political correspondent for the *New York Times*; he must have been thrilled at the play his late October six-part series on the Deans was getting around the country. A noisy crowd congregated at the Pennsylvania Depot to welcome the "incredible" pair.

Given the nasty weather that evening, a decent-sized turnout showed up at League Park, the ancient ballpark at East Sixty-sixth and Lexington. Greenlee had ensured that most of his big-time Craws were available. It was a power-packed lineup, featuring outfielders Vic Harris, Cool Papa Bell, Curt Harris (Vic's brother), and Ted Page; first baseman-manager Oscar Charleston; catcher Josh Gibson; and third baseman Judy Johnson. Sweet-tempered Josh was then at the peak of his career—not yet twenty-three and routinely pounding home runs that landed in places rarely visited by baseballs.

The Craws and the Deans put on quite a show for twelve thousand shivering souls. It was by far the biggest crowd ever to see a black team in Cleveland.[102] Diz and Paul were joined by the Rosenblums, the reigning national Class A semipro champions. The club was named after its owner, Cleveland baseball promoter Max Rosenblum. Max augmented his usual lineup by adding two big leaguers with northeastern Ohio ties: Frank Doljack, a middling outfielder in the Detroit Tigers organization who hit .269 in 192 big-league at-bats, and Johnny Mihalic, a shortstop then with the Washington Senators, who batted .244 in 69 career at-bats.

Dizzy played three innings in right, pitched three more, and even coached in the first-base box for an inning. During his stint on the mound in the fifth, sixth, and seventh, Diz was nicked for one run on four hits. The crowd buzzed when the first batter to face Diz in the fifth turned out to be none other than Satch, who promptly doubled to center. "The next two [batters] were easy," observed the *News*'s Ed McAuley, "but the veteran [Oscar] Charleston drilled a single to left and Satchel came romping home."[103] Paul didn't pitch, choosing to play right field while his big brother was on the hill.

Commenting on the game's many theatrics, the *Plain Dealer* wrote in a front-page article: "The Dean Bros. act was plenty dizzy. They clowned all over the park."[104] The crowd howled when Dizzy and Satchel took turns spoofing each other's deliveries. When Paige came to bat in the seventh, "Dizzy imitated the Negro ace's laborious windup," McAuley wrote, "got him to foul off a couple, then drilled a third strike down the middle that Satchel hardly saw."[105] Fans further chuckled when Diz hopelessly swung from the heels at a Paige fastball, contorting himself in a corkscrew. And they "roared with glee," the *Plain Dealer* wrote, "when [pitcher Dizzy] turned, and in true pantomime fashion, bawled out his brother [in right field] for not catching a fly which fell for a single."[106]

More brother-on-brother slapstick went down in the bottom of the seventh. With Dizzy in the first-base coach's box and Satch retired for the evening, Paul singled for the Rosenblums' first hit. Diz called time, signaled to the dugout for a bottle of soda, and with exaggerated flourish, offered a slug to his sibling. Then Diz ordered Paul to stay in the coach's box while Dean the Elder, trampling baseball's rulebook, took over as pinch-runner. The next hitter popped up down the third-base line, but that didn't prevent Diz from making a show of thundering toward second, then racing back to first once the catch was made. Third baseman Judy Johnson's throw across the diamond easily doubled up Diz, but "[Dizzy's] neat hook slide into the base won him another ovation," cheered the *Plain Dealer*.[107]

With a full complement of players from one of the best teams in history positioned behind him, Satch didn't need to bawl out anybody. Paige was magnificent: he struck out thirteen of the eighteen men he faced, not only shutting out the "Rosies" (as they were called in the Cleveland press) for six innings but denying them a hit. All four big leaguers—the two Deans, Mihalic, and Doljack—were among Satch's strikeout victims. Right-hander Tarleton Strong mopped up the final three innings for the Craws, giving up a single run. Satch, Josh, and company ripped the Rosies, 4-1.

The *Plain Dealer* snuck a reporter into the Rosies' dugout during the game. The correspondent was impressed that the Dean brothers were so "polite" to the "hero worshipers" surrounding them. He overhead Paul Dean say of Paige, "That guy must have something. Yeah, he's got a hell of a fastball. Yes, sir, he's got a fastball."[108] Hundreds of autograph hounds besieged Diz, Paul, and Satch after the game ended.[109]

McAuley's lead the next day spotlighted Satch's scintillating pitching. "They came to see the Deans. . . . But there was Long Satchel Paige, smashing that high, hard one through the drizzle to the tune of 13 strikeouts."[110] Other headlines zeroed in on the three-thousand-dollar windfall that the Deans purportedly collected from their one-day visit to the city.[111]

Paige's performance caused Cleveland to buzz for days. The following week's *Call and Post,* the town's African-American paper, scolded Craws' manager Charleston for taking Satch out of the game. "With the Delirious Deans in the opposing cast," *Call and Post* columnist Bill Finger maintained, "had Paige been successful in blanking all batters who faced him, all over the country daily papers would have recorded the feat. This would prove a boon for Negro baseball."[112]

Finger said he'd overheard a white fan at League Park concede that "the Craws are a big-league club. The Rosies didn't have a chance." Black stars "receive one hundredth of the write-ups given their contemporary white brother who is no better than the sepian." If the black game only got more exposure, white owners would understand the economic incentives of integrating the game, Finger pointed out. "Will the big leagues admit [Paige] and more excellent ball players who by accident of birth are colored? Some day, maybe! And while the taboo remains just that much longer . . . the tills of the ball clubs [will] be that much less full," Finger predicted.[113]

Remarkably, Cleveland's mainstream press echoed the same theme. Ed Bang of the *News* and Bill Dvorak of the *Press* all saluted Satch's dominance.

Two days after the game, *Plain Dealer* columnist James E. Doyle noted that Clevelanders were still marveling about "da'k Mistah Satchel Paige's speed trap . . . gabbing about the whiz possessed by the throwing ace of the Pittsburgh Crawfords." One reader wondered to Doyle if Paige had "fetched all the smoke from Pittsburgh over here with him." Another phoned Doyle to ask if Paige were the fastest pitcher ever to appear in League Park, a query that sent the columnist scurrying to veteran Indians catcher, coach, and future manager Steve O'Neill.

O'Neill opined that Paige was fast, but Walter Johnson was even faster. Doyle called the reader back, relayed O'Neill's observation, and heard the fan sputter, "I could have lost a bet on that one" as he hung up the receiver.[114]

Satch and the Deans could afford to lose a lot of bets as the convoy rolled toward Columbus. Doan once again stuck to his promotional modus operandi: the Deans were interviewed at the Neil House hotel while still lolling in dressing gowns.

Red Bird Stadium in Columbus had a knothole in its center-field fence. The aperture was barely bigger than a baseball; the American Association club felt confident in offering batters five thousand dollars if they could squeeze a line drive through it. Before an exhibition at Red Bird, the *Philadelphia Bulletin* would later report, Satch wagered all comers that he could throw a ball through the hole from a distance of twenty feet. After Paige missed his first five tries, the betting got fast and furious. Naturally, Satch fired it through the gap on his next three attempts and wiped up.[115]

Diz and Paul were playing with a collection of local minor leaguers buttressed by Dodger outfielder Danny Taylor (who hit .299 during the '34 season) and Enterprise, Ohio's, own Bob Kline, a right-handed pitcher (career record 30-28) then with the Washington Senators. Alas, the weather on October 22 was so bitter that only 1,650 Columbus fans showed up.[116]

"The Deans came, they saw, but didn't do much in the way of conquering," chortled the next day's *Columbus Dispatch*. Paul, defying Sam Breadon's directive, started and pitched the first two innings, giving up one run on three hits, including Curt Harris's double. Diz played third base and took a turn on the hill in the seventh and eighth, giving up a run on back-to-back singles by Curt Harris and Judy Johnson and a sacrifice fly by Bill Perkins.

Satch "put on a dazzling exhibition," enthused the *Dispatch*'s Frank M. Colley. Paige pitched the first three frames, allowing two hits and walking four. In the third, Ray Doan remembered, Satch coyly pulled one of his favorite stunts: deliberately walking the bases full with no outs.[117] With the chilled crowd roaring, Satch proceeded to whiff the next three batters: journeyman first baseman Mickey Heath, who had 46 career at-bats with the Reds in the early '30s; the Dodgers' Taylor; and former major leaguer Nick Cullop, who hit .249 in 173 at-bats with five different clubs in the '20s and '30s.[118] All nine of Paige's outs were recorded by strikeouts; the Dean squad failed to score against Satch.

So in his first nine innings on the Diz and Daf tour, Satch had struck out twenty-two batters, allowing but two hits and no runs. A pitcher listed by the *Dispatch*, perhaps erroneously, as "Barrow," hurled the last six innings for the Craws, allowing three runs on four hits and two walks.[119]

Josh Gibson, who played left that night, hit an opposite-field homer in the third with Curt Harris aboard, giving the Craws a 4-0 lead. Monte Irvin and other Negro League veterans have always said that Gibson, a right-handed hitter, packed as much power to right field as he did to left.[120] Gibson also singled and stole a base. Cy Perkins did the catching. Second sacker Johnny Russell had three hits, as did Harris.

Diz had a single, a run batted in, and must have delighted the crowd with a dramatic swipe of second. Nevertheless, the Craws won, 5-3.[121]

It was still frosty in Pittsburgh the next day, but things heated up in a hurry. Doan arranged for journeyman catcher George Susce (a tepid .228 hitter in 146 career big-league at-bats), a Pittsburgh resident, to join Diz and Paul. Red Sox outfielder Moose Solters, who hit .299 that season, and receiver Bob Garbark, a career .248 hitter who was then the property of the Cleveland Indians, were also rented for the day.[122]

Fewer than two thousand folks turned out that frigid afternoon at Forbes Field, most of them black fans eager to cheer on their Craws. They were tickled when Diz came out before the game and played catcher for Paige as Satch got warm. Dean hammed it up, shaking his glove to show how much it smarted to handle Long Tom.

Susce, who'd seen the Craws a lot, called time early in the game with Diz on the mound, the bases loaded, and the dangerous Oscar Charleston at the plate. "Heh, Diz, I don't know if you know these guys," Susce recalled saying forty years later. Diz put his arm around Susce's shoulders and said, "George, go back there" (behind the plate) and proceeded to strike out Charleston on three fastballs. "[It] shows how great Dizzy was," Susce remembered.[123]

After Diz moved to left field in midgame, the crowd chuckled when Dean pantomimed relaxing in a rocking chair, according to the *Pittsburgh Press*.[124] Despite the positive karma, the game at Forbes that afternoon is the only Paige-Dean encounter that ended up in the police blotter.

By the fall of '34, there had been hundreds of black-white exhibitions over the years. Only one, as previously noted, an Indianapolis game in 1915 between the hometown African-American ABCs and a touring white team led by the Detroit Tigers' Donie Bush, had been marred by a scuffle serious enough to precipitate a call to the riot squad.[125]

Hotheaded Oscar Charleston, then a rookie, was the principal combatant in the Indianapolis mêlée, having slugged an umpire after a disputed call. Nineteen years and at least forty pounds later, Charleston was, once again, in the thick of the Forbes Field donnybrook. Neither incident, interestingly, started as the result of a racial taunt. Instead, they were classic baseball dustups.

It all began with two outs in the bottom of the fifth and the Craws trailing, 3-1. Vic Harris rapped a swinging bunt in front of home plate and was called "safe" by the field umpire when catcher Susce threw wide of first. Dizzy, who had pitched the first two innings before moving to left, raced into the infield to claim that Harris had illegally run inside the baseline. Home plate umpire Jimmy Ahearn agreed, overruled the field umpire, and thumbed Harris "out."

Harris, who carried a grudge against Ahearn for a dubious call a decade earlier in Jeannette, Pennsylvania, went berserk. They didn't call him "Vicious Vic" for nothing; among Negro Leaguers, Harris had a well-deserved reputation for being a hothead.[126] The dugouts emptied when Harris either yanked Ahearn's facemask (Vic's version) or picked it up off the ground and clobbered the ump upside the head (the *Post-Gazette*'s version). Either way, catcher Susce took exception. Then all hell broke loose.

If, in all likelihood, manager Charleston was in the third-base coach's box, he didn't have far to run to start throwing punches, which apparently he began doing with relish. Josh Gibson, as gentle a soul as ever played the game, jumped into the fracas, putting a headlock on Susce. Ironically, Susce and Gibson were friendly; their sons attended the same integrated Pittsburgh school. Dizzy, trying to play peacemaker, attempted to separate the two catchers. Gibson was strong as an ox. Outfielder Teddy Page arrived on the scene just as Josh, without letting go of Susce, effortlessly tossed Dean aside.[127] Eye-witness estimates as to how far Dean traveled in the air from Gibson's one-armed heave range from five to fifteen feet.[128]

"Plenty of blows were delivered," Edward P. Ballinger of the *Post-Gazette* observed, "while a lot of swings missed their marks."[129] It could have gotten nasty. Umpire Ahearn apparently grabbed a bat to protect himself. Spectators hopped the rail and were not removed until extra security—billy-club-wielding "bluecoats" summoned from the nearby Oakland police station—arrived on the field. Vic Harris was handcuffed and placed into immediate custody. "I was a little fiery," Vic conceded years later.[130]

Despite all the huffing and puffing, no one was seriously hurt, although Ahearn ended up with a bump on his head, which tends to support the *Post-Gazette*'s rendering. "I can see Josh today, right now, when that was over," Teddy Page laughed decades later. "[Gibson] was kind of scratched up and had lost his cap in the scuffle, but he had a big grin on his face, you know, one of those satisfied grins, like, 'Well, that was a good one.'"[131]

Things calmed down enough to complete the game, which the Craws won, 4-3, with a two-out, three-run rally in the bottom of the eighth. Charleston doubled to right and came home when Gibson, his muscles limbered from tossing Diz like a rag doll, tagged a tape-measure home run, this one soaring over the same left-field wall that Pirate Bill Mazeroski would make famous twenty-six years later. Judy Johnson then tripled to right and scored what proved to be the winning run when Curt Harris cracked a line drive to left. Charleston had two hits, the great Gibson three. Johnson scored twice.[132]

Satch, like Diz, pitched the first two frames, giving up one run in each inning. Dizzy's double to deep left in the second drove in a score. Dean, ever the crowd pleaser, even slid into first base feet-first while grounding out.

After the game ended, umpire Ahearn wanted to press charges against Vic Harris. The cops were also hell-bent on throwing the book at Charleston and other combatants. Only some fast talking by Greenlee's guardian angel, Pittsburgh Steelers founder Art Rooney, kept Vic, Oscar, and company from spending a night in the lockup. No doubt it helped that the street-savvy Rooney, a former sandlot star, was trusted by all parties. University of Pittsburgh history professor Rob Ruck, Rooney's biographer, says that Art would have been familiar with Vic

Harris from his dealings with Greenlee. Umpire Ahearn, moreover, had been hired for dozens of games over the years by player-promoter Rooney.[133] Eventually, some sort of an accommodation was reached and all charges were dropped. In *Maybe I'll Pitch Forever*, Paige laughed: "We had some . . . high old times on that trip."[134]

Three decades later, Diz soft-pedaled the incident to *Pittsburgh Post-Gazette* sports editor Al Abrams. "Where was Paul and me when the riot was on?" Diz said in response to Abrams's 1963 query. "In the dugout, that's where. Momma Dean raised her boys to be peaceful-like." Momma Dean's peaceful-like boys may not have thrown any haymakers, but they were in the thick of the tussle.

Dizzy and Daffy's '34 black-white tour ended, it appears, with the various Dean contingents winning just four of thirteen games and tying another. The sundry versions of the Kansas City Monarchs went 2-2-1; the Philadelphia Stars went 2-0; the New York Black Yankees went 2-0; and the Pittsburgh Crawfords went 3-0.

Satch got the better of Diz in their matchups in Cleveland, Columbus, and Pittsburgh. Paige gave up just two runs, both at Forbes Field and both probably "earned," and only a handful of hits in eleven innings. Diz pitched well in the games against Paige, but allowed runs in all three appearances. Overall, Diz pitched creditably on the tour, especially considering the slipshod quality of many of his teammates. (See 1934 charts in the appendix.)

After fulfilling a couple more blackball gigs for Gus Greenlee and the Craws, Satch wed Janet Howard in Pittsburgh on October 26, surviving a boozy reception that Greenlee underwrote at the Crawford Grille. Bojangles Robinson was not only Satch's best man but entertained guests with a tap dance routine. Robinson was just one of several black luminaries cutting a rug with Satch and Janet that night. Paige then split for California to enjoy a hectic honeymoon (also paid for by Greenlee) and resume his big winter league p.c.'s.

The brothers Dean, meanwhile, scooted to New York to cash in their stardom on stage and screen. The *New York Times* reported that the brothers' salaries were the biggest ever for ballplayers appearing on Broadway, admittedly not a large category.

Diz and Paul were booked at the Roxy Theater for a week's worth of what could charitably be described as "vaudeville." Their show, such as it was, was compressed into the Roxy's usual fare; it lasted all of six minutes.

The day before they made their debut, the theater wanted the boys to pose for publicity stills with members of the chorus line. A nervous Dizzy balked at first, but finally agreed to the shoot, insisting that agent Doan "explain this to the Missus—she's likely to get very sore. She don't mind my being an actor, but she don't allow for no dancin' with show gals."[135]

Onstage, the boys stood in front of a ballpark painted on cheesy canvas. Radio announcer Ford Bond acted as host, teeing up the brothers for forgettable punch lines concocted by *New York Daily Mirror* columnist Dan Parker. The act ended with Diz bellowing, "Is Hank Greenberg in the house? Ah sure would like to strike him out once more!"[136]

Tom Meany in the *World-Telegram* wryly observed: "The Deans make no more effort to fool the audience than they do to deceive a batter. The family slogan remains, 'Plow it through there!'"[137]

The brothers moseyed over to Erasmus Field in Brooklyn one afternoon to film a short for Warner Bros. Starring slapstick comic Shemp Howard of Three Stooges fame, the film featured dialogue as shopworn as the boys' vaudeville act. "Dizzy may not know it, but he is going to show movie fans more curves than Mae West," razzed critic Edward T. Murphy of the *New York Sun*.[138] The "plot" was so amorphous that Paul told reporters, "I will not know what it is all about until I do see it."[139]

Plot or no plot, the boys collected $2,250 apiece for their cinematic venture and $1,625 a head for trodding the boards.[140] Exactly how much Wilkinson, Doan, Satch, and the Dean men made in toto on the '34 tour remains unknown. Accounts wildly vary. Bob Ray of the *Los Angeles Times* wrote that fall that Doan and his clients "cleaned up"—especially after the boys forced Doan to renegotiate terms in the wake of the big crowd in Oklahoma City.

Cardinals' treasurer Bill DeWitt, who was Dizzy's commercial agent, at least in theory, believed he'd been stiffed out of promised compensation. In '35, DeWitt sued Dizzy for $6,000 in unpaid commissions. The treasurer's suit claimed that Dean had cleared $7,000 from the '34 tour.[141] DeWitt's figure probably doesn't begin to cover the stash that Pat was stuffing into her handbag night after night. At other times, Dizzy claimed to have made a $14,000 profit from his '34 barnstorming.

In late November '34, Diz told reporters he was eager to sign his newly renegotiated Cardinals deal (a significant raise to some $20,000-plus per year) because he was broke.[142] Dean's plea of poverty was too much for St. Louis columnist Roy Stockton. Later called by the *New York Times* "the Boswell of the Gas House Gang,"[143] Stockton was skeptical that Dean had, in just a few weeks, managed to squander a fortune. Historian Robert Smith credits Stockton with helping to forge the Dean legend. Stockton, Smith wrote, was able to see beyond "Dizzy's vainglorious babbling [to] the essential sweetness of the boy's nature."[144]

According to legend, Dizzy cashed in one last time in the fall of '34 before repairing to Bradenton's links. The locale could not have been more fitting: Wrigley Field, Los Angeles's art deco replica of its famous Chicago forebear, just a few miles from Hollywood. Bill Veeck, Boston Braves outfielder Wally Berger, *Collier's*, the *Saturday Evening Post*, a distinguished group of historians assembled by the National Baseball Hall of Fame and Museum,[145] various Paige biographers and blackball scholars, not to mention Diz and Satch themselves, claim that the two pitchers met mano a mano in L.A. in early November.[146]

It was, Bill Veeck always maintained, the greatest game he ever saw. It lasted thirteen innings, with both hurlers going the distance. "Dean was superlative, holding the Paige Stars to one run and fanning 15," Veeck told *Collier's* two decades after the fact. "But Paige shut out the Dean Stars and fanned 17."[147]

As depicted by Paige devotees Rick Kenney and Jesse Stringer, Dean dissed Satch's curveball while being interviewed that fall on a West Coast radio program, alleging that Paige possessed "a great fastball but no curve."[148] Satch got wind of Dean's criticism and vowed to get even. So the first time Diz came to the plate, Satch yelped:

> "Hear say you goin' around tellin' people I ain't got a curve?"... Diz just grinned. "Well, then you tell me what this is." I threw him a curve. He swung and missed. .... I threw him two more curves and

he missed both of them too, striking out. "How's that for a guy who ain't got a curveball?" I asked.[149]

In midgame, Dean supposedly tripled off the center-field fence. "I gotcha!" Diz bleated at Satch. "No, you ain't! You're not goin' no further," Satch zinged back. Sure enough: Satch stranded Diz at third.[150]

In his 1940 profile of Paige, the *Saturday Evening Post*'s Ted Shane claimed that after Diz closed out the black team in the tenth, Satch yelped: "If you ain't gonna give us no runs, Mr. Dean, we ain't gonna give you no runs. So you better get beds and coffee ready, because we is playin' all night."[151]

They came close. Wally Berger, then an all-star slugger, said that Paige and Dean "were about the same size and they both pitched [at] about the same speed—about ninety-five miles per hour."[152]

"First, [Paige] pitched me high, then he raised it, then he brought it down," Wally remembered fifty years later. "[Paige] finally got one down a little too low and I hit it off the center-field fence."[153]

As Wally's line shot glanced off the wall, Berger said Paige chased him to second base, barking, "How'd ya hit that one?" Satch then proceeded to strike out, allegedly on nine consecutive pitches, major-league batsmen Dolph Camilli of the Phillies (16 homers and 87 RBI's in '34) and Frank Demaree of the Cubs (a career .299 hitter), plus Gene Lillard, who later had cups of coffee with the Cubs and Cardinals.[154]

Diz was every bit as stout as Satch that night, dominating the likes of Cool Papa Bell, Mule Suttles, Turkey Stearnes, Wild Bill Wright, Sammy T. Hughes, and Willie Wells, all of whom played in California that winter. The game didn't end until the thirteenth inning, when the black team finally scratched out a run against Diz—and Satch put down the white guys one last time.

As the twenty-year-old Veeck, then a college dropout, sat in the packed stands, he vowed that if he ever had the chance, he'd bring Satchel Paige to the big leagues. Barnum Bill eventually made good on his promise fourteen years later.

It's a rousing story. In many ways, it represents the denouement of the splendid Satch-Diz rivalry. Paige biographer Mark Ribowsky wrote that Satch's performance that night helped transform Dizzy Dean "from cracker to crooner for racial equality."[155]

In truth, as Robert Smith pointed out, Diz had too sweet a disposition to be much of a cracker. Moreover, Dean never became an outspoken champion of "racial equality" per se. For Diz, integrating the game was only coincidentally about righting a societal wrong. In Dean's mind, black-white games were about having a good time and making money, putting on a fun show against the best possible competition. Diz had spent most of his childhood picking cotton next to black folks and didn't see why sharing a diamond with them should kick up a fuss.

There's just one problem with this uplifting scenario: there's no public record that the game actually happened. Perhaps because it would have violated Commissioner Landis's prohibition against major leaguers barnstorming after October 31, there was no contemporaneous press coverage. But not all of Paige's performances in California were covered by the local media. And Ray Doan and Joe Pirrone were both capable of slipping a few bucks to reporters to keep a Dizzy Dean game out of the papers. Through word of mouth and a few well-placed posters, Pirrone could have filled Wrigley Field for a Diz-Satch game. Eighteen thousand fans were supposedly there that night.

If the November '34 L.A. game was just an urban myth, then why were Dean, Paige, Berger, Veeck, and others not only adamant that the game was played, but in essential agreement over its details?

We may never know the real story behind Diz and Satch's lost classic. We know for sure, however, that scores of other marvelous black-white contests took place on the West Coast from the mid-1930s through the postwar years. More than a few of them starred Satchel Paige, Dizzy Dean, and Bob Feller.

CHAPTER FIVE

Encore: Diz, Daffy, and Satch Do It Again

*Someone gave [Dizzy Dean] a baseball and it was like giving Caesar
a sword or Napoleon a cannon.*

—JIM MURRAY, COLUMNIST, *LOS ANGELES TIMES*

Ray Doan, J. L. Wilkinson, and Tom Baird were back at it in the fall of
'35, setting up a series of barnstorming matchups between the Dean
brothers and blackball's best. This time Ray enlisted old pal George
Barr, a teacher at the Doan-Hornsby umpiring school, to help coordi-
nate logistics.

Barr and Doan originally promised an even bigger go-round than
the '34 junket, but backed off when it became apparent that the Deans
had lost at least some of their commercial cachet, despite Dizzy's
remarkable 28-12 record in 1935. Diz appeared in relief fourteen times
that season, leading the National League in innings pitched with a
bone-wearying 324—thirteen more than the previous season. In two
years, Dean the Elder had won fifty-eight games, a record that put Diz
in the same rarefied air as Johnson, Mathewson, and Alexander. Paul,
his serious arm troubles still a year away, went 19-12. In their two
healthy years together, 1934–35, the Dean brothers went 96-42 with
an earned-run average barely over 3.00. The Cards won an impressive
ninety-six games in '35, but fell four short of the pennant-winning
Cubbies.

The initial Diz-Daf II itinerary called for twenty-one stops. Paul
and Diz were joined by their Cardinals' mate utility man extraordinaire Mike Ryba (career record, 52-35), and future Cards hurler Mort

Cooper (career record, 128-75), on a sojourn that began with visits to Missouri, Kansas, and Oklahoma.[1]

Ryba had been promoted to the big club that season after starring for the '34 Columbus Red Birds of the American Association. Future Hall of Famer Hack Wilson, now retired from the Cubs, and former Phillies first sacker Joe Hauser, a career .284 hitter who hadn't played in the majors for six years, also signed on for parts of the trip.

Wilkie and Baird's Monarchs, augmented by a couple of ringers, were the foils on Doan's midwestern swing. The black squad was more gifted than the club that toured with the Deans in '34: Newt Allen and Newt Joseph manned second and third base, respectively; T. J. Young handled catching duties; the outfielders were Pee Wee Dwight, Johnny "Schoolboy" Taylor, and Henry Milton; Eddie Mayweather played first; and young Willard Brown, barely twenty, handled short and also played some outfield. Even at a tender age Brown was sculpted—"just a mass of muscle," in the words of Wilkie's son Richard.[2] Chet Brewer, Lefty Beverly, and Bullet Rogan joined Satch in a deep and strong rotation—all but Beverly are now in the Hall of Fame.

Against this stellar squad Doan filled out his roster with local sandlotters. The '35 Dean-Paige go-round commenced in early October, followed a couple of weeks later by a separate Wilkie-and-Doan-choreographed tour of the heartland, this one pitting the Monarchs against three members of the freshly minted World Series champion Detroit Tigers. Second baseman Charlie Gehringer and pitchers Schoolboy Rowe and Tommy Bridges led a troupe that lost all four of its exhibitions against the Monarchs. Small wonder they were beaten: Hall of Fame shortstop Willie Wells, then of the Chicago American Giants, and capable catcher Quincy Trouppe, who'd just left the national semipro champion Bismarck, North Dakota, club, joined the Monarchs for the games against the Detroit trio. On October 18, Satch and Lefty Beverly combined to shut out the Gehringer squad before a huge crowd in Kansas City. Beau Wells had a pair of hits that night in taming the Tiger-led team, 6-0.[3]

A week later in Omaha, the Monarchs' second home, Satch pitched three shutout innings against the Gehringer club, striking out five in what became an 8-2 Monarchs victory. Gehringer scored both runs for the white all-stars. Schoolboy Rowe had more luck against the Cubs that month than he did against the Monarchs; he gave up three hits and two runs in just two innings of work. Black fans in the crowd of 5,500 chanted "You can't beat the Monarchs in Omaha!" recounted the *Defender*.[4] Maybe that's what caused the Klan to torch Omaha's ballpark the next year.　·

Quincy Trouppe wasn't the only black player returning from Dakota in the fall of '35. Satchel Paige, too, was just getting back from another amazing tour of duty for Neil Churchill's integrated Bismarck Capital Citians.

Having been outmaneuvered in '34 by his rivals in Jamestown, Churchill pledged to Trouppe that 1935 would be different. The car dealer was determined to put on the field the finest team money could buy—and have it fronted by Satchel Paige.

This time Satchel stuck around for most of Bismarck's season. Eight years later, Paige told the *Chicago Daily News* that the '35 Bismarck club was "the best team I ever saw. . . . Man, couldn't beat that team. Hit and field, and boy, did we have the pitchers." Then he lamented, "But who ever heard of them?"[5] Paige told *Collier's* in 1953 that Bismarck won 104 of 105 games in '35—which, even by Satch's tall-tale standards, was a whopper.

Paige's braggadocio notwithstanding, the 1935 Bismarck club was the most formidable racially mixed professional squad assembled prior to the 1947 integration of the big leagues. It was a sweet but all-too-brief harbinger—a snapshot of what goodwill and wealth could accomplish.

In early '35, Churchill pried away Double Duty Radcliffe from Jamestown. In fact, the auto distributor raided the Jimmies' roster so exhaustively that Jamestown chose to field an all-white squad that summer.[6] Churchill also signed black knuckleballer Barney Morris, a cagey veteran of the Negro Southern League's Monroe (Louisiana) Monarchs. After he came on board, Morris urged Churchill to retain a promising right-hander from Monroe named Hilton Lee Smith. For a bargain-basement price of $150 a month, the twenty-eight-year-old Smith followed his mentor to North Dakota and soon became a black-ball icon.　·

The Chrysler dealer wasn't done. He persuaded white slugger Vernon "Moose" Johnson, a Western League legend, to join the club.

When sober, Moose hit such gigantic shots that disbelieving black players compared him to Josh Gibson. A team photograph that season shows Moose with his right arm casually draped over Satch's left shoulder.

Churchill's '35 Capital Citians were not quite as invincible as Satch later claimed. They actually lost 14 games, against four ties and 66 wins.[7] Once Churchill set his pitching quartet—Paige, Morris, Smith, and Radcliffe—Bismarck reeled off 28 wins in 29 games.

Paige's method that summer was to start every fourth game. Twice in June, Satch beat Chet Brewer when the Monarchs rolled through the Dakotas and across the border in Manitoba. In Winnipeg, Paige struck out eighteen Monarchs as he and Chet both threw complete games.[8] Satch also remained the centerpiece of Churchill's aggressive marketing efforts. Folks bought tickets to Bismarck games with the expectation of seeing Paige pitch, if only for an inning or two—and Churchill and Satch delivered the goods. Indeed, research conducted by Kyle McNary for PitchBlackBaseball.com suggests that Paige hurled at least an inning in thirty-two straight games over a twenty-seven-day period that summer, so Satch's oft-uttered boast that he pitched every day for a month turns out to have been accurate.[9]

When it came to making a buck, Churchill was an internationalist. At one point that summer, he brought Mexico's reigning champions, Charros de la Junta, to North Dakota for a popular three-game series. With Satch winning the rubber game, Bismarck took two out of three from the Mexicans.[10]

Most of his black teammates were still living at the boardinghouse while Satch, with Churchill's help, ditched the railcar for some new digs. He now lived in a ramshackle aluminum trailer on the outskirts of town. Paige and his roommate, Ted Radcliffe, turned it into a den of iniquity—or so Duty claimed. "One woman would be goin' in as one would be goin' out," remembered Radcliffe, who, like Satch, was prone to exaggeration.[11]

Satch was so untouchable that summer—his ERA during the month of May was something on the order of 1.04—that he pulled his call-the-fielders-in routine several times. When they weren't sitting down on Satch's orders, his players would often titillate the crowd by starting toward the dugout after Paige had recorded two outs.

In August, Churchill's squad set out for Wichita, Kansas, as the star attraction in what became the city's vaunted National Baseball Congress competition. Then known as the National Semi-Pro Baseball Tournament, the Wichita competition was the brainchild of a cigar-puffing promoter and pal of J. L. Wilkinson's named Raymond "Hap" Dumont. Bob Broeg, the baseball seer of the *St. Louis Post-Dispatch*, later dubbed Dumont the "P. T. Barnum of baseball."[12]

Instead of a select semipro power or two brought in to face mainly local squads, Dumont wanted to bring the best teams in the country to Wichita. Hap gave a broad definition to "semipro"; minor-league teams and squads chock full of professional ringers were among the thirty-two clubs that Dumont invited to Wichita.

The Capital Citians were part of an eclectic mix: there were white squads from New York and Chicago; all-black teams such as the Memphis Red Sox and the makeshift "New York Tigers" (starring a home-sick twenty-three-year-old first baseman named Buck O'Neil); an all-Japanese-American nine from Stockton, California, whose pitching ace stood less than five feet tall; and an all-brothers team from Waukegan, Illinois, consisting of former minor-league third baseman Frank Stanzak and his nine siblings. The Stanzaks amazed everyone in Wichita by winning two games and almost nabbing a third.

Dumont's solicitation of interracial and black teams was remarkable, given his hometown's reputation. The state's crusading newspaper publisher William Allen White had long deplored the Ku Klux Klan's malignant influence in Wichita.[13]

At least that first year, Dumont's event was billed as both an "All-Nations Tournament" and, à la Denver, "The Little World Series." Dumont went all-out in covering his fledgling tournament in glory. Honus Wagner, Ty Cobb, and Walter Johnson were on hand, swapping stories in the box seats with Dizzy Dean's Hollywood buddy, funnyman Joe E. Brown.[14] Dumont's wizardry worked: Lawrence Stadium was packed to its nine-thousand-seat capacity or beyond for most games.

Many teams pulled into Wichita aboard chartered buses with their club names plastered on the side. But Churchill, the consummate car salesman, piled his men into the two biggest rides on his lot, a Chrysler Airflow and a Plymouth Sedan.

The caravan took a slight detour to Kansas City to pick up a special passenger: Chet Brewer of the Monarchs, whom J. L. Wilkinson was "lending" to Churchill for the Wichita tournament (no doubt for a sizable fee). With Brewer now in the rotation, Bismarck boasted an all-black and all-brilliant pitching staff: Paige, Smith, Brewer, Morris, and Radcliffe.

An hour north of Wichita, Churchill's convoy stopped in a picturesque Kansas berg named after martyred Civil War general James McPherson. There, probably by design, they met up with the Dickey Oilers, a white company club from Iowa also trekking to Wichita. Soon enough, a ballgame broke out. The *McPherson Daily Republic* was there to capture the moment, which was fortunate because Satchel was at his roguish best. The headline in the next day's *Daily Republic* read: SATCHEL STEALS SHOW.

McPherson baseball fans saw some real baseball yesterday afternoon. The Bismarck team defeated the Dickey Oilers by a 14-0 count, doing some heavy hitting when hits meant runs. The big feature of the game however, and one that was worth more than the admission price, was the show staged by the one and only Satchel Paige, colored pitcher, rated by many experts as the greatest twirler, white or black, in the country.

Satchel hadn't been used and the fans were yelling for him to take the mound. In the final inning he accommodated the spectators. He walked to the mound after waving his outfielders to stay on the bench. He struck out Ferguson and Butler, each on three pitched balls. Then the first baseman walked to the center of the diamond, leaving a hole on the right side of the infield. Weber, next Dickey batter up, rapped out a line drive through this hole that went for three bases before the ball was retrieved. Nothing daunted Paige as he then sent his infielders to the bench and with nobody but his catcher for company he pitched to Britt, who rapped one down the center of the field. Satchel got it off the ground and then ran Britt down and tagged him before he got to first for the third out. It was a "stunt" that the fans enjoyed.[15]

It wasn't the only stunt that Satch would pull over the next few days. But before the black Capital Citians could take the field, they had to find a place to stay. Much to Churchill's chagrin, a Wichita hotel refused to let Bismarck's African-American players stay with the rest of the team. Fortunately, Radcliffe and Paige knew the territory. There was a black rooming house that took boarders for three dollars a night.[16]

Despite the Jim Crow lodging arrangements, Wichita's '35 tourney enabled a multiplicity of black players to compete on an equal footing with whites—a happenstance that didn't sit well with certain people. Some teams pressured Dumont to disqualify the black players, in part because of their skin color and in part because they were too damn good. Decades later, Radcliffe chortled that Wichita's white players viewed him and Paige as "big league niggers."[17]

Wichita Eagle columnist Pete Lighter was glad that Dumont ignored the naysayers. "They say that Paige will bring victory to any club he pitches for," Lighter wrote as the tournament was getting under way. "He's the greatest colored pitcher in the country and perhaps the greatest regardless of race."[18]

Paige threw so hard in Bismarck's opening game against the Monroe Monarchs that Radcliffe "put a piece of steak in his glove so Paige wouldn't take his whole hand off," recalled one of the Stanzak brothers. Satch went the distance, striking out seventeen Little Monarchs, inspiring Negro dialect writer Octavus Roy Cohen, who was in the stands, to opine, "Folkes, youall lookin' at de best pitchah in de world. Yassah, dats him, ole Satchel Paige. You boys don't need to be discouraged—he mows de best of de big leaguers down just the same as he's a-mowing youall."[19]

The heat was so oppressive in Wichita for game two that Radcliffe had to put a wet towel on his neck between innings. Brewer started for Bismarck and pitched well, but tired in the sixth. Radcliffe, who was managing, signaled for Satch to begin throwing in the bullpen. A minute or two later, with no outs and the bases now full, Duty walked out to the mound to yank Brewer. Only then did a peeved Radcliffe realize that Satch hadn't bothered to warm up. Instead, Paige was in the bullpen playing pepper with three little white boys.

Duty nevertheless brought Satch into the game. Paige proceeded to strike out the side, purportedly on nine pitches. "Oh, he threw that day," Radcliffe remembered. "God bless him."[20]

Paige struck out seven of eight batters, Duty drove in three runs, and Trouppe hit a home run that supposedly clanked off a train chugging past the outfield wall. "You could hear it hit [the train]," Radcliffe recalled. "BOOM! We won, 8-4."[21]

In game three, Satch held the winners of the 1935 *Denver Post* tourney, United Fuel of Denver, to one run and drove in two in Bismarck's 4-1 triumph. Chet Brewer then limited an all-white squad from Shelby, North Carolina, to two hits and one run.

For the fifth game, Bismarck's opponent was the all-white Halliburton Cementers (yes, *that* Halliburton), a company club from Duncan, Oklahoma. The Cementers, augmented by former Phillies and Browns player Joe Hassler, had been cracking the ball at a prodigious rate, averaging thirteen runs in the tournament; there was much speculation that they would flatten Paige, who was working for the fifth time in eight days. But Satch went nine innings, struck out sixteen, and allowed only five hits and a solitary run.[22]

Bismarck's game six adversaries were a club from Omaha called the V-8's, which had advanced to the semifinals by beating—and beating up—the all-black Memphis Red Sox. That game was marred by a brawl in which fans poured onto the field. Only cool-headed police work forestalled a riot. Brewer had less than his best stuff against the V-8's, but didn't need it as Bismarck cruised, 15-6.

Joe E. Brown's silver screen buddy, tough guy George Raft, sat behind Bismarck's dugout for the Halliburton–Capital Citians championship game, played under Lawrence (now Lawrence-Dumont) Stadium's erratic lights. Raft, who loved to put down money on baseball and just about everything else, watched Paige give up nine hits but strand runners all night by fanning fourteen.

Haley, Trouppe, and Radcliffe broke the game open in the seventh with run-scoring doubles. Radcliffe swore that, once again, Satch whiffed the last three Cementers on three pitches each. As the final Oklahoman was being punched out after taking strike three, the umpire snarled, "Boy, you shoulda swung, 'cause you outta here!"[23]

Raft, then starring in Dashiell Hammett's noir film *The Glass Key*, bumped into Radcliffe that night. Double Duty remembered Raft saying to him, "You thought you were going to suck us in. We knew you were going to win. We didn't bet."[24] Raft may not have plunked down money, but Churchill probably needed an accountant to keep track of his manifold wagers.

The *Bismarck Tribune*'s headline the next morning shouted in bold print: BISMARCK WINS NATIONAL SEMI-PRO PENNANT. It ran right underneath another header about the latest farm relief program launched by the Agricultural Adjustment Administration.[25] The Bismarck team's share of Dumont's purse was $10,000 by some accounts, $7,000 by others.[26]

Dumont may have seemed broad-minded, but in truth the presence of black players—and the utter dominance of Bismarck's racially mixed team—had rattled people. Hap soon decreed that beginning in '37, interracial teams would be barred from playing in Wichita. All-black teams could compete, but only if they received the blessing of their state's governing body—never an easy task for a minority group.

After they grabbed the trophy in Wichita, Satch and most of the Bismarck team went barnstorming through Colorado for a couple of days with the Kansas City Monarchs. It was the last time Satch would wear a Bismarck uniform. That fall, he and Churchill parted company, on fairly amicable terms, at least by Satch's standards. Satch left that fall to resume his rivalry with the Dean brothers and revisit his favorite West Coast stomping grounds.

Bismarck continued to field a competitive—and racially mixed—team, but it was never quite the same. Churchill retired from day-to-day responsibilities in '36 to concentrate on his car business.

In 1960, to commemorate the twenty-fifth anniversary of Satch's virtuoso performance, Hap Dumont invited the fifty-four-year-old Paige to return. Delighting the crowd, Paige suited up for a valedictory turn with a local squad known as the Wichita Weller Indians. Long Rifle still had some ammunition in his right arm; he led the Indians to victory.[27]

Diz, Daf & Satch Redux got rolling on October 1 in Springfield, Missouri, just as the '35 Tigers-Cubs World Series was getting under way. In his "Sports Salad" column in the *St. Louis Post-Dispatch*, L. C. Davis quipped:

> *The Tigers taking heart of grace*
> *Full of pep and beans.*
> *Because they do not have to face*
> *Those devastating Deans.*

"I'll make more money on this trip than in a whole season with the Cards," devastating Dean No. 1 boasted in a quote picked up nationally by the Associated Press.[28] Later on the tour, Diz's braggadocio would come back to bite him.

Springfield was eager to welcome home Paul Dean and Mike Ryba, both of whom helped lead the local Cardinals to Western League championships.[29] Ryba enjoyed the company of the black players. "Every time we ran across [Ryba] it was like meeting a brother or something," Newt Allen remembered.[30]

The afternoon before the Springfield game, Ryba and the Deans held court for some good old boys at a diner. Each of the players, noted the paper, downed a bottle of beer as they traded quips.[31]

"There was nothing 'dizzy' about the big chap with the fresh, country-boy face and ingenuous manner," reported the *Leader & Press*. The reporter was surprised to find in Diz a hard-nosed businessman who had the foresight to think long-term.

"It's all right when you're tops," Diz told the paper in a feature headlined "'I'm the Tops!' Dizzy Admits—and So What?," which played on page one. "Right now everything's swell. But what does that mean? Look at [Grover Cleveland] Alexander. He was the greatest pitcher that ever lived—the greatest one in the world. He was tops, too. And look at him now. . . . Last year at Hot Springs [Alexander] had to hock his World Series ring, and his World Series pin, to buy whiskey. Look at Hornsby—he was tops, too. But the horses got him."[32] If Alexander and Hornsby, Dean's fellow Ray Doan clients, ever responded to Dizzy's salvo, history has not recorded it.

Anticipating a sellout crowd, the *Leader & Press* thoughtfully inserted this line into its game-day coverage: "A section will be reserved along the first base line for negro fans."[33] Folks sitting in the segregated seats must have enjoyed themselves that night.

The biggest crowd in the town's history, some five thousand people, jammed into White City Park to watch what turned out to be a lopsided tilt. Local hero Ryba started and was torched for six runs, all of them earned, in the first two innings. Paul came on in the third and pitched hitless ball for the next three frames, fanning three Monarchs. He was replaced by his older brother in the sixth. Diz struck out two in holding Kansas City without a hit for the remainder of the game.

Lefty Beverly whiffed eleven Springfielders over six innings, but gave up two hits to Diz, including a two-bagger. The elder Dean played right field when not on the mound. Ryba got three singles in four trips, while Paul went hitless in two tries. Beverly scattered eight hits as the Monarchs breezed, 8-2.

The fans in the Jim Crow section must have howled as Satchel Paige ambled out to the mound in the seventh. Satch closed out the game with his usual panache, fanning three and holding the white team without a base runner for the final three innings. The two Deans and Satch put on quite a performance in Springfield, pitching a combined seven innings without allowing a hit or a run.

Newt Allen, Pee Wee Dwight, and Schoolboy Taylor each had two hits for the Monarchs, as did the precocious Brown. Between them, the Newts—Allen and Joseph—scored four times.[34]

As the troupe made its way north to Columbia, Missouri, reports surfaced that Italian dictator Benito Mussolini's invasion of Ethiopia had triggered racial rioting in New York City. After Harlem residents threatened to boycott a grocery store owned by an Italian immigrant, knife fights broke out between rival street gangs. All through the '35 tour, Mussolini's conquest dominated front pages.

Every town that hosted the Dean brothers got pumped, but none more than Columbia. The *Columbia Daily Tribune*, no doubt staffed by eager-beaver graduates of the hometown journalism school at the University of Missouri, dogged the Deans' every step.

Four days before the game, the paper ran an ad hawking the big showdown as the "Greatest Baseball Attraction Ever Held in Columbia." Walk-up admissions ran seventy-five cents, with reserved seats going for a quarter. The four white professionals would play with local semipros sponsored by Columbia's downtown store owners.

Wilkie's Monarchs had been coming cross-state to the central Missouri town of thirty thousand for years. Earlier in the summer of '35, in fact, the Monarchs had thrashed the House of David in Columbia in a two-game series organized by Doan.[35]

The first subject Doan broached with the *Daily Tribune* reporter stalking the boys outside the lobby of the Daniel Boone Tavern was the amount of advance publicity the game had netted in the Columbia paper. When told that the *Daily Tribune* had been running stories all week, Doan smiled and then asked how ticket sales were going. Merchants Park, the town's old diamond out on Highway 40, would be jammed, Doan was assured. Disabled kids from the local children's clinic were invited to the game as guests of the Merchants' manager, a kindhearted gentleman named W. I. McBride.

Irked that their rooms didn't have radios, Diz, Paul, and Mike Ryba jumped into a two-door Buick parked in front of the Daniel Boone. Keeping the motor running, they rolled down the windows, cranked up the radio, and tuned into game one of the '35 Tigers-Cubs World Series. There were so many crazed wagers being tossed around that the kid reporter, trying to eavesdrop from the sidewalk, had trouble following them all. The boys were betting on practically everything: whether Lon Warneke of the Cubs or Schoolboy Rowe of the Tigers would throw a fastball or a breaking ball, the number of hits each team would get, the total amount of runs, etc.

At one point, as Warneke was giving Tigers slugger Hank Greenberg a steady diet of inside fastballs, Diz bragged that "Warneke is throwing them like I told him—trying to keep them high and inside."[36]

The reporter stuck his head inside the car long enough to ask Dizzy about Satchel Paige. "Dizzy said [Paige] was a good pitcher, and he said it in a manner to indicate he wasn't kidding," the kid wrote, perhaps not realizing he was giving Paige a dismissive compliment.[37]

Satch hadn't been with the "fast-stepping" Monarchs in Columbia when they dispatched the House of David team earlier that summer, the *Daily Tribune* noted. Perhaps influenced by Dean's evaluation, the paper described Paige as "said to be the fastest pitcher in the nation today."[38]

The two fireballers delighted the huge crowd out on Highway 40 by starting the game on the mound. Diz set down Newt Allen, Eddie Dwight, and Leroy Taylor in order in the first. But Eddie Mayweather singled to right to begin the top of the second, then took second base on catcher Ryba's passed ball. Diz stranded him there for two batters, striking out Bullet Rogan and T. J. Young, but Willard Brown's soft liner into the gap fell in front of right fielder Paul Dean—who was, the paper scolded, "no great shakes in anybody's outfield."[39] Newt Joseph then banged a liner into right that was again mishandled by Paul, plating Mayweather and Brown. Diz had another one-two-three inning in the top of the third—then repaired to center field for a couple of innings before calling it a night.

Satch, alas, pitched only one inning, making quick work of three Merchants, fanning one. Journeyman Bob Madison pitched the rest of the game for the Monarchs. Diz and the Merchants had only four hits on the evening—among them Diz's grounder in the bottom of the third that went for an infield single—yet managed to tally six runs. Madison yielded many walks in Kansas City's ragged 9-6 win.

Allen, Dwight, Mayweather, Young, Brown, and Madison all had two hits for the Monarchs, with the first three scoring twice.[40] The first two games of the '35 tour produced a decided advantage for the Monarchs. They'd outscored the Dean boys, 17-8. Things didn't change much the next day.

On October 3, Diz and Paul made good on their promise twelve months earlier to U.S. senator Elmer Thomas: they played an exhibition in Tulsa. Doan and Barr made sure their charges got worshipful play in the local press.

Banner headlines heralded the brothers' arrival. Even Satch earned his own story in the *Daily World*—this in a city whose minority neighborhood was still decimated from the bloody riot fourteen years earlier. "If 'Satchel' Paige, the speedball hurler for the Monarchs, lives up to his advance notices, there will be three Deans in the game, as Paige has often been called a 'colored Dizzy Dean,'" the paper noted the day of the game. "[Paige] is reputed to be as 'swift' as Dizzy, and also to have a good collection of puzzlers."[41]

Tulsa was atwitter at the prospect of watching the puzzle boys. Special buses transported fans from downtown to the evening game at Texas League Park. A racially mixed crowd of more than three thousand fans squeezed into the yard, with blacks relegated to the outfield bleachers. A white Tulsa kid named Jimmy Shilling, considered a promising infield prospect for the Cleveland Indians, was enlisted by Doan to play short.[42] It took another four years before Shilling made the big club; his major-league career consisted of forty-two games for the Indians and the Philadelphia Phillies.

With Diz on the mound and Ryba behind the plate, Shilling's deficiencies were exposed right away; a nervous Jimmy muffed leadoff batter Newt Allen's "easy bouncer." Diz then overpowered the second hitter, Pee Wee Dwight, as Allen swiped second and advanced to third when Ryba tossed the ball into center field. T. J. Young fought off several tough pitches before rifling a single into right field off a Dean change of pace, scoring Allen.

Rogan, batting cleanup, hit a bullet that nearly tore off the second baseman's glove, but the sandlotter held on to double Young off first. Diz retired from mound duties after one inning and moved into left field. Paul pitched the next two frames; in the second, he got Joseph and Mayweather on easy flies, sandwiched around a walk to Milton, and then struck out Paige to retire the side.

In the bottom of the third, Paul was touched for a single by Newt Allen. But Harpo escaped damage by inducing Dwight to ground out to second. Shortstop Shilling redeemed himself by going deep into the hole to rob Taylor of a hit. Paul then fanned Young.

Satch, meanwhile, was putting on a quintessential Paige performance. "Colored fans had plenty to cheer about when Paige strode to the mound," the *Daily World* noted. "'Satchel,' who is built along the elongated model of the Deans, struck out the first four all-stars to face him."[43] The next two white hitters failed to get the ball out of the infield.

When Paul dug in against Satch, Diz began "ridin' the big chucker." "'Now, now, Satchel,' quit throwing that golf ball,' Dizzy yelled as Paige fired his streaking fast one at such a pace that it looked like a blurry marble," the paper reported.[44] All Paul could manage was a groundout.

A fan sitting near the Deans' bench and within earshot of a reporter asked Diz if Paige could win in the major leagues. "'He could win anywhere,' the elder Dean replied without hesitation."[45]

Dizzy made a couple of powerful throws from his perch in left field, thrilling fans. "[Dean] zipped the ball with no thought at all of saving his arm, which is worth something like a half million dollars on the open market,"[46] marveled the paper. Dizzy the hitter never made it past first, but he did blast a Paige offering to deep center, which was a better rip than most of the white guys got against Paige that night. Paul and Diz pulled up stakes after four innings, with the score just 2-1 in favor of the Monarchs. With local players on the mound, the Monarchs had a field day, scoring ten more runs in a laugher that ended

11-3. "The colored stars might have made the game even more one-sided had they cared to do so," admitted the paper.[47]

"It was a relief," the *Daily World* concluded, "to see the 'big shots' hustle the way they did while on the field." But the correspondent wondered how long the Deans could put on such exhibitions, "playing every night as they are slated to do."[48] As it had the year before, Paul's arm was aching.

Newt "Colt" Allen, a scrappy veteran, was one of blackball's most respected leaders and a mainstay of the interracial tours of the '30s. A native of Austin, Texas, Allen played with the Monarchs for virtually all his twenty-six years in the Negro Leagues—a record of franchise longevity almost unheard of in blackball.

Allen, who went on to manage the Monarchs for a time, was proud that the black game emphasized "tricky baseball"—speed, deception, and guile, not just muscle. "We played by the 'coonsbury' rules," Newt chuckled years later. "That's just any way you think you can win, any kind of play you think you could get by on."[49]

Traveling by car, the Dean and Paige caravan made the hundred-mile journey from Tulsa to Enid in northern Oklahoma. In the early '20s, Enid had been the site of a notorious hate crime when robed Klansmen pummeled a young black man merely for walking through the white side of town.[50]

For the October 1935 visit, the Monarchs stayed in a boarding-house on the other side of the tracks while the Deans, Cooper, and Ryba holed up at the Youngblood. A reporter and photographer from the *Enid Morning News* arrived at the hotel to discover the ballplayers huddled around a radio with Doan and Barr; as in Columbia two days earlier, they were glued to the Series, this time game three.

Inning-by-inning wagers were going down, with Diz betting big on the Tigers and collecting four twelve-dollar pots.[51] "Diz and Paul were calling every strike, and almost every play during the broadcast," the *Morning News* noted.[52] The Series game was an eleven-inning thriller that wasn't decided until outfielder Jo-Jo White drove home Ducky

Medwick's sparring partner, third baseman Marv Owen, to give the Tigers a 6-5 victory.

Once the Series game ended, Diz, Paul, and Ryba hit the street in search of a barbershop but got detoured by a snooker parlor. "The three made a dive for a pool table," the *Morning News* wrote, commenting that a big crowd immediately engulfed the boys.[53]

Enid was a town of about twenty-five thousand, many of whom that night made it out to Eason Stadium. A "record crowd" packed the yard.[54]

Before the contest started, Diz and Paul put on a game of pepper that had the audience and the Monarchs tittering. Diz also put on an impromptu long-toss exhibition, repeatedly trying to reach home plate from the distant reaches of center field—a feat that may have wowed the crowd but may not have been very smart for his overworked arm.[55]

The white pros were playing with the Eason Oilers, a company team that for years competed in Wichita's National Baseball Congress. Fans were delighted when Diz started on the mound, with Ryba behind home plate. Diz pitched two scoreless innings and was replaced by Paul in the bottom of the third. The younger Dean gave up two runs an inning later. "The crowd that came out to watch the Deans in action were [*sic*] amply rewarded for the famous flingers bore down all the time that they were on the mound," enthused the *Morning News*. Dizzy struck out two Monarchs, while Paul fanned one. When not on the hill, the Deans patrolled right field.

Satch, described as "sensational" by the paper, also pitched the first two frames, striking out three. The Oilers scratched out a run against Paige in the first. Chet Brewer pitched the remainder of the game for the Monarchs, giving up four runs.

If the *Morning News*'s box score is accurate, the Deans went a combined four-for-six in the game, while Satch was held hitless. The Monarchs didn't need Paige's bat. They scored eleven runs on fourteen hits in an 11-5 romp. Willard Brown, again playing shortstop, was the hitting star; "Home Run" blasted two of his namesakes and doubled in his last at-bat. Third baseman Newt Allen, still one of blackball's fastest men at age thirty-four, served as an effective leadoff batter, scoring three runs.[56]

It was no fault of Diz's, but the '35 game tally now stood at black team four, white team zero.

On October 5, the gang moved northeast to Joplin, Missouri, a coal mining town about Enid's size just inside the border with Oklahoma and Kansas. The people of Joplin greeted the Deans with the same open arms they used fifteen years later to welcome a New York Yankee prospect named Mickey Charles Mantle. Mantle, an Oklahoman from nearby Commerce, played one season for the Class C Miners of the Western Association en route to New York City and immortality.

Joplin, another Klan haven, had seen its share of hate crimes. After one lynching, in fact, so many white Joplinites had their blood up that the town's black families were forced to flee.[57]

The community's two papers, the *Globe* and the *News-Herald*, competed to see which could flog the Satch-Diz game the hardest. A huge Saturday night crowd was expected at Miners Park, not only to hail the brothers but to salute baseball lifer Gabby Street, a Joplin native. The crusty former manager of the Cardinals, a onetime Diz antagonist, was then skippering the San Francisco club in the Pacific Coast League. Street, at one time a supposed Klansman,[58] had come home to "manage" Dizzy's squad.

Doan didn't give Gabby much to manage. Besides the three Cardinals, Street had a pedestrian lineup of semipros. The lone exception was twenty-two-year-old infielder Don Gutteridge, who'd grown up across the state line in Pittsburg, Kansas. Gutteridge, coming off an impressive season with Columbus in the American Association, was "climbing the steps of the Cardinal chain system," noted the *News-Herald*.[59] A year later, he took the final stride toward St. Louis. Gutteridge went on to a solid twelve-year career with the Cards, Browns, Red Sox, and Pirates, playing mainly second and third.

Alas, Gabby's homecoming wasn't meant to be. Rain and a severe cold front washed out the game. "Old Man Weather Stops 'Me 'n' Paul'" was the morose header in the *Globe* on Sunday morning.[60] Before the game was scrubbed, a *Globe* reporter had shadowed Dizzy all over town, trying to get the pitcher to comment on his "feud" with Street. Diz was sporting a flat-topped felt hat and a smart striped tie. "There ain't no feud between me and Gabby Street anymore," snapped Diz in the lobby of the Conner Hotel. "He's all right. He's a smart baseball manager. Yes, sir. Well, see you later."[61]

Doan pulled his charges out of Joplin early to make the three-hour trek north to Kansas City for a Sunday afternoon matchup on the Monarchs' home turf, Muehlebach Field. The promoter went all out to put a competitive team on the field in Kansas City. Diz, Paul, and Ryba were joined by Pepper Martin, Washington Senators first sacker Joey Kuhel (who batted .277 in '35), and several members of the American Association Kansas City Blues.

The *Kansas City Star* enthused, "The battle between the famous Dean brothers and Satchel Paige in a pitchers' duel has whetted the fans' interest here and officials have announced they expect a near capacity crowd."[62] Wet weather, however, produced a disappointing turnout, but the black-and-white audience got more than its money's worth.

Diz, Paul, and Ryba combined for a shutout. Dean the elder played seven innings total, three of them on the hill.[63] Satch was almost untouchable, giving up only three hits, but somehow the Dean men scratched out a run; Paige lost a 1-0 heartbreaker. Paige remembered Dean consoling him after the game by saying, "Satch, you're a better pitcher than I ever hope to be."[64]

On October 7, the Associated Press moved a story headlined "Dizzy Taciturn as Baseball Tour Flops." Diz admitted in an interview conducted at Muehlebach Field that the revenue generated on the '35 tour was only "fair" compared to the '34 swing, blaming the situation on rain and cold. The weather improved as the tour headed east—and so did Diz's spirits and pocketbook.

Once the caravan turned toward the Atlantic, sore-armed Paul went home to his new bride, the former Dorothy Sandusky, who had taken ill and was hospitalized in St. Louis.

As he had the previous year, Ray Doan worked a deal with Gus Greenlee of the Crawfords. Once again, Greenlee fielded a rugged lineup: Judy Johnson, Ray Dandridge, Cool Papa Bell, Josh Gibson, Rap Dixon, Teddy Page, Jimmy Crutchfield, and Vic Harris all played in the '35 series. Satch, however, must have taken his leave; his name does not appear in any game accounts for the remainder of the '35 swing. Maybe the Paige-Greenlee relationship had degenerated so badly at that point that Greenlee couldn't bear the thought of giving Satch more money.

Doan also contracted with additional white big leaguers to join the tour as it pointed in the direction of Philadelphia and New York. Catcher Bob Garbark of the Indians (who hit .333 in six big-league games in '35), a veteran of the '34 swing; Bill Swift (who went 15-8 that season for the Pirates); and third baseman "Jersey Joe" Stripp (who hit .306 in 109 games) of the Dodgers led the list.

At Dayton on October 9, a big crowd was delighted with a hard-fought game between the Crawfords and the Diz-led "Shroyers," a semipro club, that ended with the Craws winning, 5-2, in the tenth. Dizzy pitched the first two innings without giving up a run and then shifted to the outfield. With the score tied at two and the crowd roaring, Dizzy came to the plate in the bottom of the seventh with one out and the bases loaded. Diz hit the ball hard but the Craws' infield lived up to its reputation by turning a swift double play.[65]

The *Dayton News* wrote that the crowd left the park as "happy as if they'd seen a World Series." Dizzy's men supposedly each received $408 as their share of the gate.[66]

Two days later, at Shibe Park in Philadelphia, Dean and Greenlee's charges played an abbreviated doubleheader. The black stars touched Dizzy for a couple of early runs, collecting fourteen hits and seven tallies in all against Dean and Bill Swift. Josh Gibson tripled against Diz in game one and had two other hits on the day.[67]

The white stars managed only five hits and one run against submariner Webster McDonald of the Philadelphia Stars and Neck Stanley of the New York Black Yankees, both of whom Greenlee had recruited to moonlight for the "Crawfords." It ended 7-1 in favor of Gus's club.

Bill Swift, a native of Elmira, New York, started the second game for the white team and threw a five-inning shutout. Cool Papa Bell got the only hit, while Diz's team scraped just two hits off the New York Cubans' Frank Blake, a journeyman. The second tilt ended in a scoreless tie after five frames. It marked the first time on the '35 junket that the white team hadn't lost. The caravan immediately grabbed a train north.

On October 13 at Yankee Stadium, in front of a crowd of some twenty thousand, they played another twin bill. Remarkably, Diz went the distance in the first game, twenty-four hours after he'd pitched in Philly. It was one of the most memorable games in the entire Dean barnstorming history. Cool Papa had a pair of doubles and made a couple of crowd-pleasing plays in center. He also wowed them on the basepaths.

In the middle of game one, Bell found himself dancing off second with Josh Gibson digging in at the plate. Diz gestured toward the center fielder, Jimmy Ripple, soon to join the New York Giants, to move way back. "How far do you want me to go?" Ripple supposedly hollered at Dean.[68] The crowd began chuckling as little Jimmy, at Dean's insistence, retreated so far he was practically in the shadow of the wall. Sure enough, Gibson walloped the ball some 450 feet to center, which Ripple staggered under and speared, then heaved a throw toward the distant object that was shortstop Billy Urbanski (a career .260 hitter) of the Boston Red Sox.

Bell tagged up at second and raced to third, where coach Dick Lundy, in his day one of the Negro Leagues' best base runners, gave Cool Papa the stop sign. But as Bell hit the bag, he realized that Ripple's throw still hadn't arrived in Urbanski's glove, so Cool Papa resumed his furious dash. Bell always claimed that his slide beat Urbanski's throw home. But the umpire called him out, chiding Bell, "you don't do that against big leaguers."[69]

The only other scoring threat against Dean came in the fourth, when slick Ray Dandridge, on loan from the Newark Eagles, bashed a line drive into right-center but was thrown out trying to stretch it into a triple.[70] Diz pitched a complete-game masterpiece, allowing eight hits in a 3-0 victory that has to rank among his finest games ever. The second game was called after five innings, with Dean's club leading 1-0.[71] The Dean men had finally generated some momentum.

The next day, the exhausted troupe made its way to York, Pennsylvania. Dissension had broken out: pitcher Swift, outfielder Ripple, and infielder Tommy Thevenow (of the Pittsburgh Pirates) must have felt they'd been stiffed the night before. They demanded cash up front before taking the field. The local promoter who'd been working with Doan apparently had to dip into his own pocket to come up with the extra coin. (Ironically, two years later, Ripple and Dizzy got into such a ripsnorting fight that National League president Ford Frick fined each fifty dollars.)[72]

The black team scorched the white squad, 11-1, in the York game. Webster McDonald again dominated the Dean squad. Cool Papa claimed years later that his squad stung Diz for four early runs, with Gibson tagging tape-measure home runs in the first and again in the third. "The people started booing," Bell told John Holway, "and Diz went into the outfield for a while; he hated to just take himself out of the game." After the game ended, Bell remembered, Dean jogged past the Craws' dugout and said to Gibson, "Josh, I wish you and Satchel played with me 'n' Paul on the Cardinals. Hell, we'd win the pennant by the Fourth of July and go fishin' the rest of the season."[73]

Gibson is best known today for his bat, but Dizzy loved watching Josh operate behind the plate. "Josh was the greatest catcher back in those days," Dean reminisced in the '60s. "[Gibson] could sit on his haunches and throw you out at second base. A good receiver, a strong arm. And watch him work that pitcher: he was tops at that. He was terrific all the way around."[74] For pure genius as a hitter, Satch always put Josh on the same pedestal as Ted Williams.

Connie Mack, the domo of the Philadelphia Athletics, drove out to York that night and was so impressed by McDonald that he went looking for the submariner after the game ended. Mack found Webster still in the showers. "I'm sorry to say this," McDonald remembered Mack saying, "but I'd give half my ball club for a man like you."[75]

Perhaps not fully appreciating the brilliance of McDonald and Gibson, folks exited in an agitated mood. "York fans left Eagle Park vowing never again to patronize a major league barnstorming team," commented the *York Dispatch*. Local promoters were so irritated that they promised never to book "this type team."[76] If only the good people of York had realized that evening how many future Hall of Famers they'd had the privilege of watching.

"Dandy" Ray Dandridge was considered blackball's quickest third baseman of that generation. In the late '30s, he starred on the Newark Eagles'"Million Dollar Infield," with such standouts as Willie Wells at short, pepperpot Dick Seay at second, and Mule Suttles and sometimes Biz Mackey at first. Later, Monte Irvin and Larry Doby would join the mix.

Dandridge, a Richmond, Virginia, native also shone in Caribbean and Mexican play. In fact, Dandy pocketed so much money in Mexico he rebuffed Bill Veeck's offer to join the Indians in 1947. By 1950, Ray had enough left to be named most valuable player of the American Association's Minneapolis Miners. Dandridge never made the white big leagues but did become a scout for the San Francisco Giants. Along with the Negro Leagues' other nonpareil third baseman, Judy Johnson, Dandridge has been enshrined in Cooperstown.[77]

Sketchy records suggest that Cool Papa had five hits in the October '35 series on the East Coast. Ray Dandridge and Josh Gibson had four. For Diz's men, Jersey Joe Stripp had five safeties; hotheaded Jimmy Ripple three.[78]

The interracial contests on Diz's eastern swing ended in York. But Doan had arranged for Dizzy to continue barnstorming against white professionals and semipros in North Carolina, Tennessee, and Louisiana. The mid-October junket culminated in Dallas when the Dean-Ryba team met Doan and Wilkie's other traveling white squad, the Gehringer-Rowe club.

Things took a nasty turn in Chattanooga and New Orleans. Iffy weather and smallish crowds in both venues caused Dizzy to cancel at the last minute, disappointing fans, enraging local promoters, and triggering a wave of bad publicity. For the first time in his career, Dizzy was cast a "goat," wrote Sid Ziff a few days later in the *Los Angeles Herald and Express*.

It didn't help matters when a peevish Diz told the press he could make more money playing poker on the train than he could pitching before a few hundred paying customers. The Chattanooga walkout was especially galling, since proceeds from the game were pegged for a local children's Christmas charity. Joe Engel, the president of the Chattanooga minor league club that had organized the exhibition, wasn't shy in pressing his case against Dizzy, vowing to take the matter directly to Commissioner Landis.[79]

The *Sporting News*, which at the bidding of major-league owners abhorred barnstorming, was particularly caustic. "If the players who profit from barnstorming after the season is closed want to kill the goose that lays the golden egg," the Spink family publication editorialized on October 31, "all they need to do is to continue the tactics they have employed this fall. Dizzy Dean has come in for a lot of condemnation for the sorry part he has played, but Jerome Herman is not the only offender."[80] Another publication referred to Diz as a "big baboon."[81]

Dizzy's image had taken a hit; Doan scrambled to perform damage control. He and Pat persuaded Diz to apologize. Dizzy also promised to appear in Chattanooga and make restitution to the kids' charity. "I ain't no villain—and I can prove it," Dizzy told reporters.[82]

The *Sporting News*'s J. G. Taylor Spink, perhaps feeling guilty that his publication had been so rough on Diz's barnstorming, was willing to give Dean the benefit of the doubt. "[Dean's] still too close to the grass roots of his origins to ever go 'high-hat' on his public. Give him a chance, and 99 times out of 100 he'll turn your jeers into cheers."[83]

Documentation is incomplete but it appears that Dizzy pitched superbly in the interracial portion of his '35 tour of the Midwest and East. He threw some thirty-two innings, giving up nine runs, a number of which were not earned.

Satch, for his part, was even better. Paige worked some seventeen innings, giving up two measly runs. If both were earned, Satch's ERA for the '35 Dean swing was 1.17. The "Kansas City Monarchs" went 4-0 on the tour; the "Pittsburgh Crawfords" 3-2-1. Dean's men, it appears, won two against seven defeats and one tie.

More than eight thousand Texans, including fifteen hundred "knothole kids" who got in free, showed up at Steer Park in Dallas on October 20 to watch Diz and Lon Warneke take on Charlie Gehringer, Schoolboy Rowe, and the "American League All-Stars." Dean and Rowe each started and pitched four innings. Neither allowed a score; Diz gave up three hits, Rowe just one. After Diz and Warneke retired from mound duties, the American League squad, led by a pair of hits from Gehringer, scored five times in a 5-2 AL victory.[84]

Having pocketed a nice check in Dallas, Diz headed to California for a series of even-bigger-money contests orchestrated by Ray Doan and Joe Pirrone.

Pirrone's big coup in the fall of '35 was to bring Dean back to L.A.

for a couple of high-profile exhibitions, including another tour de force with Paige at Wrigley Field. But first, Diz was booked to appear in a major leaguer vs. minor leaguer matchup. Pirrone put together a dynamite collection of professionals, among them shortstop Arky Vaughan of the Pirates (an NL-leading .385 in his third season); Phillies' first baseman Dolph Camilli (25 homers and 88 RBIs in '35); Cardinals' utility man and outfielder Jack Rothrock (.273); outfielders Wally Berger (Braves, an NL-leading 34 homers), Ernie Orsatti (Cardinals, .240 in his last season), Tuck Stainback (Cubs, .255 in his second season), and Frank Demaree (Cubs, .325); and venerable catcher Truck Hannah, who hadn't played in the big leagues since the second Wilson administration.

Joe had outdone himself: in Vaughan and Berger, he had lassoed two of the best players in the game. Pirrone got Dizzy out to the Coast two days early—no easy task—to flog the games with the press and public. As Diz, accompanied by wife Pat, pulled into L.A. on the Southern Pacific early on October 23, he was greeted by a flock of fans and photographers. "Dizzy Dean, baseball's leading man—and prima donna—swept into Los Angeles on the front end of an Espee train yesterday and promptly announced he was all set to show the folks of this pueblo what a real pitcher looks like," zinged *Times* columnist Bob Ray.[85]

"I'll give 'em hell," Ray had Dizzy vowing as the pitcher posed for pictures later that day at Wrigley Field. Plus Pirrone booked Diz to headline a packed public rally at the new *Los Angeles Times* building. Joe also fêted Diz that night at a Pirrone's Café banquet. Dean, Vaughan, Orsatti, Berger, Demaree, and Stainback all took bows. If any black players were invited to or acknowledged at Joe's place that night, the *Times* failed to mention it.[86]

An immense crowd of eighteen thousand turned out to watch Dizzy oppose a troika of Pacific Coast Leaguers, led by the Angels' Newt Kimball. It took Kimball two more seasons before he made the Chicago Cubs. Newt ended up kicking around the National League for six seasons.

Diz tickled the Wrigley crowd by pitching for the major leaguers *and* the minor leaguers. In inimitable Dizzy fashion, he was credited with both the victory and the defeat, a bizarre juxtaposition that netted him headlines around the country. He pitched two innings at the beginning of the game for the minor leaguers, then switched hats and pitched the next six innings for the majors. In all, he gave up six runs, two to the major leaguers and four to the minor leaguers, in the 12-4 big-league win.

The *Times* was so thrilled at the specter of Dean on a local mound that the paper equipped photographer J. H. McCrory with a state-of-the-art "Miracle Eye" camera. McCrory was able to snap a single Dean delivery—from windup to follow-through—in a sequence of seven separate images that the *Times* splashed across the top of the sports section the next morning. "It Takes a 'Miracle Eye' to Follow One of Dizzy Dean's Fast Ones," boasted the caption.[87]

"The turnout must have warmed the cockles of Dizzy's heart, and sent a glow of fondness pulsing through Dizzy's wallet," columnist Ray wrote the next day. Some accounts had Dean clearing $3,000 for his evening's work; others said $3,800.

After the game Dean complained that he couldn't get his arm loose and was forced to throw too many change-ups. "But I'll have my fastball Thursday night and I'll be bearin' down because I want to beat those [black] guys," Diz said. "I'm goin' to take a workout Tuesday to get the kinks out of my arm. I hope they get Satchel Paige to pitch against me because I want to beat their best."[88] Diz got more than a rubdown; he and Pat repaired to Catalina Island.

Pat and Diz were guests of their old Hollywood pal Joe E. Brown that week. Brown proudly squired the couple around Tinsel Town, including a tour of the Warner Bros. studio, where the romantic musical *Colleen* with Dick Powell, Ruby Keeler, and Joan Blondell was being filmed. When the scene wrapped, Diz was asked what he thought. "What's so tough about lettin 'em take your picture while you're kissin' Ruby Keeler?" Dean quipped.[89]

The hype machine continued unabated for the Dean-Paige matchup, which happened to fall on Halloween night. Every day, Pirrone would tell the papers that he wasn't sure Satch would show. The "sepia sensation" was giving Joe "gray hairs," Ray wrote on October 30. If Paige couldn't pitch, curveballer Bob Griffith would get the nod, Joe told the *Times*. Except Joe identified the hurler as "Tommy Griffin," getting Schoolboy's first *and* last names wrong—an occupational hazard for Negro Leaguers.[90]

Pirrone invited reporters to watch the Giants practice the day before the big game. They put on a "dazzling" show, the *Times* said, claiming that the black guys "announced they were ready" for Dean and company.[91]

Ray's lead paragraph on game day went: "Dizzy Dean vs. Satchel Paige! That's the pitching treat in store for baseball fans who journey to Wrigley Field tonight."[92] Paige had apparently "surprised" Pirrone by arriving, unannounced, in the thick of the night. Pirrone made sure that the press knew Paige had promised to give "'Mistah Dean' a lesson in hurling."[93]

For his part, Diz pledged to "give those Giants a trimmin', and I don't care whether Satchel Paige or Suitcase Simpson [a popular cartoon character of the '30s] pitches for 'em." Then in a statement that was probably more chucklehead bravado than racial invective, Dean volunteered, "They all look alike to Ol' Diz."[94] Ol'Diz also promised, no doubt with a sly grin, that this time he wouldn't switch sides.

The Giants put forth a tough lineup. Second baseman Sammy Hughes led off, followed by third baseman Felton Snow, left fielder Turkey Stearnes, right fielder Mule Suttles, shortstop Zack Wright, catcher Biz Mackey, center fielder Bill Wright, and first sacker "Shifty Jim" West. Shifty Jim's slick work around first drew comparisons to Hal Chase, the dead-ball star whose proclivity for cheating eclipsed his artistry at first base.[95] Some seven thousand Halloweeners skipped trick-or-treating to take in the ballgame. They had to brave damp weather.

Not many exhibitions ever featured seven future members of the Hall of Fame, but this one did: Dean, Vaughan, Paige, Stearnes, Suttles, Mackey, and Bill Wright. The Ol'Diz vs. Ol'Satch shoot-out didn't quite live up to Bob Ray's billing, but it was still a good show.

Satch retired after four innings, having fanned seven. Diz, chilled by the dank air, withdrew after seven frames leading 3-2, having surrendered six hits. Angels prodigy Newt Kimball relieved Dean in the eighth and was quickly touched up for two runs. The Giants grabbed a tenuous lead, 4-3. It didn't last long.

Cubbie Demaree singled to begin the ninth. Lillard's single sent Demaree racing around second. Wild Bill Wright lived up to his moniker by uncorking an errant throw, allowing Demaree to score and Lillard to advance to third.[96]

An improbable hero emerged: Truck Hannah, the oldest guy on

the field. "Old Truck slapped out a single in the ninth inning to score Gene Lillard with the marker that gave the All-Stars a 5-to-4 verdict over the colored team," the *Times* reported.[97] Berger, who relished matchups against black players, had two extra-base hits.

The L.A. press was intoxicated by the Satch & Diz Show. On November 3, Bob Ray opined, "A really great pitcher is Satchel Paige, the Black Bullet of Negro baseball ranks, and if you don't think so ask some of those major leaguers who batted against him [last] Thursday night at Wrigley Field. . . . It was with mingled feelings of mostly relief that the members of Dizzy Dean's squad watched Mistah Paige take that long, lean, ebony right arm of his into the clubhouse."[98]

The columnist sat down with several of the white big leaguers after the Halloween night game. His piece quoted one anonymously saying: "When Satchel cuts loose with his high hard one the ball comes hopping up to the plate looking about the size of a shriveled pea, or a mustard seed."[99] Ray, because of the CWL's legacy, knew a little something about blackball, which put him well ahead of most of his peers around the country. "I don't know how [Paige] compares with such former colored aces as Rube Foster and Bullet Rogan . . . if Foster and Rogan were any faster, I just won't believe it."[100]

Ray's piece concluded by urging Angelenos to get out to Wrigley Field the next evening to watch Paige take on the CWL's White Kings. "If you've never seen Satchel in action," Ray advised, "it'll be worth your while."[101]

Satch did indeed make it worth their while. A capacity crowd on November 4 saw Satch shut out former Dodger Sloppy Thurston and his White Kings, 7-0. Paige was overpowering that night, striking out fourteen and giving up only four hits. "The lanky Negro ace was never in danger," asserted the *Times*. Satch rarely was in Southern California—especially facing white hitters.

Dizzy and Pepper Martin had plans to get away to Canada—"Let's me 'n' you go fishin' up there in Novus Scofus!" Dean had pressed Martin earlier that fall[102]—but they scrapped them so Diz and Pat could beat a retreat to Bradenton. They were pooped from their swing around the country.

CHAPTER SIX

Go West, Young Men

I was branded a Negro in the States and had to act accordingly. Everything
I did, including playing ball, was regulated by my color. . . . They wouldn't
even give me a chance in the big leagues because I was a Negro, yet they
accepted every other nationality under the sun.

—HALL OF FAME SHORTSTOP WILLIE WELLS,
CALIFORNIA WINTER LEAGUE VETERAN[1]

From the earliest days of its Gold Rush, when prospectors nervously guarded claims against outliers, California was riven by ethnic strife. Writer Bret Harte, who became famous for his yarns about panhandling, was booted from a Eureka gold miners' camp for protesting the unprovoked massacre of hundreds of Humboldt Bay Indians. A "secret" vigilante group committed the despicable crime; none of the conspirators was ever brought to justice.[2] After California became a state, its first governor tried to bar blacks from settling within its borders.[3]

Still, relations between whites and blacks were less combative in California than in most places—which helps explain why it became fertile territory for interracial baseball. Ralph Kiner, the Hall of Fame slugger who starred on the '47 Feller-Paige tour, grew up in Alhambra in the '30s, the only child of a single mom whose husband died when her son was still a toddler. From the time he was in elementary school, Kiner played sandlot ball with black kids. In a 2006 interview, Kiner said he "never gave it a second thought."[4]

As a teenager in the late '30s, Kiner played in black-white games in Griffith Park in downtown L.A., Sawtelle in West L.A., Brookside Park in Pasadena, and other diamonds across the Southland. Most of the time, all-white teams were pitted against all-black squads, but occasionally they played racially mixed games. On weekends, friends and relatives of both races would bring picnic lunches and make an afternoon of it.

As Kiner's reputation grew, he was invited to play in interracial all-star exhibitions at two of Los Angeles's larger venues: Wrigley Field in Avalon Park and White Sox (or Anderson) Park at Anderson and Fourth in Boyle Heights. Kiner distinctly remembers being impressed in those games by Goose Tatum's playfulness and Mule Suttles's power.[5]

When Kiner finally saw Satchel Paige, he was struck by the pitcher's natural gifts. "During infield practice, [Paige] and his teammates would put on a show," Kiner said, referring to "shadow ball," where infielders would pretend to catch and throw an imaginary ball and do it with such panache that it would astound the crowd. "Satchel was underrated as an athlete. He was a very good athlete," Kiner said.[6]

Early black-white baseball in California had luminous moments, but it was hardly Shangri-la. In 1914, the president of the Pacific Coast League banned black teams from using PCL parks—a decree that stuck, more or less, for nearly two decades. In 1927, Commissioner Landis tried to prevent big-league players from moonlighting in the California Winter League, in large measure because of the presence of black teams.[7]

Like many of Landis's moves against off-season barnstorming, his CWL crackdown proved futile. Big leaguers continued to winter in Southern California to stuff their wallets. Fans of both races flocked to CWL games, despite the local media's erratic and condescending coverage.

In the '20s, Los Angeles's white newspapers—the *Times* and the *Herald and Express*—tended to treat CWL Negro Leaguers the way Hollywood studios treated blacks in the movies. On those rare occasions when they deigned to cover black-white CWL games, sportswriters were dismissive. Much of that attitude changed in the early '30s when Satchel Paige's persona made the CWL a hot ticket for white fans.

Los Angeles's racial climate may have been less forbidding than that of cities back east but it was not impervious to Jim Crow. When blacks went to White Sox Park, says CWL historian William F. McNeil, they generally congregated in the bleachers—keeping a healthy distance from white fans.[8]

Satchel Paige's West Coast benefactor, Joseph L. Pirrone (his Sicilian surname was pronounced with a long "e"), was a ball of energy, a feisty little man with a big yen for public relations. Joe never tired of seeing his name in print—and "Pirrone" was in plenty of L.A. headlines from the '20s through the '50s. A man of eclectic talents, he managed to grab publicity while wearing different hats—as a sporting goods salesman, a man-about-town nightclub owner, a baseball promoter, and the domo of a World War I veterans association. He even sold cars on the side. Joe loved rubbing elbows with the elite of Hollywood and the sports world, especially when flashbulbs popped.

This obscure immigrant kid came to dominate Southern California's winter baseball scene in part because of his chutzpah and in part because of the lack of seasonal sports competition. As a young sandlotter, Pirrone recognized that the West Coast's minor leagues didn't slake L.A.'s appetite for baseball. Southern California's mild winter climate made it an ideal place to lure major and Pacific Coast leaguers looking to make extra bucks.

After overseas duty during World War I, Pirrone wangled a job with the Spalding sporting goods company. In the mid-1920s he opened Pirrone's Café near Hollywood. Featuring two floor shows each night, it became a favorite watering hole of L.A.'s glitterati. Ralph Kiner remembers what a big deal it was when older guys took him out for a night on the town that began at Joe's joint.[9]

Joe continued to lace up Spalding spikes on California diamonds well into his thirties. Beginning in 1921, the team he owned and managed, initially called the Pirrone All-Stars and later the Pirrone Café All-Stars, became a CWL fixture. Team affiliations varied from year to year, but Shell, Firestone, and the May Company (department stores) were among the companies that sponsored CWL clubs. So did the awkwardly named (given the CWL's interracial context) White King Soap Makers.

Some winters, merchant groups in Santa Monica, San Bernardino, Bakersfield, and San Diego underwrote CWL clubs. Even movie studios got involved. RKO, MGM, and others liked to have skimpy-bloused starlets throw out the first pitch, with photographers in tow.[10] George Raft, Joe E. Brown, and other Hollywood types enjoyed wagering at CWL contests.[11]

After its first decade of operation in the 1900s, the California Winter League not only permitted black teams to play, it encouraged them, because league officials soon learned that it meant better box office. It was the only professional baseball association of its day that gave blacks an opportunity to compete on equal footing with white ballplayers.

"When [African-American] teams participated in the California Winter League, attendance soared and the level of professional competition approached that of a AA league, even occasionally a AAA league," writes historian McNeil. "But when there was no [black] team in the league, games were played to near-empty grandstands, and the level of play declined."[12]

During the World War I years, no black club from back east competed in the CWL. By 1920, the CWL was foundering.[13]

Thanks to resourceful work from Pirrone and his business partner, Doc Anderson, a black entrepreneur, the league was rescued. Pirrone and Anderson made an effective team. Anderson's goal was to give L.A.'s best black semipros and sandlotters a decent facility, which he did by building 3,500-seat White Sox Park in Boyle Heights. For his part, Commissioner Pirrone cultivated blackball's powers-that-be while at the same time ensuring that the white majors' big names would continue coming West.

Following the 1920–21 season, each winter for more than two decades the CWL included at least one visiting black all-star team from back east. Negro League teams proved so popular in the CWL that Pirrone scheduled them to play two or three times the number of games played by white clubs.[14]

Some black squads, especially those headlined by Satchel Paige, would play three dozen or more games in the course of a "season"; white squads just a dozen or two. So when Pirrone anointed a "pennant winner" or a first- or second-half "champion," he was playing fast and loose—but fans and the *Times*, the *Herald and Express*, and the African-American paper the *California Eagle* didn't seem to mind.

L.A.'s black community loved Pirrone because of what the *Eagle* called his "intrepid" efforts to lure the best in blackball, but also because the CWL employed scores of black vendors, ushers, and ticket takers.[15]

Despite Pirrone's persistence, CWL coverage in L.A.'s mainstream press was spotty. All that changed, however, when two things happened: Pirrone (no doubt through some financial emoluments) got Pacific Coast League owners to drop their 1914 ban on black teams playing in PCL parks; and he negotiated with blackball domos Tom Wilson, Tom Baird, and Gus Greenlee to include Satchel Paige on the all-star teams they sent to the Coast. Through their bosses' clever bartering, Negro Leaguers soon had a sweet setup in Southern California.

Satchel Paige created art almost everywhere he performed, but the West Coast became one of his most inspired canvases. There he confronted Dean in several high-profile duels, first faced Joe DiMaggio, and met Bob Feller time and again in games that riveted the region. Beginning in 1931–32, Satch played in the CWL for substantial parts of the next five winters.

Paige was in his salad days in Southern California, still in his mid-to-late twenties and not yet ground down from grueling travel. Unlike a typical barnstorming gig, where Satch would blow into town to collect a check for a few innings of work and then hit the road immediately afterward, the CWL afforded a measure of stability. He stayed in the same place (at least in theory), probably ate a little healthier than he did on the road, and played on the same gifted team for weeks and sometimes months. Pirrone's p.c.'s and California's weather must have agreed with him, because he turned in one spectacular outing after another.

To be sure, the competition was uneven. Most white teams in the CWL were of the semipro variety, at times augmented by a professional or two. But because Pirrone had more money to toss around, his Pirrone Café lineups tended to be more potent, often featuring top-notch major and Pacific Coast leaguers.

Paige's first season in the CWL established a high bar. Tom Wilson's troupe in that era was branded the Philadelphia Royal Giants, although there was no apparent connection to the City of Brotherly

Love. Center fielder Cool Papa Bell (.415 in '31–'32 league play), first baseman Mule Suttles (.586), and shortstop Willie Wells (.417), all future Hall of Famers, anchored an athletic squad. Besides Satch, the Royal Giants' rotation included Cannonball Willis and Highpockets Trent, both of whom went 3-0, as well as Cherry Bell (1-0) and Willie Foster (9-1), Paige's future foil in the Dakotas. The *Defender* called it the "the greatest staff of pitchers ever on the Pacific Coast."[16] Small wonder that the Royal Giants reportedly went 22-2 that year.

Comfortably assuming the role of the CWL's star attraction, Satch went 6-0 in '31–'32, threw two complete-game shutouts, and scintillated his Central Avenue fan base by scorching big-league hitters. Paige made his CWL debut on October 23, 1931, opening the season by beating Pirrone's All-Stars, 8-1, in a game played under Wrigley Field's brand-new lights.

Babe Herman, ringleader of the Brooklyn Dodgers' Daffiness Boys, played a few games with Pirrone's team that winter.[17] The left-handed Herman had four at-bats on opening night and went down on strikes each time. Since Babe had hit a stunning .393 the year before, finishing second in the National League batting race to Bill Terry's .401, black fans must have been beside themselves.

"The redoubtable Satchel Paige," as the *Defender* called him the next week, struck out seven other Pirrone batsmen that night, including five of the first six hitters, allowing only five hits.[18] The Royal Giants bopped around Pirrone's starter, Sam Gibson, a journeyman right-hander then with the PCL's San Francisco Seals, for ten hits and eight runs.[19] The next season, Gibson would close out his big-league career in the bullpen of the New York Giants, going 4-8.

Two weeks later, Satch beat the White King Soaps in the first game of a doubleheader, 3-1, fanning ten and scattering five hits. Opposing him on the mound was former White Sox hurler Charlie Barnabe, winless in seven career big-league decisions. If the *Defender*'s account is accurate, Cool Papa had five hits in six at-bats in the doubleheader.[20]

The Los Angeles–based white press gave Satch and his CWL exploits scant coverage in '31 and '32. But the *Times*, the *Examiner*, and the *Herald and Express* could count noses as well as anyone. As Satch's legend grew and fan interest intensified, media coverage followed suit. Turnstiles clicked more frequently beginning in '32, when

Pirrone reduced ticket prices—bleacher seats could now be had for a quarter—and began admitting ladies for free.

Word about Satchel the showman buzzed all over the Southland. Whenever and wherever Satch pitched, a couple thousand extra CWL tickets were sold.[21] The *Eagle* loved him; back east, the *Defender* and the *Courier* soon began sharing "special correspondent" filings from the West Coast to keep readers apprised of Satch's latest triumphs.

Wilson's '32–'33 installment was labeled in most press accounts the Nashville Elite Giants—the name of his then-dormant Negro National League club. Although it went 14-2-2,[22] it wasn't as stacked as the previous year's squad. But all its position players—led by center fielder Sammy Bankhead (.371) and catcher Tommy Dukes (.357)—reportedly hit .300 or better through the course of the eighteen-game season.

Walter "Steel Arm" Davis, another future Dakotas hurler, pitched a complete-game victory that winter for the Elites, as did Andy "Pullman" Porter, who broke in that season with the Louisville Black Caps before eventually joining Wilson's reconstituted Nashville club.[23] Davis also played right field quite a bit that winter, batting a steely .359 and hitting five homers.[24]

Pirrone never had to be coaxed into putting on a show for opening day. "With a fanfare of music, loud cheering, gaudy uniforms of legionnaires, and gaily dressed femininity, the Winter League got going last Sunday," the *Eagle* reported on October 23. The '32–'33 opener was the first time that Pirrone was able to persuade White Sox Park officials to play games on the Sabbath.[25] Sunday afternoon doubleheaders soon became a CWL staple.

Satch was up to his usual tricks that winter, striking out sixty-five hitters in just forty-five innings. Again he finished the winter without a blemish, reportedly going 5-0 and pitching at least one complete-game shutout. The *Eagle* noted on November 18 that Satch beat Pirates southpaw Larry French, who led the National League that year with forty-seven appearances, and the Pirrones, 8-1. Paige gave up seven hits, three of which were stroked by former big-league infielder Fred "Pudge" Haney, the future manager of the Browns, Pirates, and Braves.

In January 1933, the *Los Angeles Times* reported that Satch fanned eighteen in disposing of Pirrone's All-Stars, 3-1. Pirrone's third baseman, believed to be onetime Chicago Cub Les Bell (a career .290 hitter), homered off Satch, spoiling Paige's bid for a shutout. That same month, the *Eagle* applauded the caliber of play in the CWL, commending Pirrone for bringing in a squad from the Texas-Mexico border that called itself the El Paso Mexicans. The El Paso club promptly went winless in its first eight games.

Pirrone outdid himself at White Sox Park to close out the CWL's '32–'33 season. A capacity crowd was treated to a motorcycle race prior to a doubleheader that pitted El Paso against a local nine known as the Redondo Mexicans. El Paso won the opener against Redondo and then faced the Elite Giants in the black team's "farewell" appearance of the season.[26] The Elites schooled the El Paso club, 4-0, with Pullman Porter pitching the bulk of the shutout. It was almost certainly the first time that blacks and Latinos had been spotlighted together in a professional baseball setting.

Porter, a towering right-hander from Little Rock, spent two decades in blackball. He was a workmanlike pitcher for the Black Caps and the Elite Giants in the '30s, but didn't make a mark until he went to Mexico in the late '30s and early '40s. Porter became a star for the 1940 Nuevo Laredo Owls, leading the Mexican League in complete games; he enjoyed similar success in the Cuban winter leagues. After the war, he rejoined the U.S. Negro Leagues, hooking up first with the Newark Eagles, then the Indianapolis Clowns.

By 1933–34, word was out among black stars about the California wintertime junket. That winter's squad, known in the *L.A. Times* as "Wilson's Elite Giants," included such stalwarts as Paige, Mule Suttles, Larry Brown, Turkey Stearnes, Steel Arm Davis, and Cannonball Willis.

Pirrone recruited a passel of white journeymen, among them infielder Bill Brubaker of the Pirates (whose only claim to fame came two years later, when he led the National League in whiffs), outfielder Smead "Smudge" Jolley (who'd led the American League in pinch-hits in 1931) of the Red Sox, shortstop Bill Knickerbocker (a Southern California kid who hit .226 in his rookie year, fifty points below his ten-year career average) of the Indians, and pitcher Lee Stine, then the property of the Chicago White Sox.

But Joe's biggest star was Norman "Buck" (né "Bobo") Newsom. Buck was something of a poor man's Dizzy Dean; he loved it when newspapermen called him "The Great Newsom." The right-hander spent the bulk of the '33 season with the Los Angeles Angels, living up to his "great" billing by being named MVP of the Pacific Coast League.[27] By late '33, Buck had been in the bigs for only a couple of brief stints, yet was already on his third major-league franchise. Another dozen or so trades were to come in Newsom's bumpy career; on five separate occasions, he toiled for the usually hapless Senators. Pirrone reveled in hyping Buck against Satch in marquee CWL match-ups. Newsom, a South Carolinian, never bothered to mask his bigotry, muttering racial epithets as he pawed the mound against black players. "I'll never go up to the big leagues until I can beat these niggers," Buck supposedly snarled one night as the Elites were hitting him hard. To which Papa Bell coolly countered, "Let's make him stay out here about two years."[28]

On October 14, 1933, Pirrone went all out in planning another opening day spectacular at White Sox Park. The *Eagle* noted that motion picture stars of both races would be on hand, along with heavyweight brawlers Jack Dempsey and Max Baer. The pugilists were treated to a fine performance by Cannonball Willis, who held Pirrone's club to six hits and helped his own cause with a run-scoring triple in a complete-game victory, 8-2.

Another overflow crowd the next day caught Satch at his best. Paige shut out the Pirrones, 10-0, allowing only three hits and five base runners.[29] Mule and Wild Bill hit homers; Wright, Wells, and Cool Papa all stole bases.

On November 9, Buck and Satch hooked up for the first time that autumn, with predictable results. "The great 'Buck' Newsome [sic] tried his luck against Tom Wilson's Colored Giants," the *Courier* reported the following week, "but lost the much-heralded mound duel to 'Satchell' [sic] Paige, the speedball strikeout king by a score of 11 to 3 here at the Whitesox Park."[30] Satch, who actually gave up single tallies in the first and third innings and trailed 2-0 before his mates erupted against Newsom, struck out thirteen Pirrone players in going the distance. Dukes took the South Carolinian deep, Stearnes and Suttles hit two doubles apiece, and Wells wowed another huge crowd with some sparkling plays at short.

The next Sunday, three days later, Pirrone arranged for a "Satchel Paige Day" at White Sox Park. Satch pitched the opener of a double-header and, between games, was showered with "numerous presents by admiring Central Avenue fans," the *Times* reported. "The largest crowd of the Winter League season turned out for the bargain bill and saw Paige live up to advance notices by holding his rivals to an infield hit up until the ninth."[31]

Larry French, who threw more career pitches against Paige than any white hurler save Dizzy Dean and Bob Feller, tossed a brave game for Pirrone, giving up only solo homers to Bankhead and Suttles before the Giants blew the game open in the eighth to win, 5-0. It was Satch's second straight complete-game shutout. Wells again starred with two doubles, although he did commit a rare error at short.

Manager Pirrone, perhaps frustrated by Paige's dominance, provided the game's comic relief. Outraged over the umpire's strike zone, Joe stormed onto the field and—in midprotest—tried to yank the ump's bow tie. "But it was one of those 'already-tied' pieces of neck-wear," the *Times* noted, "and so Pirrone was out of luck all around."[32] Joe was banished for the rest of game one but was back in the dugout for the nightcap, which saw Newsom hold the Giants to six hits and kayo eleven in winning, 4-1.

Five days later, Satch was equally stout, this time holding Sloppy Thurston and the White Kings to one hit in winning, 4-0. Satch fanned sixteen and walked only two. Forty-eight hours later, Satch was back at White Sox Park against the White Kings. This time he was mortal, striking out thirteen but issuing ten walks while losing, 4-1. A few days after Thanksgiving, Satch dueled with future major-league right-hander Johnny Babich, then the ace of Portland's club in the Pacific Coast League. In an exhibition pitting the PCL all-stars against Wilson's club, Babich held the Giants to two hits while Satch limited Babich and his mates to five. Willie Wells, whom the *Times* identified by his sometime-nickname "Beau," homered off Babich in the fourth inning for the only run of the game. Satch struck out thirteen and started a lightning-quick 1-6-3 double play. It was one of the (relatively) few double plays in history handled exclusively by future Hall of Famers: Paige to Wells to Suttles.

Thanks to Pirrone's matchmaking, Newsom and Paige met six times during the CWL's '33–'34 campaign. Newsom won only one of the contests, an ugly 10-8 affair on Christmas Day that saw Satchel hit hard for one of the few times ever on the Coast.

Perhaps the best Newsom-Paige battle came on "Buck Newsom Day" in January 1934 at White Sox Park. Buck and Satch "hooked up in a thrilling mound duel that saw the Royal Giants win a 3-2 decision over Joe Pirrone's All-Stars," the *Times* reported.

Wilson's club won 34 of 42 games that winter of '33–'34, besting Pirrone's team in the win column by thirty-one games.

Bell batted a cool .362, beating out Beau Wells by seven points to win the '33–'34 CWL batting crown, if such a thing could be awarded. Mule Suttles, who would go on to become the CWL's career home run king, hit fourteen dingers in just 157 at-bats.

Satch enjoyed a remarkable season, leading the circuit in victories (16), games pitched (20), complete games (18), winning percentage (.888), innings pitched (171), strikeouts (244), and shutouts (7). His buddy Cannonball Willis wasn't far behind, throwing 15 complete games and striking out 93 batters in 116 innings. Between them in '33–'34, Paige and Willis won 30 of the Elites' 34 victories and combined for nine shutouts.[33]

The Elites would only grow stronger in the years to come.

The '34–'35 CWL season represented some of Paige's finest work in California, although newlywed Satch didn't pull into L.A. until the Elites had already played some fifteen games. He and Janet apparently spent a fun honeymoon dancing and dining in L.A.—the happiest time of what would prove to be a turbulent marriage.

Besides Satch, proprietors Wilson, Baird, and Greenlee brought west a club laced with future Hall of Famers: slick-fielding second baseman Sammy T. Hughes of the Nashville Elites joined Cool Papa Bell (.306 on the CWL season), Willie Wells (.319), Turkey Stearnes (.423, 16 home runs), and Mule Suttles (.344, 16 home runs).

Many experts, including Monte Irvin, regard Hughes as the finest all-around second baseman in blackball history.[34] Irvin considered Sammy T., who was a rangy six-foot-three, a more accomplished fielder than Jackie Robinson and almost as lethal on the basepaths.

Hughes could handle a bat with such aplomb that Monte compared him to longtime Cubbie and Dodger (and Hall of Famer) Billy Herman, the ideal second hitter.[35]

Behind the plate in '34–'35 was Larry Brown, a supposed defensive specialist, who nevertheless hit .364 that winter. His pal Bill Wright hit .481 in seventeen games that season. Irvin compared Wild Bill's hulking physique and playing style to that of Dave Parker, the 1970s–'80s star of the Pirates and Reds.[36]

A "big three"—Pullman Porter, Cannonball Willis, and Satch—formed the backbone of the rotation. Porter won twelve games in nineteen appearances while Willis won nine, including three complete-game shutouts.

In ten appearances, Paige won eight times, going the distance in seven of them, including two shutouts. Satch struck out 104 men in just 69 innings that winter, giving up only twenty walks. The club reportedly went 12-3 before Satch arrived, 16-3 afterward.

All in all, the '34–'35 Wilson Elites were among the most powerful black all-star contingents ever assembled. They also have to be considered among the best barnstorming clubs ever, certainly on a par with Neil Churchill's integrated Bismarck squads.

Pirrone was not able to attract top-drawer talent that year; Buck Newsom chose not to play in the CWL.

Correspondent James Newton, who helped organize and promote the black CWL teams, filed regular dispatches that got huge play in the *Defender* and the *Courier*. A February 2, 1935, story in the Chicago paper was headlined "Satchel Paige Unbeaten on Coast; Hero of League."[37] The story highlighted Satch's remarkable strikeout record that winter, leaving readers the clear impression that he was beating top-level major leaguers, which wasn't accurate. CWL perennial Larry French of the Pirates, soon to be traded to the Cubs, pitched a couple of games for Pirrone that winter, but French, as usual, didn't fare well against Paige. Wilson's Elites won thirty-four out of forty.

A week later, the *Defender* ran a column that lauded Satchel's commercial appeal. "Paige's value has been established in all sections and both races are clamoring for his services. He can invade North Dakota, Wisconsin, Kansas, or Nebraska anytime he chooses and find employment awaiting his signature." But the paper also mentioned how weary Greenlee and other owners had gotten of Satch's financial demands and unreliable behavior.

Satch's pièce de résistance in Southern California that winter came in an exhibition on March 9. No doubt for a tasty p.c., he switched sides, pitching for the El Paso Mexicans. His buddies didn't hit him hard—he gave up only seven hits and struck out eleven. But the Mexicans' faulty fielding did in Satch; he lost, 7-2.

Wilson's '35–'36 club wasn't quite as fearsome, since Cool Papa, Beau Wells, Pullman Porter, and Cannonball Willis all elected to winter elsewhere. But Wilson arranged for one of his own charges, Bob "Schoolboy" Griffith, then of the Columbus Elite Giants, to pitch on the West Coast. Griffith was a six-foot-five spitballer who'd attended Tennessee State.

The Elites owner also worked deals with Tom Baird and Eddie Bolden to procure the services, respectively, of Monarchs right-hander Chet Brewer and Philadelphia Stars catcher Biz Mackey. Chet spent about two-thirds of the '35–'36 CWL season with the Elites; Mackey about half. The Elites may not have had the firepower of the previous year's edition, but they still won twenty-one of twenty-eight games, again dominating an abbreviated schedule.

Satch was even more prolific in '35–'36 than he was the previous CWL season. He appeared in sixteen contests, winning thirteen, including four complete-game shutouts. His strikeout ratio that winter wasn't quite as jaw-dropping—he whiffed "only" 113 in 94 innings—but he continued to fill ballparks whenever he pitched. A standing-room-only crowd at Wrigley Field, in fact, greeted Satch and Dizzy Dean on Halloween night in '35 (see chapter 5). Satch struck out seven in just four innings. But the Elites went down to defeat courtesy of 44-year-old Truck Hannah's ninth-inning single.

In early November 1935, the *Eagle* excitedly reported that the following Sunday had been declared "Bill 'Bojangles' Robinson Day" at Wrigley Field. Between games of an Elite Giants–Pirrone All-Stars doubleheader, the hoofer promised to compete in a foot race against whomever the black team would designate as their fastest player, which turned out to be Bill Wright.

The Bojangles–Wild Bill face-off was no ordinary sprinting contest. Wright would run one hundred yards in the conventional manner, while Robinson would simultaneously run seventy-five yards in his preferred style—backward.

Five years earlier, Robinson had set a "world record" of 13.5 seconds for the hundred-yard backward dash, the first time that such a bizarre feat was chronicled. Bojangles's record stood for a remarkable forty-seven years.[38] Even today, the world record for dashing backward one hundred yards is less than a second faster than Robinson's 1935 time.

With three thousand "wildly cheering fans looking on," the showdown ended in what was described as a "dead heat"—so the race was run again. This time, Bojangles eked out a narrow victory over winded Wild Bill.[39]

Pitching backward was a trick not even Satch would try. He put on a radiant performance in the first game, fanning seven and yielding only two hits in five innings on the mound. The Elites won, 7-0.

Despite a busy CWL schedule that winter, Satch managed to squeeze in a lucrative side trip, courtesy of the New York Yankees. On February 7, 1936, Paige headlined an exhibition in Oakland against a group of major-league and PCL all-stars. The white club was led by veteran barnstormer Dick "Rowdy Richard" Bartell, the tart-tongued shortstop of the New York Giants.

Bartell and northern California promoter Johnny Burton put together a thorny lineup for Paige that included such Bay Area stalwarts as Reds catcher Ernie Lombardi (who hit .343 during the '35 season), Cubs outfielder Augie Galan (who led the National League with 133 runs scored), first sacker Gus Suhr of the Pirates (.272), infielder Cookie Lavagetto (.290), then of the Pirates, and a twenty-one-year-old outfielder from the PCL's San Francisco Seals named Joseph Paul DiMaggio. That season DiMaggio hit .398 and drove in 154 runs. Four thousand lucky fans witnessed history that night in Oakland.

Joltin' Joe would make his Bronx debut that April. The Yankee brain trust wanted to see DiMag go up against the best, so they quietly paid Satch and catcher Ebel Brooks, a journeyman then with the New York Black Yankees, to make the trip up from L.A.[40] It's telling that the Yankees and promoter Burton still insisted on separating the races: Satch and Ebel played with an all-black squad made up of Bay Area semipros.

Years later, Bartell remembered that Satch's pitches were tough to hit—one would be an overhand riser, the next a sidearm dipper.[41] DiMaggio struggled against Paige and wasn't alone. Gus Suhr whiffed three times; Lavagetto got lassoed twice.[42]

DiMaggio's first three at-bats produced a couple of weak ground-outs and a soft fly to center. In its profile of Paige written two decades later, *Collier's* reported that Satch struck out fifteen that night.[43] Paige took a four-hitter and a 1-1 game into the tenth inning, an extraordinary feat given his pedestrian fielders.

With two outs in the bottom of the tenth, Bartell singled off Satch and swiped second. He took third when Ebel Brooks couldn't handle a fastball strike that Paige had thrown past DiMaggio. Protecting the plate with a 0-2 count, Joe hit a bounder that supposedly glanced off Satch's glove on its way to the second baseman. Joe beat the throw, allowing Bartell to score the winning run. The hometown scorekeeper deemed it a "hit."

Yankee scouts wired the home office: "DiMaggio All We Hoped He'd Be—Hit Satch One for Four."[44] DiMaggio came away awed; nineteen months later, he told the *Daily Worker* that Paige was the greatest pitcher he'd ever faced—a sentiment he reaffirmed many times over the years.[45] Joltin' Joe never became an outspoken proponent of baseball integration. But, to his credit, DiMag denounced Jim Crow.[46]

The black *Oakland Journal* sent correspondent Eddie Murphy to the Paige-DiMaggio game. "The greatest pitching attraction in the world," Murphy wrote after watching Satch in action, "is being passed up the scouts, club owners, and managers only because the doors of organized baseball are closed to him."[47]

Tom Wilson's club won twenty-three of their thirty-one CWL games in '35–'36, but it was the last year that the Nashville-based promoter and his partners were able to assemble a top-drawer team. It was also, despite Pirrone's lucre, Paige's last winter in California until midwar.

From '37 through '43, Satch preferred wintering in the Caribbean, pitching exhibitions in the Sun Belt, or going hunting and fishing.

Pirrone's CWL continued to do all right at the box office without Paige, but it was never quite the same. Chet Brewer and Schoolboy Griffith led Wilson's rotation in '36–'37, going a combined 16-2. Wilson thought he had scored a coup by securing the services of Josh Gibson that winter. The *Eagle* swooned over the prospect of blackball's peerless slugger coming to the Coast; alas, Josh didn't show. Indeed, Gibson never suited up in the CWL—one of the few prominent blackballers of that generation who didn't play in Pirrone's circuit.

Mouthy shortstop Bartell roiled things that winter when he questioned Satchel Paige's readiness for the big leagues and disparaged the black pitcher's ability. Paige wasn't everything he was cracked up to be, Bartell told white reporters. Dick claimed that he'd hit .400 against Paige in various exhibitions, including the DiMaggio game in Oakland in February of '36. After checking game accounts and eyewitnesses, the *Chicago Defender* concluded that Bartell's career batting average against Paige was actually a measly .091, with five strikeouts to boot![61] If Rowdy Richard popped off again about the inadequacies of black pitchers, it wasn't with reporters around.

Satch was once asked to comment about the success that Negro Leaguers enjoyed in the California Winter League. "We won," Satch slyly replied, "like we invented the game."[48]

CHAPTER SEVEN

Rapid Robert Meets Satch

*Now I'm gonna speak right up for Bob Rapid. First time I seen him was in
1936. I throwed against him in an exhibition game in Des Moines, Iowa
after he finished his first season with Cleveland . . . man that boy was fast.*

—SATCHEL PAIGE, *PITCHIN' MAN*

Toward the end of Bob Feller's career, columnists looked at his brusque
manner, his outsized salary, the corporation he established to exploit
his multifaceted commercial interests, his motorboat, his upscale
suburban home full of gadgetry, his pilot's license and private plane,
the collapsible motor scooter that he stowed in his Piper Cub and
rode from a Cleveland airstrip to Municipal Stadium, his preoccupa-
tion with physical fitness (which, back then, was considered weird
and narcissistic), and, most of all, his then-radical notion that major
league baseball's reserve clause should be abolished, and concluded
that Feller was full of himself. During the don't-make-waves '50s,
Feller was branded pushy and arrogant. Even the name of his corporation, Ro-Fel, Inc., struck people as egotistic.

They didn't understand him; Feller was way ahead of his time. As a
teenager, he saw that serious money could be made from barnstorming;
he worked overtime to ensure that other players—white and black—
enjoyed the financial fruits of off-season baseball, too. As a chief petty
officer during World War II he saw the inequities of a segregated navy,
recognized that integration was coming, and, not unlike Branch Rickey,
figured out ways to do good and do well at the same time.

Colleagues didn't get him, either. When Feller voluntarily headed the players' association in the '50s, he became an outspoken critic of the reserve clause, the restrictive covenant that kept major-league players bound to one organization for the bulk of their careers. He was a lonely champion for change. Stan Musial, Ralph Kiner, even Jackie Robinson all testified before Congress that the reserve clause was integral to baseball's success and shouldn't be altered.

Nearly two decades before famed labor leader Marvin Miller entered the national consciousness, Feller told a young CBS television interviewer named Mike Wallace that free agency would help, not hurt, baseball.[1] Ironically, when free agency finally came in the 1970s—ushering in a better and more lucrative era for players and owners and making baseball infinitely more interesting for fans—Feller got virtually no credit. By then, Feller had stopped being a crusader for players' rights. He had gotten older; his politics had drifted rightward. Plus he disliked Miller's confrontational style. To this day, Feller is ambivalent about his role as a labor pioneer. It wasn't a real union back then, just a loose association, Feller now argues, more than a bit disingenuously.

If Dizzy Dean and Satchel Paige seem like inventions of Mark Twain, then Robert William Andrew Feller was something out of Sinclair Lewis. The teenage Feller was the embodiment of Middle American virtue, an apple-cheeked prodigy almost too good to be true. With the Dust Bowl still swirling, Master Feller emerged from Main Street to become an American idol.

Feller's busy but unburdened boyhood along the banks of Iowa's Raccoon River was the obverse of those of his two barnstorming buddies. Bob was the adored first child of corn farmer Bill, a baseball nut, and Lena, a nurse and schoolteacher. His upbringing was so bucolic that it "sounds almost as if Ma and Pa Kettle were down the road a piece," *Sports Illustrated*'s Frank Deford wrote in a 2005 profile.[2]

The careers of Feller and Dizzy Dean were intertwined from Bobby's first day as a big-league pitcher. Bobby's debut with the Cleveland Indians came as a seventeen-year-old in a midseason exhibition against Dean's Gas House Gang in July 1936. St. Louis player-manager Frankie Frisch supposedly watched the youngster plunk the backstop while warming up and sagely scratched "Frisch" off his lineup card.

After Feller struck out eight Cardinals in just three innings, a photographer asked Dean if he'd pose with the young flamethrower. "If it's all right with him, it's all right with me," Dean said. "After what he did today, he's the guy to say."[3]

As an Indians rookie in September 1936, Feller struck out seventeen members of the Philadelphia Athletics in one game to tie Dizzy's major-league record—a feat that mesmerized the nation. The dutiful seventeen-year-old then returned to Van Meter to complete his senior year in high school. After a few days, Feller stopped wearing his Indians cap for fear that schoolmates would think he was putting on airs. His fellow seniors—all eighteen of them—elected Bobby class president.

Ray Doan, the barnstorming impresario, called the teenage Feller the "perfect American boy." Doan was so eager to get his claws into young Bobby that he pretty much dumped Dizzy Dean as a client. A decade later, Feller's supposed "perfection" did not preclude Doan, a fellow Iowan, from suing Bob for alleged breach of contract. A judge eventually threw out Doan's charges, but not before a sharp public exchange dented Feller's image. To this day, Feller, now in his nineties, has never quite shaken the perception that he got too big for his britches. In that sense, he completed the arc of a classic Lewis protagonist, supposedly forsaking the values of home and hearth for conspicuous consumption and crass pursuit of the almighty buck.

In that 2007 conversation, Feller, ever crusty, was unapologetic about making and spending money. "You can't take it with you," he proclaimed in the presence of his then-fifteen-year-old grandson. "I've never seen a Brinks truck behind a hearse."[4]

For baseball buffs unfamiliar with the Hawkeye State, "Van Meter, Iowa," has always evoked the image of an archetypal midwestern crossroads—the sort of flat-as-a-pancake place that might have inspired the biplane scene in Alfred Hitchcock's *North by Northwest*.

In truth, Bob Feller's hometown sits on bumpy terrain not far west of Des Moines. Van Meter didn't take off until late in the nineteenth century, when coal beds were discovered. Basements of some surviving homes still connect to long-abandoned mine shafts.[5]

The town is justifiably proud of its consolidated school, where elementary, intermediate, and secondary students are still housed under one roof. Much of the old-time high school has been preserved. Framed photos of long-ago graduating classes grace an older hallway.

Van Meter High's class of '37 had a sizable number of students: nineteen graduated that spring. They're the only class in town history whose commencement ceremony was broadcast live on NBC Radio. Wire service photographers also covered the event, jostling to get the best angle for a picture of class president Bobby Feller receiving his diploma.

Today, a plaque next to the school gym pays homage to Feller's legacy and to his generous donations to Van Meter's athletic programs. The baseball-football complex is named in Bob's honor. In 2003, Van Meter High won the Iowa Class 1A baseball championship—a feat trumpeted by a sign on top of the scoreboard.[6] Eight years earlier, the Bob Feller Hall of Fame and Museum had opened across town.

As kids, Satchel Paige and Dizzy Dean often didn't know where their next meal was coming from. The Fellers weren't well off by any stretch, but they could always put food on the table—not only from the seventy-five Hereford cattle and dozens of pigs in the barn, but from the apple orchard across the road and the vegetable garden in the side yard.

Paige and Dean were raised by overwhelmed single parents who had little choice but to have their kids quit school. Satch and Diz were both calculating men, but they carried education deficits with them throughout their lives. Feller, by contrast, was not only the apple of his parents' eyes—his sister Marguerite didn't come along until Bobby was ten—but he was a sharp student. Early on, he developed a voracious lifelong appetite for learning.

The Feller farm was perched on a bluff atop the Raccoon River. A dirt road in front of the house was so full of ruts and potholes that it often trapped motorists in icy weather. Bill Feller charged stranded drivers two bucks to pull their vehicle out of the muck.[7] Neighbor kids loved visiting the Fellers in the wintertime because Bob's father would hook a sleigh to their horse-drawn buggy and take youngsters careening down the road.

Bobby's dad was tall and wiry, but not nearly as broad across the shoulders as his son became. Bill had been a decent sandlotter in his day. But the real star in the family had been Bill's father-in-law, Edward Forret. Lena's dad had been a feared moundsman for the Van Meter town nine in the late 1800s, the "best durned pitcher in Ioway," folks said.[8]

When Bobby was still a toddler, his dad would sit on the davenport, encouraging his boy to wind up and fire a rubber ball. As Bobby grew older, there were endless games of catch with Dad in the barnyard when the weather was passable and inside the barn when it wasn't.

Around Bobby's eighth birthday, his dad lassoed some wire and dangled it from a tree so it hung waist-high. "In all his spare moments," Bill recalled to the Associated Press in 1936, "Bob would throw at that circle."

Every morning, rain or shine, Bobby lugged water for the farm animals from the Raccoon to the barn a couple of hundred yards away. A mutt named Tagalong dogged every step. "Sometimes, when I have been asked how I developed my fastball, I have been tempted to answer: 'Carrying water for cattle from the Raccoon River,'" Feller wrote decades later.[9] Bobby's childhood was a blur of nonstop chores and long walks to school on cold mornings. But it was also full of love and self-affirmation. There's no record that he resented the regimen that his father imposed on him. Indeed, the evidence suggests just the opposite: not unlike the young Tiger Woods, Bobby savored the hard work his dad threw at him.

When the youngster was nine, Babe Ruth and Lou Gehrig came barnstorming through Des Moines. To raise money for a local charity, the Western League Demons had Ruth and Gehrig autograph 120 baseballs, auctioning them off at five bucks apiece—a princely sum back then.

Young Bobby wanted one of those balls. He came up with a scheme that demonstrated he'd inherited his old man's entrepreneurial attitude. Dallas County's farms that fall had been overrun with gophers, endangering the alfalfa crop. Officials offered county residents a dime for each pair of exterminated gopher claws.

Bobby armed a pal with a gunnysack and instructed him to hold it over one of the gopher holes in the Fellers' alfalfa field. Then Bobby ran a hose from the exhaust pipe of his dad's '22 Dodge truck to the gopher mound, turned on the truck's ignition, and choked it full out. "I was careful," Feller remembered, "not to use up all the gas. After all, it cost Dad six cents a gallon—nine cents minus a three-cent rebate if you used it for agricultural purposes."[10] Fifty asphyxiated and declawed gophers later, Feller had his autographed ball.

Bill and Bob were in the Western League Field stands on October 29, 1928, to see the Larrupin' Lous trounce the Bustin' Babes by a score of 15-4. Ruth and Gehrig not only both hit homers, they both pitched, thrilling the Fellers.

The Fellers saw a lot of baseball in Des Moines, including games pitting the House of David against the Kansas City Monarchs. Bobby grew up watching Newt Allen, Newt Joseph, Frank Duncan, Bullet Joe Rogan, and other iconic Monarchs. He distinctly recalls seeing Satchel Paige pitch but can't identify the year.[11]

At Christmastime 1931, Bill approached his son with a wild proposition: to field their own team by building a diamond on the farm. It took months to clear and flatten the land. But by the next spring, "Oak View Park" had taken shape. Thanks to chicken wire and wood from some twenty felled oaks, the park soon had a backstop, fences, bleachers, and what Bob later told *Look* magazine was the "lumpiest infield in the Midwest."[12] Eventually, a concession stand and a hand-operated scoreboard were added. Five decades before W. P. Kinsella published his fanciful story "Shoeless Joe Jackson Comes to Iowa," Bill and Bob Feller built their own field of dreams.

Over the next few summers, Bill Feller's "Oakviews" played all comers. They also fielded a remarkably diverse lineup. Not many black kids lived in the Iowa of the 1930s, but a number of African-Americans played for and against the Oakviews, some of whom doubled as laborers on the Feller farm. If their black hirees didn't smoke around the barn, Mr. Feller paid them an extra five dollars a month.[13] Even more remarkably, Bill Feller hired black umpires to work games on the farm.[14] "Playing against black players and having them on my own team was nothing new or special to me," Feller remembered in his book *Now Pitching*.

Iowans began flocking to Oak View Park. It cost twenty-five cents to gain admittance for a single game and thirty-five cents for a week-end doubleheader—revenue that the family plowed back into field maintenance, uniforms, and equipment. They didn't make money, Bill later said, but they didn't lose money, either.[15]

Against the backdrop of farms and businesses failing all over the Midwest, the sacrifices that Bill and Lena made on their son's behalf are little short of staggering. Think of the incredulous stares the Fellers must have drawn from neighbors who were having trouble meeting their monthly bank obligations.

By age fifteen, Bobby was moonlighting with the American Legion team in Adel, the county seat. The Adel Legionnaires were led by catcher Nile Kinnick, who later became an all-American quarterback and won the Heisman Trophy at the University of Iowa. Two of the most celebrated athletes in Iowa history grew up a few miles from each other and just a couple of years apart. Feller-Kinnick proved to be an invincible battery. Nile became a naval aviator after Pearl Harbor and was killed in a training mission off the Venezuelan coast in 1943. The Hawkeyes' football stadium is named in his honor.[16]

Over the years, there have been varying stories about how Feller came to the attention of a Cleveland Indians executive named Cyril C. Slapnicka. Cy Slapnicka was a native Iowan, proud of the scouting network he'd built across the state. He wasn't the only scout to have gotten a heads-up about Feller; the Class D Des Moines Demons and other organizations were lurking, too.[17]

On July 21, 1935, Slapnicka drove out to the Feller farm, unannounced. The scene that ensued was out of a hackneyed movie script. Father and son were combining wheat when Bobby, sitting atop the tractor, spotted the tall Slapnicka weaving through the field.[18]

Bobby didn't breathe a word as Slapnicka exchanged pleasantries with Mr. Feller. The scout's stature was such that Bill recognized Cy's name and knew he represented the Indians. Slapnicka inquired about the youngster's next scheduled start. When told Bobby was slated to take the mound in Des Moines two days hence, Slapnicka allowed that he'd come by.

Slapnicka liked what he saw. A few days later, Cy again visited the Feller farm, this time armed with a crude "contract." Cleveland was offering Bobby a minor-league deal with Fargo-Moorhead of the Class D

Western League, the lowest rung in its system. Since his son was only sixteen, Bill Feller acted on Bobby's behalf.

The agreement had been scribbled on the stationery of a Des Moines hotel. It called for Bobby to join Fargo-Moorhead the following season, 1936. Feller was to receive a salary of five hundred dollars—but only if he were still on the roster at the end of the '36 season. Slapnicka's deal included a two-fisted bonus: one dollar in cash and a baseball autographed by the Indians. The only cash that changed hands in July 1935 was that solitary buck.[19]

The signing of Bobby Feller is almost always depicted in wistful hues. But in truth it was cynical at best and deceitful at worst. Slapnicka knew his Iowa roots gave him credibility with Bobby's dad that other scouts wouldn't have. Cy also knew that he was pulling a coup. When Slapnicka returned to Cleveland, he told the club's board of directors that—no snickering allowed, gentlemen—he had signed another Walter Johnson.[20]

Slapnicka knew that Feller's skills put him way beyond Class D. Even then, Cy was plotting ways to circumvent the minors and, quietly, bring Feller to the Indians. Slapnicka's dishonest brokering not only caused a flap that had to be resolved by Commissioner Landis, but cost Feller many thousands of dollars in lost salary and bonus at a time when his family sorely needed the money.

Bobby never reported to Fargo-Moorehead. Instead, Slapnicka had Feller's contract transferred to New Orleans, placing Bob's name on the "voluntarily retired" list so he could finish his junior year at Van Meter High. Major-league rules discouraged teams from signing players directly from the sandlots; prospects signed to minor-league contracts were compelled to put in time there.

Feller never showed up in New Orleans, either. Once school let out, Slapnicka sent the youngster a train ticket to Cleveland. Ostensibly, the Indians wanted Feller to hang around League Park and Municipal Stadium, the club's twin parks, selling concessions and acclimating himself to the big leagues.

The club had Feller sign a temporary deal with the Rosenblums, the crackerjack Cleveland semipro team for whom Dizzy and Paul Dean had pitched two years earlier against Satchel Paige and the Crawfords.

Bob started two games for the Rosies and nicely acquitted himself, striking out twenty-five in seventeen innings while giving up nine hits.

Fortunately for Slapnicka, the Indians had a League Park exhibition game scheduled in early July against the Gas House Gang Cardinals. Slapnicka told Feller he'd pitch the middle innings. "Just forget who they are," Cy advised the youngster. "Don't be afraid of them."[21]

The score was tied, 1-1, in the top of the fourth when Feller began warming up. Players in both dugouts craned their necks with "wild-eyed fascination," in the words of Gordon Cobbledick of the *Plain Dealer*, to watch the seventeen-year-old throw his first pitches against big-league competition.

St. Louis rookie catcher Ambrose Ogrodowski led off. Feller's first pitch was a called strike. Ogrodowski bunted Bobby's second pitch, but was thrown out by Indians' third baseman Sammy Hale.

Shortstop Leo Durocher was up next. "Keep the ball in the park, busher!" Leo lipped as he dug in. Durocher watched two fastballs crease the strike zone and, head shaking, skulked back toward the dugout. As the ump ordered him back to the plate, Durocher supposedly yelled, "You can have it [the last strike]! I feel like a stool pigeon in a shooting gallery!"[22] The Lip returned and took a halfhearted cut at strike three. Relieved that he was still in one piece, Durocher retired to the dugout to watch Arthur Garibaldi, a substitute infielder, suffer the same fate.

Feller's catcher was the Indians' manager, 45-year-old Steve O'Neill, who'd last caught for the Indians eight years before. "I'm not as spry as I used to be and you might kill me with that fastball before we're through," O'Neill kidded Feller in the dugout. "But you're great, kid." The kid's fastball left such a welt on O'Neill's left hand that, after two innings, he gave way to the bullpen catcher.[23]

As Feller left the game, quick-thinking photographers grabbed Dizzy Dean, who'd spent the afternoon lounging in the Cards' dugout in a dapper suit and floral tie. The photograph was an instant classic. In the picture, Dean, as always, is hamming it up. He's grinning ear to ear with his right arm nonchalantly draped across Feller's shoulders. The teenager's body language, on the other hand, betrays a trace of nerves. Bobby is keeping a respectful distance from the legend he'd watch pitch in the World Series two years earlier; the youngster's smile is broad but self-conscious.

———————————

The Iowa farm boy became front-page news that summer as he piled up strikeout after strikeout. American moms fell in love with Feller's chubby-cheeked countenance. "[A] face as honest and guileless as Gary Cooper's," is how St. Clair McKelway described Feller in *Life* magazine.[24]

Feller was that rare teenage phenom who achieves his promise with a minimum of angst. His first off-season was not without incident, however. Slapnicka's slippery dealings with the Fellers drew the ire of the owner of the Des Moines Demons. Lee Keyser was steamed that the Indians had signed a homegrown kid to a phony deal. Commissioner Landis's usual punishment for a major-league club that side-stepped contractual requirements was to declare the wronged player a free agent.

Sharks were circling around Van Meter that fall. Rumors suggested that Boston owner Tom Yawkey had a Red Sox executive camped out in a Des Moines hotel, ready to offer Feller two hundred thousand dollars. The Yankees were also poised to pounce.[25]

It may have taken Feller years to comprehend how badly he'd been snookered. Yet the Fellers were willing to do Slapnicka's bidding against the commissioner's office.

When Landis conducted his formal inquiry that fall, Slapnicka misrepresented the facts—and Bill and Bob willingly went along. Not only did the Fellers back up Slapnicka's shaky story, but Bill threatened to slap the commissioner with a civil suit if Landis ruled against the Indians.[26] One wonders how Slapnicka's machinations fueled young Bobby's desire to cash in on the barnstorming trail. While the commissioner deliberated, the Fellers began to do just that, cash in.

Ray Doan was a busy guy in the mid-1930s. In concert with J. L. Wilkinson, Doan often had three House of David teams on the circuit at the same time. Plus every fall Doan and Wilkie had various big-league and black troupes out stumping.[27] In early October 1936, Doan arranged for a Rogers Hornsby–led all-star team to play a five-game series in Iowa and Colorado against a black contingent that billed itself as the "Negro National League All-Stars."

Doan moved quickly to sign Feller, not only to star in barnstorming tours but to serve as a teenage faculty member at his Hot Springs academy. The promoter promised Bobby three hundred dollars for a one-game appearance against the black all-stars in Des Moines.

Hornsby and Doan also made it worthwhile for Cardinals rookie first baseman Johnny "Big Cat" Mize, who'd hit 19 homers and batted .329 that season; first sacker Gus Suhr of the Pirates (.312); third baseman Harlond Clift (.302) of the Browns, an Oklahoman whose bronzed complexion earned him the sobriquet "Darkie"; outfielder Ival "Goodie" Goodman (.284) of the Cincinnati Reds; and pitchers Big Jim Weaver (14-8) of the Pirates, Earl Caldwell (7-16) of the Browns, and Jim Winford (11-10) of the Cardinals. Emmett "Heinie" Mueller (a .282 career hitter as an outfielder) came out of retirement to barnstorm with his old mate Hornsby, playing out of position at third base.

The black squad that toured Iowa and Colorado included many of the players who had combined earlier that season to win the *Denver Post* tournament. A number of stars had, in fact, left their respective Negro League clubs in midsummer to chase bigger dollars in Denver and on the barnstorming circuit. Satchel Paige went 6-0 in Denver for a club organized by Doan and Gus Greenlee, who willingly broke up his Crawfords for a piece of the action from the Little World Series.[28]

Outfielders Cool Papa Bell, Jimmy Crutchfield, and Wild Bill Wright were along for the Doan-Hornsby tour, as were infielders Jesse Williams, Sammy T. Hughes, Newt Allen, Felton Snow, and first basemen Oscar Charleston and Shifty Jim West. Pullman Porter, Schoolboy Griffith, and Leroy Matlock joined Satchel Paige on a talented staff.[29]

Jesse Williams was one of the nimblest shortstops in blackball history, blessed with quick feet and a bat that had surprising pop. "It was every boy's dream to be a Monarch," the Kansas City veteran said late in life. "You didn't play ball until you were a Monarch."[30] Nine years after the Doan-Hornsby series, Jesse moved to second to accommodate a prospect named Jackie Robinson.

Crutchfield has been virtually forgotten today, but he was an undersized outfielder who played with grit and intelligence, earning four trips to the East-West game. "Little Big Man," as the Missourian was called, was a left-handed hitter who sprayed line drives to all fields. Historian James Riley wrote of little Jimmy: "No outfielder had better hands or better eyes in judging a ball."[31] Like Williams, Crutchfield spent two years in the army during World War II.

The series began at League Park in Des Moines on Friday evening, October 2, with Lefty Matlock pitted against Big Jim Weaver. Cool Papa led off the top of the first with a single and then promptly swiped second. Charleston scored Bell with his own single against Big Jim. Two innings later, the forty-year-old Oscar struck again, doubling in another run with a line shot into right-center that must have made second baseman Hornsby's head snap.

But the real fireworks took place later, when the hot-tempered Charleston got into an argument with white umpire Les Williams. It was only the third recorded tussle in the history of interracial exhibitions. Charleston was involved in all three—in 1915 in Indianapolis, in 1934 in Pittsburgh, and two years later in Des Moines.

Some five hundred fans came onto the field to join what sounds like a halfhearted fracas. As the next day's *Register* pointed out, at least some of the rail jumpers were pursuing autographs, not mayhem. Cops arrived to break things up, which took only a few minutes. In the top of the seventh, the black team scored three more runs; Matlock and the Negro stars cruised to a 5-2 victory.[32]

Two nights later, Hornsby's team triumphed, 2-1, before a chilled crowd at the Davenport Blue Sox's six-year-old park along the banks of the Mississippi. Paige and Porter were brilliant that night, combining on a two-hitter and striking out sixteen of Hornsby's stars.

Satch had trouble remembering names and faces, so he asked Cool Papa to remind him whenever Hornsby came to the plate. Bell's admonitions must have worked; Hornsby struck out four straight times, although it appears that at least one and possibly two of the Rajah's whiffs came against Porter.

Paige pitched five innings, gave up one hit, and struck out eight. Pullman lost the game in the ninth when Mize's fly ball to right was muffed by Wild Bill Wright. As the Big Cat lumbered around second, Wright compounded his error by throwing wildly to third, allowing Mize to score. Winford went the distance for Hornsby's squad, allowing only five hits.[33]

The teams took an overnight train to Denver, then dueled the next day in a doubleheader before an overflow crowd at sold-out Merchants Field. Despite his work the night before, Satch went the distance in the opener; Paige yielded only six hits in a 6-3 win. Hornsby again went down on strikes, puportedly for the fifth time in a row. Sammy T. Hughes homered to lead a twelve-hit attack for the Negro Leaguers.

That evening, the white team was poised to win the seven-inning second game, which would have knotted the series. They were leading 4-1 in the sixth when Charleston and Bell both delivered clutch singles, tying the game. Hughes broke the deadlock with his seventh hit of the doubleheader, a two-RBI shot that bounced into the standing-room-only crowd in center for a ground-rule double. In all, the Negro Leaguers rallied for five runs.

Hornsby came to the plate in the final inning of the nightcap with two outs, two runners on, and his club trailing, 6-4. Leroy Matlock, who'd taken over for Schoolboy Griffith, got Hornsby on a routine fly. The Rajah had a frustrating visit to Denver: he went one for eight in the doubleheader.[34]

Two days later, Doan's caravan was back in Des Moines. This time, the Pride of Van Meter was slated to go boy-to-man with the Million Dollar Stringbean.

Feller's confrontation with Paige capped off a remarkable couple of days. On Monday, October 5, town officials arranged for Feller to be fêted at a "welcome home" party. The hoopla lasted virtually all day, culminating in an exhibition played on the Van Meter High field late that afternoon. Dallas County schoolkids got the day off. "Few men in the course of a lifetime are proclaimed absolute monarchs in their own communities," gushed the next day's *Register*. "But such an honor came here Monday to 17-year-old Bobby Feller."[35]

A temporary stage large enough to accommodate a dozen or more VIPs was erected outside Van Meter's school. Somewhere between six thousand and twelve thousand Hawkeyes crowded the schoolyard—all this in a town whose permanent population was less than four hundred.

The day began with Feller receiving the symbolic keys to Van Meter from the mayor. Then Bobby received actual keys to a new truck—a gift from a group of admiring businessmen. Governor Clyde L. Herring's encomium included this: "And now he's going back to finish high school here in Van Meter. How few boys in his place would bother to do that?"[36]

But the most poignant moment occurred when Bobby's grandfather Ed Forret stood before the microphone. "I used to be kind of a ballplayer myself," allowed the old sandlot chucker. "I'm glad I've got a grandson to take my place."[37]

After the speeches ended, the crowd wandered over to the ball field for a game to raise money for a planned community building.[38] Two of Iowa's leading semipro teams staged a game so Bobby could thrill the local folks. He pitched two innings for each club, striking out eleven of thirteen batters.[39]

Des Moines back then was a city of about 150,000, less than 1 percent of whom were African-American. But Iowans loved blackball. The Monarchs and other Negro League teams packed Western League Park whenever they came to town.

Doan had Bobby appear on Des Moines radio stations to hawk the game against the Negro National League All-Stars. There's a good chance that Bob was interviewed that week by a young personality at WHO Radio named Ronald Reagan, who years later recalled chatting up the teenaged Feller. There was no need for Doan to worry about the gate. Iowans were agog at the prospect of seeing their boy Bobby go up against Satchel Paige.

Western League Park seated only a couple of thousand but it was already SRO an hour before the eight-thirty start, with fans strung out along both foul lines. Bill Feller alone requested four hundred tickets to accommodate friends and family.

The morning of the game, the *Register* lauded Leroy Matlock for shutting down Hornsby's squad the previous Friday. Regardless of who went to the mound for the black team, sports editor Sec Taylor wrote, "The major leaguers will face a good flinger."[40]

Iowans were indeed treated to good flinging. In the first inning, huge roars erupted as Satch, then Bobby, strolled to the hill. "The lights was bad and we both was strikin' out everybody," Paige recollected a dozen years later in *Pitchin' Man*. "The batters was swingin' in self-protection. I winned that game by one run."[41]

As it often was, Satch's memory was sketchy. It's true that the lights left something to be desired and that Satch and Bobby amassed a bunch of strikeouts. But neither pitcher figured in the decision; Feller and Paige each worked just three innings. The black team did eventually win, but the final tally was 4-2. Neither team scored while the opposing ace was on the mound. Satch, of course, didn't get credit for the win. His replacement, Pullman Porter, got the W.

Bobby whiffed eight of ten batters. Without naming names, Crutchfield told Bob Peterson thirty years later that certain Negro Leaguers were so intimidated by Feller that night that, à la Leo Durocher three months earlier, they "choked up."[42]

Only two balls were hit into fair territory against Feller, the *Register* reported. Sammy Hughes's dribbler to Mize down the first-base line went for a hit in the first inning when Bobby, perhaps nonplussed by all the attention, was late covering first. But Feller recovered to fan all but one of the black stars. The *Register* didn't identify strikeout victims, but Bobby almost certainly whiffed Satch—and vice versa. "[Feller] could throw hard, the young man could throw *hard*, and the lights were kind of dim anyway, and he was setting us down one right after the other," Newt Allen remembered four decades later.[43]

As soon as Feller left the game, the Negro Leaguers pounced on his replacement, Brownie Earl Caldwell (whose earned-run average that season was a dismal 6.00), for two runs. They collected eleven more hits and two more tallies against Caldwell and Mike Ryba.[44]

The *Register* acknowledged that "many experts" considered Paige the "greatest pitcher in baseball."[45] The game's greatest was greeted by a line-drive single from thirty-seven-year-old Heinie Mueller. But that was it for Hornsby's squad: Satch struck out seven of eleven batters. Hornsby batted third that night and had one hit in four appearances. The Rajah's double came after Satch retired for the evening.

"After Feller and Paige departed, things were different," the *Register* noted. "The pitches served up by the new hurlers seemed to have strings tied to them, so slow were they in comparison to the hard ones thrown by Bob and Satchel."[46]

The Negro Leaguers broke a 1-1 tie in the sixth, and scored an insurance run in the ninth when Felton Snow singled, stole second, and scored as Cool Papa's fly fell into a fog bank in right-center for a double.

Porter gave up two hits and two runs in his three innings; Griffith yielded three hits but no runs. Bell and Sammy Hughes each had three hits; Snow had two. The only big leaguer with two safeties was Ryba, described by the *Register* as the Cardinals' "jack-of-all-trades." Mize and Hornsby went a combined one for eight.[47]

Ray Doan's October 1936 junket ended with the black players dominating, winning four of five contests. The Negro Leaguers outscored the major leaguers 22-13 over the course of the series. Satch appears to have pitched a total of seventeen innings, giving up only seven hits and three runs and striking out more than one batter per frame. Leroy Matlock was also miserly, giving up five hits and two runs in ten-plus innings.[48]

Bell batted a cool .421 during the series, but was bettered by Hughes, who hit an even .500. Bill Perkins also had a solid series, garnering seven hits in twenty-two at-bats. Despite being well past his prime, Oscar Charleston continued his lifelong brilliance against white competition, going four for ten.

Although stymied by Satch, young Johnny Mize swung a big bat, leading his team with seven hits. Heinie Mueller had six safeties, tripling the output of Hornsby. The frustrations of the over-the-hill Rajah certainly did not go unnoticed in the opposing dugout.[49]

Doan wasn't through exploiting the teenage phenom. Before the weather turned in the fall of '36, he arranged for Feller to join Jimmie Foxx and an Earle Mack–organized troupe touring the Dakotas and Canada. Ironically, the kid who was signed to a Fargo contract finally got a chance to pitch there.

Feller apparently struggled in North Dakota against white minor leaguers and a couple of over-the-hill major leaguers. In fact, Doan felt compelled to dispel rumors that Feller had given up homers to three successive batters. The opposing squad had indeed gone deep three consecutive times—but *after* Feller left the game, Doan was quick to tell the *Sporting News*, perhaps worried that his new signee's aura of invincibility had taken a hit.[50]

It's evident from Doan's behavior that it didn't take long for Bobby to supplant Dizzy Dean as Ray's number-one client. With Feller, Doan got maximum gate appeal and—at least compared to Diz—minimal aggravation.

Diz and his St. Louis mate Pepper Martin were again out on the road in the fall of '36, this time without Paul. The Cards had won "only" eighty-seven games that season, finishing five games behind the pennant-winning Giants. Diz had led the NL in complete games, with twenty-eight, but wasn't quite as stout as in previous seasons. He went 24-13 (bringing his three-year win total to a lofty 82) with a 3.17 ERA. Diz had no way of knowing it, but this proved to be his last twenty-win season. For his part, Pepper hit .309 and led the league with twenty-three stolen bases.

Pepper and Diz started with a three-day swing through Kansas, Missouri, and Oklahoma, playing against white semipros and sand-lotters; they were plagued by lousy weather. A rainout in Wichita, though, didn't stop Diz from popping off against Branch Rickey and the Cardinals, skewering the organization as "Class C bush league." The next day in Oklahoma City, a sheepish Diz tried to pooh-pooh his remarks, but since the *Sporting News* was about to publish them coast-to-coast, it was too late. A fraction of the crowd that greeted the Dean brothers and the Monarchs in Oklahoma City two years earlier shivered through a quick exhibition.[51]

In Blackwell, Oklahoma, next door to Pepper's boyhood home in Osage County, the two Cardinals stopped at an ice-cream factory. In a tasty publicity move, the dairy had just named Martin its president. "I think we have somethin' here," Martin joked as he showed Dean around. "If Diz behaves himself we'll make him vice president of our chocolate department and pay him a thousand gallons a year."[52]

Oklahoma's ice-cream boys then caught a flight to one of their favorite playgrounds, the West Coast. "Two of the most-feared characters in the country are headed for California," the *Los Angeles Times* joshed. "But they will not be stopped at the border, despite the fact that they are members of that notorious 'Gas House' gang."[53]

To their annoyance, the Gas House gangsters got a crash course in California geography. Apparently confusing "Frisco" with "Fresno,"

Pepper and Diz accidently showed up—or so they claimed—in San Francisco. They hurriedly grabbed a plane south, but got to Fresno so late they missed a reception that had been thrown in their honor by local merchants. Whoever handled the boys' logistics needed a remedial course from Ray Doan.

After cashing in their Fresno p.c., Diz and Pepper hit Hollywood. Again, Joe E. Brown squired them around town. "I can't stand this city life," Diz told the *Los Angeles Times* that week. "It's too ritzy. They charge you 75 cents for a sandwich here. I can raise a whole hog for less than a dollar."[54]

On October 4, Dizzy took on a Joe Pirrone–organized Pacific Coast League squad at L.A.'s Wrigley Field. Martin and Dean were joined by their old buddy former Cardinals' outfielder Jack Rothrock (who'd spent the '36 season in the minors rehabilitating an injury), onetime Senators' infielder Johnny Kerr (lifetime batting average .266), and future big-league outfielder Buster Mills (career batting average .287).

Ten thousand Angelenos were tickled when Diz dinged a three-run homer over the left-field wall in the sixth inning, giving his team a brief 5-4 lead. Dean pitched six full frames, yielding five hits and four runs, three of them coming on pitcher Jack Salveson's homer in the fifth. Salveson was a Pacific Coast League veteran then the property of the Cleveland Indians. Jack's squad pulled out an extra-inning victory, 7-6.

"Dean's pitching was a revelation," wrote the *Times*'s stylish Braven Dyer the next day, despite Dizzy's ho-hum outing. "He is all arms and legs and whips the ball over the plate at tremendous speed. His hard one had the Coasters swinging too late and his big curve had them badly baffled."[55] Pepper's hard one hardly caused the Coasters to flinch, but Martin nevertheless took over for Diz on the mound in the seventh, absorbing the loss after giving up three more runs. "Pepper is no great shucks as a hurler," Dyer observed, "but his fast running electrified the crowd."[56]

Then Martin and Dean headed north to the Bay Area, where they played a couple of exhibitions in Oakland and San Francisco against a Pacific Coast League squad managed by local-legend-turned-pub-owner Lefty O'Doul. On October 5, Diz sat down with *San Francisco Chronicle* columnist Ed. R. Hughes. In a piece titled "The Dizzy One Hits Our Town," Dean tried to explain why Paul was suffering from arm woes—and in doing so, he bared the blasé racial prejudice of the times. "You know, Paul is a bigger man than me in every way," Dean allowed, "but he has a pain in the right shoulder and he is also lazy. About the laziest white boy I know except Ernie Lombardi, catcher of the Cincinnati team. Paul and Ernie would make a great battery." And to ensure that Italian-Americans got equally disparaging treatment, Diz went on to refer to Lombardi, a beloved Oakland product, as "that big eagle beak."[57]

After their forays to the Bay Area, Diz and Pepper headed for home via St. Louis. Diz was overdue to begin what the *Los Angeles Times* called his "holdout moan," the annual ritual in which he bargained for more money from Rickey and the Cardinals. Meeting with reporters in St. Louis on October 17, Diz said with a cackle, "Well, I've made a lot of friends in St. Louis and I would hate to leave them, but as the fellow said when the lion bit him, 'that's Africa.'" Howling at his own joke, Diz told reporters, "I got it from Joe E. Brown. Wait 'til I spring it on Pepper Martin. He'll use it every time he makes a speech."[58]

Dizzy's best barnstorming days were behind him. His arm, frayed from years of abuse and neglect, was heading in the same direction as Paul's. The mechanical changes forced by the broken toe that Diz would suffer nine months later finished the job.

CHAPTER EIGHT

Bobby and Satch Hit the Hustings

The pre-war Paige was the best I ever saw, and I'm judging him on the way he overpowered or outwitted some of the best big-league hitters of the day.

—BOB FELLER, *HOLIDAY* MAGAZINE, 1965

The marquee attraction for Joe Pirrone's '37–'38 CWL campaign was eighteen-year-old Bobby Feller. A sore arm slowed Feller's '37 regular season, his second in a big-league uniform. But once a Cleveland physician coaxed Bob's ulna bone back into its socket, Feller went on to a 9-7 record with a 3.39 ERA and 150 strikeouts in 148 innings. The Indians finished fourth in the AL standings that season, well back of Joe McCarthy's dynastic Yankees.

In mid-October, Feller made the first of many West Coast junkets to come. Bobby's California visit was the culmination of a barnstorming loop orchestrated by J. L. Wilkinson, Tom Baird, and the ever-present Ray Doan.

Young Bobby was supposedly promised a minimum of four thousand dollars, specifically, four hundred for each of ten games (or about one-fifth of what the Indians were paying him for an entire season).[1] Before winging to Southern California, Doan's tour was scheduled to swing through Peoria (icy rain forced a cancellation), Minneapolis, Davenport, Cedar Rapids, Manhattan (Kansas), Wichita, and Oklahoma City.[2] The Indians insisted that trainer Lefty Weisman keep a watchful eye on Feller's wing for the entire tour.

But first Bobby, just as he had been the year before, was fêted by the home folks in Van Meter. This time Democratic governor Nels

Kraschel joined now-senator Clyde Herring in saluting young Feller, as did the local 4-H Club. Flags and bunting again decked the town; a carnival was brought in, complete with bingo tables, fortune tellers, and a Ferris wheel.

The United Press estimated that ten thousand Iowans swarmed the Van Meter High ballyard for the exhibition game.[3] Again, Bob pitched for both the Adel nine and the Kingsbury Beer squad from Des Moines, fanning twelve of fourteen batters, many of whom he had known growing up. Only one pal managed to put a ball in fair territory against Feller—a "weak bounder" that was promptly thrown away by the nervous second sacker.[4]

Feller was joined on Doan's '37 tour by a first-rate group of stars, among them Cardinals pitcher (and chronic cutup) Lon Warneke (18-11 in '37, his first season in St. Louis), Braves hurler Lou Fette (a remarkable 20-10 in his rookie year), Pirates pitchers Mace Brown (7-2) and Big Jim Weaver (8-5), Phillies hurler George Caster (16-20), Cards slugger Johnny Mize (an impressive .364 and 113 RBIs in just his second campaign), Reds second sacker Alex Kampouris (.249), Cards sophomore shortstop Donnie Gutteridge (.271), speedy Reds outfielder Ival "Goodie" Goodman (.273), and Bucs outfielder Gus Suhr (.278 and 97 RBIs). Former Reds pitcher Lee Stine also signed on for part of the swing, as did utility man and seasoned barnstormer Mike Ryba (9-6 as a pitcher; .313 in 48 at-bats) of the Cards.

But the real headliner next to Feller was Boston Braves basher Vince DiMaggio, Joltin' Joe's older brother. Vince had just completed a respectable rookie season with the Bees, hitting twenty homers and driving in ninety-seven runs. Doan shamelessly milked Vince, providing news outlets with a steady diet of photos of the matinee-idol-handsome San Franciscan. It didn't hurt Doan's publicity push that Vince's more famous sibling was busily engaged that week in winning the Yankees' subway Series, four games to one, over the Giants.

Wilkinson and Baird ensured that most of a talented '37 Monarchs squad would be available for the Iowa, Kansas, and Oklahoma stops, among them pitcher-manager Andy Cooper (who happened to be a Wichita native), catcher-outfielder and future manager Frank Duncan, pitchers Slug Cornelius and Hilton Smith, infielder Newt Allen, infielder/outfielder Teddy Strong, speed demon outfielder Pee Wee Dwight, outfielder Henry Milton, infielder-outfielder Willard Brown, and pitcher-outfielder Bullet Joe Rogan. Even without Paige, who was toiling in the Dominican Republic that fall, Wilkinson wasn't completely unjustified in claiming that his charges could compete with the Yankees or the Giants, a boast printed October 10 by the *Wichita Eagle*.[5]

"We've been very fortunate in Wichita, having won 39 victories in 42 games here in 13 years," Wilkie told the *Eagle*, citing a statistic he knew could never be verified. "Right now we have a great team to cope with the major leaguers. The Monarchs are desirous to see just what they can do against such pitchers as Feller and Fette."[6]

Against Wilkie's black squad, Feller and company won four of the six exhibitions. At Municipal Stadium in Davenport, "fans came to see a show and the stars gave them one," enthused the *Davenport Daily Times*. The Doan men hung on for a 5-3 victory before five thousand Iowans—believed to be the biggest baseball crowd in Davenport history, most of whom were "glued to their seats until the last man was out."[7] Warneke, the starter, throttled the Monarchs for two frames, then spent the rest of the game "having one whale of a good time," cracked the *Daily Times*'s Leo Kautz. "[Warneke] autographed anything tossed his way, cavorted around the coaching box . . . and gave the crowd a big laugh when he shook hands with Umpire Duhlstein after the latter had called him out on strikes in the third inning. Lon congratulated the local arbiter for having the guts to call that third strike."[8]

Fette and Weaver continued to stymie the Monarchs through six, while the Feller all-stars got to Cornelius for two early runs. Gutteridge's triple, homer, and bunt single were the big blows for the Feller team. The diminutive Gutteridge provided the evening's other comedic moment when he deliberately stood on his tiptoes to whisper something into the ear of the six-foot-six Weaver as Big Jim pawed the mound.

The score was 5-0 until "the colored boys went to town in the seventh," reported the paper. Willard Brown's mammoth home run over the scoreboard in left-center drove in Newt Allen. The Monarchs would have had an even bigger inning were it not for Vince DiMaggio's running catch of Teddy Strong's line drive. In the bottom of the ninth, Brown smashed another line drive into left-center, this one scoring Strong. Mace Brown stranded his namesake Willard at second base as the game ended.

"'Home Run' Brown also made one of the best catches of the night in left field," commented the paper. "In the ninth inning with two out, Mize poked a honey that looked like a sure double if not a triple. But Brown came up with an almost impossible one-handed catch while running at full speed to his left for the third out."[9]

In Cedar Rapids the next night before 3,800 disappointed Iowans, Feller again rested his arm and coached first as Brown, Fette, Weaver, and Warneke eked out a 6-5 win over the Monarchs. It was so cold that players from both sides lit bonfires in front of their dugouts. Mize was the hitting hero in Cedar Rapids, driving home the winning run with a triple in the eighth.[10]

It was still frigid the following night when Feller thrilled the home folks at Des Moines' Western League Field by whiffing five Monarchs in just two innings. Doan's men held on for a 1-0 victory, although the aging Joe Rogan managed three hits against the combination of Feller, Fette, and Weaver.[11]

The game in Manhattan, Kansas, a town of eleven thousand people, took place on October 9. It was sponsored by the local merchants association, which ran ads all week in the *Manhattan Mercury* reminding businesspeople that special reserved seating was limited and that one of their favorite Cardinals, Lon Warneke, was scheduled to appear.[12] The ad included a photo of Lon sporting an enormous chaw of tobacco.

About eighteen hundred people showed up at Griffith Field that chilly Saturday night to watch Weaver, Warneke, and Brown vanquish the Monarchs, 6-3. When not on the mound, Warneke "stole the show as he kidded the players and crowd alike over the public address system."[13] The Monarchs outhit the Feller team, 9-6, with shortstop Allen collecting three safeties and Eddie Dwight and Teddy Strong two each. Goodie Goodman was the only white all-star with multiple hits, yet the Fellers pushed across three more runs than the black stars. DiMag went one for three and scored a run.

In Wichita, Wilkie and Doan must have given their buddy Hap Dumont a taste of the action, thereby guaranteeing advance publicity from Pete Lighter, sports editor of the *Eagle*. Dumont, always the showman, somehow arranged for an on-field microphone to introduce the white major leaguers at home plate before the game—an unheard-of extravagance in 1937.

"Bob Feller came to town with a reputation as a pitcher and left with an established identity as a slugger," the *Eagle* reported in an article no doubt scripted by Lighter. Two thousand hearty fans had to wait until the seventh to see Feller in action. Bobby didn't disappoint, shutting down Kansas City over the last couple of frames and fanning four. With the Monarchs leading 5-3 in the ninth, the "Iowa schoolboy" plastered a pitch over the center-field wall. It was, mused the *Eagle*, "as long a homer as was ever knocked at the city ball orchard."[14]

Bobby's all-stars still went down, 5-4, but chilled orchardgoers were rewarded for their perseverance. Teddy Strong, playing out of position at first, had three hits and scored twice. The only big leaguer with multiple hits in Wichita was Ival Goodman with two, who scored and drove in a run.

The *Eagle* punctuated its article with an obligatory bit of racial condescension. "And incidentally, Kranston, Monarch right-hander, hurled a right fine game for the colored boys, fanning six and allowing eight hits." Exactly who "Kranston" was remains a mystery; no one answering to that name or "Cranston" appeared on the roster of the Monarchs or any blackball team in the late '30s. Whoever he may have been, he did indeed pitch a fine game that night in Wichita, shutting down Vince DiMaggio.

In the same issue, columnist Lighter noted that Feller's itinerary on the West Coast included a studio test in front of motion picture executives. Lighter and his buddy Dumont happened to interview Feller at the TWA terminal. The youngster was decked out in a chocolate brown suit. When Lighter asked Feller if he was envious of colleagues in the World Series, Bobby surprised the columnist by responding, "Say, I sure would like to be in a World Series, look at all that dough!"[15]

Lighter also quizzed umpire Buddy Reynolds after the game about who was quicker: Feller or Paige. "Feller not only has more speed than Satchel Paige but a much better curveball," declared Reynolds. "Feller showed me a wonderful change of pace. The kid has everything."[16]

The kid headed off to Oklahoma City for the last leg of the hinterlands tour. Time was a wasting, since Feller had to board a flight to Los Angeles early that evening. So Bobby, whom Bus Ham and the *Daily Oklahoman* had been flacking for days, ended up pitching just one quick inning before he, Doan, and others dashed for the airport. "He lived up to his reputation, by fanning three men. Only

A baby-faced Satch warms
up for the Pittsburgh Crawfords, one of history's most
rugged teams, black or white.
Satch ditched the Craws in
1933 and again in '35 to play
interracial ball in Bismarck,
North Dakota.

George "Mule" Suttles, a strapping slugger, helped Satch's Royal Elite Giants dominate the integrated California Winter League in the 1930s.

Norman "Turkey" Stearnes was another linchpin of the black California Winter League clubs. A left-handed batsman who contorted himself into a corkscrew stance, Stearnes reportedly led the Negro National League in home runs seven times.

4

After Satch hurt his arm in 1938, J. L. Wilkinson signed Paige for his Baby Monarchs, Kansas City's traveling B team. Satch spent a year throwing slop curves until his arm recovered.

5

Satch and catcher Josh Gibson were frequent barnstorming pals and batterymates on the invincible Crawfords clubs. In October 1934, the muscular Gibson tossed Dizzy Dean like a rag doll during a tussle at Pittsburgh's Forbes Field.

"Bullet" Joe Rogan's hitting and fielding were almost as deadly as his arsenal of pitches. Bob Feller remembered that the longtime Monarch could "do anything" on a baseball field.

Right-hander Chet Brewer was a mainstay of the Monarchs before establishing his own barnstorming outfit, the Kansas City Royals. Years later Bob Feller called Bob Gibson an "exact clone" of Brewer.

James "Cool Papa" Bell owed his quicker-than-light reputation to Paige's penchant for telling tall tales. In a 1935 game against the Dean all-stars at Yankee Stadium, Bell scored from second on a sacrifice fly by Josh Gibson, only to be called out by a white umpire who chided Bell, "You don't do that against big leaguers."

Neil Churchill was a cutthroat car salesman and the driving force behind Bismarck, North Dakota's racially integrated team. In 1935, Churchill piled his players into a couple of his big sedans, trekked to Wichita, Kansas, and won the national semipro tournament with an all-black—and all-brilliant— pitching staff led by Satchel Paige.

Despite his southern upbringing, Dizzy Dean didn't understand why playing with Negro Leaguers should kick up a fuss. As a kid, he'd picked cotton shoulder-to-shoulder with black people whose desperate lot in life mirrored his own.

At the 1936 Democratic National Convention, Dizzy led the Missouri delegation's celebration when FDR was officially nominated to run again.

Satch and Diz tickled fans by imitating each other's deliveries. Each had a dramatic leg kick—a move eventually shared by barnstorming buddy Bob Feller. Even after Dean hurt his arm in 1937, he enjoyed kicking his left cleat head-high.

The reserved Paul Dean hated the nickname "Daffy." His Cardinals teammates dubbed him "Harpo" after the mute Marx Brother.

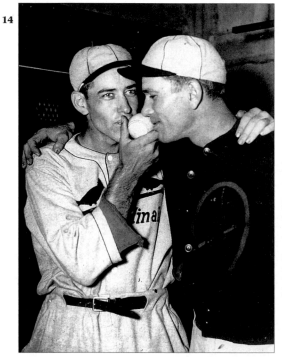

Diz made good on his boast that "me 'n' Paul" would win all four games in the 1934 World Series. The Dean boys combined for 49 wins in '34, then went barnstorming that autumn against Negro Leaguers, among them Satch and the Crawfords.

Thirty thousand fans, most of them black, jammed Chicago's Wrigley Field in May 1942 to watch Ol' Satch and his Monarchs take on Ol' Diz and a group of servicemen "all-stars." It was the first time that the Wrigley family permitted a Negro League team to use its park. Satch's squad won, 3–1.

Satch and Diz pose with army private Cecil Travis, late of the Washington Senators, before the May 1942 exhibition at Wrigley Field. When Paige struck out the smooth-swinging Travis the following week in Washington, D.C., black fans went crazy.

Pepper Martin was not only Dean's teammate on the Cards' infamous Gas House Gang but an intrepid barnstormer. While barnstorming, Diz and Pepper liked to hype the gate by walking downtown and hollering at each other.

Bob Feller was among the first prominent big-leaguers to enlist in World War II, earning eight battle stars on the USS *Alabama* as a gunnery specialist. To recoup some of the money he forfeited during the war, Feller devised "racial rivalry" tours with Paige.

Farm kid Feller spent thousands of hours honing his pitching skills in the barnyard with his father. The Fellers built their own "field of dreams," complete with a backstop, fences, a concession stand—and black players from nearby Des Moines. Their barn is now on the National Register of Historic Places.

The careers of Feller and Dean were intertwined from day one. Bob's major league debut came in July 1936 in a midseason exhibition against Dizzy and the rest of the Gas House Gang.

The Satchel Paige All-Stars traveled in separate but ostensibly equal style on their October 1946 tour with Bob Feller's All-Stars. Together, they criss-crossed the country, often playing in two different cities on the same day.

Satch was dejected that Branch Rickey and the Brooklyn Dodgers chose infielder Jackie Robinson, thirteen years Paige's junior, to break the color barrier. Although they were (briefly) Monarchs teammates and on occasion barnstormed together, Paige and Robinson were never close.

Hall of Fame slugger Ralph Kiner, who starred on the 1947 Feller-Paige tour, grew up playing interracial ball in Southern California. Kiner said of the Negro Leaguers, "We didn't think they were of our quality. But we were proved wrong."

A member of the Newark Eagles' "Million Dollar Infield," Ray Dandridge was one of blackball's slickest third basemen. "Dandy" made so much money playing ball in Mexico that he rebuffed Bill Veeck's offer to join the Indians in 1947.

As a teenaged Newark Eagle in the early 1940s, second baseman Larry Doby (right) teamed with shortstop Monte Irvin to form a precocious double-play combo. Both were converted to outfielders once they joined the integrated majors.

In 1947, Doby, shown here as a Newark Eagle, became the American League's first black player. A year later Satchel Paige would join Larry on the Cleveland Indians.

Iconoclastic owner Bill Veeck signed Paige to play in three cities: Cleveland, St. Louis, and Miami, challenging racial attitudes and setting box-office records.

By the time Feller and Paige became teammates on the 1948 Indians, they had barnstormed together all over the country. They first met in Des Moines, Iowa, in October 1936 when Feller was just seventeen.

"I am the proudest man on the earth today," Satch said when he was inducted into the Hall of Fame in August 1971. Initially, baseball authorities wanted to establish a separate wing for Negro Leaguers. "The only change," Satch cracked, "is that baseball has turned Paige from a second-class citizen to a second-class immortal." Officials eventually came to their senses.

a walk handed the third Negro batter [third baseman Pat Patterson] marred [Feller's] brief appearance." But the whole enterprise, at least in Ham's eyes, was marred by the big leaguers' apathetic performance sans Feller.

"The Negro club won going away, 10 to 0, as a handful of shivering fans booed lustily whenever they could muster that much energy," snarled the *Daily Oklahoman* in an article headlined, "Negroes Win Farce." After Feller left the game, the paper sniffed, "everyone might as well have gone home."[17]

It's too bad Ham couldn't have taken the long view, because he failed to salute some spectacular batwork. Teddy Strong continued his impressive hitting with three safeties, three runs, and two RBIs; Pee Wee Dwight had four hits and scored twice. In all, the Monarchs pounded Lou Fette and Jim Weaver for 16 hits. Kansas City scored 10 runs in the first six innings, aided by five miscues by the white team.[18]

Although his gutty performance went unacknowledged by the *Daily Oklahoman*, Hilton Smith went the distance for the Monarchs, holding the all-stars to just three hits, two of them by Vince DiMaggio, and one walk.[19]

Ham ran a sidebar that morning titled "Good Pay!"[20] It noted that Feller's jaunt to the West Coast would net him a cool $1,200 in guaranteed money for just one appearance. Doan and Feller were apparently so proud of their deal making that they couldn't help but share details—real or exaggerated—with the press.

Angelenos treated young Feller's arrival with the pomp of a royal visit; Prince Robert got adulatory coverage. Braven Dyer in the *Times* wrote that "during his short span of two seasons, the raw farm boy from Iowa has displayed more consistent sheer strikeout ability than any pitcher in the history of baseball."[21] Bill Henry, also of the *Times*, saluted Bobby as "quiet, polite, and sensible. He hasn't picked up any ambition to be a big city wisecracker and apparently has nothing resembling a swelled head."[22]

The treatment Feller got in L.A. in October 1937 would have swelled anyone's head. On the day before he was scheduled to pitch, he was the guest of honor at a luncheon hosted by civic and business leaders at the Hotel Hayward. At Doan's urging, Bobby did a series of

interviews with L.A. radio stations. The capper came later that evening when the youngster was introduced to actor Clark Gable,[23] then
was photographed sitting ringside at a boxing match.[24]

In a week, Feller had gone from the farm in Van Meter to Hollywood stardom. Indeed, the eighteen-year-old woke up the next morning to this heady account in the *Times*: "Feller, whose darting dips to
the plate are the fastest things on earth outside of the streamline train,
will uncoil his sinewy right arm to send the first bullet pitch toward
the catcher at 8 p.m."[25]

Doan and Pirrone had arranged for Feller to face a creditable squad
of white professionals playing under the banner of the "Arky Vaughan
All-Stars." Infielders Vaughan of the Pirates and Lin Storti (career big-
league average .227), formerly with the Browns, plus future Cubbie
Steve Mesner, were among the bigger names. Shortstop Bill Knickerbocker, Feller's pal from the Indians, and an all-but-washed-up Babe
Herman played on Feller's team.[26]

Lefty Weisman, Feller's masseur, also made the trek to the Coast.
Weisman had no professional training in orthopedics. He'd come
to the Indians seventeen years before at the invitation of the Tribe's
then-manager, Tris Speaker. Speaker and Weisman had been friendly
since Speaker's early days in Boston, when the center fielder spotted
the Jewish immigrant kid panhandling on a South End street corner.
Once Speaker became the Indians manager, he made good on a promise to young Weisman, bringing him to Cleveland to perform odd
jobs in the clubhouse. Over time, Lefty became the Indians trainer; by
most accounts, he became a pretty good one.[27]

His charge's arm was in fine shape that night at Wrigley Field. A
huge racially mixed throng saw Feller strike out ten batters over five
innings. He gave up one run in what proved to be a 7-2 win over
Arky's gang. Since the Indians had imposed an October 13 cutoff
on Bob's barnstorming, it was time for him to return to Van Meter.
But the youngster could do arithmetic. The number of black faces in
Wrigley's stands that night wasn't lost on him. Feller saw the money
that could be made on the West Coast. Before getting back on the
plane, Doan escorted Bobby to a winter league game in Bakersfield,
where Feller reportedly got 75 percent of the gate just for taking a
bow.[28]

While Feller was wowing them in Southern California, Satchel Paige was plying the Midwest with a group of black players he'd enlisted in the Caribbean. Satch's 1937 sojourn to the Dominican Republic is one of the most celebrated—and chuckled over—moments of his career. Agents of Dominican strongman Rafael Trujillo tracked down Paige in the spring of '37, supposedly flashing a suitcase stuffed with cash to woo Satch. Paige once again jumped his contract with the Craws; this time he was slapped with a "lifetime" suspension from Greenlee and other disgusted Negro League club owners.

Paige persuaded Cool Papa Bell, Sammy Bankhead, and Leroy Matlock to jump to the Dominican with him; Josh Gibson joined them in midseason.[29] Chet Brewer and Schoolboy Griffith were already in the D.R. for the thirty-game season when Satch and the other Negro League mercenaries arrived. Legend has it that during a game with the pennant on the line, Generalissimo Trujillo ordered heavily armed soldiers to surround the field. Satch always claimed that, fearful for his life, he struck out five of the last six batters, clinching the championship for the Trujillos. It makes for an amusing anecdote, although various eyewitnesses said that Satch's account exaggerated both the danger and his role in the Trujillos' triumph.[30] Nevertheless, years later when someone remarked to Satch that Dominican *beísbol* was a "spiritual" experience, Paige retorted, "Them guns wasn't spiritual. But they nearly made a spirit out of me."[31]

With Abe Saperstein's help, blacklisted Satch took his buddies from Dominican ball onto the barnstorming circuit, securing an invitation to compete in one of Satch's favorite venues, the *Denver Post* tourney. Satch and his amigos barely broke a sweat in the Little World Series, beating a Texas company squad known as the Bay Refiners for the title. The Refiners' player-manager was the Lone Star State's Rogers Hornsby, who again struggled—as he had so often—against black pitchers. The racist Rajah struck out three times in the finals against Schoolboy Griffith.[32]

Satch's Dominican stars also played in a couple of heavily publicized games that September at the Polo Grounds in Harlem. Before a crowd of twenty thousand, a blackball all-star squad led by pitcher Johnny Taylor beat Satch, 1-0, when Shifty Jim West hit an opposite-field homer off Paige in the ninth. Paige was said to be so angry that he stormed off the field and locked himself in his hotel room. A few days later Satch and his Dominican stars got their revenge, beating Taylor and his stars, 9-4, in another game at Coogan's Bluff.[33]

It doesn't appear that Dizzy Dean barnstormed in the fall of '37. Ol' Diz was still nursing the arm he'd damaged after suffering a broken toe in that summer's all-star game. At that point, Diz didn't realize that he'd never regain his luster. To keep himself busy, Dean purchased a filling station in Bradenton. He liked to hang out at the garage, sporting a hat with "Diz" stitched on the front, pulling up a crate, and swapping stories with the locals. That fall, the impish sportswriter Tom Meany inquired: "I wonder if Diz, as part of the service, dusts off his customers?"[34]

Not long after Master Feller's appearance in California in the fall of '37, a skinny kid from San Diego also made his CWL debut. Theodore Samuel Williams was all of nineteen years of age when he played four games for a team jointly sponsored by a credit card company and a Southern California hotel. The future Splendid Splinter got four hits in those contests, all against a CWL team headed by San Diego pitching legend Herman "Old Folks" Pillette. Old Folks spent twenty-nine years pitching all over the country, including a three-year stint with Ty Cobb and the Detroit Tigers in the early '20s.

Pillette was twenty-three years Williams's senior, but that didn't stop The Kid from walloping a home run that was heralded by the *San Diego Union* as one of the "lustiest" in city history.[35] Williams batted .287 in 14 CWL at-bats that season—not a bad showing but not quite a barometer of what was to come.[36]

Without Satch as a gate lure, the CWL in the late '30s wasn't quite as lusty as it had been. By then, Biz Mackey had taken over as field manager for Tom Wilson's wintertime club. Wild Bill Wright, Shifty Jim West, and Sammy T. Hughes were still making the annual foray, but Turkey Stearnes stopped coming. Mule Suttles skipped the '38–'39 season but came back the following winter for a few games.

Bob Feller's visits to the Coast continued to generate much excitement. After it was announced in early fall '39 that Feller would again be coming out to L.A., the *Times* sent columnist Bob Ray back east for an exclusive interview. Ray marveled at the now-twenty-year-old's maturity on the mound. Feller had won 24 games for the Indians in the '39 season, leading the American League in victories and strike-outs, with 246. His '39 prowess followed a 17-11 record in '38, when he led the league in whiffs with 240. Remarkably, before his twenty-first birthday, Bob Feller had won 55 games in the big leagues.

"Whereas he used to rare [*sic*] back and power the ball right past the batters, Bob now uses his 'fogger' on special occasions to get out of jams," Ray wrote. "He has developed a cracking curve that is one of the best in the business and he mixes 'em up more now when he's pitching. [H]is calmness in the clutch now belies his 20 years."[37]

Ray's colleague at the *Times*, Paul Zimmerman, was also taken by the youngster's relaxed presence around adults. "The old gag about taking the boy out of the farm, but being unable to take the farm out of the boy, didn't hold water in [Feller's] case," Zimmerman wrote.[38]

Zimmerman also commended Feller for turning down fifteen hundred dollars to endorse cigarettes. Feller feels "he owes it to his youthful worshipers to keep his name out of tobacco ads"[39]—a pang of conscience that never bothered Dizzy Dean and would never have bothered Satch if given a chance. Republic Pictures, producers of the *Hit Parade* series then popular as a prefeature warm-up, set up another screen test for Feller. Two years earlier, Republic had hired Joe DiMaggio after Joltin' Joe tested favorably in front of studio execs.[40]

Just as he was two years before on his first visit to the Coast, Bob was honored at a luncheon with L.A. community leaders and newspapermen. Doan and Pirrone again assembled a first-rate supporting cast for Feller, but this time, instead of a makeshift professional lineup, they had Bob face the best the CWL had to offer: Tom Wilson's Royal Giants.

Lou Novikoff (career batting average for the Cubs and Phillies, .282), the "Mad Russian," then a slugging outfielder with the PCL's Angels, was recruited to play with Feller, as were outfielders Frank Demaree (.304 in '39), by then with the Giants, and Fern Bell (.286 in 83 games) of the Pirates, plus well-traveled utility infielder Red Kress (.250 in 64 games), then of the Pirates.

Instead of Wrigley Field or White Sox Park, the CWL's usual L.A. venues, the Feller-Giants game was held at roomier Gilmore Park, home to the PCL's Hollywood Stars. For the first time in their CWL experience, Wilson's Giants were using Gilmore as their "home" field for the bulk of the '39–'40 season.[41]

The Giants put forth a decent if unspectacular lineup. Wild Bill Wright played center and his pal Mule Suttles manned right, with Bill Hoskins, who hit .303 on the CWL season, in left. Marlin Carter played short with Jake Dunn at second, Jesse Walker at third, and Shifty Jim West at first. Pepper Bassett (.308 in 26 CWL at-bats that winter) was behind the plate with Bill Harvey (2-1 that CWL season), then Terris McDuffie (5-3), on the hill.

McDuffie was a burly right-hander who spent fifteen years in the Negro Leagues. His pitching helped the Homestead Grays to the '41 postseason. He also figured in one of the major leagues' contrived stabs at integration. As World War II was winding down, McDuffie and stylish first sacker Dave "Showboat" Thomas were invited to try out for the Dodgers; the "audition" was widely viewed as a cheap Branch Rickey publicity stunt aimed at mollifying Brooklyn's minority population. A few weeks later, though, Rickey stunned Brooklyn and the world by signing Jackie Robinson. Unlike Jackie, Terris and Showboat never made it to the show.

A black-and-white capacity crowd of seven thousand crammed into Gilmore on October 13, 1939, to watch Feller go, as promised, seven full innings. Bob's fastball caused fourteen Royal Giants to flail—but it still wasn't enough as the major leaguers went down to defeat, 5-2.

Because of Landis's edict that major leaguers could barnstorm for only ten days after the end of the regular season, Bob's extracurricular activities were over for '39. After a quick trip to San Francisco, Feller headed back to the farm.[42]

Dizzy Dean's right arm never really recovered from the trauma it suffered in the summer of '37. The lithe pitching motion that caused Branch Rickey's heart to skip a beat was was sadly reduced to a gruesome lunge. "I ain't what I used to be," Diz conceded when someone asked asked him about his throwing arm. "But hell, who is?"[43]

Dean couldn't fog it anymore but on occasion he could still fool hitters with an assortment of slop balls. In '38, Rickey sold Diz to the archrival Cubs for $185,000—quite a sum for a pitcher Branch knew was damaged goods. From '38 through '40, Diz was able to go only a combined 16-8. Despite trying all manner of treatments and cures, he was in almost constant pain.

Diz's last heroic moment came at Chicago's Wrigley Field in game two of the 1938 World Series between the Cubs and the Yankees. Of Dean's performance, columnist Joe Williams wrote, "First it was astonishing, next incredible, then just plain annoying to see Dean take one Yankee hitter after another and make a first-class sap out of him."[44]

In the top of the second with Lou Gehrig and Joe DiMaggio both on base, Cubs third sacker Stan Hack collided with shortstop Billy Jurges while trying to field an infield squibber. With the left side of his infield sprawled in the dirt, Diz had to chase down the wayward ball as Gehrig and DiMaggio wheeled around third to score. But those two runs were all that the Yankees mustered through seven innings.

Yankee starter Lefty Gomez, meanwhile, gave up nine hits—two of which were collected by Dizzy. Both times he reached first, Diz flexed his muscles at Gomez, pantomiming a Charles Atlas bit to irk the Yankees. Alas, the Bombers had the last laugh. In the top of the eighth, Frankie Crosetti hit a two-run homer off Diz to put the Yankees ahead to stay. The Yankees won that afternoon, 6-3, en route to a four-game sweep of the Series.

Two years later the Cubs sent Dean down to Tulsa in the Texas League. As he had a decade earlier, Diz packed them in all over the Southwest. But it was all for naught: he couldn't get his arm or rhythm back.

From then on, Dean's barnstorming was sporadic; on occasion, especially if the money was big enough, he would hit the road. But he was strictly a ceremonial pitcher; he'd throw an inning or two, then hit the dugout or chat up fans in the stands. The Monarchs' George Giles recalled playing against Dean in a 1939 exhibition in Nebraska, which suggests there may have been other Dean-Monarchs games that fall, but no record has been found.[45]

In '41, after a brief stint as a coach for the the Cubs, Diz accepted a job broadcasting Cardinals and Browns home games on radio. As Dean's biographer Vince Staten put it, "He would still be pitching, only now it would be pitching a product, Griesedieck Brothers Brewery Falstaff Beer."[46]

Dizzy the broadcaster hated reading advertising copy; he often stumbled over polysyllabic words, although that might have been part of his country boy shtick. While shilling for Falstaff, Dean preferred to wing it. Sometimes he got the gist of the copy; other times he veered off into aimless stories, but he helped sell a lot of beer.

He also became an even bigger folk hero, taking what *Time* called his "corn pone idiom" onto the airwaves.[47] Listening to Diz broadcast a baseball game, the *St. Louis Globe-Democrat* editorialized, "is a pleasant interlude. It is a mélange of grammatical errors, vaudeville, observations of his 'hongriness' and his yearning for a helping of fried chicken, plus a routine calling of strikes and balls."[48] Cardinals Nation back then strung from the Deep South through the Great Plains. Listeners in the breadbasket understood Diz when he threw out such incomparable lines as "The batter is a-sendin' a tall can o'corn out into center."[49]

A commotion in the stands once caused Diz to observe that a group of people had gathered around "some fat lady." When a horrified advertising executive in the broadcast booth told Dean off-air that the woman was royalty, Diz cracked into the microphone, "I've just been informed that the fat lady is the Queen of the Netherlands."[50]

After a schoolteacher complained about Diz's repeated use of *ain't,* Dean rejoined, "A lot of people that ain't sayin' ain't ain't eatin'"— although he later admitted the line originated with his late friend Will Rogers.[51] During the all–St. Louis World Series in 1944, Commissioner Landis insisted that Dean be removed from the national broadcast team, calling his syntax "unfit for a national broadcaster." Responded Diz, "How can that commissar say I ain't eligible to broadcast? I ain't never met anybody that didn't know what 'ain't' means!"[52]

When two years later a Missouri education association sent a complaint to the Federal Communications Commission about Dean's diction, the Cards and Browns were smart enough to recognize a public relations bonanza. Within days, their radio stations were flooded with supportive letters and telegrams; publications large and small rushed to Diz's defense.

"Exposure to shattered syntax as perpetrated by Dizzy may encourage a certain degree of laxity among his young hearers—and adults as well," wrote the editors of the *Globe-Democrat*, "but their interest is in the game, not in the linguistic precision of the broadcast. The imperfections of his speech may be remembered and copied, but we doubt it."[53] Added Norman Cousins in the lofty *Saturday Review of Literature*: "Never before in history have man and machine been so perfectly wedded to each other as Diz and his microphone. . . . Abuse of English is the standard occupational disease of the national pastime—a disease which, if cured, would do irreparable damage to the patient."[54]

In his classic baseball poem "Line-up for Yesterday," Ogden Nash coined this encomium to Diz:

> *D is for Dean*
> *The grammatical Diz*
> *When they asked, "Who is tops?"*
> *Said correctly, "I is."*[55]

By the late '30s, the California Winter League was facing competition from elsewhere in the hemisphere. Winter circuits in the Dominican Republic and Puerto Rico were siphoning much of the Negro Leagues' top talent. A professional Mexican association formed in 1937 also impinged on the CWL. The onset of World War II further depleted CWL rosters, both black and white.

Instead of playing two or three dozen games a year, by '40–'41 Pirrone winnowed the CWL season to a dozen contests or fewer. Joined by his old buddies Cool Papa Bell, by then forty, and Buck Leonard, thirty-six, Satchel Paige, then thirty-seven, rejoined the CWL for the '43–'44 season. Once again Satch got great box office across the Southland, albeit for only five appearances. Paige ended up with three wins against one loss, striking out thirty-five in thirty innings—not quite the pace of his salad years, but not bad for a pitcher his age. The Giants won "only" seven of twelve games that winter, well off their usual winning percentage.

Brewer soon created his own traveling team, dubbed it the "Kansas City Royals," and managed to attract some top-flight ballplayers. Monarchs Bill Simms, Bonnie Serrell, and Willard Brown played for Brewer's CWL Royals, as did Quincy Trouppe. Yet in the six CWL games that Chet and company played in the winter of '43–'44, they won only three.[56]

For the third year running, Bob Feller in 1941 led the American League in victories, this time with 25, bringing his win total for '39–'41 to a Mathewsonian 76. Unlike the previous season, when Bob barn-stormed for a few days with an Earle Mack troupe that played white minor leaguers in Montana and North Dakota,[57] no tour was planned for the '41 off-season.

Instead, Feller accepted two early October gigs: his usual homecoming carnival in Van Meter and a big-money matchup against Satchel Paige and the Monarchs at Sportsman's Park in St. Louis arranged by Wilkinson and Doan.

Several thousand African-American fans sat in the segregated right-field bleachers to root on their man Satch, but Bobby "had much the better of it," the *Globe-Democrat*'s Robert L. Burnes reported. Satch struggled in the first inning against a middling "all-star" team that included such Cardinals as outfielder Joe Grace (career batting average: .283), infielder Frank "Creepy" Crespi (.263), first baseman Johnny "Hippity" Hopp (.296), and catcher Walker Cooper (.285), plus infielders Emmett Mueller (.253) of the Phils and Johnny Lucadello of the Browns (.264). Despite persistent claims to the contrary in books and articles over the years, Cardinal rookie Stan Musial did not play that afternoon.

Lucadello's triple off the screen in right field was the big blow against Satch in the bottom of the first, driving in Crespi and Mueller. Burnes criticized Satch the next day for trying to slip curveballs past the big-league hitters after getting them down in the count 0-2, a pattern that Satch fell into from time to time. Paige's "relative ability in the pitching business has long been debated," Burnes sniffed, concluding that Feller's fastball was quicker than Satch's—at least that day.[58]

Bobby went five innings and gave up a run only because catcher Cooper was slow in chasing a wild pitch. In the bottom of the first, Feller fired "three smokers" to whiff the esteemed Willard Brown, whom Burnes the next day identified as "Willie." Satch gave up all four runs in the first two of his four innings. His successor, Hilton Smith, was terrific, holding the white club to four hits and no runs in his four-inning stint.[59]

Feller returned to Iowa that fall to be with his ailing father. Bill Feller had been diagnosed some time before with inoperable brain cancer.

Bob brought him to see the finest specialists at the Mayo Clinic but nothing could be done. By late '41, the family knew his condition was grave. The Fellers certainly could have used the big bonus money that the Yankees or Red Sox would have given Bob if, five years earlier, Landis had declared the youngster a free agent. Instead, young Bob was about to make a far more profound sacrifice. That October afternoon in St. Louis was the last time he would win a game in a big-league ballpark for four long years.

CHAPTER NINE

Black-White Ball
Goes to War

*I wouldn't waste my time teaching my child to hate. I wouldn't want
him to waste his life like that. I'd want him to live in peace.
If you hate, you get all tore up.*

—JOE "PIG" GREENE, 92ND INFANTRY DIVISION,
CATCHER, KANSAS CITY MONARCHS[1]

A year before Mickey Vernon passed away, he was asked about the racial realities of his youth. The onetime all-star first baseman for the Washington Senators and the Cleveland Indians, then eighty-nine, shrugged his shoulders, shifted uncomfortably in his chair, and recounted this story.

In the waning days of World War II, Navy Special Aide (1st Class) Vernon was stationed on tiny Ulithi atoll in the Pacific. The island was no more than a mile long and a few hundred yards wide, yet the navy was careful to keep sleeping quarters strictly segregated. When they weren't loading ships bound for Iwo Jima or Okinawa, the men—black and white together—played ball on a field the Seabees carved out of the jungle.

The skills of one black seaman jumped out at Vernon. He was a South Carolina youngster named Lawrence Eugene Doby. Larry Doby was familiar with Mickey Vernon, by then a veteran of five hundred games in the big leagues. But Vernon had never heard of the nineteen-year-old prodigy. Nor did Mickey know much about Larry's team, the Newark Eagles, nor, for that matter, the Negro Leagues. So awed was Mickey by Doby's all-around game that Vernon wrote to his boss, Senators owner Clark Griffith, urging the club to consider signing Doby if integration were to come to the majors.

Outdoor movies were shown almost every night on Ulithi. Blacks could go to the makeshift theater as long as they sat on benches in the back. Most nights, Doby and Vernon found themselves skipping the show. Instead, they'd hang out together in front of Vernon's tent, oiling their gloves and swapping stories. Doby would regale Vernon with tales about how tough it was to hit Satchel Paige and Hilton Smith and Chet Brewer. Vernon would counter with tales about Bobby Feller and Hal Newhouser and Spud Chandler.[2]

When Doby became the American League's first black player in 1947, he thanked Mickey for his encouragement during the war. Perhaps because of Doby's insights, Vernon was one of the few white hitters who enjoyed occasional success against Paige.

All these years later, it remains a powerful vignette: two young men thousands of miles from home, one black, one white, in the eleventh hour of the Allies' great crusade, defying Jim Crow by just sitting around talking baseball.

World War II, not surprisingly, changed the complexion of interracial ball. Feller, barnstorming's biggest draw, joined the navy two days after Pearl Harbor—the first prominent star to enlist. So many Monarchs and other Negro Leaguers served in the armed forces that, by midwar, Wilkinson and Doan were hard-pressed to mount their usual postseason tours.

Satchel Paige and Dizzy Dean never joined up. Dean's draft status, in fact, became something of a cause célèbre in '42. A perforated eardrum, coupled with Diz's army stint as a teenager, relieved public pressure. In 1944, Satch, who had given conflicting information about his age to the draft board, was apparently classified 1-A, but never called.

In the late summer of '44, Paige, no doubt guided by the savvy Abe Saperstein, achieved a public relations coup by demanding that a substantial percentage of the proceeds from that year's East-West game go to aid injured servicemen.[3] Columnist Joe Bostic of the *People's Voice* believed that Paige and Saperstein were angry because their financial demands for the East-West game had not been met. But Satch and Abe realized their goal. Unlike the '42 Paige-Dean exhibition in Chicago, a decent amount of the '44 East-West game revenue did go to wartime charities—and Satch generated some sweet publicity to boot.

Paige frequently visited hospitals; wounded soldiers and sailors couldn't wait to touch his fabled right arm. At an army infirmary in San Francisco, Satch met an injured serviceman who once played for the House of David. The two of them had a great time chuckling about the old days. In January 1945, the *Defender's* Al Monroe reported that Satch was one of several black celebrities slated to take an overseas USO tour. Paige was to be joined by UCLA football star Kenny Washington, boxing champion Henry Armstrong, and Olympic gold medalist Jesse Owens.[4]

Often partnered with Dizzy Dean, Paige appeared at exhibitions to raise money for war bonds and other charities. In Dayton, Ohio, in the summer of '44, Diz and Satch entertained a big black-white crowd. "We was . . . playin' at Ducks Park," Diz remembered years later, "when I popped a blue darter [Deanese for a line drive] over first and got myself three bases outta it. The fans were yellin' their head off for me when Ol' Satch walks over and says to me, 'I hope all your friends brought plenty to eat, Diz, because if they wait for you to score, they're gonna be here past dark. You ain't goin' no further.' Then [Paige] fanned the next three."[5] Paige's teammates that day in Dayton were racially mixed, like the crowd.

Diz, too, lent his name and image to the war effort, urging folks on the home front to donate cigarettes to GIs overseas or support other service charities. In '43, Diz joined broadcaster Red Barber, saloon-keeper Toots Shor, and entertainer Frank Sinatra in asking for contributions so that the *Sporting News* could be made available to soldiers and sailors on the front lines.[6]

World War II unleashed forces that not even the game's entrenched reactionaries could dissipate. The phony predicate upon which Jim Crow baseball rested was demolished. As Wendell Smith put it in '42, "[The] big league is perpetuating the very things thousands of Americans are overseas fighting to end, namely, racial discrimination and segregation."[7]

All-black service teams, such as the Black Bluejackets of Great Lakes

Naval Training Station, more than held their own against white military teams stocked with major leaguers. As the war dragged on, moreover, the lengths to which the major leagues scrambled to remain Caucasian became patently ludicrous.

Joe Nuxhall, a fifteen-year-old left-handed pitcher, was plucked out of high school by the Cincinnati Reds. The St. Louis Browns gave a contract to Pete Gray, an outfielder whose right arm had been severed in a childhood trucking accident. "How do you think I felt when I saw a one-armed outfielder?" hissed Monarchs ace Chet Brewer late in life.[8]

America's hypocrisy on racial issues was never more jarring. During the war, the NAACP redoubled its efforts to curb segregation. At ballparks across the country, civil rights advocates handed out "Stop Lynching" buttons. The Congress of Industrial Organizations, moreover, established the End Jim Crow in Baseball Committee.[9] African-American protesters outside Yankee Stadium brandished signs that read, "If we're able to stop bullets, why not balls?"[10]

The men on the rosters for the May 1942 Dean–Paige exhibition in Chicago did much to contribute to V-E and V-J. It's unknown if Zany Zeke Bonura, the onetime Cub and White Sox first sacker, tried to rekindle his romance with the Comiskey lass while back in Chicago in May 1942. If he did, he broke her heart all over again; within a few months Bonura had been posted to Oran, Algeria.[11]

German field marshal Erwin Rommel's Deutsches Afrika Korps was still a menacing presence in North Africa, but that didn't stop the army from putting Zeke in charge of a baseball program for enlisted personnel. They picked the right man. Within months, Bonura had forty-four teams competing in several different leagues and was tabbed the "Czar of North African baseball."[12]

Bonura's program made such an invaluable contribution to esprit de corps that in October 1943, General Dwight D. Eisenhower directed that Zeke, by then a corporal, be awarded a Legion of Merit.[13] Zeke cheekily asked the Allied supreme commander to sign a couple of dozen balls. Ike, a baseball buff, obliged.

Corporal Bonura arranged for the autographed mementos to be

presented to members of the Casablanca Yankees, who'd won the North African World Series over the Algiers Street Walkers, two games to none. The Casa Yanks were led by ace hurler "Hunkie" Wojtczak, who threw a one-hitter in the series opener. *Stars and Stripes* and newsreel cameras were there to capture the moment.[14]

Private Cecil Travis was eventually assigned to the army's 76th Division, spending most of '43 and '44 training in England. In January 1945, in the immediate aftermath of the Battle of the Bulge, the 76th crossed the channel and was rushed into the bitter cold of the Ardennes. Fighting almost nonstop, Cecil and his comrades shoved the Werhmacht's 212th Volksgrenadier Division through Belgium and Luxembourg.

On February 7, the 76th engineered a surprise nighttime assault and crossed the Sauer River. They entered Germany in the teeth of the heavily fortified Siegfried Line. The 76th fought for another three months, battling trench foot as they trudged through snow and ice, then mud. Cecil and his comrades silenced more than a hundred pillboxes, liberated thirty-three villages, captured 2,400 enemy soldiers, drove 126 miles into German territory, and earned a personal commendation from General George C. Patton.[15]

Travis was one of thousands of soldiers in the Ardennes to suffer from frostbite. Two of the toes on his left foot—his plant foot in the batter's box—were so severely damaged that his leg never regained its strength. After two frustrating seasons, Travis retired from baseball.

Many white Georgians of Cecil's generation would never have volunteered anything civil about a black man. Indeed, Cecil confessed later in life that he had no idea in the early '40s that his Senators shared Griffith Stadium with a Negro League team. But when asked about Satchel Paige after the 1942 exhibitions in Chicago and Washington, Travis said, "He's powerfully smart and he's got good motion. He don't give you anything good to hit, and he gets hep to a batter's weakness quick."[16]

The sweetest moment in Willard Brown's baseball life happened some four thousand miles from Muehlebach Field in Kansas City. Brown and Leon Day, the ace of the Newark Eagles staff, whom the *Courier*'s Ches Washington ranked in the same class as Paige, were part of the all-black 818th Amphibian Battalion. Their unit landed at Normandy—"scared to death" in Day's words—on D-Day plus six.

Although members of the 818th had received combat training, like almost all black soldiers in Europe they were kept away from the front lines. Instead, they guarded prisoners or hauled fuel and ammunition. Still, the 818th had its share of harrowing moments.

After hostilities ended, the 818th and other outfits had time to play ball. Leon, Willard, and mates waxed other service squads, advancing all the way to the European Theater of Operations (ETO) championship against General Patton's prized Third Army team.[17]

The ETO finals took place at what had been ground zero for the Third Reich: the Luitpoldhain, the massive Nuremberg stadium where Joseph Goebbels and Albert Speer once organized Nazi rallies. Army engineers carved out a crude diamond on the same field where Leni Riefenstahl filmed her chilling masterpiece *Triumph of the Will*.[18] One hundred thousand battle-weary G.I.s, many of them beered up and betting heavily, crammed into Hitler's old arena for the ETO championship.

Patton's staff, never one to wage a fight unprepared, made sure that Third Army big leaguers Harry "the Hat" Walker of the St. Louis Cardinals, Ben Zientara of the Cincinnati Reds, and Maurice Van Robays and Johnny Wyrostek of the Pittsburgh Pirates were ready to go in Nuremberg. They weren't enough.

Willard Brown reportedly drove in both runs for the 818th, while Day nursed a 2-1 lead into the bottom of the ninth. The Third Army's leadoff batter tripled, so the tying run was standing ninety feet from home plate with the meat of Patton's lineup due up. Day later told Negro Leagues historian Henry Metcalfe that he whiffed Walker and Wyrostek, both left-handed hitters, on three pitches each. Zientara was a righty but didn't fare any better. Alas, the reaction of "Old Blood and Guts," the grandson and namesake of a Confederate officer killed at the Third Battle of Winchester and the son and namesake of an unreconstructed white supremacist, was not recorded.

The 818th then accepted a challenge from both the Third Army and the champions of the Mediterranean Theater of Operations, the all-black 92nd Infantry Division, to compete in the G.I. World Series, a round-robin tournament in Marseilles. The 92nd's squad was headed by Willard Brown's longtime teammate Monarchs catcher Joe "Pig" Greene.

Leon, Willard, and company again disposed of the Third Army, this time before fifty thousand servicemen in a soccer stadium.[19] After the first game in Marseilles, Day and Brown were surprised to learn that some of Patton's white charges, including Harry Walker, had wangled their way onto the 818th's team for the championship contest against the 92nd.[20]

Walker had earned a Purple Heart and a Bronze Star on Patton's front lines. He was the younger brother of Fred "Dixie" Walker, the prickly white Mississippian who, two years later in the Dodger clubhouse, would treat Jackie Robinson with scorn. With Harry the Hat, the pride of Pascagoula, playing in the outfield next to Home Run Brown, a proud black man from Shreveport, the ETO's hastily integrated squad beat back the MTO champs. The army may not have been integrated, but its champion baseball team was.

But the fun in the south of France was just beginning. Day, Brown, and other members of the 818th then joined forces with Greene and the 92nd once again to take on Patton's boys. This time the Third Army guys thought they had it wired. Patton's squad secured the services of the ultimate ringer, future big-league hurler (and barnstorming perennial) Ewell "the Whip" Blackwell. But Blackwell's sidearm shooter didn't intimidate Brown or Greene. Willard smashed two homers over the makeshift center-field fence, Joe belted one of his own, Day threw with his usual verve, and the all-black squad pummeled Patton's men, 8-0.[21]

Pig Greene was one of blackball's premier catchers when he was pressed into duty with the 92nd Infantry Division, successors to the "Buffalo Soldiers," the famed all-black frontier cavalry. Assigned to General Mark Clark's Fifth Army, the 92nd was one of the few African-American units in Europe to see combat.[22] Greene spent eight months on the front lines as part of a company that operated a 57-millimeter antitank gun. He earned several decorations for valor in the 92nd's fight against crack Panzer troops.[23]

One night in early 1945, Joe Greene and seven other men volunteered to sneak close to enemy lines to dig a cannon emplacement. At dawn, the Germans began raining artillery shells. A projectile slammed into the ground a few feet from Greene's foxhole. The concussion was so intense that he was tossed into the air. But Greene was lucky: the shrapnel missed his vital parts, although he spent three weeks recuperating in a field hospital.[24]

On April 29, 1945, Greene's unit entered Milan's Piazzale Loreto and cut down the bodies of Italian dictator Benito Mussolini, his mistress, Clara Petacci, and a dozen other Fascist leaders. Having been shot by Italian partisans, their mutilated corpses were hanging upside down from a ramshackle gallows—a macabre scene all too familiar to black Americans. "They had them hanging up, but we had to take them down," Greene remembered.[25]

While he was fighting fascism Greene couldn't fraternize with white soldiers. In much of America he couldn't vote, or frequent a lunch counter, or sip out of a "whites only" water fountain. His skin color prevented him from playing organized baseball—or from earning a decent living in practically any profession.

Yet the country that denied him his basic rights not only ordered him to put his life on the line but entrusted him with one of the most harrowing jobs in combat—firing at close range at heavily armored Panzer and Panther tanks. Some 330 Buffalo Soldiers were killed in the line of duty; another 2,800 were wounded—Joe Greene among them—or declared missing in action.[26]

The motto of the Buffalo Soldiers was etched into their unit's insignia. It read: "Deeds Not Words."

After its shakedown cruise along the Nova Scotia coast, Chief Petty Officer Bob Feller's battleship, the USS *Alabama*, was sent to the Royal Navy base at Scapa Flow to provide convoy protection for the British Home Fleet. Six times the *Alabama* ventured north of the Arctic Circle.

While on shore leave in the northernmost reaches of Scotland, Feller's shipmates liked to hang out in pubs, swilling warm beer. But farmhand Feller, a teetotaler, befriended a local family that owned a Jersey cow. In exchange for milking the animal, the family would give Feller several quarts, which he stashed in a refrigerator on board ship.[27]

After it was sent through the Panama Canal in late '43, the *Alabama* crossed the equator some forty-four times, zigzagging to elude enemy submarines. In the spring of 1944, the *Alabama* and its sister ship the *Indiana* docked for repairs at Majuro Atoll in the Marshall Islands. Each vessel carried some 2,900 men—or six times the population of Van Meter, Iowa.[28]

The sailors on the twin battle wagons needed rest and relaxation; for months, they'd been engaged in continuous action. A few weeks earlier, the two ships had provided cover for the aircraft carrier *Enterprise* as its task force moved against Japanese-held islands near the coast of New Guinea.

Shore leave on Majuro gave chief gunnery specialist Feller a chance to work on the latest addition to his pitching arsenal, a slider. The *Alabama*'s recreation officer spotted an abandoned ball field on a nearby island. The Seabees did their best to smooth out an infield, but it was still full of rocks when the *Indiana* men issued a challenge to their counterparts. Navy war correspondent Eugene Kinkead, a staff writer at the *New Yorker* before and after the war, happened to be assigned to the *Indiana*.

Kinkead scribbled notes that afternoon and was smart enough to save them. Two years later, they came in handy when Feller no-hit Joe DiMaggio, Tommy Henrich, Charlie "King Kong" Keller, and all the other Bronx Bombers at Yankee Stadium. Recognizing the ironic juxtaposition, Kinkead wrote a piece contrasting Bob's no-no in the Bronx with his performance in somewhat less urbane conditions on Majuro.

"A steady trade wind blew gusts of white coral dust over the infield," Kinkead wrote of the South Pacific game in the May 11, 1946, *New Yorker*. Burlap sacks served as ersatz bases, a hunk of wood impersonated home plate, and strips of chicken wire made for a makeshift backstop. Feller was wearing dungarees, a gray sweatshirt, a cap Kinkead described as "nondescript," and, as near as the correspondent could tell, his navy-issue black shoes in lieu of baseball cleats.

"The most dangerous [hitter] on the *Indiana* team," Kinkead recalled, "was the second baseman, a monstrous enlisted man with huge hands who wore nothing but sneakers and khaki shorts and an impressive matting of hair on his chest. He looked like a slugger." Kinkead sat on the *Indiana* side, near a seaman from Brooklyn who, as the game progressed, insisted on giving Feller lip. "'Oh, yuh joik!' he kept repeating during the second inning at close to a hundred and twenty decibels. 'Yuh couldn't beat Detroit and yuh can't beat us. Yuh stink!'"[29]

Somehow the rec officer was able to procure a rosin bag. Feller, sweating in the tropical heat, occasionally grabbed the bag to dry his hand. "'That's right! Pick up yuh little rosin bag, Robert!' howled the heckler, as though he'd caught Feller in the act of spiking the third baseman," Kinkead wrote.

It was clear to Kinkead that Feller was well off top form. In the fifth inning, the *Indiana* guys managed to load the bases with no outs. Up to the hunk of wood strode the hairy-chested second sacker. "He stood easily at the plate, like an amiable orangutan, his large bat a toothpick in his hands. The *Indiana* side was in an uproar. 'Yuh through!' shouted the Brooklyn man. . . . Just then out of the scrub bordering left field popped a fast-running pig, followed by a pack of knife-brandishing sailors in full cry. They dashed across the diamond in a swirl of dust and disappeared among the palm trees along right field. Feller stared after them bewilderingly for a moment, then wiped his forehead with a grimy hand and pitched again to the big fellow."[30]

The second baseman drew a base on balls. But it was the only run Feller allowed. "It was really quite a triumph," concluded the writer.

After Feller and his *Alabama* mates held off the *Indiana* nine, a gaggle of sailors approached the pitcher and asked him about his future. "He said he thought with a little luck he might get back in form," recalled Kinkead.[31]

A few days later, the battleships left Majuro to join Operation Forager, the invasion of Saipan. In the midst of the *Alabama*'s bombardment of enemy strongholds, Feller spotted a sailor adrift in the water. He alerted Sky Control, which dispatched a destroyer to rescue the man. The lucky seaman later sought out Feller to thank him.

For the remainder of '44, the *Alabama* had no more pleasant side trips. It fought in both battles of the Philippine Sea, as well as supporting Marine landings at Palau, Ulithi, and Yap. At Leyte Gulf, the largest naval engagement in history, the *Alabama* was assigned to protect the *Enterprise*, Admiral Bull Halsey's flagship.

At one point, the navy gave Feller permission to take an extended leave in Honolulu to appear in a service all-star game. But Feller declined, telling his commanding officer that he had an obligation to stay with his crew.

Kamikaze attacks endangered Feller's last few months aboard the *Alabama*. On October 14, 1944, the *Alabama* narrowly averted being struck by a series of suicide bombers. Feller later compared the kamikaze pilots to "blind, maddened bulls" in a barnyard.[32]

Bob earned five campaign ribbons, six citations for gallantry, and eight battle stars. To this day, he's proud that the *Alabama* was the only Pacific Theater battleship to have neither absorbed a direct hit nor lost a man to enemy action. So proud, in fact, that in a 2007 interview, he repeated the assertion, word for word, three times in the span of two hours.

"I'm no hero," Feller told Fay Vincent for Vincent's oral history *The Only Game in Town*. "The heroes never returned. The survivors returned. And that's the way I sincerely feel about it."[33]

The USS *Alabama* now serves as a floating museum in Mobile Bay, where it's anchored not far from the boyhood home of Satchel Paige.

CHAPTER TEN

Feller and Satch Celebrate V-J Day

I taught Bobby Feller a little something, too, only it didn't take.
He tried to throw my hesitation pitch and dern near threw his back out.
Ain't many men that can throw a ball like that.

—SATCHEL PAIGE, *HOLIDAY* MAGAZINE, 1965

J. Edgar Hoover's Federal Bureau of Investigation had so thoroughly infiltrated the American Communist Party during World War II that almost every gathering was placed under surveillance. In July 1945, the FBI's Boston field office reported that, at a regional convention, New England Communists had resolved to agitate on behalf of ending racial segregation in major-league baseball.

Among the issues discussed at the conference was the scheduled Braves Field appearance later that summer of Satchel Paige and the Kansas City Monarchs (then including Jackie Robinson) to play workers from the Charlestown Navy Yard. After debating which Beantown franchise needed black stars more—the Braves (who won a dismal 67 games that season) or the Red Sox (an almost-as-bad 71)—the Marxists vowed to pass out fliers protesting Jim Crow baseball during the Monarchs' visit.[1]

Less than a year after V-J Day, four black World War II veterans and their families moved into an apartment building in a Chicago neighborhood known as Airport Homes. The enclave around the Midway airfield was ethnic working class; like many Chicago neighborhoods, it had long resisted integration.

When word spread about the black intrusion, hundreds of white residents began protesting. Things quickly devolved into what one observer called a "seething cauldron."[2] Chicago's police spent the first two days of the crisis with heads burrowed as white rioters kept the terrified families trapped in their apartments. Only after civil rights and labor activists threatened to arm themselves and march into Airport Homes did the cops budge. A few days later, the police evicted the families and sent them back to the city's Black Belt.[3]

For many blacks, the postwar years were galling, a cruel betrayal of the American promise. A million African Americans had served in uniform. Having helped vanquish fascism, they hoped to build better lives for themselves and their families. Yet they returned to a society that remained belligerent to people of color. Educational opportunities for blacks were dim, job prospects dimmer. Especially in the South, it was difficult for returning black servicemen to obtain benefits promised by the GI Bill.[4]

Despite the stubbornness of Jim Crow in the postwar years, baseball remained the one American institution where racial integration was openly—and passionately—debated. Such prominent white columnists as King Features' Jimmy Cannon, the *Washington Post*'s Shirley Povich, the Hearst syndicate's Bob Considine, even Hearst's über right-winger Westbrook Pegler, had long lobbied for an end to baseball's color barrier.

They were no longer appealing to deaf ears. In late 1944, when major-league club owners chose U.S. senator Happy Chandler, Democrat of Kentucky, to succeed the deceased Kenesaw Mountain Landis, they knew they were appointing a commissioner who wouldn't stand in the way of the game's desegregation. "If they can fight and die on Okinawa and Guadalcanal in the South Pacific, they can play baseball in America," Chandler told the *Pittsburgh Courier*'s Ric Roberts.[5]

But the driving force behind big-league integration was the *Courier*'s indefatigable Wendell Smith. Not unlike his friend Sam Lacy of the *Afro-American*, Smith didn't merely write about Negro Leaguers; he served as their champion. By early '45, Smith had contacted several big-league organizations, quietly arranging tryouts. Smith wasn't necessarily pushing blackball's most gifted players. Instead, he chose young men who, in his judgment, were capable of handling the pressure of being a pathbreaker.

In April 1945, Smith set up an audition at Fenway Park for infielders Jackie Robinson of the Monarchs and Marvin Williams of the Philadelphia Stars, as well as outfielder Sam Jethroe of the Cleveland Buckeyes. Tom Yawkey, the owner of the Red Sox, was a South Carolinian whose primitive racial views hamstrung his franchise for the next two decades. Yawkey was never going to make history by signing a black player—and Smith surely knew it.[6]

All along, Smith had sensed that Branch Rickey and Walter O'Malley of the Brooklyn Dodgers were his most promising candidates among the game's white power brokers. For decades, Rickey had closely followed blackball, often watching Negro League games.

As a player at Ohio Wesleyan College, Rickey had witnessed a black teammate being spurned by a hotel. Rickey said he never forgot the young man's humiliation. As he looked at Ebbets Field's dwindling attendance, as well as Brooklyn's changing demographics, he concluded that his franchise required a shake-up.

But the Mahatma needed a pretext before making a move. When, at Smith's behest, Rickey first sat down with Robinson, it was supposedly because the Dodgers were interested in establishing a new league for black players. Only after deliberations got serious did Rickey come clean about his real intentions. Thinking ahead, Rickey had already begun investigating the prospect of moving the Dodgers' 1946 spring training camp from Florida to the Caribbean to escape the depredations of Jim Crow.[7]

World War II, ironically, had been a boon to black baseball. Many Negro League franchises set attendance marks. For the first time, hundreds of thousands of black fans had some spending money thanks to jobs in government agencies and munitions factories. "Even the white folks was comin' out," Satchel Paige remembered.[8]

The Rickey-Robinson gambit played out in the press just as Satch and Bob Feller were gearing up for a triumphant postwar tour of the West Coast. Wendell Smith, Sam Lacy, J. L. Wilkinson, and other perceptive observers of the blackball scene knew that the collapse of baseball's color barrier would likely spell the demise of the Negro Leagues.

"Four hundred and fifty-five years after Columbus eagerly discovered America," the *Washington Post*'s Povich wrote after Jackie debuted with the Dodgers, "major league baseball reluctantly discovered the American Negro."

Buck O'Neil served in a navy construction battalion during World War II. He was doing typical black seaman work—unloading crates—when a petty officer shared the news that had just come over the radio: Brooklyn had signed Robinson.[9] Buck knew that big-league integration would disrupt his livelihood. He also knew there were more deserving blackballers. But Buck told interviewers that he couldn't stop smiling for days.

Not surprisingly, Satchel Paige was ambivalent about big-league integration. Satch was one of baseball's best-compensated players of either race in the '30s and '40s; he knew his income would decline if the color barrier fell.

Like many blacks of his generation, Satch subscribed to Booker T. Washington's go-along-to-get-ahead acceptance of racial inequality. "You might as well be honest about it," Paige said in the early '40s regarding the prospect of integration in baseball. "There would be plenty of problems, not only in the South, where the colored boys wouldn't be able to stay and travel with the teams in spring training, but in the North, where they couldn't stay or eat with them in many places. All the nice statements in the world from both sides aren't going to knock out Jim Crow."[10]

Satch may not have been an outspoken champion of integration, but he was hardly the obsequious Uncle Tom his detractors have painted. The path Paige chose took no small amount of courage, as fellow Negro Leaguer and Hall of Famer Monte Irvin argued in a 2007 interview. As Irvin put it, Satchel forged his "own unique way."[11] Longtime Negro Leagues catcher Frazier "Slow" Robinson said in his memoirs that Paige "proved that the black ballplayer could play major league baseball by barnstorming against all those white teams." Satch, Slow Robinson wrote, "loosened up things" for the integration to come.[12]

In the middle of the '37 World Series, after watching the New York Giants staff get strafed by Yankee hitters three games in a row, Satch dashed off a telegram to Giants manager Bill Terry: "Giants seem to be in trouble. Try Ethiopian pitchers."[13]

At a big July 4, 1941, matchup in St. Louis, Paige refused to take the field unless officials allowed blacks to sit in box seats at Sportsman's Park. Satch won the standoff: organizers finally relented. For the first time in St. Louis baseball history, the races at least partly commingled at the home park of the Cardinals and Browns. The city's biggest blackball crowd ever, nearly twenty thousand people, enjoyed the Monarchs' 11-2 trampling of the Chicago American Giants.[14]

Paige's constant travel put black baseball on a more competitive footing with the white major leagues. For two decades, Satch was the Negro Leagues' foremost attraction. "People came from miles around to see [Paige]," Irvin remembered.[15] All those hundreds of thousands of miles Paige traversed on back roads—and the hostility he overcame along the way—created new horizons for black players.

Satchel made white club owners, scouts, and fans appreciate the caliber of ball being played in the Negro Leagues, and forced them to confront the absurdity of denying these men the chance to compete in the big leagues. "We cannot explain how the eventual integration of major league baseball would have been different without the earlier experience of Paige and others," social historian Terrie Aamodt has written, "but it would likely have begun even more slowly and have taken longer to accomplish."[16]

As the *Alabama* sortied across the Pacific, it dawned on Chief Petty Officer Feller that one way to recoup some of the money he and other servicemen-ballplayers had sacrificed during the war was to orchestrate a series of interracial barnstorming games. Feller called them "racial rivalry" contests—and despite the phrase's disquieting connotation in today's world, he still calls them that.

Why not do the tours right, Feller thought, with bigger names in bigger markets, complete with big-time promotion and family-friendly side entertainment? And to maximize profits, Feller vowed to underwrite the whole enterprise himself. To the extent possible, middlemen—club owners, promoters, and booking agents—would be eliminated. Feller wouldn't need Ray Doan to do the organizing; he'd do it himself. He also wouldn't rely on the usual cabal of blackball operatives to promote the tour; he'd take on those responsibilities, too. And to increase the number of games, thereby generating additional revenue, he'd use airplanes to hop from market to market.

When the *Alabama* was sent to Puget Sound to be overhauled in early '45, the navy elected to take Feller out of action, too. Rather than sail with his ship for what proved to be the last half year of war, Feller drew Stateside duty.

Retired catcher Mickey Cochrane had for two years been the director of baseball operations at Great Lakes Naval Training Station outside Chicago. But in the late winter of '45, Lieutenant Commander Cochrane was rotated to active duty in the Pacific. The navy determined, with a cunning eye toward publicity, that Feller was the perfect replacement. Feller's status as an enlisted man who ranked far below a lieutenant commander apparently didn't deter the brass.

Bob reported to Great Lakes in February 1945 and found some solid ballplayers awaiting him. Infielders Ken Keltner of the Indians and Pinky Higgins of the Tigers, catcher (and future Feller detractor) Walker Cooper, then with the Cardinals, pitcher Denny Galehouse, then with the St. Louis Browns, and pitcher Johnny Gorsica, soon to rejoin the Tigers, were among the major leaguers stationed at Great Lakes.[17]

It took a few months, but the star of the Majuro Atoll game got himself back into shape. As part of its publicity tour in May, Bob and his Great Lakes squad played a Sunday afternoon game in Moline, Illinois, against a sandlot nine headed by none other than Dizzy Dean. The day before the game, the *Moline Daily Dispatch* ran a huge photo of Feller under a banner headline: "Quad-City Fans Awaiting Feller-Dean Clash." It promised to be a "super-baseball attraction," the paper predicted, featuring "two of the greatest hurlers in modern day history."[18] Proceeds from the game would benefit a youth work program sponsored by the Moline Optimists Club.

The next day, before a jam-packed crowd of five thousand at Browning Field, Diz showed up wearing a drab-looking uniform with just "Dizzy Dean" inscribed on the jersey—his generic barnstorming outfit. When the sandlot club's catcher didn't show, the Great Lakes guys lent Diz's squad their second-string receiver.

Ol' Diz put on a fun show for the Quad Citians. He pitched two innings, went two for three at the plate, including a single against Feller, engineered the back half of a double steal (again against Feller!), and manned first from frames three through six. While on the mound, Diz slopped the ball around but yielded only two hits and no runs. Not bad for a guy who hadn't played much for four-plus years.

Feller wowed the fans, many of whom had traveled across the Mississippi from Bob's native Iowa. "Feller turned in a neat five innings of hurling for the Sailors, whiffing 12 and giving up only five hits and one run before retiring," reported the *Daily Dispatch*. Bob even drove in Pinky Higgins with Great Lakes's first run by lining a sacrifice fly in the fourth.

In the bottom of the sixth, Diz dusted off an old barnstorming routine after his grounder to shortstop got him thrown out "by a country mile," the paper said. Dean refused to leave the field, titillating the crowd by taking a lead off first—then throwing his arms up and feigning indignation when the ump motioned him toward the dugout.[19]

Two months later, in front of ten thousand rowdy sailors, CPO Feller pitched a no-hitter, striking out ten minor leaguers. In all, Bob threw about one hundred innings that spring and summer.

A few days after Nagasaki, Feller was discharged. The war had cost him, Bob calculated, about a quarter of a million dollars. "The trick," Feller confided to his wife, "was to make it up."[20] By then a self-educated entrepreneur, Bob was never reticent about telling people that his right arm was a "perishable commodity." He set out to leverage that commodity as aggressively as circumstances would allow.

On August 22, 1945, Cleveland gave Feller a heartfelt homecoming, complete with a downtown parade, gubernatorial and mayoral proclamations, a VIP luncheon, appearances by local demigods Cy Young and Tris Speaker, a jeep for use on the Iowa farm, and a new contract from the Indians. Headlined a Cleveland paper, "This Is What We've All Been Waiting For!"[21]

It's a shame his Majuro tormentor didn't get to see Feller's first start, which happened to be against the Detroit Tigers, the team the

Indiana's heckler claimed Bobby couldn't beat. Remarkably, Feller went the distance against the Tigers, striking out twelve and allowing only four hits—none after the fourth inning—and two runs in beating Prince Hal Newhouser. Feller even showcased his new slider. A couple of weeks later he shut out the Tigers, permitting only one hit. It was his sixth career one-hitter; seven more were to follow.

Feller got in eight more starts for the Tribe in the fall of '45, winning five, losing three, and ringing up a remarkable 2.50 ERA.[22] He also persuaded Commissioner Chandler to expand the permissible big-league barnstorming season from ten to thirty days that October.[23] Chandler couldn't say no to a war hero, especially when Feller told the commissioner that Bob would organize, free of charge, an instructional training session for fellow veterans the following spring.

Feller and Paige weren't the only barnstormers celebrating V-J Day. Pete Gray, the one-armed outfielder whose perseverance captivated fans, also toured that October. Gray led a big-league all-star team through the Midwest and out to the Coast, playing both white and black clubs. One of the Bay Area black squads that Gray played that fall, in fact, had a one-armed outfielder of its own.[24]

That same fall of '45, Biz Mackey put together a squad of Negro Leaguers that included Roy Campanella, Biz's protégé, as well as infielder-outfielder Monte Irvin, pitcher Don Newcombe, and shortstop Willie Wells. Biz's stars played a five-game series in Brooklyn and Newark against a white all-star ensemble led by former Reds third baseman (and future Dodger manager) Chuck Dressen. Dressen's squad featured, among others, Brooklyn pitcher Ralph Branca, Tiger pitcher Virgil "Fire" Trucks, and Dodgers second baseman Eddie Stanky. Dressen's guys took three of the games, with the fifth and final contest called a scoreless tie after five innings.[25]

There wasn't time that autumn for Feller to institute his grand barnstorming scheme, so Bob again turned to perennial organizer Ray Doan. Doan, in turn, hired Charlie DeWitt, Bill's brother. Charlie was then a minority owner and traveling secretary of the St. Louis Browns. DeWitt not only lent a hand to the Feller-Paige swing that fall; he also helped orchestrate Pete Gray's junket.

On September 20, 1945, the *Sporting News* reported that Feller would give a series of Doan-coordinated exhibitions on the West Coast against service teams, Pacific Coast League all-star clubs, and black squads. Doan also announced that, together with DeWitt, he was organizing an American League versus National League all-stars tour of the Plains and Midwest. A catastrophe was narrowly averted in early October when a train carrying Jeff Heath and Allie Reynolds of the Indians wrecked outside Great Falls, Montana. Although the engineer and the fireman were killed, the ballplayers on board escaped unhurt.[26]

Paige and Jackie Robinson, newly signed by the Dodgers, both played a few games in the fall of '45 for the latest installment of Chet Brewer's Kansas City Royals. Brewer's club hopscotched the Coast playing a variety of black and white teams, including Feller's.

On relatively short notice, Doan and Feller cobbled together a dynamite tour—one that, for the first time in baseball history, relied almost exclusively on air travel. Bob and company bounced from Southern California to northern California to the Pacific Northwest to Texas—and back again. The *Sporting News* made no mention of Feller renewing his West Coast rivalry with Paige, but that's exactly what happened.

On October 2 in Los Angeles, so many people showed up at Wrigley Field to salute former CPO Feller and Paige that ten thousand fans were turned away.[27] The huge crush of both blacks and whites didn't happen by accident. Doan and DeWitt had placed banner ads in the L.A. papers urging fans to get tickets in advance to see "Satchel Paige: Greatest Colored Pitcher" take on "Bob Feller, American League Strikeout King."[28]

L.A.'s columnists also jumped into the fray, albeit with the press's tendency to engage in distasteful racial stereotypes. The *Times*'s Braven Dyer chose to hype the Feller-Paige matchup by recounting his favorite yarn about Satch. While wintering in Venezuela a few years earlier, Paige was playing the outfield, oblivious to a covey of snakes that had taken residence near the ballpark's fence.

"When Paige pranced out to the pasture," Dyer wrote, "he casually noticed what he took to be a pile of iron pipe near the fence and thought no more about it. The guy at bat whacked a long one which bounced from the grass to the fence and then rolled along the 'iron pipe.' Satch ambled over and just as he reached for the ball, the 'pipe' moved. Paige found himself looking onto the eyes of a restless boa constrictor. Satch never bothered about the ball. He just lit out for the bench and never stopped until he had plunged headfirst into the dugout."[29]

Dyer's story of the wide-eyed black man frantically running to save his skin came, of course, from Satch himself. Paige knew that stories reinforcing white people's views of blacks—no matter how unflattering—helped put people in the ballpark. Satch told the Venezuela snake story on himself dozens of times, often changing the identity of the reptile and the circumstances under which he spotted it, but almost always including the "feets don't fail me now!" race and headlong dive into the dugout. A few days after Dyer's column, the *Seattle Post-Intelligencer*'s Royal Brougham recounted a similar version.[30]

Before the CWL went of out business, it enjoyed a bit of a revival thanks to the postwar Feller-Paige games. But it became a league for semipros and wannabes. The CWL's desultory end should neither diminish its luster nor the role that Satchel Paige played in making it one of the most vibrant professional circuits in history.

The various iterations of the black Giants won more than 60 percent of their games, capturing the CWL "pennant" (admittedly an arbitrary measure) in thirteen of sixteen years. The only CWL flag snagged by Pirrone's Café squad came in '41–'42 after most of the bigtime black players stopped coming west.[31]

In his CWL career, Paige averaged twelve strikeouts for every nine innings pitched—a remarkable record, regardless of competition. In seventy-seven appearances, he went 56-7, shutting out opponents seventeen times—marks that were Hall of Fame caliber.

From early autumn 1931 to December 1933, Satch didn't lose a CWL game. He wasn't up against chumps all the time, either. Paige often was matched against the best Pirrone could muster—major leaguers such as Buck Newsom, Larry French, and Sloppy Thurston.

Other black hurlers enjoyed success on the Coast, but not quite at the same rarefied level as Satch. Chet Brewer went 43-13 in the CWL, Bullet Joe Rogan 42-14, and Cannonball Willis 41-9.

Two of blackball's iconic sluggers—Mule Suttles and Turkey

Stearnes—also put up imposing numbers on the Coast. The Mule mauled 64 homers in 450 career CWL at-bats over nine years, hitting French at a .389 clip. Turkey tagged 56 CWL homers over ten years, batting .448 against Newsom and .378 against Thurston.[32]

White major leaguers also had inspired moments playing in Pirrone's circuit. Wally Berger bashed ten homers in just fifty-one career at-bats, with many of those plate appearances coming against black-ball's best pitchers.[33]

All these years later, the questions remain vexing. Why didn't major league baseball learn something from Pirrone's interracial success? Instead of undermining the CWL, why didn't Landis and the owners try somehow to emulate it?

The bitter truth is that their racial animus was too deeply rooted. Landis and his owners were convinced that integration meant fewer people in the stands—when, in fact, the CWL and other interracial barnstorming proved the opposite. As baseball historian Bill McNeil argues, their parochialism set back by at least two decades the cause of racial integration in major league baseball.[34]

Courtesy of Doan and California Winter League domos Joe Pirrone and Bill Feistner, Feller was playing with a Pacific Coast League all-star team. Jack Salveson, a longtime PCL hurler from Fullerton, was on Feller's staff. Salveson at that point belonged to Bob's Cleveland Indians; it would prove to be Jack's last go-round as a big leaguer.

Bob's infield included future big leaguer Eddie Bockman (career big-league batting average: .230) from Santa Ana, who kicked around with the Giants, Indians, and Pirates for parts of four years; Gerry Priddy (a career .265 hitter), an L.A. native who had a respectable eleven-year run with the Yankees, Senators, Browns, and Tigers; and Glen "Rip" Russell (.245), another L.A. product, who played parts of six seasons for the Cubs and Red Sox.

Satch was backed by a decent group of black stars, playing under the banner of Brewer's Royals. L.A. icon Jackie Robinson played short, with Jesse Williams at second, Wild Bill Wright in center, and Herb Souell at third. Booker McDaniels, Pullman Porter, and, on select occasions, Brewer himself, were available to pitch.

Paige and Feller publicly agreed to go five innings each—and, for once, they stuck to their pledge. Satch got the better of Bob, striking out ten over his five frames and departing with a 2-1 lead. Feller also nicely acquitted himself, fanning six, containing the explosive Robinson, and giving up just a pair of runs.

Salveson relieved Feller and kept the Royals in check. Satch was replaced first by Pullman Porter, who gave up one run, and then Brewer, who gave up two more in the PCL all-stars' 4-2 win. The *Chicago Defender*'s Lawrence F. LaMar described Jackie Robinson as a "sparkplug of action on the playing field" and called his base running "marvelous."[35] Bill Wright recalled that Robinson doubled down the right-field line that night, although there was no mention of such a hit in the press's sketchy account.[36]

The respective headlines in the *Defender* and the *Los Angeles Times* provide a telling commentary. "Paige Outpitches Feller; Loses"[37] was how the black paper—accurately—portrayed the story. "Feller All-Stars Whip Paige, 4-2"[38] is how it was—inaccurately—played in the *Times*. Each pitching star earned fourteen hundred dollars for five innings of work, claimed the *Defender*[39]—or more than Feller had earned for an entire year's service in the U.S. Navy.

But it's what transpired in the locker room that night, not the field of play, that netted Feller publicity that tarnished his image. After the game, Paul Zimmerman of the *Times* quizzed Bob about Dodger signee Robinson's big-league potential. Jackie was a good athlete but too muscle-bound to be an effective major-league hitter, Feller told the reporter. Robinson's football physique would make him susceptible to fastballs. "[Robinson] couldn't hit an inside pitch to save his neck," Bob ungraciously claimed.

But that rebuke was mild compared to what followed: "If [Robinson] were a white man, I doubt if they would consider him big-league material."[40] Later that fall, Feller told Wendell Smith, "I hope [Robinson] makes good. But I don't think he will."[41]

To be sure, Feller wasn't alone in expressing doubt about Jackie's baseball abilities. In early November 1945, the *Defender*'s Al Monroe quoted "Old Timers"—presumably veteran Negro Leaguers requesting anonymity—as saying that Robinson lacked the skills to make it in the major leagues. Monroe's sources called Jackie an "average ball-player who is vedy [*sic*] fast but woefully weak in reaching for outside pitches. Bob Feller of the majors says the same thing."[42]

Actually, Feller said something quite different, but said it in such a belligerent way that it triggered a firestorm in the African-American community at the very time when Bob's farsightedness was giving black players a chance to prove their mettle. Feller could have chosen to apologize for his remarks, especially when it became apparent in the spring of '46 that Robinson, then with the Dodgers' AAA club the Montreal Royals, was ticketed for stardom. Instead, Feller—stubborn to the point of pigheadedness—took a bad situation and made it worse.

In September 1946, as Jackie was wrapping up the International League batting crown with a .349 average and leading the circuit in runs scored with 113, reporter Sam Maltin of the *Montreal Herald* wrote Feller an "open letter" that was published in the *Courier* and referenced in other papers. After taking Feller to task for his criticism of Robinson eleven months before, Maltin wrote:

> As a pitcher, you must realize that your fellow [International League] hurlers must have tried various offerings on the gifted Robinson—including inside pitches. Seldom has Jackie failed to connect in some way. His strikeout record is one of the lowest in the league.[43]

If Maltin's public scolding chastened Feller, there was no evidence a few weeks later when Bob was being interviewed by the *Sporting News*. Toward the end of the '46 tour, reporter Steve George asked Feller if any of the blackballers Bob had seen over the past decade were capable of making the white majors.

"Haven't seen one—not one," snapped Feller, who surely knew that, once again, he was stirring a hornets' nest.

"Maybe [Satchel] Paige when he was young. When you name him you're done. Some are good hitters. Some can field pretty good. Most of them are fast. But I have seen none who combines the qualities of a big-league ballplayer."

Taken aback, George asked, "Not even Jackie Robinson?"

"Not even Jackie Robinson," Feller jabbed.[44]

Bob would have been better off hewing to Leo Durocher's view. When asked a couple of years before if black stars were good enough for the majors, Leo allowed, "Hell, yes, I've seen a million of 'em."

The Lip's future charge, Jackie Robinson, not surprisingly, bristled in October 1945 when Feller fired his first shot. In San Diego a week after Zimmerman's original piece appeared, Feller and Robinson had a blow-up before another Royals-Feller exhibition. A disagreement surfaced that evening over how much money the black players had been promised. Some accounts suggest that Chet Brewer and Robinson were concerned that they were getting "okey-dokeyed" by Feller and Doan—receiving a percentage of the net rather than a percentage of the gross, as had been promised. Robinson threatened to lead a boycott of the game unless more money was put up.

When Feller got wind of the brewing mutiny, he stormed into the black team's clubhouse at Lane Field, confronted Robinson, and demanded that the Royals take the field—or else. Harsh words were exchanged, words that, sadly, the two protagonists never forgot.

"There are 13,000 fans [the actual paid attendance was 9,107] out there who have paid to see us play ball—all of us," Feller barked at Robinson, at least according to Bob's *Now Pitching* autobiography. "And if you're not out there to lead off when I'm finished my warm-ups, I'm calling [Commissioner] Chandler at his home in Kentucky. This is the major leagues, and you don't pull that stuff up here, not right before a game."[45]

Well, it wasn't the major leagues—it was an exhibition in a minor-league park with a bunch of Pacific Coast Leaguers. Jackie was doing something that Feller, the prickly players' advocate, should have admired: standing up for his rights. Robinson wasn't alone in believing that black players got shortchanged in interracial contests. Chet Brewer later claimed that during the '46 California series, Feller shorted Satchel Paige out of some $2,400. When Chet pointed out the discrepancy to Paige, who in turn took the complaint to Feller, Bob got angry and stayed angry, Brewer told interviewers.[46]

Sure enough, in the fall of '46, Paige did end up suing Feller for $1,711.88, charging that Bob doled out pay based on net, not gross. Paige and Feller eventually settled their differences out of court, but not before a spate of embarrassing publicity.[47]

"I played two games against Feller on the coast last month. If you lined up ten of us [black ballplayers], I'll bet [Feller] couldn't pick me out of the bunch," a still-angry Robinson told Jimmy Cannon in the fall of '45, a sentiment later echoed by blackballer (and '46 tour veteran) Gene Benson.[48] Cannon would soon become an outspoken Feller critic.

Feller should have been a hero to the journalistic champions of integration; instead, Bob became something of a heel. It didn't help Bob's cause that he never took back his Robinson reproach. In 1949, Feller further inflamed passions by telling *Ebony* magazine that few black players could "make the grade" in the big leagues—an inexplicable statement from a player whose teammates Larry Doby and Satchel Paige had helped the previous year to deliver Cleveland's first World Series championship in three decades.[49]

The closest Bob came to a mea culpa was in January 1962, when it was clear that he and Robinson would go into Cooperstown together later that year. "It pains me to confess this," Feller wrote in a bylined *Saturday Evening Post* article, but he'd missed the mark on Jackie.[50] In the late '80s, while being interviewed by baseball historian Art Rust Jr., Feller said that his remarks about Robinson had been "tongue-in-cheek," an absurd assertion given how emphatic and how repeated Bob's denigration had been.[51] Feller's exchange with Rust suggests that, all those decades later, Bob still had the guilts about Jackie.

In subsequent years, Feller stressed to various historians that he wouldn't abide bigotry among his barnstorming troupers. "I wouldn't have them [bigots] on my team," Feller told biographer John Sickels.[52] But Feller did extend invitations to the race-baiting Bobo Newsom and Jeff Heath. In August 1947, after pinch-hitter Willard Brown borrowed Heath's bat while they were teammates on the St. Louis Browns and hit the first home run in American League history struck by a black man, Heath grabbed the offending instrument and smashed it to smithereens. It was "the moment when [Willard] watched pure hatred crashing against a dugout wall," Joe Posnanski wrote in *The Soul of Baseball: A Road Trip through Buck O'Neil's America*.[53]

Feller's ambivalence toward his own role as a racial pioneer is captured in two contradictory statements made three decades apart. In the late '30s, he told black barnstormers that they'd given much to baseball but that baseball had not given much to them. Thirty years later, as he was being honored as the greatest living right-handed pitcher, Feller was asked about the state of race relations in baseball. "I don't think baseball owes colored people anything. I don't think colored people owe baseball anything, either." When Jackie Robinson was told of Feller's comment, Robinson retorted, "I don't think Bob has grown any more from 1947. He has his head in the sand."[54]

In truth, Feller was neither the civil rights champion portrayed by Jim Murray nor the insensitive lout painted by Jimmy Cannon. Bob was a calculating businessman who didn't hesitate to seize opportunities to make money. Black-white barnstorming, in his mind, was a commercial enterprise, not a social undertaking.

Still, he had a good heart, paid black barnstormers well, treated them (for the most part) with dignity, and—at least for the world of the 1940s—displayed a sophisticated social conscience. Like a lot of middle-aged white Americans in the turbulent '60s, though, Feller's politics took a rightward turn. The man who had done so much to spotlight black ballplayers began reveling in political incorrectness. When asked in 2007 about the Jim Crow travel arrangements on his tours, Feller said more than a little defiantly, "Look. We knew it was wrong . . . but we just didn't think that way back then."[55]

Despite Feller's bumpy relations with Robinson, his October 1945 tour remained a hot ticket. Feller's verbal joust with Robinson in San Diego didn't seem to faze him. Bob pitched five shutout innings against the Royals that night, giving up only three hits and striking out ten. Paige did him one better, whiffing eleven and yielding only one hit in a 5-0 Royals win. "Having proved to the satisfaction of big leaguers that a hitch of three and one-half years in the Navy didn't take away any of his ability or box office appeal, Bob Feller will arrive here this morning for two games in the Bay Area," the *San Francisco Chronicle* reported on October 4. In northern California and the Pacific Northwest, Paige and Feller essentially operated as solo practitioners, hooking up with local squads. Neither the PCL all-stars nor the Royals were on the marquee for Bay Area games.

On October 5, twelve thousand Bay Area denizens jammed into Seals Stadium to watch Paige again stymie Giants shortstop Dick Bartell, by then finishing up his rowdy eighteen-year career. Also enlisted that day was Iowan Bunny Simmons, who had caught Feller back in his American Legion days and was completing a stint in the service. San Francisco's own Augie Galan (who hit .307 in '45), then with the Dodgers, was pressed into duty. To ensure that Satch had a decent receiver, Paul Hardy, a member of the Chicago American Giants and a "noted catcher in colored circles," was signed for the game.[56] Feller's men won 11-0, but did all their scoring after Satch departed.[57]

Two days later, Seattle's Junior Chamber of Commerce brought in Feller and Paige as gate attractions for a Sunday afternoon fundraiser at Sicks' Stadium. The cause could not have been more poignant: proceeds went to purchase recreational equipment for thousands of convalescing servicemen in the Seattle area.

Nearly three hundred wounded sailors and soldiers from the Seattle Naval and Madigan hospitals were the Jaycees' guests. Uniformed personnel and their kids got in for free. Bob and Satch played with squads from the Sand Point Naval Air Station and the Seattle Coast Guard operating base.

Both the "NavalAirs" and the "Operators," as they were called in Seattle's *Post-Intelligencer* and the *Times*, were stacked with onetime minor leaguers. The Operators, in fact, were managed by former and future Cubbie Marv Rickert, an outfielder who hit .247 in 402 big-league games. A paid crowd of nearly 9,500 turned out to honor Bob, Satch, and the wounded warriors. It was unprecedented for Paige to play with white teammates in the Feller exhibitions—but Satch did that afternoon.

Even though Feller was a navy man, the Jaycees insisted that a coin be flipped to determine which star pitched for which team. "The advantage supposedly will go to the team that draws Feller," the *Times* calculated the morning of the game. "[Feller] has promised to go five or six innings, while the ancient Paige will be able to muster only three or four."[58]

The *Times* got it wrong on both counts. Sand Point won the coin toss, so Feller did indeed get to pitch with the NavalAirs. But Paige and what the *Post-Intelligencer* called his "uncanny slants" got the better of Bob—and Satch went five innings, the same distance as Feller. Satch was sensational, yielding only one hit, which, naturally, was a single to Feller. "[I]t was Ol' Satch who stole the show," the *Post-Intelligencer's* Royal Brougham opined, "with a surprising assortment of stuff for a geezer going on fifty."[59] (Satch was actually going on forty.)

Both runs that Feller allowed came in the first, when a line drive glanced off his knee. But to his credit, Bob stayed in the game and pitched shutout ball until being relieved by Jack Salveson in the sixth. When the "world's two greatest pitchers," as Brougham called them, departed the game, the score stood 2-1 in favor of Satch and his Operators. A coast guardsman named Ray Orteig blanked Sand Point over the last four innings, while the Operators got to Salveson and Naval-Air hurler Jack Wilder for four more runs. The Coasties won, 6-1.

If either service team in Seattle was racially integrated beyond coast guardsman-for-a-day Satch, the papers didn't mention it. All that changed the next day.

"Geezer" Satch and his young pals Bobby and Jack dashed across the Cascades for their next contest in the tiny central Washington town of Wenatchee. They again matched up with service teams: Satch with the Puget Sound (or Bremerton) Navy Yard, Bob for the Fort George Wright army squad out of Spokane. By court order, the Navy Yard workforce had, in midwar, been desegregated. Its baseball squad was similarly integrated.

Like the game in Seattle, the Wenatchee exhibition was the brain-child of local Jaycees. Wenatchee's young merchants were in the midst of waging a public relations campaign to land a minor-league franchise.[60] Somehow the Jaycees provided Doan and DeWitt enough money to snare Feller and Paige.

Wenatchee was then a town of some ten thousand. It may have been the proud capital of apple country but it wasn't used to this level of excitement. The town's newspaper, the *Wenatchee World*, buzzed all week in anticipation of Bob's and Satch's arrival. Native Pacific north-westerner Clifford "Lefty" Chambers, who went on to a six-year big-league career (48-53, ERA 4.29), was stationed at Fort Wright. Lefty was slated to take over once Feller and Salveson had finished their duties.

The *World's* story the next day was headlined "Fans Marvel at Speed of Two Hurlers."[61] Spectators at Recreation Park murmured as first Feller, then Paige, whipped the ball past overmatched batsmen. It was a lopsided affair: the army men with Feller, Salveson, and Chambers beat up on the Puget Sound navy workers—but only after Satch left the game. Paige pitched the first four innings, whiffing four and shutting down Fort Wright on just one hit, a double by a G.I. named DePoiso, who had a story to tell his grandchildren. Alas, after Satch departed, the Navy Yard defense collapsed; its pitchers got swamped for 11 runs.

Feller, complaining that he "couldn't get loose" in the chill, pitched three innings and didn't give up so much as a "loud foul," the *World* commented. Bobby struck out seven—then watched Salveson and Chambers complete the shutout. The navy men managed only two hits, both against Salveson.[62] The Jaycees' gambit eventually worked: Wenatchee secured a franchise in the Class B Western International League, now known as the Northwest League.

After the Wenatchee game, the three headliners hurried back to Seattle to grab a flight to the Bay Area, where the previous week's rained-out game had been rescheduled. On the afternoon of October 10, Satch and Bob hung around Feller's room at the St. Francis in San Francisco, listening to the radio as Hal Newhouser and his Tigers beat Hank Borowy and the Chicago Cubs, 9-3, to clinch the '45 Series, four games to three.[63]

The next night in Oakland, the conventional racial dynamic was restored. Feller played with a white all-star squad of major and minor leaguers, while Satch hooked up with an outfit known as the Oakland Colored Giants, the same squad that had taken on Pete Gray's team a few days earlier. Feller pitched no-hit ball for five innings, facing the minimum of fifteen batters and striking out seven. Paige, the *Sporting News* said, "was touched for eight blows and two runs in the five [innings] he worked." But Satch's team lucked out when Salveson was strafed for nine hits in the final four innings. Jack gave up one run in the eighth and three more in the ninth, allowing Paige's squad to escape with a 4-3 win.[64]

Satch took a break from Doan's tour for the next few days as Feller and Salveson traveled to Utah and Texas. Feller thrilled members of a Salt

Lake City industrial league team by helping them beat a rival squad on October 13. Bob fanned nine Salt Lake sandlotters and walked just one in five innings. Salveson took over for the final four innings to lock down a 3-2 victory for Bob's squad. Clarence "Hooks" Iott (career record 3-9), a former St. Louis Brown still on active duty, yielded four hits to Feller's club.

Doan loved working the autumnal Texas circuit because it meant decent weather and big crowds. But racial tension made it tough if not impossible for blacks to play there, so Doan arranged for Feller to be joined by Yankee hurler Spurgeon "Spud" Chandler, who'd spent almost two full years in the service. On October 14 in Dallas, Feller and Chandler played for a Fort Worth semipro team. Feller pitched four scoreless innings and Chandler mopped up in a 2-1 win over a Dallas-based outfit.

The next night in Fort Worth, turnabout was fair play, as Bob and Spud pitched for the Dallas team, leading them to an 8-4 extra-inning win over the Fort Worth club. Feller and Chandler each pitched four shutout innings.[65]

Feller flew back to the Coast and resumed his interracial exhibitions against Satch and Chet Brewer's Royals. On Wednesday evening, October 24, before another crowd in excess of ten thousand in San Diego, the Royals defeated Feller's team, 3-2, despite Bob's yeoman performance. Bob struck out fourteen in just six innings, giving up a solitary hit. When Feller gave way to Salveson, Bob was leading Satch, 1-0. The defense disintegrated behind Salveson, committing five errors and allowing three unearned runs. Satch nearly matched Feller by pitching six innings, giving up five hits, one run, and striking out seven.[66]

The Feller-Paige rematch at Wrigley in L.A. on October 26 drew an even bigger crowd than the earlier Wrigley game. It was getting close to Feller's twenty-seventh birthday, so Bob's California pals surprised him with a three-decker birthday cake.

Some twenty-six thousand Angelenos shoehorned themselves into the park at Forty-first and Avalon. For press consumption, Feller and Paige both vowed to go the full nine. But each worked "only" seven— and each put on a show. Feller whiffed thirteen Royals and allowed only four hits. Satch kayoed eight and permitted just five safeties.

The game went ten innings before Feller's men scratched across the go-ahead tally, winning 3-2. Onetime Detroit Tiger Joe Wood Jr., the son of "Smoky Joe," the legendary Red Sox pitcher, scored the deciding run after tripling in the tenth.

In all, nearly sixty thousand fans paid to see Paige and Feller pitch at Wrigley Field that fall—which meant each ballplayer made a pretty penny on the gate percentage.

Two days later, up the coast in Oakland before 5,400 customers, Satch didn't show as apparently expected, but Feller pitched six stout innings for a Pacific Coast League all-star team. The PCL stars were again playing the Oakland Colored Giants, whom they beat in a squeaker, 2-1. Bob allowed only five hits in fanning ten.[67]

Then Feller packed his bags to return home to Waukegan, Illinois, his wife's hometown. They were expecting their first child later that year.

Just as barnstorming wound down at the end of October 1945, the *Sporting News* chose to editorialize on Branch Rickey's signing of Jackie Robinson. Over the years, the publication run by the Spink family had been reliably reactionary, but this time it outdid itself.

"There is not a single Negro player with major league possibilities for 1946. Satchel Paige, of course, is barred by his age. Nor could he afford to accept a major contract, even if he were ten years younger," the paper fumed in a statement that proved to be wrong on all three counts.

"Robinson, at 28, is reported to possess baseball abilities which, were he white, would make him eligible for a trial with, let us say, the Brooklyn Dodgers' Class B farm at Newport News, if he were six years younger," it concluded.[68] The Spink family had one-upped Feller—not only disparaging Jackie's talent but impugning the Dodgers for signing Robinson in the first place.

The same issue of the *Sporting News* highlighted a similarly themed screed from Joe Williams. The *New York World-Telegram* columnist, an acerbic Georgian, wrote, "I have seen the Negro make sure and steady advances. I have also seen him cruelly victimized by pressure groups, social frauds, and political demagogues." Exactly what outside forces were "victimizing" African Americans, Williams didn't say. But clearly he meant such feckless do-gooders as the NAACP, the Urban League, and the recently widowed Eleanor Roosevelt.

Williams then took direct aim at interracial barnstorming and the men who cashed in from it, chief among them Dizzy Dean. "[T]here are any number of southern players who apparently have no social scruples against playing with or against Negroes in the off-season and exhibition games when the opportunity to pick up stray dollars is inviting. An example is Dizzy Dean, who makes a business of touring with Satchel Paige. These men in no way help to clarify the issue."[69]

If Williams thought the Dean-Paige barnstorming exhibited untidy "social scruples," he would have been aghast to learn what Bob Feller was dreaming up for the following autumn.

CHAPTER ELEVEN

Going Airborne: The Feller-Paige '46 Tour

On the mound and off, [Satchel Paige's] clownishness was mixed with a warrior's hardened diffidence; he knew he was the attraction, the champion, and the conqueror.

—HENRY METCALFE, NEGRO LEAGUES HISTORIAN

In January 1946, Feller made good on his promise to Commissioner Chandler to run a low-cost training camp for World War II veterans with aspirations to get back in the game. He opened the camp in Tampa, Florida, and enlisted first-rate counselors, among them Connie Mack, Joe DiMaggio, Spud Chandler, Tommy Bridges, Lou Boudreau, Bill Dickey, and Bob's old pal Dizzy Dean. Bob also arranged for his corporate sponsor, Wilson Sporting Goods, as well as Hillerich & Bradsby, the makers of Louisville Slugger bats, to donate equipment.

The *Sporting News* and other publications gave Feller's camp plenty of exposure. No tuition was charged, but campers were expected to pay for lodging, which the Tampa Chamber of Commerce provided at a discounted rate of thirteen dollars per week.[1] Feller later said he invested $2,500 of his own money, none of which was reimbursed. No-nonsense Bob even imposed a midnight curfew and banned alcohol—strictures that, if applied to counselors, must have cramped Dean's style.

A majority of the campers were onetime minor leaguers or semipros home from the war determined to give the game one last shot. The three-week session attracted some 180 ballplayers, 66 of whom ended up signing professional contracts—a success rate significantly higher than the Doan-Hornsby camps in Arkansas and Mississippi. Feller remains, to this day, justifiably proud of his "Free School," as the *Sporting News* called it.[2]

While waiting to take the field at the 1946 All-Star Game at Fenway Park, James Barton "Mickey" Vernon was sitting in the clubhouse, feeling a bit overwhelmed. It was the first All-Star Game appearance for the Senators' first baseman; he was awed to be in the same locker room as Joe and Dom DiMaggio, Charlie "King Kong" Keller, and Boston's Splendid Splinter himself, Ted Williams.

Mickey felt a tap on his shoulder. It was fellow navy veteran Bob Feller, the American League's starting pitcher in the All-Star Game. Feller told Vernon that he was organizing a barnstorming tour that fall and wanted Mickey to be part of it. Vernon was leading the AL in batting at the All-Star break. "If you're still leading the league at the end of the season," Feller told Vernon, "I'll give you a $750 bonus to come tour with me."

Vernon and Feller shook hands on the spot. Sure enough, Mickey went on to finish first in the league with a .353 batting average, besting Williams by 11 percentage points. On day one of their '46 tour, Feller handed Mickey a check for $750—which represented close to 10 percent of what the Senators paid Vernon that season. "I thought I'd died and gone to heaven," Mickey laughed in an interview sixty-one years later.[3] Six other '46 AL all-stars went touring with Feller and Vernon under the big top that fall.

Jackie Robinson, coming off a season when he led his Montreal Royals to both the International League pennant and the minor league "Little World Series" championship, also had his own troupe in '46, which included (at various points) such stellar black players as Roy Campanella, Buck Leonard, Ted Strong, and Larry Doby.

But Jackie's tour wasn't nearly as well planned or promoted as Feller's. Robinson guaranteed his stars five thousand dollars each; when crowds proved disappointing, he had to dip into his signing bonus from the Brooklyn Dodgers to make payroll. Jackie also came up a few bodies short at different times. One of the guys Robinson pressed into duty was his white teammate and fellow Dodger farmhand Al Campanis.[4] The future front office executive, who four decades later humiliated himself and his fabled franchise by publicly questioning whether blacks had the "necessities" to manage at the big-league level, actually helped integrate the game as a barnstormer.

After Feller's father passed away and he returned from the Pacific, he didn't shy away from squawking about the game's inequities—or from getting money while the getting was good. The *Cleveland News*'s Hal Lebovitz and other reporters marveled at the change in Feller's personality. Gone was the wide-eyed farm boy, replaced by a hard-edged man who didn't hesitate to steer a conversation to his advantage. Perhaps because he'd been callously exploited as a teenager, Feller became a sponge in the dugout and the clubhouse, absorbing everything about the game's finances. Over time, he became the owners' bête noire—one of the few players of his generation to develop an expertise in baseball's economics.

Even today, Feller may not be able to remember details of specific barnstorming games, but he takes pride in recalling the balance sheet from his 1946 venture. Feller calls it the "most successful barnstorming tour in the history of baseball."[5] Since he ended up turning an immense profit, he's justified in making the claim.

It was the most ambitious baseball undertaking since John McGraw and Charles Comiskey dreamed up their round-the-world junket in 1913. No one had ever attempted to use airplanes to crisscross the country, playing a game in one market early in the afternoon, then going airborne to play a second game that night hundreds of miles away. Nor had a player ever taken it upon himself to organize a tour from top to bottom—from personnel and logistics to marketing and public relations. When fellow barnstormers learned that Feller was underwriting the whole gig himself, they were incredulous. Bob later said the '46 effort cost him fifty thousand dollars up front.[6] It turned out to be worth every penny.

Unlike Feller's '45 swing, when Bob played for the most part with minor leaguers, servicemen, and sandlotters, the '46 tour would feature big-league baseball's best players. Feller recruited all-stars from both leagues, many of whom were seasoned barnstormers, purportedly paying the big stars $6,000 and the lesser lights around $1,700.[7] Bob later told Shirley Povich of the *Washington Post* that Mickey Vernon cleared upward of $3,000 for his share of the '46 tour—more than a third of what the Senators were paying Mickey.[8]

To fortify his pitching staff, he snagged Bobo Newsom (14-13, with a 2.93 ERA in '46) and knuckleballer Dutch Leonard (10-10, 3.56) of the Washington Senators, along with Johnny Sain (20-14, 2.21) of the Boston Braves, and Spud Chandler (20-8, 2.10) of the New York Yankees—a forbidding rotation in anyone's book. On the tour's eve, Bobo backed out, so Feller added pitcher and future manager Freddie Hutchinson of the Detroit Tigers (14-11, 3.09).

Batting champ Vernon of the Nats (.353, 85 RBIs) handled first. At second was Brownie Johnny Berardino (.265), a former *Our Gang* child star who quit baseball in the early '50s to return to showbiz. Eventually Berardino became a beloved soap opera character, Dr. Steve Hardy, the heartthrob of *General Hospital.*

At shortstop was the Yankees' slick fielder Phil Rizzuto (.257). At third was Bob's teammate and navy buddy Kenny Keltner (.241). The outfielders were Jeff Heath (.278, 84 RBIs) of the Browns, Charlie Keller (.275, 113) of the Yankees, Sam Chapman of the Athletics (.261, 67), and the nonpareil Stan Musial (.365, 103) of the Cardinals.

In landing Musial, Feller had secured the services of both leagues' reigning batting champs. But before Stan the Man could join the tour, he had to complete what became a classic seven-game World Series against Ted Williams and the Boston Red Sox. Behind Feller's plate were Jim Hegan (.236) of the Indians, Frankie Hayes (.233) of the White Sox, and Bob's old roomie and batterymate, supposedly reformed party boy "Rollickin' Rollie" Hemsley (.223), then with the Phillies.

Hal Newhouser and Ted Williams also profited from the Feller tour. After being solicited by Feller—southpaw Newhouser had *averaged* 27 wins the previous three seasons, while Williams had hit .342 and led the league with 142 runs scored in '46—each was paid ten thousand dollars that season *not* to barnstorm. Detroit owner Spike Briggs and Red Sox mogul Tom Yawkey were worried about their meal tickets getting hurt—or perishing in an airplane crash.[9]

At the last second, Feller added his Cleveland mate Bob Lemon. Lemon could both pitch (four wins on the mound that season) and play the field. Cleveland institution Lefty Weisman signed on as trainer.

To get the best the Negro Leagues had to offer, Feller turned to Kansas City Monarchs owners J. L. Wilkinson and Tom Baird, along with the Monarchs' field manager, veteran barnstormer (and still occasional catcher) Frank Duncan.

Satch, of course, was the premier guy on Feller's list. In early September, twenty-three thousand fans at Yankee Stadium saw Paige pitch a complete-game masterpiece against Goose Tatum and the Indianapolis Clowns. After the game, Paige was asked by the *Defender* how he was feeling. "'I'm practicing up for Bob Feller and that series that is coming up,' Satch replied with a big grin."[10]

Feller's tour was the fulfillment of a dream for Paige. For once, someone else was doing the hard work. Paige would travel like a prince and he was guaranteed handsome pay—for far less aggravation than he was used to.

Joining Satch were five of his teammates on the Monarchs: hurler Hilton Smith, Henry Thompson, Willard "Home Run" Brown, Chico Renfroe, and Buck O'Neil. O'Neil was reported to have eked out the '46 Negro American League batting crown by just two points over his teammate Brown (.350 to .348).

Three members of the Negro National League champion Newark Eagles would join the tour: Monte Irvin, Leonard Pearson, and Max Manning.

The Philadelphia Stars contributed pitcher Barney Brown, a southpaw, and Frank Austin, a shortstop. Austin purportedly hit .390 in winning the NNL batting championship as a rookie in 1944.

Paige's first-string catcher was his old Bismarck buddy, the thirty-three-year-old Quincy Trouppe, who by then was managing the Cleveland Buckeyes of the Negro American League. Trouppe was credited with a .313 batting average in '46, good for fifth place among NAL hitters, according to reports. Trouppe's Buckeye charge Sammy Jethroe would man center field. Third base would be handled by the Homestead Grays' Howard Easterling, who'd returned from three years in the Pacific to bat over .300. Slick Artie Wilson of the Birmingham Black Barons played short.

Supposedly to keep Satchel on time and out of trouble, Duncan and Feller hired William "Dizzy" Dismukes as business manager for the black club. Dismukes had been a fine sidearmed pitcher back in the '10s and '20s and had gone on to become a respected front office executive and traveling secretary for the Chicago American Giants and Kansas City Monarchs.[11]

It was a solid club, to be sure, but not exactly a "Who's Who of Negro Baseball," as Feller's press release claimed. Nor was Satch's '46 squad a match for the Crawfords of the mid-'30s or the Bismarck team that Neil Churchill assembled for the '35 Wichita tournament. Josh Gibson was not invited; by then, his chronic drinking had become a problem, and within four months, Gibson would be dead. Roy Campanella and Grays' first sacker Buck Leonard also rebuffed Satch's offer. Jackie Robinson, too, was not happy with the financial terms presented by Paige, Feller, and Wilkinson, which prompted Jackie to organize his own tour.[12]

Feller vowed to do everything first-class. It took months of work on off days during the '46 season, but Bob leased two state-of-the-art DC-3s from Flying Tigers Airlines and had them paint "Bob Feller All-Stars" on one fuselage, "Satchel Paige All-Stars" on the other. He booked reservations at the finest hotels—for white players, anyway. His people made sure that Satch and company made alternative arrangements at decent places. Months in advance, Feller lined up ballparks and others facilities. Years later, he laughed that his hundreds of long-distance calls that year jacked up AT&T's dividends.

Feller paid his players well, black or white—at least a hundred dollars a game, plus a generous per diem. For most white players, that was good money, a substantial percentage of their annual income. For the black players save Paige, it was the biggest payday they'd ever made or could hope to make.[13]

Remembered Buck O'Neil, "I was excited to be chosen for the Satchel Paige All-Stars because I knew I'd be making more money in one month than I had made in the last six." O'Neil also recognized that, in the wake of Robinson's signing, the tour provided other blacks with a chance "to prove ourselves against [white] big leaguers."[14] No one knew it at the time, but eight future members of the Hall of Fame were along for the '46 tour: Feller, Paige, Musial, Lemon, Rizzuto, Smith, Irvin, and Willard Brown.

Before packing their bags, though, the Monarchs and Eagles had some unfinished business. The 1946 Colored World Series between these two teams took place over seven games in four separate cities: New York (the Polo Grounds), Newark (Ruppert Field), Chicago (Comiskey Park), and Kansas City (Blues Stadium).

Satch, no doubt distracted, brought less than his best stuff, going 1-1 with an 8.00 ERA. Much to the chagrin of Buck O'Neil and other Monarchs, Satch skipped out on game seven. O'Neill speculated that Paige was meeting with Bob Feller to go over details for the tour, which was starting the next day in Pittsburgh.[15] Pitcher Max Manning also went 1-1 in the series, won by his Eagles, four games to three. After the Colored Series ended, Effa Manley, the owner of the Eagles, bragged, "I believe we could have beaten the winner of the white World Series, too."[16] It's a shame they didn't play; the '46 Eagles might have given the Stan Musial–Enos Slaughter Cardinals a pretty good run for their money.

Feller again worked his magic with Commissioner Chandler, securing Happy's permission not only to barnstorm for thirty full days but to begin the tour during the Bosox-Cards World Series. Baseball's ban against junketeering during the Series had been on the books—and more or less enforced—since Judge Landis's original crackdown more than two decades earlier. Given the vehemence of club owners, it was no small thing to get Chandler to waive it. A year later, though, the commissioner and the owners would insist that no barnstorming begin until the postseason concluded.[17]

The program from the 1946 tour spotlighted the military service of the white all-stars. Feller, Lemon, Musial, Vernon, Keltner, Chapman, Rizzuto, Berardino, and Hemsley had all been in the navy. Hegan had served in the coast guard, Keller in the merchant marine. The program failed, however, to acknowledge the wartime sacrifice of the Negro Leaguers. There was nary a word about Hank Thompson getting wounded in the Ardennes or Willard Brown's heroics in the push across France and Belgium.

Buck O'Neil had served in the navy. Hilton Smith had been a State-side officer in the army. In addition to Thompson and Brown, Easterling, Duncan, and Barney Brown had all served in the army's European Theater. Monte Irvin had also been in the army, as had Rufus Lewis, a righty pitcher on the tour. Their Eagles teammate Max Manning had served in the quartermaster corps of the Army Air Corps.[18]

Seven decades later, Feller told Fay Vincent, "We were interested in one thing, making money. I mean what else is there? Yes, we put on a good show; there was racial rivalry, not amongst the players, but amongst the fans. And we [had] a few laughs."[19]

A few years earlier, Feller had told John Sickels much the same: "We made a lot of money—everybody smiled all the way to the bank. And that was all there was to it. Nothing more, nothing less."[20]

Feller's old confidant *Cleveland News* columnist Ed McAuley had long been intrigued by blackball. In October 1934, McAuley had been among the Cleveland writers entranced by Satchel Paige's near-perfect performance against the Dean brothers and the Rosenblums.

Twelve years later, on the eve of Bob's tour, McAuley penned a column expressing "curiosity regarding the caliber of the colored cast" that Feller and company would be facing. "Colored players are on their way into major league baseball," McAuley wrote on September 27, 1946. "Feller's tour should be something of a preview." Citing Jackie Robinson's '46 success for Montreal in the International League, McAuley argued:

> Most qualified observers believe that few of the present-day colored stars could compete on even terms with American and National Leaguers. If this is true, it is only because the Negro athletes have not had the benefit of such training as has been lavished on their white contemporaries. It is ridiculous to suggest that a race which has produced super-stars in boxing, football, basketball, and track, would not prove equally successful if given the same opportunity in baseball.[21]

It was one grueling odyssey: Feller scheduled thirty-five games, some two-thirds of them against the Satchel Paige Negro All-Stars, in twenty-seven days, thirty-one separate towns in seventeen different states, necessitating thirteen thousand miles' worth of travel—all statistics that PR man Burton Hawkins continually hyped in his press bulletins.

The itinerary called for big-market games in six major-league cities, as well as visits to four "high minor" markets, plus a healthy agglomeration of games on the West Coast.[22] Four same-day, multicity doubleheaders were part of the mix—a first for white major leaguers.

To live up to Hawkins's hype, Satch and Bob would start games whenever possible, making a meaningful (more than token) appearance in each park. Feller, never one to pass up an easy score, even squeezed in four games against an Earle Mack–led group of West Coast minor leaguers. Bob also managed, in midtour, to fly from California to New Jersey to pick up a personal appearance check of two thousand dollars at a convention of milk producers. But Bob's pièce de résistance in '46 was scheduling a game in tiny Versailles, Kentucky, Happy Chandler's hometown—part of the I-scratch-your-back-you-scratch-mine pact Feller had reached with the new commish.

There was much excitement about the Feller-Paige tour in the black media. "'Fireball' Bob Feller is not going to play the Negro Big League All-Stars cheap," the *Defender* proclaimed on September 28. "When [Feller] lines his team up against Satchel Paige's squad . . . [Feller] will have a lineup that sounds like the teams that played in the American and National League All-Star game at Boston this year."[23]

The "tan stars," the *Defender* averred, "are also getting together." Paige would have an "aggregation of the leading performers from both circuits in his lineup." The game "between the great Satchel Paige and the equally as great Bob Feller" at Comiskey in early October would be a "natural," the paper concluded.[24]

Feller validated his billing by fanning six Detroit Tigers in five innings on September 28, the last game of the regular season, the day before the tour was scheduled to begin. His six whiffs eclipsed by two Rube Waddell's major-league record of 346 strikeouts in a single season, a mark that had stood for four decades. (Much to Feller's chagrin, baseball statisticians later added three whiffs to Rube's total, so technically Bob did not break Waddell's record.)

No matter how methodical, Feller's planning couldn't account for weather. It was unseasonably chilly in early fall in the Northeast and Midwest. Nor could Bob and his advisers anticipate labor unrest in the markets they visited. A power utility workers' strike forced the Feller-

Paige game in Pittsburgh to be moved to the afternoon, hurting the gate. A streetcar workers' walkout made it difficult for fans in Columbus to get to the park. An airline pilots' strike forced Feller, eager to catch his flight to Atlantic City, to start a game early in Sacramento, even before many spectators had arrived. And a dockworkers' dispute in Honolulu complicated Feller's finale.[25]

Once Feller got word of the utility strike in Pittsburgh, the tour's first game was hastily rescheduled for Monday afternoon, September 30, at Forbes Field—the park where, twelve years before, a scuffle had broken out between teams headlined by Satch and Dizzy Dean. A crowd of 4,592 "shivered through football weather"[26]—dank cold and fog—to watch Bob and Satch go head-to-head for three innings. When each departed, the game was knotted at one.

Bob whiffed three Negro Leaguers; Satch did him one better. Feller allowed two hits, Paige just one, but the white all-stars managed to score Phil Rizzuto in the first after Scooter coaxed a walk, was sacrified to second, and came home on Keller's RBI single. Barney Brown, described by the hometown *Courier* as one of "Negro baseball's most artistic moundsmen," replaced Satch in the fourth and gave up only one hit, standing "the major leaguers on their ear" the rest of the way.[27]

Paige's "sepia mates," as the *Courier* called them, broke the tie in the top of the seventh when, with Feller's Cleveland teammate Bob Lemon on the mound, Hank Thompson walked and stole second. Thompson scored when aging third baseman Herb Souell, by then answering to the nickname "Baldy," banged one up the middle.[28] Easterling and Trouppe each had doubles for Satch's squad. Lemon ended up with the loss, although he pitched well, giving up just two hits. Lefty Brown got the win, aided by shortstop Rizzuto's two errors.

On Tuesday, October 1, the caravan moved west across the border to Ohio, where Feller had arranged the tour's first twin-market doubleheader. Playing an afternoon game, followed by a game under the lights an hour or two away, was standard operating procedure for the black guys, but hopping on a bus and rushing to another ballyard must have been a strange experience for the white players.

More rotten weather—and with it, disappointing turnouts—awaited. Another smallish crowd of some three thousand showed in Youngstown to watch the afternoon game, which quickly degenerated into an 11-2 rout for Feller's club. Johnny Berardino, Jeff Heath, and Spud Chandler all homered. Remarkably enough, the same three pitchers, Feller, Chandler, and Bob Lemon, worked both ends of the doubleheader.

The nightcap, an hour north at Cleveland's Municipal Stadium, provided the tour with one of its more affecting moments. Of the ten thousand "rabid fans" who "braved the chilly blasts of the lake-front stadium," roughly two-thirds were black, estimated the *Call and Post*, Cleveland's African-American paper.

"A roar of pride rose from the partisan crowd when old Satchel strolled to the mound in the first inning," the paper reported the following week. "His first pitch, a slow curve, was a ball. His second pitch, a fast breaking inshoot, was a called strike. When his third pitch, a tantalizing curve, broke across for a strike, the crowd went wild."[29]

Alas, Satch couldn't quite match Feller's dominance. The first batter Bobby faced, bat magician Artie Wilson, snuck a perfect bunt down the third base line. And that was it for the Negro Leaguers that night. They wouldn't get another hit off the white team until two outs in the bottom of the ninth. The final score was 5-0.[30]

Arthur Lee Wilson was a wiry little shortstop with exceptional range. A native Alabamian, Artie was thrilled when the homestate Black Barons signed him in the early '40s. Soon Wilson, a left-handed hitter, was lacing opposite-field line drives all over Negro American League ballparks. In 1948, Wilson was credited with hitting .402 in NAL play, so he's sometimes called the last player to have hit .400 for an entire season. That same year, Artie helped mentor seventeen-year-old Black Baron Willie Mays, who was just breaking into professional ball.

Wilson in many ways personifies the frustrations experienced by Negro Leaguers during the early days of integration. In late '48, the Yankees acquired him for their Newark Bears farm club but offered such a measly salary that Wilson jumped to the San Diego Padres of the Pacific Coast League. When the Yankees lodged a protest with Commissioner Chandler, Wilson's San Diego contract was voided. Eventually he was sold to the PCL's Oakland franchise, where he became the first African-American to play full-time with the Oaks. There he roomed with future Yankee Billy Martin. Wilson led the Oaks to the 1950 PCL pennant, topping the league in hits and runs.

The next year, Wilson finally got a chance with the team that signed his mentee Mays—the New York Giants. Wilson stuck for only a few big-league games, batting .182 in 22 career at-bats. But he returned to the PCL and became a legend, winning three more batting crowns for Portland and Sacramento. In 2003, Artie Wilson was elected to the PCL Hall of Fame.[31]

At Comiskey Park on the evening of Wednesday, October 2, the weather warmed up—and so did the crowd and the quality of the competition. Urged on by the hometown *Defender*, a huge African-American turnout (perhaps as much as 70 percent of the gate, Feller later estimated[32]) swelled the audience to twenty-two thousand. There were so many walk-up ticket buyers, and so few vendors, that Rapid Robert himself jumped in to man the turnstiles.

Fay Young of the *Defender* was irritated that only a handful of ushers were on the premises. Many of the folks who shelled out two dollars for prime tickets never found their seats, Young complained. More than a few paying customers "sat in the grandstand or went home disgusted." Other enterprising fans got into the park by slipping a buck to a cop; one member of Chicago's finest, Young wrote, "bragged that he cleaned up $150."[33]

Those Chicagoans able to find seats were treated to a fine ballgame. Feller's team won, 6-5. Bob and Satch each pitched three scoreless innings, giving up just one hit apiece. Feller walked two and fanned one; Satch didn't walk anybody and struck out three.

The Paiges' 5-1 lead disappeared when the Fellers rallied for five runs in the eighth, keyed by Jeff Heath's home run. Johnny Sain got the win, even though he was bopped around for five runs. Gentry "Jeff" Jessup took the loss for Satch's team—which "disgusted all the Negro fans," Young wrote, because Jessup pitched for the local American Giants and got strafed.[34]

Early on October 3, Feller made good on his promise to Commissioner Chandler. Some four thousand excited Kentuckians jammed into Versailles's Memorial Field, a yard designed to seat less then one-fourth that number. It's probably not a coincidence that Paige's team was not invited to play in Kentucky. Feller may have been looking to save a few bucks on travel, but it's more likely that Chandler worried that the specter of a black-white contest would stir too much hostility in his segregated hometown.

Chandler hosted a reception for Feller and mates at his home— then applauded when Bobby, who'd played the first seven innings of the game in left field, took the mound to close out a victory over local minor leaguers.

The Flying Tiger then whisked Bobby and his teammates to Cincinnati, long reputed to be among the North's most racist cities. Since most of Feller's travelers were American Leaguers, the *Cincinnati Enquirer* noted the day of the game that many of the white stars had never played at Crosley Field.[35] The paper all but ignored the black team.

A crowd of eleven thousand saw the Feller squad shut out Satch's men, 3-0, to take a four-to-one lead in games played. Bob pitched the first three frames; the only hit he surrendered was a single to center by Satch. Paige pitched two innings, giving up a run in the opener when Rizzuto led off with a single, was sacrificed to second by Johnny Berardino, and came home on Mickey Vernon's single.

An error by second baseman Chico Renfroe of the Monarchs led to another Feller run in the fifth. Dutch Leonard threw five-hit ball over the final six innings while Rufus Lewis, a Newark Eagles righty, nicely acquitted himself, too, allowing only four hits. Each team had only six safeties but the Feller stars made them count.

The two-plane convoy then flew to New York. Satch's and Bob's teams entertained a robust Yankee Stadium crowd of some twenty-two thousand, about half of whom were African-American.[36] Feller's team won 4-2 in the tenth when Frankie Hayes doubled off the venerable Barney Brown. Neither Feller nor Paige pitched that night, preferring to save their Bronx exploits for the big Sunday afternoon matchup two days hence. Instead, Spud Chandler threw the first five innings and left with the score tied at one. Bob Lemon came on in the sixth and turned out to be the hitting hero as well, lining a Brown fastball into the short porch in right field to knot the game at two and allowing Hayes to win the game two innings later. Brown, who had "pitched well throughout," said the *New York Times,* took a tough loss.[37]

PR man Hawkins had done a good job flacking the October 5 game at Newark's Ruppert Stadium, the Yankees' minor-league outpost. All week, Burt peppered the *Star-Ledger* and *Evening News* with releases and little ads. A wild game ensued before a nice crowd of thirteen thousand, with the white team emerging on top, 13-10, but Quincy Trouppe grabbed the glory. No box score has been found, but the *Star-Ledger* reported that Feller pitched the first two innings, allowing two hits and fanning one. The black team was trailing 13-3 when it suddenly stampeded for seven runs in the ninth, three of them coming home on Trouppe's second home run of the game.[38]

On Sunday afternoon, October 6, it was back to Yankee Stadium, where 27,462 fans—reputedly the biggest crowd ever to watch a black squad in Gotham—saw Satch pitch five shutout innings. The *Courier*'s correspondent Haskel Cole led with "The Satchel Paige–Bob Feller show hit Yankee Stadium full blast Sunday afternoon, when the colored all-stars shellacked the American Leaguers, 4-0." Satch's men "jumped blazin' Bob for the winning run in the second frame on Troupe's [*sic*] walk, Easterling's sacrifice, and Benson's single off Keltner's glove."[39]

Feller also threw five innings, giving up four hits and two runs, one of them a monstrous homer to right by left-handed slugger Hank Thompson. Scuffball artist Neck Stanley, who'd pitched against Dizzy Dean's stars in Brooklyn and Paterson in '34, hurled the last four innings, striking out Berardino and Vernon back-to-back with two runners on base in the top of the eighth. Stanley ended the game by fooling Frankie Hayes with a wicked emery ball.

Stanley's subterfuge did not go down well with the white guys. Feller's men were so perturbed by Neck's "cheating" (spitters and scuffers were outlawed in organized baseball but never banned in blackball) that Bob told Satch to dump him from the roster, which Paige promptly did. It was Neck's first and only appearance in the '46 campaign.[40]

Spud Chandler, who came on for Feller in the sixth, was touched for two runs in the eighth. Trouppe opened the inning with a single against Chandler and came around to score on Howard Easterling's massive triple to center. Spud's wild pitch chased Easterling home.[41]

After the final out, the teams raced off to LaGuardia Airport, from where DC-3s flew them to Baltimore. A few hours later, Satch's squad completed a two-city doubleheader sweep by beating Feller's club, 7-4, before a near-capacity—and still segregated—crowd of some five thousand at Bugle Field. Feller, surely exhausted from his earlier per-formance in New York, pitched just one inning. Johnny Sain again struggled, giving up one tally in the third and three more in the fourth. Bob Lemon came on in the sixth and had trouble finding the plate. Buck O'Neil tripled to deep left center, and Sam Jethroe had the black team's only other extra-base hit, a run-scoring double. Gentry Jessup got the win, giving up eight hits in going the distance. Between them, Sain and Lemon gave up six runs, with Lemon taking the loss.[42]

From Baltimore, it was off to Columbus, Ohio, where a good-sized crowd of nine thousand at Red Bird Stadium watched Feller strike out five in three innings, giving up only a single to Hank Thompson. Still, Satch's men won, 4-3.

By this time on the tour, Feller had no shortage of detractors. Jim Ogle, the "Sports Reflections" columnist in the *Newark Star-Ledger*, spoke for many columnists when the caravan reached Jersey. "[W]e think that Rapid Robert is taking a gamble with his valuable right arm. No mat-ter how strong, the human body can only stand so much punishment and there seems to be little sense to the punishment that Bob is deal-ing out to himself. . . . Bob's team is playing two games a day in some spots. . . . What is he trying to do? He can't need money that badly."[43]

Feller met with reporters in New York and answered his critics. "I'm looking out for Feller, physically and otherwise," Bob said. "'I'm not working too hard on this junket. I'm just getting the ball up to the plate. I didn't take too many chances near the end of the season, either, even though I worked so often. Don't worry, I'm not going to hurt this thing,' he emphasized, raising his right elbow."[44]

Old pal Rollickin' Rollie Hemsley also spoke up for Feller, calling Bob "a lot smarter now than he used to be. . . . In addition to his hop-ping fast ball he has developed a fine slider and change of pace."

Hemsley had "considerable praise," United Press reported, for Satchel Paige. "Back in 1929, when I was just a punk breaking in with the Pittsburgh Pirates, Paige showed me plenty of speed," Rollie said. "[Paige is] not so fast now but he still has plenty of speed. He claims to be 38. I'd guess he was closer to 48," Rollie chortled. Paige's actual age was 40.[45]

Paige had his toughest outing of the tour on October 8 in Dayton, giving up six runs on five hits in the first. Four thousand paying customers saw Jeff Heath hit a three-run homer off Satch; Keltner and Hayes also drove in runs in the opening frame. The Monarchs' Lefty LaMarque, who joined the club in midtour, took over for Satch in the fourth and shut down the Fellers until the ninth.

Feller pitched three shutout innings, then watched Spud Chandler get knocked around in the fourth. First Buck O'Neil, then Howard Easterling, banged run-scoring triples. The 6-6 tie was broken in the top of the ninth when King Kong Keller drove in Yankee teammate Rizzuto. Bob Lemon got the last three outs for Feller's squad, which won a thriller, 7-6.

Feller's squad took a quick side trip to Louisville to play a minor-league outfit managed by future Pirates and Braves skipper Billy Herman. Bob's team won, 7-2, but Louisvillians were delighted when a local kid, Mike Gast, outpitched Feller for the first few innings. Gast never made it to the majors.[46]

Richmond, Indiana, a town of forty thousand halfway between Dayton and Indianapolis, somehow attracted the next game. Tucked just outside the Ohio line, Richmond had a "schizophrenic" racial identity, says local historian Doris Ashbrook. The town was founded in the early nineteenth century by southern Quakers, who migrated west to escape the taint of slavery. Early on, the town welcomed freed blacks, several of whom became respected merchants. Richmond evolved into a hotbed of abolitionism and a furtive stop on the Underground Railroad. Remarkably, by the 1880s, the local high school was racially integrated—almost unheard-of in Indiana back then.[47]

But by the second decade of the twentieth century, the Klan's corrosive influence had infected the town. Movie theaters, hotels, and restaurants became Jim Crow and stayed segregated through the World War II years.

The Feller-Paige exhibition was treated as a big event by the local *Palladium-Item*, which ran one article after another the week of the game. The coverage was so extensive it provides us with one of the few detailed vignettes of the '46 tour.

On that momentous Thursday morning, Richmond's mayor and

other notables rolled out the red carpet for the Feller-Paige entourage as the DC-3s taxied to the terminal at Municipal Airport. Since Richmond's ball field didn't have a locker room, organizers arranged for private autos to transport players to the local YMCA. After the game ended, they reversed course and hustled players back to the Y to shower—then got them over to the airport so the white guys could catch their flight to Davenport, Iowa.[48]

Although the paper had predicted a huge turnout, a "disappointing crowd" of 2,280 eastern Indianans and western Ohioans showed up at Municipal Stadium, the home of the Richmond Roses of the Class D Ohio State League. Comic Jackie Price put on a hilarious pregame show, simultaneously pitching two balls to two different catchers and snagging long flies in the outfield while careering in a jeep. Fans were thrilled when players from both teams autographed balls, books, scraps of paper, and anything else.

The next day's *Palladium-Item* ran a big picture of Johnny Berardino in his Browns uniform surrounded by a gaggle of youngsters. At one point during the game a young fan dove for a foul ball on top of the big leaguers' dugout. The youngster corralled the ball but slipped off the edge of the dugout roof, landing "on the back of three players." With the crowd roaring, the players autographed the kid's ball for him before sending him back to his seat.[49]

Municipal Stadium's public address announcer further pleased customers by giving inning-by-inning updates of game four of the Red Sox–Cardinals World Series, a 12-3 St. Louis laugher.[50]

"Old Satch Paige," the paper said, "did not twirl any as he was complaining of a slight cold."[51] Old Satch ended up taking the afternoon off. Nevertheless, Paige took a turn in the batting cage before the game and surprised a reporter by consistently bashing shots into the outfield. With Paige out, his squad was short on hurlers. Satch's old pal Lefty Brown, himself pushing forty, stepped into the breach and pitched creditable ball for six innings, giving up five runs.

Feller pleased the crowd by pitching the first two innings. Weary from throwing the night before in Louisville, Bob got roughed up for eight hits. The Paiges got to Feller for three quick runs in the first and two more in the second. Feller repaired to the Y, where Weisman gave him a rubdown. Bob returned to the dugout in street clothes and "did his share of [bench] jockeying," the paper noted.[52]

Feller's squad chipped away at Barney Brown (misidentified in the *Palladium-Item* the next day as "Willard") and Lefty's successor, the bespectacled Max Manning, tying the score at five in the seventh. A few batters later, Kenny Keltner's sacrifice fly put the Fellers ahead. They won, 7-5. Artie Wilson had three hits in a losing cause. Hank Thompson, saluted by the *Palladium-Item* as having played "some sparkling ball at the keystone sack," had two hits, as did Buck O'Neil and Quincy Trouppe. Feller's old pal Hemsley, never much of a batter, had one hit against Manning, two against Brown, and drove in a run.[53]

The private car caravan drove at breakneck speed to get the white team showered and back to the airport, so they could point the plane toward Davenport. Feller fared better that night before three thousand fellow Iowans. He started the game against the Davenport Cubs of the Three-I League, going four innings, striking out six, and giving up just two hits and no runs. But the highlight of the evening came when native Hawkeye Feller hit one out of the park. As near as can be determined, it was Feller's only round-tripper on the '46 tour.[54]

The next day was more of the same: another two-state doubleheader was slated for Feller's guys; this time, both contests were against minor leaguers. After the Pride of Van Meter was warmly greeted at Des Moines' Western League Park, winning 9-1, he got the news that bad weather had moved into the Twin Cities, canceling that night's game in St. Paul.

Burton Hawkins proudly announced in midtour that Feller's all-stars had attracted nearly 150,000 fans in their first fifteen dates—and had gone 8-4 in their twelve games against the Paige stars. The *Sporting News* trumpeted both facts in its October 16 issue.

On October 12, the interracial troupe pulled another two-city doubleheader, with visits to western Iowa and Kansas. In Council Bluffs, on the eastern bank of the Missouri across from Omaha, the Fellers won, 3-2, before a crowd of 4,100. Frankie Hayes reached first base against Satch early in the game, only to be literally "caught napping." Somehow the rotund catcher known as "Blimp" fell asleep as he took a lead. Satch didn't bother to throw to first baseman Buck O'Neil; Paige just jogged over from the mound and tagged Frankie "out" as the crowd howled.[55]

After a short flight, Feller and Paige discovered a crowd twice that size awaiting them at Satch's 1935 stomping grounds, Lawrence-Dumont Stadium in Wichita. Feller's team again won, 5-3. Bob started and gave up doubles to Hank Thompson and Johnny Davis; Davis's shot soared over Sam Chapman's head in center. It was the only run Bob allowed in his three-inning stint.

Satch threw nothing but goose eggs for three innings but Gentry Jessup gave up three in the top of the fourth. Jim Hegan's single put the Fellers ahead; Keller later homered to cinch the game.[56] In the bottom of the ninth, Johnny Sain ended a threat by striking out two Paige men with runners on base.[57]

The most dramatic contest of the tour took place the next day in Kansas City, but only because the originally scheduled venue, Sportsman's Park in St. Louis, was busy hosting game six of the World Series. Once the Series was extended, Feller and Hawkins scrambled to add a second game to their Kansas City itinerary.

In game one, longtime Monarch Hilton Smith pitched brilliantly in front of 2,800 home folks, but was trailing, 2-0, in the bottom of the ninth when Newark Eagles outfielder Johnny Davis smashed a game-winning three-run homer to left off Spud Chandler. As he paraded around the bases, the muscular Davis grabbed shortstop Phil Rizzuto, playfully slung him over a shoulder, and, to the delight of the crowd, carried little Scooter around third and headed home. "We both slid in at home plate together," big Johnny chuckled a half century later.[58]

It was a wondrous American moment: Fiero Francis Rizzuto, the immigrant kid known in those less sensitive days as "Little Dago," the son of a Brooklyn streetcar conductor, cavorting with a half-black, half–Native American street kid who'd grown up across the East River in an orphanage. The heartland crowd never gave the ballplayers' ancestries a second thought as they stood and cheered.

The affable Davis never made the white majors, but he had big-league talent. Perhaps too many gifts, Monte Irvin told historian James Riley. Had Davis not divided his time among pitching, catching, and playing the outfield, Johnny might have starred in the majors, Irvin believed.[59]

Davis's mixed heritage earned him nicknames like "Cherokee" and "Geronimo" in the Negro Leagues; later, in the Pacific Coast League of the '50s, he was known as "the Big Chief." Abandoned at an early age, Davis grew up in New York's Catholic protectory. Johnny joined one of the best teams in blackball history, the wartime Newark Eagles of Leon Day, Max Manning, Monte Irvin, Larry Doby, and Willie Wells. At the '44 East-West Game, Davis tied Buck Leonard for second in the home run derby, both behind Josh Gibson.

After finishing the Paige-Feller tour in '46, Johnny headed south to pitch in the Puerto Rican League. Remarkably, he went 7-4 with a 2.42 ERA that winter. The closest the Big Chief got to the bigs was in 1952 with the PCL's San Diego Padres. Davis was hitting well that season and being seriously scouted by the Chicago White Sox until he broke his leg. Johnny continued to play on the Coast for another few years.[60]

Feller's team got a measure of revenge the following night before a crowd of nearly six thousand at Muehlebach Field. Bob pitched well in a 4-1 victory.

The next day it was off to Denver for a split-game doubleheader. Bob's white squad first took on an American Legion team at Merchants Field then, in classic Feller fashion, cleared the stands and charged fans a new fee to watch Bob's boys play a squad sponsored by a local jewelry store.[61]

From Denver, the team flew to the West Coast, where Feller had interracial games set up in Los Angeles, San Francisco, San Diego, and Long Beach, plus four additional contests against the Earle Mack–organized squad of Pacific Coast Leaguers. Bob's stars would no longer be playing the "Satchel Paige Negro All-Stars," per se. Instead, to save money, Feller had arranged for Satch to hook back up with Chet Brewer's Kansas City Royals, who were once again wintering in Southern California.

Most of Satch's fellow travelers left the tour in Kansas City. On the Coast, Paige was joined by a Royals lineup that had Monarchs icon Jesse Williams playing short and leading off—then giving way to, among others, veteran Negro Leaguer Bubba Hyde in center, Eddie Stone of the Pittsburgh Crawfords at third, Dave Hoskins of the Homestead Grays in left, and Birmingham Black Baron Ed Steele in right. Pitchers Booker McDaniels and Jim Williams, both of the Monarchs, rounded out a decent but not spectacular club—certainly not the caliber of the players who'd been flying around with Paige and Feller for three weeks.

On Tuesday, October 15, Satchel Paige sat with columnist Dave Lewis of the *Long Beach Independent* for a rare mainstream media interview. Paige bragged to Lewis that he'd gone unbeaten, 21-0, that season in Negro League play, which contradicted other claims he made that his '46 blackball record was 24-2. Satch also told Lewis that he'd pitched sixty-four consecutive innings without being scored upon that summer, a fanciful claim that had little or no basis in fact and couldn't be documented.

Lewis correctly identified Satch's age as forty, which suggests that, contrary to Bill Veeck's folklore, Paige knew how old he was. "Don't let 'em tell you I'm too old to pitch," Satch said, citing his performance in the Monarchs' NAL pennant-clinching victory. "There were 18,000 in the stands [that day] and I just wanted to let 'em know old Satch still had it."[62]

Lewis, naturally, felt obliged to retell Satch's encounter with the snake in Venezuela. "Although [Paige] claims his fastball has lost none of its blinding speed," Lewis opined, "even his most ardent admirers have to admit that Satch hasn't the zip he flashed in his prime, although he still can leave a trail of smoke when he burns it in there." In the old days, maintained Lewis, Paige threw only "two kinds of balls—hard and harder. The batter didn't see 'em. The umpire didn't see. Nobody saw 'em. The catcher felt 'em hit his glove with numbing force."[63]

A noisy and mainly African-American crowd of 22,577 greeted Bob and Satch at Wrigley Field on the evening of October 16. Paige must have numbed catcher Buster Haywood's glove plenty. Satch struck out seven in five innings but not, alas, Cardinals star Stan Musial, who finally latched on to the tour after collecting an anemic $3,757 for dispatching the Red Sox. Stan the Man's Cardinals, fueled by Enos

"Country" Slaughter's mad dash home in the bottom of the eighth inning in game seven, had beaten back Boston the previous day.

Musial went zero for two against Satch and flew out three times in the game overall while coaxing one walk. The other batting champ, Mickey Vernon, also went hitless. Satch fanned Mickey at least once, but gave up the only extra-base hit of the evening to Johnny Berardino, who smacked a Paige fastball over the left-field wall in the first.

Feller yielded three runs, none apparently earned, pitching five-hit ball through five innings. Bob also fanned seven in notching the win, as his all-stars held on, 4-3.

The two stars that night were relievers Bob Lemon and Booker McDaniels, neither of whom allowed a hit over four innings. It was a sloppily played game, with Vernon, Jeff Heath, and Sam Chapman all committing errors.

In the locker room after the game, Musial commiserated with reporters about the Cardinals' paltry winning share in the Series, claiming that "I should have been out here [barnstorming with Feller] the whole time." Stan's words caused a tremor in Commissioner Chandler's office, which issued a quick rebuke. But between Musial's criticism and the success of Feller's tour, major-league owners were shamed into increasing World Series shares the next year.[64]

The "big-top barnstormers," as the *Times* called them, headed down the coast to San Diego, another popular locale for Paige and Feller. They put on a great show before a sold-out crowd of nearly eleven thousand. Each pitched five innings, with Feller shutting down the Royals but striking out only two.

Satch allowed a solo homer to Jeff Heath in the third and was touched for another run in the fourth when World Series hero Musial got his first hit on the junket and was driven home by Kenny Keltner's double. That was all the scoring; the game ended 2-0.[65]

In the years before big-league integration, Stan Musial played only a handful of games against Negro League opponents. But he'd grown up in Donora, a steel town that was as integrated as any in the western Pennsylvania of the early twentieth century. A couple of decades later,

Donora produced Ken Griffey Sr., a multiskilled African-American out-fielder who became an integral part of Cincinnati's Big Red Machine—and the father of one of the greatest players in history.

Like most major-league hitters, Musial had trouble deciphering Paige. Mickey Vernon reminisced in 2007 that hitting Paige required aggressiveness on the one hand, and patience on the other.[66] To get around on Satch, a batter had to commit early yet somehow adjust late, because Paige's Bee Ball had such movement and was so hard to "find." Among renowned left-handed white hitters, Vernon and Char-lie Gehringer—both of whom stood more or less flat-footed in the bat-ter's box—had some luck against Paige. But Musial, Mize, and most other lefties struggled. As he always had, Satch would "read" a lefty's knees—and pitch to his weaknesses.

Feller's troupe traveled thirteen thousand miles in '46 without inci-dent. But as their DC-3 tried to gain altitude after leaving San Diego's airstrip, one of its engines began ominously sputtering. "It scared the bejesus out of my wife and I," recalled Mickey Vernon sixty-one years later. "The two of us turned white. So did most everyone else."[67] Fell-er's pilots did a good job turning around the aircraft and safely landed it back in San Diego.

Bob, always quick-witted, immediately got on the phone and arranged for a bus to take the group up to Los Angeles, impressing Vernon.[68] But his ballplayers and their spouses were shaken by the incident. The next year, apparently responding to popular demand, Feller directed his pilots not to fly over mountain ranges.

Bob's men detoured to Sacramento on the evening of October 21 to play a Pacific Coast League squad managed by northern California's own "Smilin' Stan" Hack, the longtime Cubbie third sacker. Feller was in a hurry that night, because he had to catch a plane to collect his two-thousand-dollar appearance fee from the National Dairymen Association's gathering in Atlantic City. Bob actually started the game a few minutes early so he could get to the airport on time. Hundreds of fans were still filing into the park as the game began.

Feller fanned four in just two innings but gave up two quick runs

in the top of the first, no doubt causing palpitations among his sched-
ulers. Bob's secretaries had commandeered a taxi, which was waiting
outside the clubhouse with its motor idling. With Bob yielding to Sain
and Dutch Leonard, the game ended 4-3 in favor of the big leaguers. Somehow Bob was able to make it to the airport, fly more than
three thousand miles, grip and grin in Atlantic City, grab another
flight west, and rejoin his comrades in California within twenty-four
hours—no mean feat in 1946, never mind today.

It was while Bob hurriedly changed into a business suit in the Sacramento locker room that Steve George, a freelance reporter working for the *Sporting News,* asked Feller those fateful questions about
black players' potential to make the "big-league grade."[69] Perhaps
Bob should have thought through his answer before snarling that
"I haven't seen one—not one" who had the skills to make it in the
majors. Three days before he was scheduled to start another three-
game series against Jackie Robinson, Chet Brewer, and the Royals,
Feller chose to pour salt into the wound one more time.

With Bob and his men otherwise occupied, Brewer's Royals swept
a Wrigley Field doubleheader on October 20 against a ragtag group of
white minor and major leaguers led by first baseman Chuck Stevens of
the St. Louis Browns (career batting average .251). Feller's men, with
Bob now back, traveled down the Coast to play the PCL's Hollywood
Stars in an exhibition at San Bernardino, losing 3-2.[70]

Up and down the California coast on three successive nights, Bob
renewed what had become his heated rivalry with Jackie Robinson.
Jackie's team had been on the midwestern circuit for a couple of
weeks, drawing mediocre gates. At one point, Robinson's club played
a group of white major leaguers captained by the seventy-two-year-
old Honus Wagner, who presumably directed action from the dugout
and not from his old perch at shortstop.

For Feller and Robinson, the desire to make money trumped their
mutual dislike. Before a smallish crowd in San Francisco on the 23rd,
Feller's squad beat Jackie's club, 6-0, permitting only two hits.

The next night the two teams grappled in San Diego, with Feller's
troupe again coming out on top, 4-2. The *Pittsburgh Courier* was on
hand to describe the action. "On Thursday night [in San Diego] Jack-

ie's valiants led the game 2-1 up to two outs in the eighth when Stan Musial singled, Charlie Keller doubled off the right field wall, and both scored on Jeff Heath's single to center."[71]

Another heartbreaker awaited "Jackie's valiants" at the finale the following night at Wrigley Field. "Friday night's game was a thriller and left the fans literally hanging from the rafters," the *Courier* wrote, "when the Robinsons came from behind to score three runs and go down swinging in the ninth with two men on."[72]

Twelve thousand "screaming" fans saw Feller pitch a perfect game for the first five innings, striking out 10 of 15 batters. But it was Robinson's strenuous objections to the ball-and-strike calls of a PCL umpire, not Rapid Robert's performance, that grabbed headlines in the *Sporting News*.

Today, Robinson is justly praised for grace under pressure. But that night in his hometown, still seething over Feller's criticism and perhaps nervous about the presence of Dodger manager Leo Durocher, Jackie took loud exception to several umpiring calls. Halley Hardy, the sports editor of the black *Los Angeles Tribune*, called Robinson's protests "unnecessary and uncalled for," adding, "Jackie has a lot to learn if that is a sample of the way he expects to conduct himself in major league baseball."[73] Robinson, who had kept his anger in check during the '46 International League season, may well have been frustrated that night by his inability to hit Feller. He struck out twice, going zero for three.

The next night, Feller and Paige were scheduled to meet in Long Beach. But Satch didn't show. By then, Paige had prepared his lawsuit against Feller; sources told the *Sporting News* that Feller had bilked Satch of $3,500. But a few days later, when Paige actually filed the suit, it was for less than half that amount. Whatever the explanation for the shortfall it did not deter Paige from going barnstorming with Feller the following year.

In Long Beach, instead of a black squad, Feller's men ended up playing the majors-minors contingent that had played the Royals six days before. A two-run shot by Bob Lemon with Rollie Hemsley aboard in the eighth won the game for the Fellers, 2-1. Feller pitched four innings, giving up a solo homer to journeyman outfielder Jack Graham, then the property of the New York Giants.[74]

According to the *Sporting News*, rainy weather scrubbed scheduled games in Portland and Vancouver. After the Long Beach contest, Bob and his wife, Virginia, flew on to Hawaii for some well-earned R&R—but Bob appeared (at least briefly) in two more exhibitions in Honolulu. The Fellers were joined on their Hawaii excursion by Jackie Price, Charlie Keller, and Stan Musial, cashing in on his newly earned World Series fame.[75] Bob Lemon continued touring on the Coast, tapping several members of the Feller squad.

"Sure I'm tired," Feller told the *Sporting News*. "My arm is in great shape, though. . . . After all, you know, a fellow is only young once, and I'm going to make as much money as I can, while I can."[76]

The biggest barnstorming extravaganza in history had come to an end. Feller's stars played before some 250,000 paying customers in the fall of '46—the vast majority of them attending the interracial contests against Satch. The Feller team's record in black-white contests was 17 wins and 5 losses in what turned out to be nineteen games against the Satchel Paige Negro All-Stars (where Feller's men went 14-5) and 3-0 against the Robinson-Brewer club. With a few games remaining on the tour, Feller's official chronicler, Burton Hawkins, told the *Sporting News* that Bob's club had won 13 of 18 against black opponents—which, in all likelihood, was accurate. Satch's '46 team didn't have the pitching depth to compete with Feller, Lemon, Chandler, Sain, and company.

Feller's '46 tour left a huge legacy—and not just the one in Bob's bank account. By using airplanes, Feller opened major-league baseball's eyes to the possibility of geographic expansion and quicker travel. He also brought big-time baseball to the West Coast. The Feller swing encouraged columnist Vincent X. Flaherty and a bevy of civic officials to begin compiling data about California's suitability for big-league franchises.

But most important, Feller gave sorely needed exposure to blackball and its artisans. In New York, Chicago, and Los Angeles, racially mixed crowds of twenty thousand or more warmly greeted black stars. Fans throughout the heartland braved icy weather to cheer for African-American players as well as white. Major-league scouts were in the stands at many of the '46 games, scribbling notes.

Indeed, seven members of Satch's traveling stars eventually made it to the bigs: Satch, Hank Thompson, Monte Irvin, Willard Brown, Quincy Trouppe, Artie Wilson, and Sammy Jethroe. Several other '46 blackballers, Johnny Davis among them, ended up playing in the high minors.

Feller made upward of seventy-five thousand dollars in profit—a huge payday in 1946 America and a margin that must have driven Ray Doan to distraction. Bob had worked hard on what turned out to be an all-consuming project; he'd earned the dough. Along the way, he made a lot of people happy—and put money in a lot of people's pockets.

For years, Feller told various writers and historians that he kept scorebooks from the '46 tour, along with local press clippings and other contemporaneous materials. But when asked about them in 2007, all Feller did was wink, smile, and hand over a reproduction of the "Bob Feller's All-Stars Souvenir Program."

CHAPTER TWELVE

Bobby and Satch's (Almost) Farewell Tour

Harry Truman's salary raise has earned him new fame.
He's the first President of the United States to rate as big a
pay check as Bob Feller.

—SHIRLEY POVICH, COLUMNIST, *WASHINGTON POST*

In August 1947, as Bob Feller and Satchel Paige were gearing up for a third successive barnstorming tour, the *Afro-American*'s Sam Lacy listed the old-time blackballers who, in the mold of the men who had broken the color barrier that season, Jackie Robinson and Larry Doby, would have been "cinches" to make it in the integrated majors. Among the immortals on Lacy's list were slick-fielding first baseman Ben Taylor, superb center fielder (and later first baseman) Oscar Charleston, agile shortstops Pop Lloyd and Dick Lundy, and a beat-up old pitcher named Leroy Paige.[1] It may never have occurred to Lacy that Satchel, then starting his fifth decade in life, would still have enough left to star in the big leagues—but Ol' Satch did.

Two weeks after Lacy's column appeared, Paige was in Champaign, Illinois, pitching against a local plumbers union team, a typical postwar barnstorming gig for Satch, when he leaked word that, the year before, the New York Yankees had come calling. But the Bombers' contract offer was so feeble that Satch was offended. "I make more than that now," Satch sniffed to the *Sporting News*, "and I don't have to account to nobody."[2]

On September 28, 1947, another guy who didn't like accounting to anyone, Jay Hanna "Dizzy" Dean, made his last appearance on a major-league mound. It came, fittingly enough, at Sportsman's Park, the site of so many of his triumphs. But this time Diz was wearing the drab colors of the St. Louis Browns, not the red-and-blue brilliance of the Cardinals.

It was the last weekend of the regular season. The Brownies were capping off yet another dismal campaign—manager Muddy Ruel's men went 59-95 that year—when Diz the broadcaster hatched a publicity stunt.

Dean's ploy worked. A crowd of some sixteen thousand—one of the Browns' better box office showings all season—turned out to watch Diz, still only thirty-six, heave his first big-league pitches in more than six years. Somehow Dean kept a Rudy York–led White Sox club at bay for four innings. Diz walked only one and gave up just three hits, one of them a mere infield straggler.

In the bottom of the third, Dean was working on a shutout when he waddled to the plate wielding a blue-striped bat. Umpire Cal Hubbard, playing Dizzy's foil, shook his head and ordered Dean back to the bat rack. To the crowd's amusement, Diz defiantly returned with a red-striped model—but somehow this one passed Hubbard's muster. Dean promptly banged a line-drive single to left off Steady Eddie Lopat but strained a thigh muscle as he rounded first.[3]

With his leg smarting, Dean pulled himself out of the game an inning later. Dean's "teammates" included two of Feller's favorite barnstormers, infielder Johnny Berardino and outfielder Jeff Heath. Between them, Heath and Berardino accounted for five hits and both of St. Louis's runs that afternoon. Alas, Browns reliever Glenn Moulder gave up a three-run homer to Chisox third baseman Cass Michaels in the top of the ninth; the Browns ended up losing, 5-2.[4] Berardino and Heath once more packed their bags to go touring; Sox hurler Lopat did the same.

From time to time if the p.c. was right, Diz would still show up at minor-league and sandlot parks in his old Cardinals colors (or, sometimes, in a uniform adorned only with "Dizzy Dean" on the front), chat up spectators, hijack the public address microphone, jaw with batters and umpires, scrape the mud off the rubber, peer in for the sign, kick his left leg high, and throw a few tosses. But he never again tried to compete in a major-league game.

Just as it had the year before, Feller's chronic barnstorming was causing columnists to question his judgment. "Pitching four innings every day—sometimes twice a day—during his barnstorming trip makes Bob Feller penny-wise pound-foolish in our book. He could well be cutting years off his career," the *Los Angeles Times*'s Al Wolf wrote that fall.[5] Wolf wasn't alone: the *Sporting News* and other publications suggested that Feller's "greed" was jeopardizing the Indians' future.

In his first autobiography, *Bob Feller's Strikeout Story*, published that same year, Feller pooh-poohed charges that barnstorming was ruining his arm. It was just the opposite, Feller wrote. By throwing so many innings, Bob claimed to be proudly replicating the workhorse habits of "Iron Man" Joe McGinnity and Cy Young, the turn-of-the-century idols whom columnists of the '40s often cited as evidence that modern pitchers were too soft.

Many years later, Feller enjoyed pointing out that he pitched well in excess of four hundred innings in '46—and nearly as many in '47. Even with all that strain, Iron Man Bob went on to pitch nine more seasons for the Indians. Like Satch, Feller was fortunate to have been given preternatural strength in his right shoulder and elbow. Barnstorming clearly contributed to the fraying of the Dean brothers' arms, but somehow Feller and Paige were immune.

Feller's 1947 production didn't have quite the pizzazz of his 1946 barnstorming tour. There were fewer games against black opponents, fewer games overall, and considerably less press hoopla at the front end, although Bob again retained the services of comic Jackie Price. This time, '47 barnstormer Ralph Kiner recalled six decades later, Price was joined for at least part of the tour by Jackie's protégé Max Patkin.[6] Over the next few decades, Max the Clown would go on to become a beloved and ubiquitous presence on the professional baseball circuit. Patkin achieved such stardom that he earned a cameo appearance in the 1988 film *Bull Durham,* where he got to dance with Susan Sarandon's character. Indians trainer Lefty Weisman again signed on to massage Feller's arm.[7]

Instead of reprising the Satchel Paige Negro All-Stars and having them fly in tandem with his squad, Bob saved money by negotiating with Chet Brewer and his partner, black businessman Marshall Armstrong, to hook up with the Kansas City Royals—but only on the West Coast. Of the twenty-three games planned for Feller's '47 junket, only eight featured black opponents. Most of the time Feller's club would play white major- or minor-league all-star squads cobbled together for the occasion. The most ambitious part of the itinerary would come late in the tour, when Feller, much to the consternation of major-league owners, accepted Mexican League president Jorge Pasquel's invitation to play a series of games in Mexico.

Bob again contracted with Flying Tigers to provide his team with a DC-3. The players being ferried around by Feller's charter weren't quite in the same class as the '46 ensemble; nevertheless, it was a reputable group. Beefy outfielder Kiner, who'd already slugged seventy-four homers in just two seasons with the Pittsburgh Pirates, represented a real coup, as did fellow outfielder Andy Pafko of the Chicago Cubs, coming off a .302 season.

Pafko was indebted to Feller for giving him the opportunity to make some extra money. "Bob treated all of us swell," Andy told the *Chicago Daily Tribune*'s Arch Ward after the tour ended. "[Feller's] a shrewd businessman, too, and he is going to capitalize on his name while he's able."[8] Former Feller roomie Jeff Heath (.251 with 85 RBIs in '47), Willard Brown's adversary in the Browns' dugout, handled another outfield spot.

Infielders included Johnny Berardino (.261 in '47) of the Browns, "Eppie" Miller (.268) of the Reds, Gerry Priddy (.214 that season but a .265 career hitter) of the Senators, Feller's old barnstorming pal Kenny Keltner (.257) of the Indians, and first sacker Ferris "Burrhead" Fain (.291 in his rookie season) of the Philadelphia Athletics. Another Tribesman, '46 tour veteran Jim Hegan (.247), assumed catching duties.

Chisox left-hander Lopat (16-13 with a 2.81 ERA) buttressed Feller on the rubber, as did A's hurlers Phil Marchildon (19-9, 3.22) and Bill McCahan (10-5, 3.32 with a no-hitter to boot), and Cleveland's jack-of-all-trades Bob Lemon (11-4, 3.44 ERA as a pitcher; .321 in 47 games as a hitter). When the caravan hit California, other major leaguers would be added, among them Yankee right-hander Allie Reynolds, the part-Cherokee "Super Chief," who had gone 19-8 that season with a 3.20 ERA.

While being interviewed in 2007, Feller said that crowds in the Deep South would not accept blacks appearing on the same playing field as whites. When it was pointed out that St. Louis, a place that had hosted a well-attended Paige-Feller game in '41, was as Jim Crow as any southern city back then, Feller shrugged and repeated that he and his business advisers believed that interracial games would not work down South.[9] With that in mind, Feller's '46 tour had visited border states but sidestepped markets farther south.

It pained Feller to forgo potential cash, so at the outset of the '47 tour he set up games against white squads in Atlanta, Birmingham, Memphis, New Orleans, Houston, Dallas, and Oklahoma City.[10] In Birmingham, Feller's stars played a team headed by Harry Walker, the feisty Mississippian who two years earlier had inadvertently integrated service ball in the south of France. Detroit Tiger Virgil "Fire" Trucks and St. Louis Cardinal Murray Dickson combined to shut out the Feller stars in Birmingham, 3-0.[11]

Four days later in Dallas, Ralph Kiner crushed a first-inning three-run homer to pace Feller's men to a 5-2 victory over a squad led by former major-league catcher and future manager and front-office executive Paul Richards.[12] Kiner's bat, which had produced fifty-one homers during the regular season, stayed red-hot throughout the tour. After the Dallas game, Feller's gang flew out to the Coast once again to take on Chet Brewer's Royals.

On October 14, the grand Feller-Royals rivalry was resumed in San Diego. A Lene Field crowd of 5,500 in the navy town greeted the Pacific war hero and watched him pitch the middle innings of an 11-3 romp.

Gene Richardson's slop curves and change-ups didn't fool Kiner and company, as Feller's all-stars scorched the lefty for nine runs in the second and third innings. The Royals managed ten hits off a Pacific Coast Leaguer, Feller, and Canadian Phil Marchildon, but scored only three times. It doesn't appear that Satch pitched that evening.[13]

At least one other white major-league all-star team was plying the Coast that October. A group headed by Ewell "the Whip" Blackwell, the Cincinnati Reds' six-foot-six sidearmer who'd led both leagues in wins that season with 22, worked the California circuit against the Royals and other teams—albeit without the formal structure of the California Winter League, which had disbanded.

"The beanpole slinger," as the *Los Angeles Times*'s Al Wolf called Blackwell, had grown up in nearby San Dimas. Earlier that season, the beanpole had nearly duplicated the feat of Johnny "Double No-Hit" Vander Meer by pitching a no-hitter immediately followed by a one-hitter. Angelenos couldn't wait to see the local kid take on the Royals, especially since fellow beanpole Satchel Paige was slated to be Blackwell's opponent.

Paige and Blackwell's Wrigley Field money match on October 23, 1947, bracketed by another Paige-Ewell contest the following weekend, was the brainchild of Long Beach–based promoter Bill Feistner, a sometime-rival, sometime-ally of Joe Pirrone's. Feistner that fall had phased out the CWL in favor of a series of big-name exhibitions. Bill left his imprint all over Southern California that autumn, doing the organizing for Brewer, Blackwell, and Feller. Sixteen years after Satch first started coming to L.A., Paige could still pack them in like no one else.

Feistner helped Blackwell assemble a solid squad of major leaguers, many of whom were native Californians. Third baseman Bob Dillinger (.294 in '47) of Glendale and the St. Louis Browns, outfielder Peanuts Lowrey (.281) of Culver City and the Cubs, outfielder George "Catfish" Metkovich (.254) of Angel's Camp and the Indians, outfielder Zeke Zarilla (.224 in '47 but a .276 career hitter) of L.A. and the Browns, catcher Roy Partee (.231) of L.A. and the Red Sox, and second baseman Johnny Berardino (.261) of L.A. and the Browns (moonlighting from the Feller tour), all backed up Blackwell in the two-gamer against the Royals. Feistner also coaxed Yankees outfielder and World Series hero Johnny Lindell (.275 that season but a glittering 9-for-18 with 7 RBIs against the Dodgers the previous week) into coming out to the Coast. The Phillies' Jesse Flores (4-13 but a 3.39 ERA), who happened to be of light-skinned Mexican ancestry, was available out of the bullpen.

Brewer and Armstrong ensured that the '47 Royals would be stocked with quality players. Perennial Monarchs barnstormer Jesse Williams, back to playing shortstop since Jackie Robinson had moved on to the Dodgers, led off. Jesse's teammates, catcher Joe "Pig" Greene, who'd been scouted but not signed by the Yankees, and lefty change-up artist Gene Richardson, also starred on the '47 edition of the Royals.[14]

The Royals boasted four members of the 1947 Negro American League champion Birmingham Black Barons: outfielder Ed Steele; pitchers "Jo" Williams and Jimmy Newberry; and infielder extraordinaire Lorenzo "Piper" Davis. Like the Indianapolis Clowns and the Harlem Globetrotters, the Black Barons were controlled by Abe Saperstein, whose hands and wallet were all over black sports back then.

Davis, who'd grown up in Piper, Alabama (hence the moniker), was the consummate Negro Leaguer—born five years too soon. Lithe and quick, he was so accomplished at basketball that he played four years for Saperstein's 'Trotters. When Davis manned second for the Black Barons, he and shortstop Artie Wilson formed one of the deadliest double-play combinations in baseball history. In '48 and '49, Piper managed the Black Barons; he was Willie Mays's first professional boss.

In 1950, Davis became the first black player signed by Tom Yawkey's Boston Red Sox. But Piper never advanced in Yawkey's organization and ended up, as so many aging black stars did back then, playing on the West Coast, where racial attitudes were somewhat more relaxed. Throughout the '50s, Piper was a perennial all-star for the Pacific Coast League's Oakland Oaks and Los Angeles Angels.[15]

Another renowned Globetrotter played for the '47 Royals on the Coast. Reece "Goose" Tatum, a gangly Arkansan credited with inventing basketball's hook shot, was the team's first sacker. Goose scooped errant throws with the same alacrity he used in his dribbling routines, which became one of the 'Trotters' signature acts. While warming up before baseball games, Tatum loved to show off by catching fly balls behind his back.

By '47, Goose was a year-round Saperstein minion, working for

Abe's Clowns in the summertime and barnstorming with the 'Trotters the rest of the time. Tatum's two hits in the '47 East-West Classic caught the attention of major-league scouts, but Goose demurred, preferring to stay a two-sport barnstormer. He became a beloved 'Trotter and an unofficial American diplomat, entertaining millions of people and generating much goodwill around the world.[16]

It took Goose, Piper, Pig, Satch, and company thirteen innings to put away the Blackwell All-Stars, 4-3, on October 23. Tatum had struggled all night, failing to get a ball out of the infield, when he came to the plate in the bottom of the thirteenth with the score 3-2 in favor of the Blackwells. Ed Steele was at third and Piper Davis at second when Goose poked a curveball from the Phillies' Flores into center. Both runners scored, making a winner of Jimmy Newberry, who went on to star in both Japan and the Manitoba-Dakota League.[17]

Blackwell, who didn't fare any better that night than he did two years before, pitching against black service teams in the south of France, walked four, gave up three hits, and yielded two runs in four innings. Satch, on the other hand, was up to his usual California tricks, shutting out the white squad over four innings, whiffing nine, and allowing just two singles. Satch also drove in the Royals' second run with a second-inning single off one of the Whip's shooters. Jesse Williams was the only member of the Royals with two hits, although seven other Brewer men had safeties. Ed Steele's thirteenth-inning double set the stage for Tatum's heroics.

A decent Sunday afternoon crowd of nearly 7,500 showed up at Wrigley to watch the Paige-Blackwell rematch. Ewell's submarine ball again had trouble finding the plate. Blackwell walked three and yielded four hits but limited the Royals to two runs over five innings. Nevertheless, the Royals snatched another win, 3-2. Zeke Zarilla thrilled his L.A. pals by hitting a two-run fourth-inning homer off Paige. Satch, who struck out five and gave up two hits, departed the game in the bottom of the fourth, trailing 2-1.[18]

Promoter Feistner must have been short a pitcher, because Johnny Lindell took over for Blackwell in the sixth. Lindell, who closed out his career as a hurler for the Pittsburgh Pirates and Philadelphia Phillies (going 6-17 in '53), pitched all right, giving up three hits and walking two. But an error by first baseman Catfish Metkovich triggered a Royals rally in the ninth. Outfielder Bob Abernathy drove in the winning run.[19]

Alhambra's own Ralph Kiner rocked the ball on the Coast, as he did throughout the '47 tour. Kiner is a genial soul, quick with a smile and a story to match—as any fan of "Kiner's Korner," the long-running interview program that Ralph hosted as a New York Mets broadcaster, can attest. When asked his impressions of black players on the '47 tour, Kiner, at age eighty-five, said, "Well, we thought they were good players, for sure, but better entertainers. Goose Tatum we really enjoyed watching. We didn't think they [black players] were of our quality. But we were proved wrong."

Satchel Paige could really put on a show in infield practice, Kiner remembered, marveling all those years later at Satch's athletic gifts. "We took the games pretty seriously," Kiner said. "And so did the colored players."[20]

Nevertheless, Kiner doesn't recall ever discussing with tour teammates the societal inequities facing blacks. "We just didn't think or talk that way back then," he said, a bit apologetically. Nor does Ralph remember anything "derogatory"—his word—being said about black players, but added: "We underestimated the impact that blacks would have on the game. Everyone knew that Josh Gibson and Oscar Charleston had been good enough to play in the majors. But most of us thought the guys we were playing against weren't all that good. We were wrong."[21]

Feller, Kiner, and the rest had two mid-October clashes set with the Royals, both on the familiar turf of Wrigley Field; a third was added in early November. On October 15, Feller's squad was slated to face the Brooklyn Dodgers' Dan Bankhead, Sammy's younger brother (career big-league record 9-5), who hadn't pitched in the just-concluded Dodgers-Yankees World Series but had been used as a pinch-runner. There was a mix-up between promoter Feistner and Bankhead over up-front money and travel arrangements, so Bankhead never left his home in Memphis.

Fortunately for Feistner, the Million Dollar Stringbean happened to be in Southern California, rested and ready. How much Satch squeezed out of Feistner will never be known but this much is certain: under the circumstances, Paige would not have come cheap. "When I saw all those folks out in the stands, I decided I'd better pitch," Satch wrote in *Maybe I'll Pitch Forever*. "You don't make about fifteen thousand mad when you want them to come out the next time."[22] Wrigley fans that night must have been thrilled to see Paige on the mound.

Bobby and his old nemesis went right to work. Each pitched four innings. Paige seemed quicker than Feller that night, the *Times* said, striking out seven and giving up just two hits and one walk. Feller gave up four hits and one walk, but struck out only two. Still, "the Cleveland fireballer had it in the clutches," the *Times* noted the next day. "Displaying his speed and slider which gave him 20 victories this season, Feller took complete command when threatened. . . . Feller didn't appear at all tired and his stuff had plenty of zip."[23]

Paige's stuff had plenty of zip, too, but he ended up with the loss when Keltner singled in the fourth and later scored on Jeff Heath's sacrifice fly. Jo Williams came on in the fifth and pitched well, giving up just one more run in the Fellers' 2-1 victory.

Kiner was overpowered by Paige in his first two at-bats, but he made up for it by slashing a double off Williams in the top of the seventh that "nicked the left field bricks," the *Times* reported. Heath then drove in his second run of the game with a solid single, scoring Kiner.[24]

The barnstormers headed north to chase more money in the Bay Area. It doesn't appear that Paige pitched either in Oakland, where the Royals lost to the Fellers, 6-1, or in San Francisco, where Brewer's men went down, 7-2. Before 6,500 in Oakland, Feller hurled four scoreless innings and fanned five. The next night across the bay, Feller pitched four more scoreless innings and whiffed seven. Kiner cracked yet another three-run homer in San Francisco.[25]

Game five of the Royals-Feller series took place at Wrigley on Sunday afternoon, October 19. A mainly African-American crowd of 12,000-plus watched Bob and Satch go five innings each. Again, Paige outpitched Feller and again, the white team won a hard-fought 2-1 victory.

Paige fanned Ralph Kiner twice and kayoed six other batters over five innings. Satch allowed only three hits—singles to Andy Pafko and Gerry Priddy and a double to Jim Hegan—and didn't walk anybody. Satch departed leading, 1-0.

Feller gave up a run in the second when Goose Tatum drove in Bill Hoskins. But that was it for the Royals. Bob, too, gave up just three hits.

McCahan pitched well in relief of Feller, yielding only one hit and two walks over the final four innings. Williams also threw well for the Royals, but gave up solo homers to Pafko in the sixth and Priddy in the seventh—all the runs that Feller's men needed. Hoskins and Tatum each stole second in a losing cause.[26]

But Paige's masterful pitching was the real story. Over nine innings in two games against Feller's squad, Satch had struck out fifteen, giving up a solitary run on just five hits. "You never heard such talk," Satch recalled in his autobiography. "All those writers out on the Coast couldn't believe I wasn't in the majors, the way I was showing. I couldn't understand it, either."[27]

For the next few days, Feller arranged for his stars to make some quick cash in Bakersfield and Ventura by playing against "merchants" squads, which turned out to be a hodgepodge of local minor leaguers and sandlotters sprinkled with a few of Bob's big leaguers. Feller's "team" won in Bakersfield, 8-6, and in Ventura, 3-0, where Bob and Steady Eddie Lopat combined for the shutout.[28]

As the gang was making its way to the airport to head off to Mexico City, Bob suddenly got word that the two Mexican squads he planned to play had abruptly disbanded. Feller immediately called Ken Parker, the Pacific Coast League promoter who'd been supplying fill-ins for Bob's team all week. It cost Feller a small fortune, but out of his own pocket he flew a batch of PCL players to Mexico City. The Mexico games went off without a hitch.

Jorge Pasquel's franchises may have been foundering, but that didn't stop the Mexican League strongman from "lavishly"[29] entertaining his guests. Kiner, still a bachelor, had no trouble 59 years later remembering the wine, women, and song in Mexico City.[30] The first four games were contested in spacious Mexican League Park; the final three were played in smaller venues in Tampico, Torreón, and Guadalajara.

For the second year running, Feller's plane experienced engine trouble. Unlike the previous episode, when the airborne plane had to turn around, this time the problem occurred on the ground. After a considerable delay, it was fixed, but several of Feller's barnstormers left the tour early, worried that the DC-3 wasn't reliable.[31]

Feller and Paige combined for one last payday in California in the fall of '47 before calling it quits. Many of Bob's troupers had gone home after the Mexico trip, but by tapping major leaguers wintering on the Coast, Feller was able to field a decent team. Center fielder Peanuts Lowrey (.281 in '47) of Culver City and the Cubs and second baseman Eddie Bockman (.258) of Santa Ana and the Indians were among the big leaguers pressed into duty, along with two veterans of the '46 majors-minors squad: first sacker Chuck Stevens (a .251 career hitter), a former—and, oddly, future—Brownie, and journeyman outfielder Jack Graham (a .231 career batsman), an ex-Giant and Dodger.

While Bob's men played in Mexico, Chet Brewer had kept his Royals busily engaged in California. Brewer's entire roster, sans Goose, who had left to join the Globetrotters, was available for the Feller finale.

Feistner and his two headliners knew how to hype a gate. Almost twelve years to the day after Satch's much-ballyhooed Halloween shootout with Dizzy Dean, the L.A. papers ran banner advertisements urging fans to witness the Feller vs. Paige "Finish Duel."[32]

Each of the "perennial winter league enemies," as the *Times* called Feller and Paige on November 2, pledged go at least seven innings in the Sunday afternoon matchup "in an effort to settle the question of who is the best twirler." Were it up to Feller, the *Times* averred, "it will be a nine-inning personal duel."[33] Just to add a little spice to the pregame smack, Feller publicly questioned whether Paige could still go the full nine innings.[34]

If Satch took any offense from Feller's comment, he didn't share it with the press. Nevertheless, it wasn't lost on Paige that the white majors had signed a number of Negro Leaguer hurlers—such as Dan Bankhead—whose skills weren't anywhere close to Satchel's, even though Paige had celebrated his forty-first birthday.[35] "All I had to do was go nine, I kept thinking," Satch remembered. "By the time the game came up, I'd really worked myself up over it. I drove out to the ballpark and smoked about five cigarettes just getting there."[36] With major-league scouts in attendance, Satch knew he had a stage and wanted to seize it.

Seize it he did: A majority-black crowd of more than nine thousand cheered as Paige put on a bravura performance. "The ageless Paige fanned 15 men and allowed only four hits and was never in danger of having a run scored against him," the *Times* reported the next day. "If he wasn't striking the opposition out, his mates were backing him up in great style, something that Feller didn't have to aid him."[37]

Bob's patchwork infield betrayed him in the third and again in the fourth. Errors by Stevens and Bockman led to three unearned runs. "At other times," wrote the *Times*, "balls went for hits that might just as easily have been fielded."[38]

But the blows walloped by Piper Davis and Joe Greene couldn't be fielded by anyone; they went for solo homers. Brewer's men recorded eleven hits in eight innings against Feller, including a double by second baseman Ray Neil. Jesse Williams and Ed Steele each had two hits and an RBI. The final score was 8-0.

Only three Feller men got hits off Paige: Lemon, Priddy, and Bob Sturgeon. Shortstop Sturgeon, who'd lost three years to navy duty, would play in only thirty-four more big-league games.

Sturgeon was typical of the batters Satch dominated that day. Still, the complete-game four-hitter must have caught the attention of scouts—as did Satch's other marvelous work in California that fall. In his matchups against Feller and Blackwell, Paige pitched seventeen innings, giving up just one earned run and fanning no fewer than thirty batsmen. Satch struck out Kiner and Berardino three times and got Pafko, Lemon, Lowrey, and Metkovich twice.[39]

Paige's dominance certainly grabbed the fancy of *Herald-Examiner* columnist Vincent X. Flaherty. "The eternal Satchel Paige shuffled out there on Wrigley Field the other night and gave the customers a pretty fair sample of the stuff that makes him one of the most remarkable figures in baseball history," Flaherty wrote a couple of days after the game. Having watched Satchel pitch for many years on the Coast, Flaherty was something of a connoisseur.

"[Paige] pitched to 'em like he owned 'em. Never was poor old Satch better than he was the other night. The fast ball that supposedly deserted him and bequeathed him to the old gentlemen's home, was cracking across the plate," Flaherty quipped. "[Paige] pulls the string on his pitches and give 'em the soft stuff. But he is forevermore giving 'em something they don't expect."[40] The columnist couldn't understand why a big-league club hadn't signed the man now known as the Methuselah of the Mound.

After pitching one last time at Wrigley in November 1947 against a collection of white minor leaguers, Satch split for the Caribbean winter leagues. The November 2, 1947, game in Los Angeles marked the last time Feller and Paige would face one another in a barnstorming showdown. As Feller told the *Sporting News* in the fall of '47, major-league integration had taken the novelty from interracial barnstorming. On occasion as the years went by—if the cash on the barrelhead was big enough—Feller and Paige could be coaxed into showing up and pitching a few innings, as they did in Tijuana, Mexico, in the fall of '49. But the glory days of baseball's two fastest pitchers matching fireball for fireball in barnstorming duels were over.

A few hours after the November 2 Feller-Paige game ended, Wrigley Field's night watchman attempted to get in on the action. Apparently under the impression that Wrigley's vault still contained more than fifteen thousand dollars in receipts (it didn't; Feller had already divvied up the dough), the watchman jimmied open the door-sized safe. When he discovered only a pittance of cash, the dejected guard tied himself up and waited for the sun to rise. That morning he told police that masked gunmen toting submachine guns had gotten the jump on him. The cops didn't buy his story; the guard was arrested on "suspicion of burglary."[41]

As Wrigley's watchman learned to his dismay, barnstorming tours were no longer big moneymakers. Instead of the huge margins generated by the '46 tour, Feller's '47 tour barely scraped by. Some accounts suggest that Feller actually went into the red in '47 to the tune of about five thousand dollars.[42] Having to fly a bunch of Pacific Coast Leaguers from L.A. to Mexico City dented Bob's balance sheet.

Bob told the press that fall that unless major-league baseball relaxed its rules to allow barnstorming during the World Series, post-season junketeering wasn't worth it. "Late Start Dooms Tours—Feller," headlined the *Sporting News* in December.[43] The following year, Feller didn't have time to go barnstorming. He was busily engaged in the World Series against the Boston Braves along with his new teammate Satchel Paige, now holding court in the bullpen.

Satch Becomes a Rookie

Baseball opened doors for me. When I felt low and disgusted it gave me a lift. . . . Because of this great National game, I have lived a life comparable to the wealthiest man in the United States.

—NEGRO LEAGUES CATCHER QUINCY TROUPPE

Bob and Virginia Feller were often presented in popular magazines as the ideal American couple. Photo spreads would show Bob and his vivacious wife aboard their motorboat, or admiring Bob's plane, or marveling at some contraption in their ultramodern home outside Cleveland—a handsome suburban pair enjoying the fruits of America's postwar affluence.

It was a mirage. Just as the young Feller was not the perfect American boy, the marriage of Bob and Virginia Feller wasn't exactly idyllic. Virginia had battled drug addiction since the 1947 birth of their second son. A botched blood transfusion led to a dependence on painkillers. She couldn't shake the addiction, despite multiple trips to the Mayo Clinic, extended stays in treatment centers, and myriad "cures" prescribed by friends and loved ones.

Substance abuse back then was considered a character weakness, not a disabling disease. Watching his wife get hooked on pills must have mystified a young-man-in-a-hurry like Bob. He'd been raised on the verities of hard work and self-discipline. Virginia's challenge could be overcome, Bob surely thought, if she would just put her mind to it. He'd watched old pals like Rollie Hemsley kick the bottle—but somehow his own wife seemed to lack the resolve to stop taking drugs.

Virginia's substance abuse darkened Feller's life. A few years after watching his dad die an agonizing death, Feller had to deal with the effect of his wife's addiction on their three young boys. To complicate matters, Feller was business partners with Virginia's father; they had joint investments, plus her dad helped organize Bob's commercial enterprise, Ro-Fel, Inc., and served as one of its officers.

As Virginia's problems mounted, so did Bob's bills. He estimated that he spent hundreds of thousands of dollars on pills and treatments that didn't work. "It all went down the drain," he bitterly recalled in his 1990 autobiography.[1]

Feller hired a live-in nanny to look after the boys and take care of the house. Eventually Virginia's condition got so bad that when Bob left their home to go on road or business trips, he would hide the pills. "I called home every few days to tell her where she would find her next doses," Feller wrote. "It was a real-life version of that scene in *Lost Weekend* when Ray Milland finds the bottle of liquor that had been hidden from him in the chandelier."[2]

Bob stayed with Virginia for nearly a quarter century after she developed her addiction, waiting for his sons to grow up before obtaining a divorce. Virginia's issues eviscerated his savings, causing him severe financial problems after his playing days ended in 1956. He piled up so many debts that, eventually, he had no choice but to sell his house and hit the road, making ends meet by reprising his barnstorming act.

No wonder the latter-day Feller could be so prickly. It wasn't easy being Bob Feller. Despite the big paydays and glittering photo ops, he had never had anything close to a "normal" life. Adults wanting to cash in on his incandescent talent—from Ray Doan to Cy Slapnicka—denied him his adolescence. War and his father's terminal illness disrupted his twenties. Finally, his wife's substance abuse impinged on what should have been the happy time of fatherhood in his thirties, forties, and fifties.

One of the greatest pitchers in history was, in retirement, reduced to flying off to one small town after another to pick up a few hundred bucks hurling an inning or two against a bush-league squad or members of the local meatcutters' union. In that sense, Feller was like Paige: until his legs gave out, he never really stopped barnstorming.

Dizzy Dean would have done the same, but Diz's bum arm and big belly wouldn't let him.

In 1948 Cleveland Indians owner Bill Veeck thought that signing Satchel Paige would make both baseball and financial sense. Although Veeck later admitted that he'd been eyeing Paige all through '46 and '47—and discussing with Abe Saperstein the prospect of procuring Satch—it took until mid-1948 before Veeck finally made it happen. Paige had even sent Veeck a telegram in '47 asking for a tryout. Barnum Bill later explained that he didn't sign Satch in '47 because the Indians were having a mediocre year and he didn't want to "waste" Paige's brilliance—which sounds like convenient 20-20 hindsight.

No matter: when Veeck called Saperstein in July 1948, the Indians were in a four-way pennant chase with the Athletics, Red Sox, and Yankees. The Tribe needed to buoy its bullpen and strengthen its staff. The story goes that Veeck quietly approached Bob Feller and asked if Satch still had it. "He had it the last time I saw him," Feller said, referring to the November '47 game in Los Angeles. "I think he could help us a lot."[3] Saperstein told Veeck that he could get Satch cheap, as long as Paige's agent—Saperstein—got a finder's fee. By some accounts, Abe pocketed fifteen thousand dollars for delivering Satch to the Indians; others say ten thousand. Either way, Saperstein was well compensated. When Abe's letter arrived, Satch and his wife, Lahoma, jumped up and down with joy.

Veeck set up a tryout at Municipal Stadium without divulging the name of the pitching prospect to shortstop-manager Lou Boudreau. It was the morning of July 6, 1948—coincidentally, a day before Satch's forty-second birthday. Boudreau, already in uniform, did a double take when he saw Satch, Veeck, and Saperstein sitting in the dugout. He thought the playful Veeck was trying to pull a fast one.

Once Lou gained his bearings, he asked Paige, "Can you still throw like you used to?"

"I got as fast a ball as anybody pitchin' now, but I got to admit it's not half as fast as it used to be," Satch answered, at least according to his autobiography. "But I can still pitch it where I want to."[4]

It was suggested that Satch run a little to get loosened up. Paige began jogging but sheepishly quit after about seventy-five yards. "You know, Mister Lou," as Paige always called Boudreau, "this is an awful big ballpark. I guess I just won't run after all."[5]

Boudreau grabbed a catcher's mitt, squatted behind the plate, and urged Satch to pour it on. "That's some control," Boudreau said after Paige threw about fifty pitches. "You didn't miss the strike zone more than four times."[6]

Lou, still flirting with .400 on his way to a .355 average that season, picked up a bat and took a few cuts against Paige. The eventual 1948 American League Most Valuable Player had trouble getting the ball out of the infield. Veeck and Saperstein had hobbled into the outfield grass to shag Boudreau's hits—but there were no hits to track down. "Don't let him get away, Will," Boudreau whispered to Veeck. "We could use him."[7]

Veeck signed Paige the next day to a ten-thousand-dollar contract for the remainder of the '48 season. As they shook hands, Veeck said, "Satch, I'm just sorry you didn't come up in your prime. You'd have been one of the greatest right-handers baseball has ever known if you had."[8] Veeck had realized the dream he envisioned fourteen years earlier sitting in the stands at L.A.'s Wrigley Field—bringing Satchel Paige to the big leagues. By joining Larry Doby in Cleveland's clubhouse, Paige was now one of just four African Americans in the majors—and the only black pitcher in the American League.

When stunned reporters that evening asked how he'd fare in the majors, Satch offered a vintage Paigeism: "The plate's the same size."[9]

Led by the *News*'s Ed McAuley, Cleveland columnists were a tad skeptical but largely favorable—and so were Tom Meany and Jimmy Cannon. Meany, who contributed to the controversial left-wing magazine *PM*, admitted he'd never heard of Jackie Robinson before the Dodgers inked him. But with Paige, "it's different. The Satchmo has been a pitching legend for a long time."[10]

The Spinks of St. Louis, predictably, had a harsher take. The *Sporting News* mavens didn't try to conceal their contempt. This time, Veeck the Showman had gone too far. "To sign a hurler at Paige's age is to demean the standards of baseball in the big circuits. Further complicating the situation is the suspicion that if Satchel were white, he would not have drawn a second thought from Veeck," hissed J. G. Taylor Spink.[11]

For decades Paige had been cruelly denied the opportunity to pitch in the big leagues because of his skin color. Now he was taking a substantial pay cut to play in the majors and being accused of manipulating his racial identity.

But Satch had the last laugh. Years later, when Paige was read Spink's diatribe, he ribbed, "I demeaned the big circuits considerable that year. I won six and lost one."

In an open letter to Spink, the *Courier*'s Ric Roberts called Veeck's gesture "beautiful," then trilled: "Give Paige his hour of triumph; let the thronging thousands see him in the plush-lined, gold-plated backdrop of the majors."[12]

The '48 Indians weren't exactly gold-plated, but when Satch learned that his Monarchs bosses, J. L. Wilkinson and Tom Baird, hadn't gotten any recompense for his signing, he asked Veeck to remedy the situation. Barnum Bill managed to come up with five thousand dollars, which Wilkie and Baird apparently split. It was five thousand more than the Monarchs duo ever got from Branch Rickey and the Dodgers for Jackie Robinson. Effa Manley, the owner of the Newark Eagles, maintained that the white majors "stole" her players. Rickey and others raided the Negro Leagues with impunity and never paid a dime to club owners.

Veeck conceded to various journalists over the years that he was amazed by the massive numbers of fans that Satch lured. On July 9, Satch became the first black pitcher in American League history when he relieved his barnstorming rival Bob Lemon in the fifth inning of a game against the St. Louis Browns, trailing 4-1. Satch later claimed that thirty-five thousand fans stood in roaring tribute for a good ten minutes, but that's an exaggeration. It is true, however, that a mass of photographers was awaiting his arrival, their flashbulbs popping as Paige strode to the hill. "Pitch loose like you always do," Boudreau advised as he handed Satch the ball before returning to shortstop.

Oddly, the first two batters Satch faced, Chuck Stevens and Gerry Priddy, were both veterans of the California off-season circuit. At least they'd seen Satch and had some inkling as to what was coming. Stevens singled and Priddy sacrificed him to second—but that's as far as the Browns went. It took Satch just five more pitches to record the last two outs of the inning, including a called strikeout. Satch shut down the Brownies before coming out in the eighth to another big roar.

Paige displayed the full repertoire in his debut, including multiple windups and the Hesitation. "With a carload of different pitches," wrote the Cleveland *Plain Dealer*, "[Satchel] showed how it's done in as grand a coming-out party as any ball player ever had."[13]

That party was tame compared to what was to come.

It took the American League two quick weeks to nullify Satch's secret weapon. A few days after he joined the Indians, Paige again wheeled out his corkscrew-windup-punctuated-by-the-dramatic-pause move against the Dodgers in a midseason exhibition, whiffing the likes of Gil Hodges, Erv Palica, and Tom Brown. AL president Will Harridge arbitrarily ruled that the Hesitation gave Satch an unfair advantage, even though it appeared to be within the rules of the game. Harridge instructed his umps not to give Satch any leeway. But even without it, Satch pitched well, appearing in relief eight times in July and going 1-1 with a tiny ERA.

When Boudreau said he would start Satch in an early August game against the Senators, fans stampeded the Municipal Stadium box office. Seventy-two thousand people showed up that night to be part of history, overwhelming ticket sellers and concessionaires. That night Veeck's vendors ran out of just about everything except baseballs.

Satch, understandably, came out skittish, walking two batters in the top of the first before giving up a bases-clearing triple to Ed Stewart. Quickly it was 2-0, Washington. "Don't worry none," Satch assured Boudreau in the Indians dugout. "That ol' control ain't gonna be missing anymore. You just leave me in there."[14]

Boudreau followed instructions; Satch rewarded him with an excellent outing, pitching into the seventh and giving up only one more run. When the Indians rallied, Satch won his first big-league start. He'd also pitched the Tribe into first place that night.

Much of the familiar Satch mythology was spawned during his three months with the Indians in '48. Paige drove Boudreau and Cleveland general manager Hank Greenberg crazy by showing up late—or not showing up at all. If his arthritic toe started barking, Satch said he knew it was going to rain and he wouldn't bother to come to the park.

One afternoon in New York, Paige was late getting to the Grand Central Terminal and missed the Indians' train to Boston. But a sympathetic porter told Satch that he'd seen Feller miss the train, too, so Paige breathed a little easier as he caught a flight to Beantown. Unbenownst to Satch (or any teammate), Bob had taken an express train to New Haven, Connecticut, and jumped onto the Indians' train there; Feller's sleuthing had gone undetected. When Paige greeted the team as it arrived in the lobby of the Kenmore Hotel, he was shocked to discover Feller. As an irked Boudreau slapped Satch with a hundred-dollar fine, Paige protested that Feller had also missed the train. Boudreau informed Satch that Feller had been sitting right next to him as they pulled into South Station and demanded the hundred bucks.

"Satch could never figure that one out," Feller wrote in 1991. "He looked at me out of the corner of his eye the rest of the time he played for the Indians."[15]

Paige suffered from a nervous stomach. During games, Cleveland trainer Lefty Weisman would slip Paige some bicarbonate of soda. One night, Weisman called in sick, so there was nobody to quell Satch's distress. Paige called time-out and repaired to the dugout; catcher Jim Hegan signaled for someone to grab the trainer's medicine kit. Bob Lemon started fumbling through Weisman's bag.

"What does Lefty usually give you, Satch?" Lemon inquired.

"Somethin' white," Satch replied.

Lemon tossed a white pill into a cup of water; Satch drank the fizzing potion down, "emitting a burp," Arch Ward of the *Chicago Daily Tribune* later wrote, which "could be heard in the 14th row."[16] Nobody was exactly sure what "medication" Lemon had plucked out of the bag. But Hegan, Boudreau, and others were convinced that Satch was a raging hypochondriac.

Paige was used to pitching every day, so it frustrated him to be idle between mound appearances. Satch started sneaking into the locker room to grab naps. One afternoon at Sportsman's Park, he was surprised to be jostled awake by old barnstorming buddy Dizzy Dean.

"What's the matter, boy, you tired from overwork?" Satch recalled Diz asking.

"Diz, I'm tired from underwork. This is the first time in twenty years I've gone four or five days without pitching."[17]

Paige's somnolent days didn't last long; Boudreau used him with greater regularity as the pennant race heated up.

Satch's next start came on familiar turf—Comiskey Park in Chicago, where the Lean One had starred in so many East-West games. But Paige had never seen Comiskey like this. More than fifty-one thousand fans—the Chisox's first sellout in three years and their biggest nighttime crowd ever—crammed themselves into the South Side park. Another fifteen thousand people were turned away. Joe Louis was among the African-American luminaries honoring Paige in a pregame ceremony that night.

Paige lit up Comiskey, throwing a nine-inning shutout at the White Sox and winning 5-0. But it wasn't a cakewalk; until the top of the ninth, Satch's lead was only 2-0. In only his second start in the big leagues, Paige had thrown a complete game goose egg. "No single player," exulted Cleveland's African-American *Call and Post,* "has been able to pack 'em in as has Paige."

But not even as enthusiastic a cheerleader as the *Call and Post* could have predicted what would happen next. On August 20, Satch again got a start at Cleveland's Municipal Stadium. Nearly seventy-nine thousand people showed up, crowding its aisles, jumping up and down in its seats, and drinking every drop of its beer.

That night was Satch reincarnate. Facing a Chicago club that, though in last place, was still led by Luke Appling, a future Hall of Famer, Satch again flummoxed the Chisox, shutting them out on just three hits. Tribe fans went crazy—none more so than the club's owner.

As soon as Paige dispatched the last Chicago hitter in the top of the ninth, Veeck was on the line to Western Union, dictating a telegram to J. G. Taylor Spink: "Paige pitching—no runs, three hits. Definitely in line for the *Sporting News*'s Rookie of the Year award. Regards, Bill Veeck."[18]

All told, some 210,000 fans paid to see Satch pitch in his first three major-league starts. To be sure, a good portion of all three crowds was

African-American, but tens of thousands of white fans turned out to see how the living legend would hold up against big leaguers. Satch pitched a total of 72-plus innings in '48, striking out forty-five batters. It wasn't quite the dominance of his palmy days in L.A.—but what other forty-two-year-old "rookie" could have pulled it off?

"You know, we didn't win by any six games," Veeck later told the Chicago Urban League in remarks quoted by Fay Young. "If any one of these six victories turned in by Paige had been a defeat, we wouldn't have played in the World Series, we wouldn't have been American League champions."[19]

Satch cracked another barrier that summer and fall. Paige became a favorite in the Cleveland clubhouse, pulling pranks and practical jokes; he could give a hotfoot with the best of them. The easygoing Satch experienced little of the hostility that the more uptight Larry Doby had encountered the year before. Satch shot craps with Kenny Keltner and flipped dimes with Gene Bearden and the other guys in the bullpen. He could also take a joke, laughing when Feller gave him an "ice cream sandwich" with a bar of soap in the middle.

Doby worried that Paige's loud clothes and flashy lifestyle would embarrass other black major leaguers. Larry wasn't shy about lecturing Paige to curb his penchant for fooling around. "Supposedly I roomed with Satch," Larry chuckled years later, "but I roomed with his luggage."[20]

Veeck and Doby both recalled that a variety of women would show up to claim the game ticket that Satch liked to leave for "Mrs. Paige." Satch brushed off Doby's apprehensions, calling him an "old lady." Courtesy of Veeck, Paige was able to skip the team bus and drive to road games in a rented Cadillac. Boudreau and Greenberg were annoyed, especially when Paige puttered behind the bus, then dramatically passed it while blinking his lights and blaring his horn.[21]

Satch appeared in twenty-one games down the stretch and was a huge reason why the Indians held off both the Red Sox (by one slim game) and the Yankees. He won six games, saved another, and held opponents to a 2.48 ERA.

J. G. Taylor Spink actually wrote a sort of mea culpa that fall as Cleveland won its first pennant in twenty-eight years, the longest drought of any team in the American League. Ironically, Feller and Paige, the great barnstorming pair, experienced frustration in the '48 Fall Classic.

The Indians won a riveting six-game Series over the Boston Braves, who were led by Warren Spahn and Johnny Sain (of "pray for rain" fame) without significant contributions from the two fireballers. Feller, in fact, was charged with both of the Tribe's defeats. In the Series opener, he lost a 1-0 heartbreaker to barnstorming pal Sain when the second-base umpire incorrectly ruled that the Braves' Phil Masi had eluded Feller's pickoff throw to shortstop Boudreau. In game five, Feller failed to survive the seventh inning, getting pounded for eight hits in an eventual 11-5 loss.

Satch, too, appeared in game five—but only for two-thirds of an inning and only after the score was lopsided. Still, Paige was the only Cleveland pitcher that day not roughed up for a run.

Paige was, however, roughed up by the umpires. Arbiter George Barr, Ray Doan's old business partner, was familiar with Satch's peculiarities from the '35 tour. Before Satch even threw a pitch, Barr warned Paige not to wet his fingertips, lest Satch throw an illegal spitter. A lot of Negro Leaguers threw spitters and scuffers—but not Satch, at least not usually.

A few pitches later, umpire Bill Grieve piled on, calling Satch for a balk because Grieve didn't like the way Satch waggled his fingers while stretching with a runner on first.[22] Despite the umps' deliberate, and quite likely malicious, effort to make Paige's life uncomfortable, Satch retired the Braves without further damage. Another color barrier had been broken: Satch became the first African-American to pitch in a World Series.

The next afternoon, black-white barnstorming vet Bob Lemon, with relief help from Gene Bearden, pinned down the clincher, 4-3. It was Cleveland's first Series championship since 1920 and the last the team has won to date.

Even though Satch had been with the club for less than half the season, his teammates voted him a full World Series share.

A few weeks after the '48 season ended, Cleveland baseball writers held their annual "Ribs and Roast" banquet. Since the city was still giddy over the Indians' Series triumph, the place was packed. Through various skits and speeches, reporters poked gentle fun at Veeck, Green-berg, and Boudreau, all of whom were in the audience.

But the scribes saved their best spoof for someone who wasn't there: Satchel Paige. They dressed one of their own in an oversized Indians uniform and floppy clown shoes (that old joke!); then black-ened "Satchel's" face Al Jolson–style, making sure to keep the area around the eyes bright white to reinforce the stereotype. In the onstage sketch, "Satchel" keeps asking a fellow journalist imperson-ating Veeck, "How much money do Ah get?" When "Veeck" ignores him, "Paige" complains in an exaggerated dialect, "Ah guess money ain't impo'tant 'round here."[23] The Paige-Veeck routine was such a big hit it was pictured in that week's issue of *Sporting News*. One won-ders how Cleveland writers would have treated Satch had he gone 1-6 down the stretch, instead of the other way around.

Once the Series ended, Van Meter held its traditional homecoming for Feller. But the weather was so nasty that "only" fifteen hundred people (still four times the size of the town's population) showed up. Earlier that year, Feller had been forced to testify in Ray Doan's lawsuit for allegedly violating his 1945 barnstorming contract. A federal judge dismissed Doan's claims in June 1948; Doan threatened to appeal, but nothing came of it beyond more aggravating publicity.

Satch, of course, was back on the barnstorming trail right away. The white headliner opposite Satch was Indians rookie left-hander Bearden, a knuckleballing Arkansan who'd been untouchable that season, winning twenty games and leading the American League with a 2.43 ERA. Affable Gene was from Lexa, a Mississippi River town across the state from Dizzy Dean's birthplace, Lucas.

"Everybody was rooting for Gene to make it," recalled Feller.[24] Bearden had been severely wounded in July 1943 when his light cruiser, the USS *Helena*, was torpedoed off the Solomon Islands. Gene's knuckler completely buffaloed the Braves during the postseason. Bearden pitched ten and two-thirds innings without allowing a run, winning the third game of the Series, 2-0.

Satch and Gene had a playful friendship; they genuinely enjoyed each other's company. At one point late in the '48 season, the *Chicago Daily Tribune*'s Arch Ward reported that the two were "barbering" in

the Cleveland dugout. "Paige was recalling barnstorm games of yester-
year and telling how he pitched to some of the former major league
stars. 'Just what kind of a pitch,' asked Bearden, 'was Connie Mack's
weakness?'"[25] Satch went way back—but not to the 1890s.

Handsome Gene's stature as World Series hero and the AL's rookie
of the year gave him cachet for the California winter circuit—especially when partnered with Bob Lemon, another twenty-game winner
for the champs.[26]

On October 24, 1948, Satch was honored at another "Satchel Paige
Night" at L.A.'s Wrigley Field—sixteen years after the first one. Naturally, Paige showed up late. But the majority-black crowd of nearly
fourteen thousand shrieked as Satch was showered with presents from
local merchants, including a couple of thousand-dollar gift certificates. Playing with his old pals from the Royals, Paige then blanked
Bearden's team for three innings, striking out four and shutting down
such familiar barnstormers as Johnny Berardino and Zeke Zarilla. A
Royals lineup that included Jesse Williams at short and the forty-four-
year-old Cool Papa Bell in center had its way with Bearden, bruising
him for seven hits and three runs in five innings.[27] The Royals won,
4-3, as Bell and Williams each scored.

On Halloween night a week later, Jackie Robinson surprised Angelenos—and perhaps Satch, too—by joining Lemon and Bearden's
squad against Paige and the Royals. With black America's most revered
athlete now ironically playing for the white squad, interracial ball had
come full circle. Perhaps wanting to give young Jackie a glimpse of the
glory days, in the second inning Satch and Cool Papa pulled off one
last bit of homage to Rube Foster and blackball.

With Lemon on the mound and Bell dancing off first, Satch pushed
a bunt to the left side. As the third baseman scooped up the ball and
threw across the diamond to retire Satch, Cool Papa rounded second
and never hesitated while bolting toward third. Catcher Roy Partee,
then of the St. Louis Browns, suddenly realized that third was uncov-
ered and began lumbering up the baseline. Partee had taken the bait:
by the time pitcher Lemon realized that home plate, too, was now
unguarded, Cool Papa was already peeling around third. Even in his
fifth decade, Bell had enough left to outrace Partee and Lemon as they
scrambled to cover home. Bell scored easily. He had two hits that day
in the Royals' 8-4 defeat.[28]

Satch and Gene hit the interracial circuit together quite a bit over the next couple of off-seasons. In '49 they worked the Texas loop, which until then had always been considered off-limits for black-white ball. Satch could also be counted on to make blackball appearances, either as a solo artist or in concert with Chet Brewer's Royals, who still played the West Coast most falls.

In late October 1949, Feller did a brief valedictory swing through California, apparently at the behest of Abe Saperstein.[29] Abe had arranged for Feller's new teammate, slugger Luke Easter, to head a black all-star team that planned to hit the West Coast circuit. Saperstein's problem was that there was no white major league outfit for Easter's group to play: Bob Lemon's troupe was already paired up with Brewer's Royals.

So Abe persuaded Feller at the last minute to come west with a pedestrian squad that included Bob's old running mate Jack Salveson and twenty-four-year-old infielder and future manager Gene Mauch (career batting average .239), then the property of the Cubs. "Lucious Luke's" black lineup included the Bankhead brothers, Dan and Sammy, as well as Cool Papa Bell—but not Paige, who was busy touring the Southwest that fall with Bearden.

Feller's eleventh-hour gambit annoyed Lemon, the *Sporting News* reported, because it further depleted an already thin market. Sure enough, Vincent X. Flaherty of the *Los Angeles Examiner* noted, neither squad that October "created any gate panics" in Southern California.[30]

"Barnstorming's glory days were over," Feller admitted that week to Paul Zimmerman of the *Los Angeles Times*. "This fall exhibition business used to be quite a deal. But the way things have been going this time the players are just getting a nice trip out of it and that's all.[31] To drum up interest at Wrigley Field, Feller and Saperstein had Easter compete in a heavily hyped pregame home run contest against Ralph Kiner and Gus "Ozark Ike" Zernial, then of the White Sox. Still, the gate was disappointing.

Abe coaxed Satch out to Tijuana in early November 1949 for a black-white matchup that had the feel of the old days. Lemon and Feller also made the trip to Mexico to meet up with their compadre.

It was one of Feller and Paige's last West Coast appearances together. Sadly, no box score or game account has survived.

In October 1951, Bearden and Paige went barnstorming again, this time in a tour that took them from Ontario and the upper Midwest down through Missouri and Texas. In Benton Harbor, Michigan, the home of the House of David, Paige once more hurled against the bearded team that he had faced dozens of times over the years. No doubt he regaled Bearden with stories of pitching *with* the House of David and *against* the Monarchs in the *Denver Post* tourney seventeen years before. In Ballwin, Missouri, just outside St. Louis, Gene and Satch found themselves on the same diamond with veterans of the All-American Girls Professional Baseball League.[32]

Until old age and emphysema caught up to him, Satch never really stopped barnstorming.

At a couple of points as the years went by, Bob Feller and Jackie Robinson came close to burying the hatchet. In July 1962, as Feller arrived at the Cooperstown airport to be inducted into the Hall of Fame in the same ceremony as Robinson, Jackie was waiting for him. He gave Bob a ride into the village. Feller appreciated the gesture and told Jackie he was honored that they were going into the Hall together. Jackie reciprocated.

But as baseball and society continued to struggle over racial equality, the proud-to-be-politically-incorrect Feller would make provocative statements, which would, in turn, extract a response from Jackie, which would elicit another salvo from Bob—and pretty soon they'd be warring again. Feller could never get past Robinson's obstinacy in California in '45 and '46, repeatedly calling Jackie "bush league"— about the harshest invective one player can use against another. Robinson, in turn, would accuse Feller of having his "head in the sand" on racial issues. As the years went on, the controversy sparked more unflattering press coverage for Feller.

Instead of being saluted for easing the game's integration, Feller was labeled a racist in certain circles. But Feller was far from bigoted. To be sure, he could be stubborn and bullheaded. Maybe he and Robinson couldn't get along because they were so much alike. Sadly, they were still quarreling when Robinson died of diabetes at fifty-three.[33]

Paige's adult life was almost as tempestuous as his childhood. His 1934 marriage to Janet Howard never really took; after the wild wedding reception at Gus Greenlee's Crawford Grille, it was all downhill. They didn't officially divorce until the early '40s, although they hadn't lived together as husband and wife for several years. They had no children.

Paige returned from the Caribbean in the late '30s with Lucy, a woman he introduced as his "wife"—although he was still technically wed to Janet. He apparently did marry her in Puerto Rico in the winter of 1940–41, which means Satch was, in effect, a bigamist for a year or two, but he was never prosecuted. His marriage to Lucy, too, soon ended in divorce. She suffered from a debilitating mental illness; many years later she committed suicide in Puerto Rico.

During the war, Paige was browsing in a Kansas City drugstore when he spotted a beautiful young woman working behind the counter. Lahoma Brown was a tough-as-nails twenty-one-year-old single mother, originally from Oklahoma. She seemed to bring out the best in Paige. After their wedding a few years later, she got him to settle down—at least at times, although it doesn't appear that Paige ever stuck to the vow of fidelity. She made him buy a home in a nice Kansas City neighborhood, become a regular churchgoer, put away some money, and appreciate the joys of children. Together, they had seven kids and many grandchildren, all of whom Satch doted on.

Not unlike Colonel Tom Parker and Elvis Presley in the same era, Bill Veeck and Satchel Paige became one of the great promoter-entertainer combinations in American popular culture. Usually abetted by Abe Saperstein, Barnum Bill and Satch broke barriers, tweaked noses, and kicked up a few rhubarbs—but still laughed all the way to the bank.

After Veeck was forced to sell the Indians in the wake of his 1949 divorce settlement, the Tribe's new ownership, tired of Satchel's antics, dumped Paige. It took Veeck a couple of years to accumulate the capital necessary to buy another club. The only franchise available in the early '50s was the pathetic St. Louis Browns. Quipped sportswriter

John Lardner: "Many critics were surprised to learn that the Browns could be bought because they didn't know that the Browns had ever been owned."[34]

Again, Veeck called Satch. Paige spent most of the 1951–1953 seasons with a club that never climbed more than a few games out of the American League's cellar. Satch was the Browns' only black player; given St. Louis's edgy racial climate, he was reasonably well received. Veeck, by his own admission, erred in hiring Rogers Hornsby to manage the '52 Browns. The Rajah still treated Satch with the same disdain he had shown sixteen years earlier on the barnstorming trail through Iowa and Colorado. Before an exhibition game in San Antonio, Hornsby fined Satch for showing up late to the park, ignoring Satch's explanation that no cab in the segregated city would pick up a black man.

Whenever Paige started at Sportsman's Park, the Browns doubled their usual attendance. Considering the lackluster quality of his teammates, Satch pitched well, compiling an ERA of 3.07 in '52 and 3.53 in '53. In '52, he became the first African-American pitcher selected for the All-Star Game; a year later, he did it again. But his employment pattern also repeated itself. After the '53 season, Veeck sold the club to businessmen who moved it to Baltimore, where it became the Orioles. Satch was again told his services were no longer needed.

In the mid-1950s, Veeck became a trusted adviser to the owners of the Miami Marlins of the International League, the Philadelphia Phillies' AAA team. When Veeck urged the Marlins manager, Don Osborn, to sign Paige, the skipper balked, convinced that Ol' Satch was over the hill. At Paige's tryout, Veeck told Osborn to trot out his nine best hitters; Veeck would give the manager ten bucks for every hit his men got. A few minutes later, Osborn's wallet was empty and Paige had signed on as a Marlin. As was his wont, Satch inked a percentage of the gate—which turned out to be a smart move.

On August 7, 1956, the largest crowd in minor-league baseball history—more than fifty-seven thousand people—paid to see fifty-year-old Paige defeat the Columbus, Ohio, AAA team at the Orange Bowl. The old dog learned a new trick that summer: Osborn, a onetime minor league pitcher, taught Paige the proper mechanics of a curveball. Armed with a new weapon, Satch proceeded to dominate IL hitters in '56, finishing with eleven wins and an ERA of 1.86. But Paige still missed curfews and team buses with so often that it angered the Marlins' front office.[35] After Paige's box office appeal wore off, they parted company. Satch went back to the barnstorming circuit (he kept touring well into his sixties) and even did a turn for a minor-league club in Portland, Oregon.

In 1965, as a PR ploy, owner Charlie Finley of the Kansas City Athletics signed the fifty-nine-year-old Satch, providing him with his own oversized rocking chair for the bullpen. Remarkably, Satch pitched three shutout innings against the Red Sox, giving up only one hit, a single by Hall of Famer Carl Yastrzemski.

Three years later, the Atlanta Braves signed Satch as a pitching coach, allowing him to put in another 158 days as a major leaguer so he could qualify for a $250-a-month pension. The Braves, then new to Atlanta, hoped that the specter of Satch sitting in the bullpen might attract some fans into the ballpark. Things had come full circle: Paige, denied the chance to pitch in the big leagues for all those years, was now being used as a marketing lure in a formerly Jim Crow city. Just to let Satch know there were no hard feelings, *Time*'s article on the Braves' move referred to him as "old Satchelfoots"[36]—three decades after the same publication called him "long, dark Leroy."

In 1981, ABC produced *Don't Look Back,* a made-for-television movie ostensibly about Satch's life. It was supposed to be directed by feisty actor George C. Scott—a blackball buff who'd long been smitten with Satch. But within days Scott quit over artistic differences with the network's production team.[37] Starring Lou Gossett Jr. in the title role, the movie is predictably dull but not, as these things go, awful. The few scenes devoted to interracial barnstorming get the facts so bollixed up they're difficult to follow—although "Charlie Gehringer" is shown lacing a double against Satch, which, heaven knows, actually did happen a few times. Paige went to his grave muttering about Gehringer.

Satch wasn't the only one enamored of Hollywood. Early in their marriage, Dizzy and Pat Dean loved visiting Tinsel Town and palling around with Joe E. Brown and other movie stars. In 1952, Twentieth Century-Fox fulfilled one of Dizzy Dean's dreams by putting out *The Pride of St. Louis,* which purported to be the story of Dizzy's rags-to-riches life. Dan Dailey played Diz, Joanne Dru played Pat, and squeaky-voiced Richard Crenna, in his big-screen debut, played Paul.

In classic Hollywood—and Dean family—fashion, the movie played fast and loose with the facts. Diz's passion for barnstorming is short-shrifted in the film. But the money was good so Diz didn't squawk. "Jeez," he said, "they're gonna give me 50,000 smackers just fer livin'!"

Paul at first didn't like the idea of a movie being made about their lives. "You ought to be proud," Diz scolded his brother, "that they want to make a picture story about a couple of sockwads like me and you." His share of the film rights allowed Paul to buy a nice spread in North Texas.[38]

A couple of days into shooting, Dan Dailey suffered a nervous collapse; production was shut down for a few weeks so he could recover. "He's only been me for two days," Diz cracked, "and already he's nuts!"

Lord knows they tried over the decades, but major-league owners could never quite smother barnstorming. Ironically, the very issues that they'd staunchly resisted for so long—racial integration, geographic expansion, higher salaries, and wider broadcasting—killed barnstorming for them. Better roads and more advanced radio and television broadcasting rendered rural areas less isolated and brought big-time baseball closer to fans.

In '46, there were some 17,000 television sets in the United States. Three years later, Americans were buying more than 250,000 sets *a month*.[39] When commercial networks began broadcasting the World Series and the "game of the week" (later featuring Dizzy Dean behind the mic), it became less of a thrill for small-town folks to see major-league players at the local yard. The *Sporting News* took note of this trend in the fall of '51 when it ran a story headlined "Series TV Blamed as Barnstormers Lose Gate Appeal."[40] The popularity of the Caribbean winter leagues also contributed to the demise of off-season ball on the West Coast.

African-American fans, moreover, now wanted to watch black players who had made it in the bigs, not those still toiling in the remnants of the Negro Leagues. Bob Feller himself attributed barnstorming's decline to big-league integration. Black-versus-white games, Feller said in '51, "produced such hard-fought contests."[41] Now that blacks were in the majors, the competitive edge was missing from barnstorming and with it, Feller believed, interracial barnstorming's commercial appeal.

The most successful barnstorming tours in the '50s were those headed by black big leaguers Jackie Robinson, Willie Mays, and Roy Campanella. Often featuring pals such as Monte Irvin, Don Newcombe, and Luke Easter, the Robinson-Mays-Campanella tours targeted black audiences north and south.

Since white players began making somewhat better money in the '50s and '60s, they didn't rely as much on off-season cash. Still, some white stars continued barnstorming, with mediocre results. Following his record-breaking season in 1961, slugger Roger Maris stumped the Carolinas, but crowds proved disappointing. Among the last big-time barnstorming ventures was Willie Mays's junket in '62; again, attendance was sporadic, even with the Say-Hey Kid coming off a World Series appearance.[42]

Once barnstorming declined, "something colorful and picaresque" disappeared from the American scene, Robert Cole has written.[43] Black-white exhibitions, especially, had an edgy, almost forbidden quality— a little like sneaking off to an all-night jazz club on the wrong side of the tracks.

Interracial games were one of the few events of the pre–World War II era that brought together blacks and whites—albeit briefly. How many heartland Americans in the '30s and '40s would have seen gifted African-American ballplayers were it not for black-white barnstorming?

In 1953, as Paige was winding down his stint with the Browns, Richard Donovan of *Collier's* magazine published a three-part series about him. Donovan's journalism contained the usual Paige hyperbole, but it was far better researched and more sensitive than earlier caricatures in the *Saturday Evening Post* or *Life*. "[Satchel's] face mystifies many fans who peer at it to discover the secrets of time," Donovan observed.

> Head on, it seems to belong to a cheerful man about thirty. From another angle, it looks melancholy and old, as though Paige had walked too long in a world made up exclusively of pickpockets.

From a third angle, it seems a frontispiece for the great book of experience, with expressions of wisdom, restrained violence, cunning and easy humor crossing it in slow succession.

After Donovan filed his piece about the man with the cunning face, the writer realized that his notebook had plenty of leftover material—especially the little bon mots that Satch was fond of saying or that had been attributed to him by friends and teammates. Some of the aphorisms Satch had actually uttered; others Donovan cobbled together from different sources.

At the last second *Collier's* added a sidebar called "Paige's Rules for Staying Young." They weren't really Satchel's "rules," per se, and Paige had never organized them as such. No matter: they became such a big hit they eclipsed Donovan's narrative. Over time, Satchel's sayings became part of the American language; to this day, they form the most enduring part of his legacy.

1. Avoid fried meats, which angry up the blood.
2. If your stomach disputes you, lie down and pacify it with cool thoughts.
3. Keep the juices flowing by jangling around gently as you move.
4. Go very light on the vices, such as carrying on in society—the social ramble ain't restful.
5. Avoid running at all times.
6. And don't look back. Something might be gaining on you.

Paige was so overwhelmed by the public's reaction that he had his "rules" printed on business cards, which he proudly handed out in airports and train stations. Like everything about Satch's life, his adages are part real and part fable, part school of hard knocks and part whimsy. It's a shame Paige couldn't have found a way to trademark "don't look back," because it's been so widely used and abused. It's become the phrase that people instantly associate with him.

But Donovan missed a couple of Satch's truly inspired sayings. The first riffed off the jokes about Paige's age. Television host Johnny Carson loved to quote it. "How old would you be [although Carson usually said 'be's'] if you didn't know how old you actually was?" The other is pure existential Satch: "No man can avoid being born aver-age—but ain't no man got to be common." Of all of his adages, this last one is the most profound and defiant: it comes closest to captur-ing the essence of Satchel's spirit.

Dizzy Dean was elected to the Baseball Hall of Fame in 1953, thir-teen years after he last won a game in the big leagues. In his accep-tance speech, Diz got big laughs by once again playing the lovable lunkhead, the character that Will Rogers couldn't get enough of. "The good Lord was good to me," Diz jibed that day in Cooperstown. "He gave me a strong body, a good right arm, and a weak mind."[44]

Perhaps more than any figure in baseball, Ted Williams was respon-sible for getting Negro Leaguers into the Hall of Fame. As the Splendid Splinter was being enshrined in Cooperstown thirteen years after Diz, he surprised his audience by evoking the memory of the black players he'd first seen as a San Diego teenager.

"The other day Willie Mays hit his 522nd home run," Williams said from the podium. "He has gone past me, and he's pushing, and I say to him, 'go get 'em, Willie.' Baseball gives every American boy a chance to excel. Not just to be as good as anybody else but to be better. This is the nature of man and the name of the game. I hope someday Satchel Paige and Josh Gibson will be voted into the Hall of Fame as symbols of the great Negro players who are not here only because they weren't given the chance."[45]

Bob Feller, too, began calling on the Hall to correct the histori-cal injustice; other influential figures, among them columnists Jim Murray and Arthur Daley, joined the chorus. They were buttressed by the 1970 publication of *Only the Ball Was White*, Bob Peterson's book that triggered renewed interest in the glory days of blackball. Com-missioner Bowie Kuhn and a special Baseball Writers Association of America (BBWAA) committee determined in '71 that Negro Leaguers would indeed be admitted to the Hall—but that their plaques would be located in a separate wing of the museum, apart from the white legends of the game.

The hue and cry against Cooperstown's myopia was immediate. Critics seized on the irony of the Hall and BBWAA perpetuating the

very evil—"separate but equal"—that they were supposed to be eradi-
cating. Satch made it clear that he was honored to get into the Hall
under any circumstances but preferred to go in through the front
door—not the entrance reserved for tradesmen of color. "The only
change," Satch mused in one of his better lines, "is that baseball has
turned Paige from a second-class citizen to a second-class immortal."[46]
Officials finally came to their senses and eliminated the separate wing.

On August 9, 1971, Satch was officially inducted. "I am the proudest man on the earth today," Satch said. He got laughs when he joked,
"They'd make fun about my not running, about being slow to get out
to the mound, but I never rushed myself. I knew that they couldn't
start play until I got out there."[47] The Negro Leagues boasted many
"Satches and Joshes," Paige told the crowd that day.

One of the old-timers in that same Hall of Fame class of '71 was
Rube Marquard, the deadball era southpaw. A half century earlier, Marquard had been fined by his irate boss, Charles Ebbets of the Brooklyn Dodgers, for having had the temerity to pitch against a blackball
team. It was unclear in 1920 whether Ebbets was angry at Rube for
violating a team rule—or for getting cuffed around by Atlantic City's
Bacharach Giants.

Later in life Hilton Lee Smith bristled when people hailed him as
"Satchel's Relief" or "Satchel's Caddie." Being stuck in Paige's shadow
all those years had cost him recognition and money, Smith believed.
"Next morning [after a game]," Hilton once confided, "I'd read in the
paper that 'Satchel and the Monarchs Win Again,'" with nary a reference to Smith.[48]

In the 1960s, Hilton Smith and Satchel Paige happened to settle
in the same Kansas City neighborhood. As the years went by, though,
they rarely saw each other. A decade after Satchel was enshrined in
the Hall of Fame, Smith contracted terminal cancer and, with his time
dwindling, became obsessed with attaining the same honor.[49]

Smith's best friend in baseball, Buck O'Neil, promised his ailing pal
that he would do everything in his power to help Hilton gain admission to Cooperstown. That day came in 2001—eighteen years after the
man whose curveball was known as El Diablo passed away.

The plaques of Hilton Smith, Willard Brown, Mule Suttles, Turkey Stearnes, Oscar Charleston, Cool Papa Bell, and other esteemed black barnstormers now hang near Satchel's in Cooperstown.

One of the last times that Satchel Paige met Bob Feller on a pitching mound was July 8, 1973, in Tulsa, Oklahoma. Thirty-seven years had passed since Bobby, then seventeen, and Satch, then thirty, first dueled.

That summer Satch had been serving as a part-time pitching coach for the AAA Tulsa Oilers of the American Association. The team owners had been egging Paige to coax a few extra fans into Oiler Park. Satch, then sixty-seven, consented to an old-timers' game. The excited Oilers extended invitations to Feller, then fifty-four; Cool Papa Bell, a spry seventy; native Oklahoman Allie Reynolds, then fifty-eight; and in a truly inspired gesture, the Dean brothers. Dizzy couldn't make it to Tulsa but Paul, a few weeks shy of his sixtieth birthday, drove up from his Texas ranch. Satch's black "all-stars" were scheduled to play a three-inning exhibition against Feller's white "all-stars" before a Sunday evening Tulsa-Evansville twinight doubleheader.

Old Oiler Park is located some six miles from the site of the 1921 Tulsa race riot.[50] To pay their respects to Satch and Cool Papa, hundreds of African Americans walked through the turnstiles that night. They were the children and grandchildren of people who, during the Klan's rampage a half century before, had been denied treatment at the city's hospitals. Since the park's Jim Crow restrictions had been lifted some years earlier, black Tulsans sat amid descendants of Klansmen.

The second-biggest crowd of the season, more than four thousand people of both races, howled as Bell and other old-timers got caught in one pickle after another on the basepaths, eluding the tag until collapsing from exhaustion.[51] While on the mound, Satch took it easy in the hot Tulsa sun—but so did Feller, Reynolds, and Dean, according to the *Tulsa World*. Paul took a bow and lobbed a few pitches. It had been forty years since the Dean boys and Satch first barnstormed together. The teams Paul played for didn't often beat Satch's—but this one did that night. The "Fellers" beat the "Paiges," 3-0.

The day of the game, the *World* highlighted one of Dizzy's classic quotes about Paige: "My fastball looked like a change of pace alongside that li'l pistol-bullet Satch shoots up to the plate."[52]

Satchel Paige died nine years, almost to the day, after the Tulsa exhibition. The last few years weren't easy; he suffered from emphysema. All those hundreds of thousands of miles swallowing grimy highway air contributed to his illness, he believed.

The *Washington Post* eulogized Satch by invoking one of his inimitable sayings. "I never threw an illegal pitch. The trouble is, once in a while I toss one that ain't never been seen by this generation."[53] Satch was fond of telling people, "I ain't never had a job; I just always played baseball."

Dizzy died in 1974 from a massive coronary suffered while at a golf tournament in Nevada. *Newsweek* paid tribute to him by exhuming one of his oldies-but-goodies from the '30s: "Anybody who's ever had the privilege of seein' me play ball knows that I am the greatest pitcher in the world. And them that ain't been fortunate enough to have a gander at Ol' Diz in action can just look at the records."[54] By his sixties, Diz was seriously overweight, nearing three hundred pounds. During a round of golf in the '50s, President Eisenhower asked Diz why he'd let himself get so heavy. "Well, it's like this, Mr. President," Dean said, noting that he couldn't afford to eat much in his first twenty years of life. "Now that I'm makin' some money, I'm makin' sure that I eat enough to make up for the lean years."[55]

Thirteen years after Dizzy died, blackball legend Piper Davis, who as a kid saw Dean pitch in the '31 Dixie series, offered a heartfelt testimonial. "When Diz was good, he was as good as Satchel," Piper told baseball historian Allen Barra in 1987. "I'll say something else for [Dean's] memory too—he was respectful of the Negro Leaguers, and I guess that came from his relationship with Satch. You never heard black players call Diz 'a cracker.' If all the guys in white folks' ball been like Diz, we'd all have been better off."[56]

Bob Feller had a healthy appetite for fattening his bank account, which explains why he barnstormed against blacks with such regularity. When Feller is asked today about interracial barnstorming, he steers the conversation to dollars and cents; he's clearly uncomfortable appraising the societal import of black-white exhibitions in the '30s and '40s. As columnist Jim Murray put it after Paige's death, Feller was an "unlikely emancipator. No one is going to suggest [Feller] for inclusion on Mt. Rushmore. But his contribution to the game, whether due to his own ego or greed, is a lot more considerable than his 266 victories."

Like Dizzy Dean, Feller always went out of his way to salute Paige's brilliance. "When [Feller] let Satchel prove it," Murray wrote, "[Bob] did as much as anyone to break down hypocritical barriers."[57] Bob's role as a barrier breaker constitutes a more enduring part of his legacy than three no-hitters and forty-six shutouts.

Once fantasy camps became popular in the 1990s, the Cleveland Indians tapped their (now former) spring training facility in Winter Haven, Florida, to host middle-aged wannabes. For years, Bob Feller was a celebrity counselor. Most octogenarians, especially Hall of Famers, would have hung out in the dugout telling stories or limited their duties to keeping the beer cold.

Not Rapid Robert. During the scrimmage on the last day, Feller insisted on pitching to every camper. There's an illuminating YouTube video, in fact, that shows a fortysomething Tribe fan lining a one-hopper off Feller's shin. Bob, then in his early eighties, doesn't bother to rub the welt as the ball goes careening and the batter lurches toward first, no doubt horrified that he's bruised a Cleveland icon but still thrilled that he's gotten on base against Blazin' Bob.

In 1945, Feller had shown similar grit when pitching against Satch in Seattle. But that was in front of hundreds of wounded servicemen and surrounded on the field by active-duty naval aviators and coast guardsmen. The Winter Haven moment, by contrast, came in an empty park, witnessed only by pudgy accountants and lawyers. Yet Feller soldiered on.

The video shows that Bob's left leg kick—the signature move Feller shared with barnstorming pals Satchel Paige and Dizzy Dean—was, by then, almost nil, of course. Still, it's not hard to imagine young Bobby arching his back to let one rip against the Monarchs on a chilly October evening in Wichita—or on a balmy afternoon on the Majuro Atoll with that seaman from Brooklyn bleating in his ear.

A concrete partition sat in the middle of the Winter Haven complex. As a kid, Feller spent endless hours chucking a ball against the side of the family barn. He did it so well that the shed overlooking the Racoon River is now where it belongs: in the National Register of Historic Places.

Seventy years later in Florida, Feller repeated the ritual—firing the ball against the concrete divider and fielding the bounce, firing and fielding, over and over again.[58] The old man had reverted to the boy.

When the time came to face those campers, Bob was determined to put on a good show—just as he, Satch, and Diz had all over the country for all those years before crowds black and white.

Acknowledgments

Writers of popular history find themselves deeply obligated to reference librarians, who, fortunately, tend to be a merciful lot. Dozens of research professionals across the country—from Wenatchee, Washington, to Paterson, New Jersey—dug up long-ago news clips about barnstorming exhibitions they'd never heard of. Many were tickled to learn that Satchel Paige, Dizzy Dean, and Bob Feller once graced their local ballyards.

Karen Wente of the Moline (Illinois) Public Library went above and beyond the call of duty in documenting a Quad City Optimists Club fund-raiser played just after V-E Day between a Great Lakes Naval Training Station squad, captained by Chief Petty Officer Bob Feller, and a sandlot club captained by Dizzy Dean. Doris Ashbrook at the Richmond (Indiana) Public Library was similarly dogged in finding clips on the Feller-Paige visit to her town in 1946.

David Kelly, the Library of Congress's resident baseball guru, again proved invaluable, as did his colleagues in the Newspaper and Current Periodicals Room—my second home for the last two years. I'm also indebted to the fine people who staff the reference desks at the Georgetown University Library and the four different branches of the Fairfax County (Virginia) Public Library that I tapped for this book. John Vernon, formerly with the National Archives, provided guidance, as did his friend Bill Wallace, the curator of Commissioner Happy Chandler's papers at the University of Kentucky Library. There's a reason John Updike called libraries "citadels of light."

One proud research nugget came courtesy of Karen Steinauer and Matt Piersol at the Nebraska Historical Society, with a nudge from old pal Ann Baker at the University of Nebraska Press. Karen and Matt unearthed the *Oxford Standard*'s coverage of the first recorded contest between Dean and the Kansas City Monarchs—an article that probably hadn't seen the light of day in three-quarters of a century. Other state historical societies, notably in Missouri, Oklahoma, North Dakota, and Ohio, also delivered in the clutch. Barry Lewis, a reporter at the *Tulsa World*, did much-appreciated digging, as did his friend noted Tulsa baseball buff Wayne McCombs, and my fellow dead(ball)-head Mike Sowell, a professor of journalism at Oklahoma State University.

John Holway, my northern Virginia neighbor, has spent much of his admirable life chronicling the Negro Leagues. John and his books were indispensable, as was Bill McNeil, the éminence grise of the California Winter League, and his associate Los Angeles history aficionado Sesar Carreno. So, too, were members of the Society for American Baseball Research's Negro Leagues Committee, among them Larry Lester, James Riley, Phil Dixon, and Dick Clark. Other SABR-ites were extremely helpful, including my old Cleveland friend Fred Schuld. Larry Hogan, who helped direct the Hall of Fame's project on the Negro Leagues and, each fall, hosts the Pop Lloyd conference, was a great resource, as was Thomas Barthel, the author of *Baseball Barnstorming and Exhibition Games: 1901–1962*. Speaking of the Hall of Fame, Tim Wiles, Jim Gates, Freddy Berowski, Pat Kelly, Jenny Ambrose, Lindsay Prescott, and Gabriel Schecter all generously gave of their time.

Professor Leslie Heaphy of Kent State University, a great blackball historian and coordinator of the yearly Malloy Conference, could not have been more responsive. The same can be said for University of Pittsburgh professor Rob Ruck, Art Rooney's biographer and an expert on the city's multicultural history.

Neil Lanctot, my fellow Simon & Schuster author and the biographer of Roy Campanella, provided important perspective, as did Bob Luke, Willie Wells's biographer.

Professor Jules Tygiel of San Francisco State University, whose work on the societal import of Jackie Robinson is brilliant, spent time on the phone with me, despite being gravely ill with cancer. Sadly, Dr. Tygiel died in 2008.

Hall of Famers Bob Feller, Monte Irvin, and Ralph Kiner all graciously agreed to be interviewed, as did Mickey Vernon, who passed away a year after we talked. No wonder President Eisenhower loved Mickey; he was a complete gentleman. Former Negro Leaguers Doc Glenn, Mahlon Duckett, Lionel Evelyn, Armando Vazquez, and many others genially shared their recollections, as did Satchel Paige's son Robert.

Legendary Negro Leagues umpire Bob Motley, author of *Ruling over Monarchs, Giants, and Stars* (a gift from old friends Holly and Jim Smith), was a delight to interview, as was his son Byron. Ray Doswell at the Negro Leagues Baseball Museum and Hall of Fame in Kansas City, Missouri, helped track down information.

Larry Tye, Satchel Paige's fine biographer, magnanimously shared his barnstorming research as did historian Allen Barra. Accomplished baseball writer Paul Dickson helped point me toward key resources.

Paul Dean's daughter Alma Dean Bozeman, who's named after the paternal grandmother she never knew, generously provided insights into Uncle Diz, as did her son Gary.

Ed Hartig, distinguished chronicler of the Chicago Cubs, Timuel Black, a nine-decade resident of the Black Belt and veteran of the 308th Quartermaster Corps during World War II, and Michael Flug, a senior archivist from the Chicago Public Library, shared their thoughts on Chicago's stormy racial history.

In Van Meter, Iowa, Delores Jones and Scott Havick at the Bob Feller Museum were helpful. Trey Armistead, a physics teacher at Van Meter High, kindly gave me a tour of Bob's alma mater and filled me in on the town's history. In Jackson, Mississippi, Michael Rubenstein, executive director of the Mississippi Sports Hall of Fame (which has an excellent Dizzy Dean exhibit), was helpful.

In Allentown, Pennsylvania, the late historian Bob Peterson's widow, Peg, son Tom, and daughter Margie were all wonderful, digging through boxes and giving me full access to Bob's files and books. Bob happened to grow up in my hometown, Warren, Pennsylvania, and graduated from Warren High in 1943 with my mother, Anne Marie Harrington. Another product of Warren County, Chuck Clawsen, who like Bob Peterson was a fine sandlot catcher in his day, related his memories of Josh Gibson and the Homestead Grays barnstorming through town.

In Philadelphia, Babe Ruth biographer Bill Jenkinson provided voluminous data on Ruth's interracial barnstorming. Old friend and neighbor Julie Dahlen, a proud native of Tulsa, shared her knowledge of Tulsa's awful 1921 race riot. Another old pal, Rich Marcus, recounted his experience with Bob Feller at a Cleveland Indians fantasy camp.

Please note that many photos in the book come from the Ben and Alma Jones Archives. Ben is the last of the great renaissance men: a literary scholar, a jazz buff, a song stylist, the actor who played Cooter on the *Dukes of Hazzard* television series, a former Democratic congressman from Georgia, a gentleman farmer in Rappahannock County, Virginia, and, most recently, the man who channels Dizzy Dean in a hilarious and touching one-man show. He's also done a clever musical adaptation of Dizzy's life. Out of the goodness of their hearts, Ben and Alma allowed me to borrow their immense collection of Dean and Paige memorabilia.

My editor at Simon & Schuster, Bob Bender, could not have been a better guy to work with: unfailingly kind, patient, and thorough—but tough when he needed to be.

I owe my biggest debt of gratitude to Elizabeth and our Triple A's— Allyson, Andrew, and Abigail. When I started researching interracial barnstorming, Abby was in second grade. Now when she needs help with her advanced math homework, I take one look—and tell her to go see Mommy or one of her siblings.

Appendix

1933 SATCH VS. DIZ IN LOS ANGELES

LOS ANGELES, OCT. 16, WHITE SOX PARK

Attendance: 10,000

Outcome: 2–1, Pirrone Stars

Satch	Diz
3 ins.	3 ins.
0 runs	1 run
?? hits	2 hits
?? Ks	?? Ks

SATCH VS. DIZZY 1934

CLEVELAND, OCT. 21, LEAGUE PARK

Attendance: 12,000

Outcome: 4–1, "Craws"

Satch	Diz
6 ins.	3 ins.
0 runs	1 run
0 hits	4 hits
13 Ks	4 Ks

COLUMBUS, OCT. 22, RED BIRD STADIUM

Attendance: 1,650

Outcome: 5–3, "Craws"

Satch	Diz
3 ins.	2 ins.
0 runs	1 run
2 hits	2 hits
9 Ks	1 K

PITTSBURGH, OCT. 23, FORBES FIELD

Attendance: 2,000

Outcome: 4–3, "Craws"

Satch	Diz
2 ins.	2 ins.
2 runs	0 runs
3 hits	1 hit
3 Ks	1 K

LOS ANGELES "LOST CLASSIC," EARLY NOV., WRIGLEY FIELD

Attendance: 18,000

Outcome: 1–0, "Giants"

Satch	Diz
13 ins.	13 ins.
0 runs	1 run
17 Ks	15 Ks

SATCH VS. DIZZY 1935

SPRINGFIELD, MO., OCT. 1, WHITE CITY PARK

Attendance: 5,000

Outcome: 8–2, "Monarchs"

Satch	Diz
3 ins.	3 ins.
0 runs	0 runs
0 hits	0 hits
3 Ks	2 Ks

COLUMBIA, MO., OCT. 2, MERCHANTS PARK
Attendance: 6,000
Outcome: 9–6, "Monarchs"

Satch	Diz
1 in.	3 ins.
0 runs	2 runs
0 hits	3 hits
1 K	2 Ks

TULSA, OCT. 3, TEXAS LEAGUE PARK
Attendance: 3,000
Outcome: 11–3, "Monarchs"

Satch	Diz
2 ins.	1 in.
0 runs	1 run
0 hits	1 hit
4 Ks	1 K

ENID, OKLA., OCT. 4, EASON STADIUM
Attendance: 5,000
Outcome: 11–5, "Monarchs"

Satch	Diz
2 ins.	2 ins.
0 runs	0 runs
0 hits	0 hits
3 Ks	2 Ks

JOPLIN, MO., OCT. 5, MINERS PARK
rained out

KANSAS CITY, MO., OCT. 6, MUEHLEBACH FIELD
Attendance: 7,000
Outcome: 1–0, Dean Stars

Satch	Diz
9 ins.	3 ins.
1 run	0 runs
3 hits	0 hits

LOS ANGELES, OCT. 31, WRIGLEY FIELD

Attendance: 7,000

Outcome: 5–4, Dean Stars

Satch	Diz
4 ins.	7 ins.
?? runs	2 runs
?? hits	6 hits
7 Ks	?? Ks

1936 SATCH VS. BOBBY IN DES MOINES

DES MOINES, OCT. 6, WESTERN LEAGUE PARK

Attendance: 5,000

Outcome: 4–2, Paige Stars

Satch	Bob
3 ins.	3 ins.
0 runs	0 runs
1 hit	1 hit
7 Ks	8 Ks

SATCH VS. BOBBY 1941

ST. LOUIS, SPORTSMAN'S PARK

Attendance: (est. 10,000)

Satch	Bob
4 ins.	5 ins.
4 runs	1 run

SATCH VS. BOBBY 1945

LOS ANGELES, OCT. 2, WRIGLEY FIELD

Attendance: 26,000
Outcome: 4–2, Feller–PCL Stars

Satch	Bob
5 ins.	5 ins.
1 run	2 runs
?? hits	?? hits
10 Ks	6 Ks

SAN FRANCISCO, OCT. 5, SEALS STADIUM

Attendance: 12,000
11–0, Feller Stars

SAN DIEGO, OCT. 3, 1945

Attendance: 9,107
Outcome: 5–0, Royals

Satch	Bob
5 ins.	5 ins.
0 runs	0 runs
1 hit	3 hits
11 Ks	10 Ks

SEATTLE, OCT. 7, SICKS' STADIUM

Attendance: 10,000
Outcome: 6–1, Paige–Coast Guardsmen

Satch	Bob
5 ins.	5 ins.
1 run	2 runs

WENATCHEE, WASH., OCT. 8, RECREATION PARK

Attendance: 5,000
Outcome: 11–0, Feller–Fort Wright

Satch	Bob
4 ins.	3 ins.
0 runs	0 runs
1 hit	0 hits
4 Ks	7 Ks

OAKLAND, OCT. 10, OAKS BALL PARK

Attendance: ??

Outcome: 4–3, Oakland Colored Giants

Satch	Bob
5 ins.	5 ins.
2 runs	0 runs
8 hits	0 hits
?? Ks	7 Ks

SAN DIEGO, OCT. 24, LANE FIELD

Attendance: 13,000

Outcome: 4–2, Royals

Satch	Bob
6 ins.	6 ins.
1 run	0 runs
5 hits	1 hit
7 Ks	14 Ks

LOS ANGELES, OCT. 26, WRIGLEY FIELD

Attendance: 26,000

Outcome: 3–2, Feller Stars

Satch	Bob
7 ins.	7 ins.
5 hits	4 hits
8 Ks	13 Ks

SATCH VS. BOBBY 1946

PITTSBURGH, SEPT. 30, FORBES FIELD

Attendance: 4,592

Outcome: 3–1, Paige Stars

Satch	Bob
3 ins.	3 ins.
1 run	1 run
1 hit	2 hits
4 Ks	3 Ks

CLEVELAND, OCT. 1, MUNICIPAL STADIUM

Attendance: 9,700

Outcome: 5–0, Feller Stars

Satch	Bob
?? ins.	4 ins.
?? runs	0 runs
?? hits	1 hit
?? Ks	?? Ks

CHICAGO, OCT. 2, COMISKEY PARK

Attendance: 22,000

Outcome: 6–5, Feller Stars

Satch	Bob
3 ins.	3 ins.
0 runs	0 runs
1 hit	1 hit
3 Ks	1 K

CINCINNATI, OCT. 3, CROSLEY FIELD

Attendance: 11,000

Outcome: 3–0, Feller Stars

Satch	Bob
2 ins.	3 ins.
1 run	1 run

NEW YORK, OCT. 6, YANKEE STADIUM

Attendance: 27,462

Outcome: 4–0, Paige Stars

Satch	Bob
5 ins.	5 ins.
0 runs	2 runs
4 hits	4 hits
4 Ks	0 Ks

DAYTON, OHIO, OCT. 8, HUDSON FIELD

Attendance: (est. 4,000)

Outcome: 7–6, Feller Stars

Satch	Bob
3 ins.	3 ins.
6 runs	0 runs
5 hits	?? hits
?? Ks	?? Ks

COUNCIL BLUFF, IOWA, OCT. 12, MEMORIAL FIELD

Attendance: 4,100

3–2, Feller Stars

WICHITA, KANS., OCT. 12, LAWRENCE-STADIUM

Attendance: 8,000

Outcome: 5–3, Feller Stars

Satch	Bob
3 ins.	3 ins.
0 runs	1 run

LOS ANGELES, OCT. 16, WRIGLEY FIELD

Attendance: 22,577

Outcome: 4–3, Feller Stars

Satch	Bob
5 ins.	5 ins.
1 run	3 runs
?? hits	5 hits
7 Ks	7 Ks

SAN DIEGO, OCT. 17, LANE FIELD

Attendance: 11,000

Outcome: 2–0, Feller Stars

Satch	Bob
5 ins.	5 ins.
2 runs	0 runs

SATCH VS. BOBBY 1947

LOS ANGELES, OCT. 15, WRIGLEY FIELD

Attendance: 15,000
Outcome: Feller Stars, 2–1

Satch	Bob
4 ins.	4 ins.
1 run	0 runs
2 hits	4 hits
7 Ks	2 Ks

LOS ANGELES, OCT. 19, WRIGLEY FIELD

Attendance: 12,160
Outcome: Feller Stars, 2–1

Satch	Bob
5 ins.	?? ins.
0 runs	1 run
3 hits	3 hits
8 Ks	?? Ks

LOS ANGELES, NOV. 2, WRIGLEY FIELD

Attendance: 9,145
Outcome: Paige-Royals, 8–0

Satch	Bob
9 ins.	8 ins.
0 runs	5 runs
4 hits	11 hits
15 Ks	3 Ks

Notes

PROLOGUE: MAY 1942

1. history.sandiego.edu/gen/WW2Timeline.
2. *Los Angeles Times,* January 24, 1969, column by Jim Murray.
3. Interview with Michael Flug, senior archivist, Chicago Public Library, January 2007.
4. *Pittsburgh Courier,* June 5, 1942, column by Wendell Smith.
5. Stanley "Doc" Glenn, *Don't Let Anyone Take Your Joy Away,* p. 17.
6. *St. Louis Globe-Democrat,* October 6, 1941, article by Robert F. Burnes.
7. *Chicago Defender,* May 31, 1942, column by Eddie Gant.
8. John "Buck" O'Neil, *I Was Right on Time,* p. 119.
9. *Chicago Defender,* May 23, 1942.
10. *Los Angeles Times,* October 22, 1944.
11. BaseballLibrary.com, Willard Brown entry.
12. Bob Motley, *Ruling Over Monarchs, Giants, and Stars,* p. 107.
13. *Chicago Daily Tribune,* May 22, 1942.
14. BaseballLibrary.com, Zeke Bonura entry.
15. Ibid.
16. Irish Elk, mcns.blogspot.com.
17. Neil Lanctot, *Negro League Baseball: The Rise and Ruin of a Black Institution,* p. 114.
18. *Chicago Defender,* May 23, 1942.
19. John Holway, *The Complete Book of Baseball's Negro Leagues: The Other Half of Baseball History,* p. 287.
20. Robert Gregory, *Diz: The Story of Dizzy Dean and Baseball During the Great Depression,* p. 209.
21. Interview with Ben Jones, Dizzy Dean scholar and interpreter, April 2007.
22. Gregory, p. 234.
23. Ibid., pp. 244–45.

24. Donn Rogosin, *Invisible Men: Life in Baseball's Negro Leagues,* p. 131.

25. Ibid.

26. Jim Reisler, *Black Writers/Black Baseball,* p. 107.

27. Mark Ribowsky, *Don't Look Back: Satchel Paige in the Shadows of Baseball,* p. 124.

28. Monte Irvin, *Few and Chosen: Defining Negro Leagues Greatness,* p. 129.

29. Leroy (Satchel) Paige, as told to David Lipman, *Maybe I'll Pitch Forever,* p. 91.

30. Larry Tye, *Satchel: The Life and Times of an American Legend,* p. 91.

31. Jules Tygiel, *Extra Bases: Reflections on Jackie Robinson, Race, and Baseball History,* p. 33.

32. John Holway, *Voices from the Great Black Baseball Leagues,* p. 107.

33. Irvin, *Few and Chosen,* p. 130.

34. Rogosin, *Invisible Men,* p. 132.

35. *New York Star,* July 21, 1948, column by Tom Meany.

36. Tye, *Satchel Paige,* p. 82.

37. Larry Hogan, ed., *Shades of Glory,* p. 407.

38. Thom Loverro, *Encyclopedia of Negro League Baseball,* p. 228.

39. John Holway, *Josh and Satch,* p. x1.

40. *Saturday Evening Post,* July 27, 1940, article by Ted Shane.

41. Tygiel, *Extra Bases,* p. 27.

42. As quoted in Vince Staten, *Ol' Diz: A Biography of Dizzy Dean,* p. 222.

43. *New York Times,* November 15, 1930, column by John Kieran.

44. As quoted in Charles Alexander, *Breaking the Slump: Baseball in the Depression Era,* p. 105.

45. Tye, *Satchel,* p. 91.

46. *New York Times,* April 5, 1992.

47. Jules Tygiel, *Jackie Robinson and His Legacy,* p. 27.

48. *Los Angeles Times,* August 14, 1955, article by Dizzy Dean.

49. *Chicago Daily News,* May 23, 1942, article by Associated Press.

50. *Chicago Herald American,* May 25, 1942.

51. Ibid.

52. *Chicago Daily News,* May 25, 1942.

53. Holway, *Voices,* p. 283.

54. Peterson, *Only the Ball Was White,* p. 129.

55. Holway, *Josh and Satch,* p. 84.

56. *Washington Post,* July 8, 1948, column by Shirley Povich.

57. Motley, *Ruling Over Monarchs,* p. 89.

58. *Chicago Defender,* October 26, 1946, column by Fay Young.

59. Ibid., May 30, 1942.

60. Ibid.

61. *Chicago Daily News,* May 25, 1942.

62. *Chicago Defender,* May 30, 1942.

63. Holway, *Voices,* p. 283.

64. *Chicago Defender,* May 30, 1942.
65. *Chicago Daily Tribune,* May 25, 1942.
66. *Chicago Defender,* July 10, 1954, column by Fay Young.
67. *Chicago Daily Tribune,* May 25, 1942.
68. *Chicago Defender,* June 13, 1942.
69. *New York Times,* June 5, 1942.
70. *Chicago Defender,* June 13, 1942, column by Eddie Gant.
71. *Pittsburgh Courier,* June 6, 1942, article by Wendell Smith.
72. As quoted in Rob Kirkpatrick, *Cecil Travis of the Washington Senators,* p. 122.
73. *Chicago Defender,* May 30, 1942, column by Fay Young.
74. *Los Angeles Times,* June 10, 1982, column by Jim Murray.
75. *Chicago Defender,* May 16, 1942.
76. *Chicago Defender,* May 23, 1942.
77. Ken Burns's documentary *Baseball,* interview with Buck O'Neil.
78. *Bill Mazeroski's Baseball Journal,* "Josh, Satch, Cool Papa, and the Black Wagner," by Robert Peterson.
79. *Sporting News,* October 15, 1971.
80. *Baseball History 4,* "Ersatz Octobers: Baseball Barnstorming," by Robert Cole, p. 77.
81. Ibid., p. 88.
82. *Los Angeles Times,* June 10, 1982, column by Jim Murray.
83. As quoted in journals.cambridge.org.

CHAPTER ONE: INTERRACIAL BARNSTORMING BEFORE SATCH

1. Herman Wouk, *Inside, Outside,* p. 34.
2. Tygiel, *Extra Bases,* p. 67.
3. William Safire, *Safire's New Political Dictionary,* pp. 45–46.
4. Thomas Barthel, *Baseball Barnstorming and Exhibition Games, 1901–1962,* p. 13.
5. Tygiel, *Extra Bases,* p. 140.
6. Leslie Heaphy, ed., *Satchel Paige and Company: Essays on the Kansas City Monarchs, Their Greatest Star, and the Negro Leagues,* p. 50.
7. Barthel, *Baseball Barnstorming,* p. 13.
8. Heaphy, ed., *The Negro Leagues,* p. 10.
9. Ibid., p. 15.
10. Holway, *Complete Book,* p. 18.
11. Ibid., p. 23.
12. Mark Ribowsky, *Complete History of the Negro Leagues,* p. 60.
13. Holway, *Complete Book,* p. 86.
14. Ibid.
15. Ken Burns's PBS documentary *Baseball.*

16. Phil Dixon with Patrick J. Hannigan, *The Negro Baseball Leagues: A Photographic History,* p. 171.
17. Tygiel, *Extra Bases,* p. 79.
18. Holway, *Complete Book,* p. 65.
19. Ribowsky, *Complete History,* p. 63.
20. Rogosin, *Invisible Men,* p. 8.
21. O'Neil, *I Was Right on Time,* p. 26.
22. William F. McNeil, *The California Winter League: America's First Integrated Baseball League,* p. 13.
23. Rogosin, *Invisible Men,* p. 34.
24. *Chicago Defender,* October 30, 1915.
25. Holway, *Complete Book,* p. 108.
26. Irvin, *Few and Chosen,* p. 99.
27. Ibid.
28. Holway, *Complete Book,* p. 104.
29. Heaphy, ed., *Satchel Paige and Company,* p. 113.
30. Janet Bruce, *The Kansas City Monarchs: Champions of Black Baseball,* p. 15.
31. Ibid.
32. Holway, *Complete Book,* p. 104.
33. Rogosin, *Invisible Men,* p. 18.
34. Heaphy, ed., *Satchel Paige and Company,* p. 116.
35. *Newsweek,* October 25, 1999.
36. Tygiel, *Extra Bases,* p. 61.
37. Ibid., p. 183.
38. Jules Tygiel as quoted in *Shades of Glory,* ed., Lawrence Hogan, p. viii.
39. Leigh Montville, *The Big Bam,* p. 21.
40. Interview with Ruth scholar and biographer Bill Jenkinson, February 2007.
41. *Philadelphia North American,* October 5, 1920.
42. Hogan, ed., *Shades of Glory,* p. 130.
43. *Chicago Defender,* December 10, 1931.
44. *Buffalo Express,* October 11, 1920.
45. *New York Times,* October 12, 1920.
46. *Chicago Defender,* October 26, 1946, column by Fay Young.
47. Reisler, *Black Writers/Black Baseball,* p. 7.
48. Interview with Neil Lanctot, December 2006.
49. Taped interview between Monte Irvin and Bob Peterson, Hall of Fame.
50. Burns's PBS documentary *Baseball.*
51. Reisler, *Black Writers/Black Baseball,* p. 9.
52. Rogosin, *Invisible Men,* p. 123.
53. Barthel, *Baseball Barnstorming,* pp. 95–97.
54. Cole, "Ersatz Octobers," p. 79.
55. Barthel, *Baseball Barnstorming,* p. 96.

56. Ibid., p. 105.
57. Ibid., pp. 125–30.
58. *Pittsburgh Courier,* December 4, 1943.

CHAPTER TWO: SATCH HITS THE CHITLIN' CIRCUIT

1. Lanctot, *Negro League Baseball,* p. 156.
2. Taped interview between Bob Peterson and Jimmy Crutchfield, Hall of Fame.
3. Glenn, *Don't Let Anyone Take Your Joy Away,* p. 3.
4. *Philadelphia Daily News,* August 6, 2004
5. Glenn, *Don't Let Anyone Take Your Joy Away,* p. 41.
6. Tye, *Satchel,* p. 38.
7. Colorado.edu/ibs/Eb/Alston/Econ454/lecture.
8. Rogosin, *Invisible Men,* p. 91.
9. Alexander, *Breaking the Slump,* p. 4.
10. Ibid., p. 5.
11. Timothy M. Gay, *Tris Speaker: The Rough-and-Tumble Life of a Baseball Legend,* pp. 3–4.
12. *Chicago Defender,* November 4, 1939.
13. Holway, *Voices,* p. 103.
14. *Miami Herald,* February 10, 1971.
15. Interview with Ben Jones, April 2007.
16. *Saturday Evening Post,* July 27, 1940, article by Ted Shane.
17. Cleveland *Plain Dealer,* December 10, 1978.
18. *Collier's Magazine,* "The Fabulous Satchel Paige," three-part series by Richard Donovan, May 30, 1953.
19. Ibid., June 13, 1953.
20. Alan J. Pollock, *Barnstorming to Heaven: Syd Pollock and His Great Black Teams,* p. 139.
21. Irvin, *Few and Chosen,* p. 133.
22. Cleveland *Plain Dealer,* June 9, 1982.
23. Ribowsky, *Complete History,* p. 224.
24. *Holiday Magazine,* August 1965.
25. *San Francisco Examiner,* March 4, 1969.
26. *New York Daily News,* February 12, 1981.
27. *Holiday Magazine,* August 1965.
28. *Ebony,* March 1969.
29. Ribowsky, *Don't Look Back,* p. 66.
30. Irvin, *Few and Chosen,* p. 130.
31. Quincy Trouppe, *Twenty Years Too Soon: Prelude to Major-League Integrated Baseball,* p. 55.
32. O'Neil, *I Was Right on Time,* p. 101.
33. Paige, *Maybe I'll Pitch Forever,* p. 12.

34. O'Neil, *I Was Right on Time,* p. 111.
35. Paige, *Maybe I'll Pitch Forever,* p. 15.
36. Ibid., pp. 17–18.
37. Ibid., p. 22.
38. *Miami Herald,* February 10, 1971, article by Ed Storin.
39. Paige, *Maybe I'll Pitch Forever,* p. 23.
40. Ibid., p. 24.
41. Ibid., p. 25.
42. Ribowsky, *Don't Look Back,* p. 34.
43. *USA Today,* August 27, 2007.
44. Paige, *Maybe I'll Pitch Forever,* p. 42.
45. Ribowsky, *Don't Look Back,* p. 40.
46. Paige, *Maybe I'll Pitch Forever,* p. 47.
47. Heaphy, ed., *Satchel Paige and Company,* p. 209.
48. Ribowsky, *Don't Look Back,* p. 112.
49. *Mansfield (Ohio) News Journal,* August 17, 1998.
50. *Bill Mazeroski's Baseball Journal,* "Satch, Josh, Cool Papa, and the Black Wagner," by Robert Peterson.
51. Paige, *Maybe I'll Pitch Forever,* p. 52.
52. *New York Times,* February 10, 1971, column by Arthur Daley.
53. Holway, *Complete Book,* p. 270.
54. Irvin, *Few and Chosen,* p. 120.
55. James A. Riley, *The Biographical Encyclopedia of the Negro Baseball Leagues,* Crutchfield entry.
56. Cole, "Ersatz Octobers," p. 77.
57. Holway, *Complete Book,* p. 296.
58. Ibid.
59. *Pittsburgh Courier,* October 8, 1932.
60. Sam Lacy, as quoted in *Blackball News,* December 7, 1999.
61. Trouppe, *20 Years Too Soon,* p. 46.
62. PitchBlackBaseball.com, North Dakota's Integrated Baseball History, "Satchel Arrives."
63. Recorded interview with Ted Radcliffe, Hall of Fame, 1995.
64. Paige, *Maybe I'll Pitch Forever,* p. 88.
65. PitchBlackBaseball.com, "Satchel Arrives."
66. Paige, *Maybe I'll Pitch Forever,* p. 88.
67. PitchBlackBaseball.com, "Satchel Arrives."
68. Ibid.
69. Ibid.
70. Ibid.
71. *Chicago Defender,* August 19, 1933.
72. Ibid., September 9, 1933.
73. PitchBlackBaseball.com, "Satchel Arrives."
74. Paige, *Maybe I'll Pitch Forever,* p. 89.

75. Ibid.

76. Ibid.

77. Heaphy, ed., *Satchel Paige and Company,* p. 66.

78. PitchBlackBaseball.com, "Satchel Arrives."

79. Trouppe, *20 Years Too Soon,* p. 50.

80. Paige, *Maybe I'll Pitch Forever,* p. 88.

81. *Collier's Magazine,* June 6, 1953.

82. Ribowsky, *Don't Look Back,* p. 114.

CHAPTER THREE: THE LEAN ONE MEETS THE DIZZY ONE

1. *Omaha World-Herald,* October 5, 1933.

2. *Oxford (Neb.) Standard,* October 5, 1933.

3. Ibid.

4. Taped interview between Bob Peterson and Jimmy Crutchfield, Hall of Fame.

5. Bruce, *The Kansas City Monarchs,* p. 21.

6. Irvin, *Few and Chosen,* p. 135.

7. Fay Vincent, *The Only Game in Town,* p. 47.

8. John B. Holway, *Black Diamonds: Life in the Negro Leagues from the Men Who Lived It,* p. 26.

9. John B. Holway, *Blackball Stars: Negro League Pioneers,* p. 167.

10. *Oxford (Neb.) Standard,* October 5, 1933.

11. BaseballLibrary.com, Brewer entry.

12. Vincent, *The Only Game in Town,* p. 12.

13. Holway, *Black Diamonds,* p. 30.

14. Ibid., p. 30.

15. Ibid., p. 65.

16. *Oxford (Neb.) Standard,* October 5, 1933.

17. psacard.com/articles.

18. Red Smith as quoted in *The Baseball Hall of Fame 50th Anniversary Book,* pp. 171–72.

19. *New York World-Telegram,* February 18, 1942, column by Joe Williams.

20. *Los Angeles Times,* July 18, 1974, column by Jim Murray.

21. Staten, *Ol' Diz,* p. 12.

22. *Sporting News,* January 23, 1941.

23. Interview with Alma Dean Bozeman, February 2008.

24. Ibid.

25. Ira L. Smith, *Baseball's Famous Pitchers,* p. 222.

26. As quoted in Staten, *Ol' Diz,* p. 22.

27. *St. Louis Post-Dispatch,* October 7, 1934.

28. Interview with Gary Bozeman, February 2008.

29. Ibid.

30. Cooperstown/Home Plate Press, *Baseball's Immortals,* p. 3.

31. Gregory, *Diz,* p. 29.

32. Ibid., p. 30.

33. Ibid., p. 35.

34. Ibid., p. 33.

35. Interview with Alma Dean Bozeman, February 2008.

36. Gregory, *Diz,* p. 36.

37. *New York Times,* September 7, 1958, column by Arthur Daley.

38. Ibid.

39. Gregory, *Diz,* p. 42.

40. As quoted in the *New York Times,* July 17, 1974.

41. Gregory, *Diz,* p. 48.

42. Ibid., p. 47.

43. Ibid., p. 48.

44. Ibid., pp. 48–49.

45. *Philadelphia Bulletin,* July 21, 1961, column by Red Smith.

46. Staten, *Ol' Diz,* p. 57.

47. Gregory, *Diz,* p. 58.

48. Ibid., p. 60.

49. *Washington Post,* December 8, 1940.

50. *Saturday Evening Post,* March 16, 1935.

51. Gregory, *Diz,* p. 66.

52. *Sporting News,* December 25, 1931.

53. Gregory, *Diz,* p. 75.

54. Barthel, *Baseball Barnstorming,* p. 121.

55. Gregory, *Diz,* p. 75.

56. Ibid., p. 76.

57. *St. Joseph's Gazette,* October 6, 1933.

58. Ibid.

59. *Omaha World-Herald,* October 7, 1933.

60. Ibid.

61. Dennis Hoffman presentation to Society for American Baseball Research meeting, July 2008.

62. *Kansas City Star,* October 8, 1933.

63. Ibid., October 5.

64. *Wichita Eagle,* October 11, 1934.

65. *Saturday Evening Post,* July 27, 1940, article by Ted Shane.

66. McNeil, *The California Winter League,* p. 162–65.

67. Ibid., p. 162.

68. BaseballLibrary.com, Stearnes entry.

69. Ibid., Suttles entry.

70. Recorded interview with Monte Irvin, Hall of Fame.

71. BaseballLibrary.com, Wells entry.

72. *Los Angeles Times,* October 16, 1933, article by Bob Ray.

73. Ibid.

74. Ibid., October 17, 1933.
75. McNeil, *The California Winter League,* p. 166.
76. *Houston Post,* October 20, 1933, p. 8.
77. *Washington Post,* October 21, 1933, Associated Press article.

CHAPTER FOUR: "PLENTY DIZZY":
DIZ, DAFFY, AND SATCH IN 1934

1. *Chicago Defender,* October 6, 1934.
2. Ibid.
3. *St. Louis Globe-Democrat,* October 10, 1934.
4. Associated Press, October 9, 1934, article by Charles W. Dunkley.
5. As quoted in Gregory, *Diz,* p. 11.
6. Ibid.
7. *Brooklyn Eagle,* October 16, 1934, Associated Press article.
8. Staten, *Ol' Diz,* p. 145.
9. *Daily Oklahoman,* October 10, 1934.
10. Gregory, p. 21
11. Heaphy, ed., *Satchel Paige and Company,* p. 209.
12. Ribowsky, *Complete History,* p. 180.
13. Barthel, *Baseball Barnstorming,* p. 139.
14. Ribowsky, *Don't Look Back,* p. 127.
15. Dixon with Hannigan, *The Negro Baseball Leagues,* p. 12.
16. Ibid., p. 170.
17. *Sporting News,* September 29, 1948.
18. Henry Metcalfe, *A Game for All Races: An Illustrated History of the Negro Leagues,* p. 106.
19. Heaphy, ed., *Satchel Paige and Company,* p. 209.
20. Dixon with Hannigan, *The Negro Baseball Leagues,* p. 170.
21. Holway, *Complete Book,* p. 309.
22. Ribowsky, *Don't Look Back,* p. 127.
23. Holway, *Complete Book,* p. 311.
24. *St. Louis Post-Dispatch,* September 22, 1934.
25. *Cleveland News,* October 20, 1934.
26. Gregory, *Diz,* p. 246.
27. *Philadelphia Inquirer,* October 17, 1934.
28. Gregory, *Diz,* p. 123.
29. Barthel, *Baseball Barnstorming,* p. 136.
30. *Chicago Daily Tribune,* January 16, 1937.
31. *Kansas City Star,* October 10, 1934, Associated Press article.
32. Barthel, *Baseball Barnstorming,* p. 136.
33. *Brooklyn Eagle,* October 11, 1934.
34. Interview with Barry Lewis, *Tulsa World,* January 2007.
35. Interview with Tulsa native Julie Dahlen, March 2007.

36. *Columbia* (Mo.) *Daily Tribune,* September 30, 1935.
37. Interview with Barry Lewis, *Tulsa World,* January 2007.
38. *Daily Oklahoman,* October 8, 1934.
39. Ibid., October 11, 1934.
40. Ibid.
41. Ibid.
42. Ibid., October 10, 1934.
43. Holway, *Voices,* p. 283.
44. Barthel, *Baseball Barnstorming,* p. 137.
45. *Daily Oklahoman,* October 11, 1934.
46. *Wichita Eagle,* October 12, 1934.
47. Ibid.
48. Ibid.
49. Ibid., October 11, 1934.
50. Ibid., October 12, 1934.
51. Taped interview with Ted Radcliffe, Baseball Hall of Fame.
52. Baseball-reference.com, Trent entry.
53. *Wichita Eagle,* October 12, 1934.
54. *Kansas City Star,* October 12, 1934.
55. Ibid.
56. Ibid.
57. *Des Moines Register,* October 14, 1934.
58. Ibid.
59. *Chicago Defender,* October 20, 1934.
60. *Chicago Daily Tribune,* October 15, 1934.
61. Ibid.
62. *Chicago Defender,* October 20, 1934.
63. Ibid.
64. *Milwaukee Journal,* October 16, 1934.
65. *Dallas Morning News,* October 19, 1934, Associated Press article.
66. *Milwaukee Journal,* October 16, 1934.
67. Ibid.
68. Ibid.
69. Cole, "Ersatz Octobers," p. 88.
70. *Philadelphia Inquirer,* October 16, 1934.
71. Ibid.
72. *Los Angeles Times,* October 17, 1934, Associated Press article.
73. Ibid.
74. Lanctot, *Negro League Baseball,* p. 5.
75. Holway, *Complete Book,* p. 306.
76. Holway, *Blackball Stars,* p. 201.
77. *Philadelphia Inquirer,* October 16, 1934.
78. *Philadelphia Record,* October 16, 1934.
79. *Brooklyn Eagle,* October 18, 1934.

80. *New York World-Telegram,* October 17, 1934, column by Dan Daniel.

81. *New York Daily News,* October 17, 1934.

82. Ibid., column by Jimmy Powers.

83. E-mail from Brooklyn Historical Society, November 2008.

84. *Brooklyn Eagle,* October 18, 1934.

85. Ibid.

86. Ibid.

87. *New York Herald Tribune,* October 18, 1934.

88. *New York World-Telegram,* October 18, 1934.

89. Ibid.

90. *Brooklyn Eagle,* October 18, 1934.

91. Ibid.

92. Gregory, *Diz,* p. 242.

93. John Holway, Society for American Baseball Research, *Baseball Journal,* Beckwith entry.

94. Ibid.

95. *Brooklyn Eagle,* October 18, 1934.

96. *Baltimore Sun,* October 18, 1934.

97. *Columbus Dispatch,* October 21, 1934, Associated Press article.

98. *Paterson Morning News,* October 20, 1934.

99. Ibid.

100. *Pittsburgh Courier,* October 13, 1934.

101. *Cleveland News,* October 20, 1934.

102. *Cleveland Call and Post,* October 27, 1934.

103. *Cleveland News,* October 21, 1934.

104. Cleveland *Plain Dealer,* October 22, 1934.

105. *Cleveland News,* October 21, 1934.

106. Cleveland *Plain Dealer,* October 22, 1934.

107. Ibid.

108. Cleveland *Plain Dealer,* October 22, 1934.

109. *Cleveland Call and Post,* October 27, 1934.

110. *Cleveland News,* October 21, 1934.

111. Cleveland *Plain Dealer,* October 22, 1934.

112. *Cleveland Call and Post,* October 27, 1934.

113. Ibid.

114. Cleveland *Plain Dealer,* October 23, 1934.

115. *Philadelphia Bulletin,* August 13, 1968.

116. *Columbus Dispatch,* October 22, 1934.

117. *Sporting News,* September 29, 1948.

118. Hogan, ed., *Shades of Glory,* p. 272.

119. *Columbus Dispatch,* October 23, 1934.

120. Taped interview with Monte Irvin, Hall of Fame.

121. *Columbus Dispatch,* October 23, 1934.

122. Holway, *Blackball Stars,* p. 115.

123. Ibid.

124. *Pittsburgh Press,* October 24, 1934.

125. Holway, *Complete Book,* p. 108.

126. Irvin, *Few and Chosen,* p. 83.

127. Holway, *Josh and Satch,* p. 68.

128. Holway, *Complete Book,* p. 315.

129. *Pittsburgh Post-Gazette,* October 24, 1934.

130. Holway, *Complete Book,* p. 315.

131. Holway, *Josh and Satch,* pp. 68–69.

132. *Pittsburgh Post-Gazette,* October 24, 1934.

133. E-mail from Rooney biographer Rob Ruck, November 14, 2006.

134. Paige, *Maybe I'll Pitch Forever,* p. 92.

135. Staten, *Ol' Diz,* pp. 154–55.

136. Ibid., p. 155.

137. Ibid.

138. *New York Sun,* November 3, 1934.

139. Staten, *Ol' Diz,* p. 155.

140. Ibid., p. 157.

141. Ibid.

142. *Chicago Daily Tribune,* December 6, 1934.

143. *New York Times,* April 5, 1992.

144. Robert Smith, *Baseball in the Afternoon: Tales from a Bygone Era,* p. 423.

145. A special Negro Leagues committee that produced *Shades of Glory.*

146. Holway, *Josh and Satch,* p. 69.

147. *Collier's Magazine,* June 6, 1953.

148. Heaphy, ed., *Satchel Paige and Company,* pp. 82–83.

149. Ibid.

150. Holway, *Josh and Satch,* p. 69.

151. *Saturday Evening Post,* July 27, 1940, article by Ted Shane.

152. Ribowsky, *Don't Look Back,* p. 121.

153. Diamondangle.com, Berger recollection.

154. Ribowsky, *Don't Look Back,* p. 121.

155. Ibid.

CHAPTER FIVE: ENCORE: DIZ, DAFFY, AND SATCH DO IT AGAIN

1. Holway, *Complete Book,* p. 322.

2. Holway, *Black Diamonds,* p. 108.

3. Holway, *Complete Book,* p. 322.

4. *Chicago Defender,* October 26, 1935.

5. *Chicago Daily News,* June 18, 1943, as quoted in PitchBlackBaseball.com.

6. Heaphy, ed., *Satchel Paige and Company,* p. 60.

7. Ibid., p. 63.

8. Ibid., p. 209.
9. PitchBlackBaseball.com, North Dakota's Integrated Baseball History, research by Kyle McNary.
10. Heaphy, ed., *Satchel Paige and Company*, p. 60.
11. Ribowsky, *Don't Look Back*, p. 127.
12. Heaphy, ed., *Satchel Paige and Company*, p. 91.
13. Kancoll.org, William Allen White entry.
14. PitchBlackBaseball.com, North Dakota's Integrated Baseball History, "1935: National Champs."
15. Ibid.
16. Ribowsky, *Don't Look Back*, p. 130.
17. Ibid.
18. Heaphy, ed., *Satchel Paige and Company*, p. 93.
19. PitchBlackBaseball.com, North Dakota's Integrated Baseball History, "1935: National Champs."
20. Ibid.
21. Ibid.
22. Ibid.
23. Ibid.
24. Ibid.
25. *Bismarck Tribune,* August 24, 1935.
26. Heaphy, ed., *Satchel Paige and Company*, p. 90.
27. PitchBlackBaseball.com, North Dakota's Integrated Baseball History, "1935: National Champs."
28. *Washington Post,* October 9, 1935, Associated Press article.
29. *Joplin (Mo.) Globe,* October 9, 1935.
30. Holway, *Voices,* p. 100.
31. *Springfield (Mo.) Leader & Press,* October 2, 1935.
32. Ibid.
33. Ibid.
34. Ibid.
35. *Columbia (Mo.) Daily Tribune,* September 30, 1935.
36. Ibid., October 2, 1935.
37. Ibid.
38. Ibid.
39. Ibid., October 3, 1935.
40. Ibid.
41. *Tulsa Daily World,* October 3, 1935.
42. Ibid.
43. Ibid., October 4, 1935.
44. Ibid.
45. Ibid.
46. Ibid.
47. Ibid.

48. Ibid.
49. Tygiel, *Extra Bases,* p. 65.
50. *Enid (Okla.) Daily News,* December 9, 1921.
51. *Joplin (Mo.) Globe,* October 6, 1935.
52. *Enid (Okla.) Morning News,* October 5, 1935.
53. Ibid.
54. Ibid.
55. Gregory, *Diz,* p. 301.
56. *Enid (Okla.) Morning News,* October 5, 1935.
57. Joplin Public Library.org.
58. Harvard Gazette Online, April 16, 2009, article by Corydon Ireland.
59. *Joplin (Mo.) News-Herald,* October 5, 1935.
60. *Joplin (Mo.) Globe,* October 5, 1935.
61. Ibid.
62. *Kansas City Star,* October 4, 1935.
63. *Washington Post,* October 9, 1935, Associated Press article.
64. Holway, *Josh and Satch,* p. 83.
65. *Dayton Daily News,* October 10, 1935.
66. Holway, *Complete Book,* p. 323.
67. Holway, *Josh and Satch,* p. 67.
68. Holway, *Voices,* p. 124.
69. Ibid.
70. Holway, *Complete Book,* p. 323.
71. Ibid.
72. *New York Daily News,* May 21, 1937.
73. Holway, *Josh and Satch,* p. 68.
74. Ibid., p. 74.
75. Holway, *Voices,* p. 87.
76. *York Dispatch,* October 13, 1935.
77. Baseball-records.com, Dandridge entry.
78. Holway, *Complete Book,* p. 324.
79. *Los Angeles Herald and Express,* October 23, 1935.
80. *Sporting News,* October 31, 1935.
81. Gregory, *Diz,* p. 278.
82. *Los Angeles Herald and Express,* October 23, 1935.
83. As quoted in Gregory, p. 279.
84. *Dallas Morning News,* October 21, 1935.
85. *Los Angeles Times,* October 24, 1935.
86. Ibid., October 30, 1935.
87. Ibid., October 28, 1935.
88. Ibid., October 29, 1935.
89. Gregory, *Diz,* p. 279.
90. *Los Angeles Times,* October 30, 1935.
91. Ibid.

92. Ibid., October 31, 1935.
93. Ibid.
94. Ibid.
95. *Washington Post,* July 31, 1940, column by Bob Considine.
96. *Los Angeles Times,* November 1, 1935.
97. Ibid.
98. Ibid.
99. Ibid., November 3, 1935.
100. Ibid.
101. Ibid.
102. Gregory, *Diz,* p. 279.

CHAPTER SIX: GO WEST, YOUNG MEN

1. As quoted in Reisler, *Black Writers/Black Baseball,* p. 12.
2. Warren A. Beck and David A. Williams, *California: A History of the Golden State,* p. 234.
3. McNeil, *The California Winter League,* p. 12.
4. Interview with Ralph Kiner, December 2006.
5. Ibid.
6. Ibid.
7. McNeil, *The California Winter League,* p. 14.
8. Interview with Bill McNeil, March 2007.
9. Interview with Ralph Kiner, December 2006.
10. McNeil, pp. 144–46.
11. *Washington Post,* October 27, 1937.
12. McNeil, *The California Winter League,* p. 66.
13. Ibid.
14. Ibid., p. 67.
15. *California Eagle,* December 16, 1927.
16. *Chicago Defender,* November 7, 1931.
17. Ibid., October 31, 1931.
18. McNeil, *The California Winter League,* p. 155.
19. *Chicago Defender,* October 24, 1931.
20. Ibid., November 7, 1931.
21. McNeil, *The California Winter League,* p. 163.
22. Ibid., p. 160.
23. Baseball-records.com, Pullman Porter entry.
24. McNeil, *The California Winter League,* p. 160.
25. Ibid., p. 157.
26. *California Eagle,* January 6, 1933.
27. McNeil, *The California Winter League,* p. 164.
28. Tye, *Satchel,* p. 87.
29. *Chicago Defender,* November 4, 1933.

30. *Pittsburgh Courier,* November 11, 1933.
31. *Los Angeles Times,* November 13, 1933.
32. Ibid.
33. McNeil, *The California Winter League,* p. 166.
34. Irvin, *Few and Chosen,* p. 41.
35. Ibid., p. 42.
36. Ibid., p. 115.
37. *Chicago Defender,* February 2, 1935.
38. Recordholders.org, 100-yard dash running backward.
39. *California Eagle,* November 15, 1935.
40. *Collier's,* May 30, 1953.
41. Holway, *Complete Book,* p. 324.
42. Ribowsky, *Don't Look Back,* p. 137.
43. *Collier's,* May 30, 1953.
44. Ribowsky, *Complete History,* p. 199.
45. *Daily Worker,* September 13, 1937.
46. *Chicago Defender,* January 8, 1938.
47. As quoted in Kathryn Long Humphrey, *Satchel Paige,* p. 36.
48. Tye, *Satchel,* p. 87.

CHAPTER SEVEN: RAPID ROBERT MEETS SATCH

1. Interview between Mike Wallace and Bob Feller, CBS-TV, 1957 (You-Tube).
2. *Sports Illustrated,* August 4, 2005, article by Frank Deford.
3. John Sickels, *Bob Feller: Ace of the Greatest Generation,* p. 35.
4. Interview with Bob Feller, March 2007, Winter Haven, Florida.
5. Interview with Trey Armistead, November 2007, teacher, Van Meter High School.
6. Ibid.
7. Sickels, *Bob Feller,* p. 7.
8. Gene Schoor, *Bob Feller: Hall of Fame Strikeout Star,* p. 8.
9. Sickels, *Bob Feller,* p. 7.
10. Ibid., p. 12.
11. Interview with Bob Feller, March 2007, Winter Haven, Florida.
12. *Look,* March 6, 1956, p. 39.
13. Vincent, *The Only Game in Town,* p. 46.
14. Bob Feller with Bill Gilbert, *Now Pitching: Bob Feller,* p. 140.
15. Sickels, *Bob Feller,* p. 17.
16. Ibid., pp. 18–24.
17. Ibid., p. 25.
18. Ibid.
19. Feller with Gilbert, *Now Pitching,* pp. 37–38.
20. Sickels, *Bob Feller,* p. 29.

21. Ibid., p. 33.
22. *Look,* March 6, 1958, p. 38.
23. Ibid.
24. *Life,* May 12, 1941, article by St. Clair McElway.
25. Sickels, *Bob Feller,* pp. 50–52.
26. Ibid., pp. 52–54.
27. Barthel, *Baseball Barnstorming,* p. 141.
28. Heaphy, ed., *Satchel Paige and Company,* p. 66.
29. Holway, *Complete Book,* p. 333.
30. Bruce, *The Kansas City Monarchs,* p. 40.
31. Leslie A. Heaphy, *The Negro Leagues, 1869–1960,* p. 115.
32. *Des Moines Register,* October 3, 1936.
33. *Davenport Daily Times,* October 5, 1936.
34. *Denver Post,* October 6, 1936.
35. *Des Moines Register,* October 7, 1936.
36. Ibid.
37. Ibid.
38. Barthel, *Baseball Barnstorming,* p. 142.
39. *Des Moines Register,* October 7, 1936.
40. Ibid.
41. Satchel Paige with Hal Lebovitz, *Pitchin' Man,* p. 73.
42. Bob Peterson's taped interview with Jimmy Crutchfield, Hall of Fame.
43. Holway, *Voices,* p. 101.
44. *Des Moines Register,* October 8, 1936.
45. Ibid.
46. Ibid.
47. Ibid.
48. Holway, *Complete Book,* p. 333.
49. Ibid., p. 334.
50. *Sporting News,* November 12, 1936.
51. Ibid., October 8, 1936.
52. Gregory, *Diz,* p. 302.
53. *Los Angeles Times,* October 1, 1936.
54. Ibid., October 4, 1936.
55. Ibid., October 5, 1936.
56. Ibid.
57. *San Francisco Chronicle,* October 6, 1936.
58. *Los Angeles Times,* October 16, 1936.

CHAPTER EIGHT: BOBBY AND SATCH

1. *Los Angeles Times,* September 25, 1937.
2. *Sporting News,* October 21, 1937.
3. *Davenport Daily Times,* October 6, 1937.

4. *Des Moines Register,* October 6, 1937.

5. *Wichita Eagle,* October 10, 1937.

6. Ibid.

7. *Davenport Daily Times,* October 6, 1937.

8. Ibid.

9. Ibid.

10. *Des Moines Register,* October 8, 1937.

11. Holway, *Complete Book,* p. 349.

12. *Manhattan Mercury,* October 6, 1937.

13. Ibid., October 11, 1937.

14. *Wichita Eagle,* October 11, 1937.

15. Ibid.

16. Ibid.

17. *Daily Oklahoman,* October 12, 1937.

18. Ibid.

19. Ibid.

20. Ibid.

21. *Los Angeles Times,* October 12, 1937.

22. Ibid.

23. Interview with Bob Feller, March 2007.

24. *Los Angeles Times,* October 13, 1937.

25. Ibid.

26. *Sporting News,* October 21, 1937.

27. Gay, *Tris Speaker,* pp. 266–69.

28. *Los Angeles Times,* October 14, 1937.

29. Holway, *Complete Book,* p. 337.

30. Ibid.

31. *Journal of Sport History,* 20, no. 1 (Spring 1993), review of *Sugar Ball: The American Game, the Dominican Dream,* by Alan Klein.

32. Holway, *Complete Book,* p. 346.

33. Ibid.

34. As quoted in Gregory, *Diz,* p. 338.

35. McNeil, *The California Winter League,* p. 189.

36. Ibid., p. 186.

37. *Los Angeles Times,* October 11, 1939.

38. Ibid.

39. Ibid.

40. Ibid., October 10, 1939.

41. McNeil, *The California Winter League,* p. 196.

42. Barthel, *Baseball Barnstorming,* p. 132.

43. Baseball-almanac.com, Dizzy Dean quotations.

44. As quoted in Gregory, *Diz,* p. 355.

45. Barthel, *Baseball Barnstorming,* p. 132.

46. Staten, *Ol' Diz,* p. 205.

47. *Time*, April 24, 1950.
48. As quoted in Staten, *Ol' Diz*, p. 221.
49. Ibid., p. 222.
50. Ibid., p. 219.
51. Ibid., p. 220.
52. Ibid., p. 18.
53. As quoted in ibid., p. 221.
54. As quoted in ibid., p. 220.
55. Ibid., p. 220.
56. McNeil, pp. 215–16.
57. Barthel, *Baseball Barnstorming*, p. 144.
58. *St. Louis Globe-Democrat*, October 6, 1941, article by Robert L. Burnes.
59. Ibid.

CHAPTER NINE: BLACK-WHITE BALL GOES TO WAR

1. As quoted in Holway, *Voices*, p. 312.
2. Interview with Mickey Vernon, February 2007.
3. Reisler, *Black Writers/Black Baseball*, p. 91.
4. *Chicago Defender*, January 20, 1945.
5. Gregory, *Diz*, p. 376.
6. Ibid.
7. As quoted in Bruce, *The Kansas City Monarchs*, pp. 108–9.
8. Tygiel, *Extra Bases*, p. 69.
9. Ibid., p. 74.
10. Ibid., p. 69.
11. Baseballlibrary.com, Bonura entry.
12. *Stars and Stripes*, October 25, 1943, North African edition.
13. Ibid.
14. Ibid.
15. 76thDivision.com.
16. Kirkpatrick, *Cecil Travis*, p. 122.
17. Metcalfe, *A Game for All Races*, pp. 115–18.
18. historyplace.com/worldwar2/triumph/tr-will.htm.
19. Rogosin, *Invisible Men*, p. 57.
20. Metcalfe, *A Game for All Races*, pp. 115–18.
21. Ibid.
22. Holway, *Voices*, pp. 307–13.
23. Ibid.
24. Ibid.
25. Ibid.
26. historynet.com/african-american-92nd-infantry-division.
27. Interview with Bob Feller, March 2007.
28. Feller with Gilbert, *Now Pitching*, p. 117.

29. *New Yorker,* May 11, 1946, article by Eugene Kinkead.
30. Ibid.
31. Ibid.
32. Feller with Gilbert, *Now Pitching,* pp. 117–19.
33. Vincent, *The Only Game in Town,* p. 44.

CHAPTER TEN: FELLER AND SATCH CELEBRATE V-J DAY

1. *Boston Globe,* July 21, 1945.
2. Roosevelt.edu/Chicagohistory.
3. Interview with Michael Flug, December 2006.
4. *Journal of Social History,* Spring 1998.
5. Bruce, *The Kansas City Monarchs,* p. 111.
6. Ibid., pp. 111–12.
7. *Pittsburgh Courier,* September 26, 1946.
8. Organization of American Historians website, "The Negro Leagues," by Jules Tygiel.
9. Holway, *Complete Book,* referenced in foreword by Buck O'Neil, p. 7.
10. Reisler, *Black Writers/Black Baseball,* p. 134.
11. Interview with Monte Irvin, February 2007.
12. Frazier "Slow" Robinson, *Catching Dreams,* p. 124.
13. Alexander, *Breaking the Slump,* p. 226.
14. Ribowsky, *Don't Look Back,* pp. 197–203.
15. Dixon and Hannigan, *The Negro Baseball Leagues,* p. 11.
16. Heaphy, ed., *Satchel Paige and Company,* p. 16.
17. Feller with Gilbert, *Now Pitching,* p. 120.
18. *Moline (Ill.) Daily Dispatch,* May 19, 1945.
19. Ibid.
20. Barthel, *Baseball Barnstorming,* p. 145.
21. Vincent, *The Only Game in Town,* p. 45.
22. Sickels, *Bob Feller,* p. 136.
23. *Los Angeles Times,* September 16, 1945.
24. Cole, "Ersatz Octobers," p. 90.
25. Holway, *Complete Book,* p. 428.
26. Barthel, *Baseball Barnstorming,* p. 146.
27. *Pittsburgh Courier,* September 26, 1945.
28. *Los Angeles Times,* September 30, 1945.
29. Ibid.
30. *Seattle Post-Intelligencer,* October 5, 1945.
31. McNeil, *The California Winter League,* p. 237.
32. Ibid., p. 238.
33. Ibid., p. 239.
34. Ibid., p. 221.
35. *Chicago Defender,* October 13, 1945.

36. Holway, *Complete Book,* p. 428.

37. *Chicago Defender,* October 13, 1945.

38. *Los Angeles Times,* October 3, 1945.

39. *Chicago Defender,* October 13, 1945.

40. As quoted in Sickels, *Bob Feller,* p. 158.

41. As quoted in Tygiel, *Baseball's Great Experiment,* p. 76.

42. *Chicago Defender,* November 10, 1945, column by Al Monroe.

43. *Pittsburgh Courier,* September 21, 1946.

44. *Sporting News,* October 30, 1946.

45. Feller with Gilbert, *Now Pitching,* p. 141.

46. Ribowsky, *Don't Look Back,* p. 242.

47. *Chicago Defender,* November 9, 1946.

48. Tygiel, *Baseball's Great Experiment,* p. 76.

49. Sickels, *Bob Feller,* p. 160.

50. *Saturday Evening Post,* January 27, 1962.

51. Sickels, *Bob Feller,* p. 157.

52. Ibid., p. 161.

53. Joe Posnanski, *The Soul of Baseball: A Road Trip Through Buck O'Neil's America,* p. 113.

54. Sickels, *Bob Feller,* pp. 260–61.

55. Interview with Bob Feller, March 2007.

56. *San Francisco Chronicle,* October 4, 1945.

57. *Sporting News,* October 11, 1945.

58. *Seattle Times,* October 7, 1945.

59. *Seattle Post-Intelligencer,* October 7, 1945.

60. *Wenatchee (Wash.) World,* October 8, 1945.

61. Ibid., October 9, 1945.

62. Ibid.

63. Humphrey, *Satchel Paige,* p. 53.

64. *Sporting News,* October 11, 1945.

65. Ibid.

66. Ibid., November 1, 1945.

67. Ibid.

68. Ibid.

69. Ibid.

CHAPTER ELEVEN: GOING AIRBORNE: THE FELLER-PAIGE '46 TOUR

1. *Sporting News,* November 15, 1945.

2. Sickels, *Bob Feller,* pp. 137–39.

3. Interview with Mickey Vernon, February 2009.

4. Tygiel, *Baseball's Great Experiment,* p. 163.

5. Interview with Bob Feller, March 2007.

6. Sickels, *Bob Feller,* p. 151.
9. Feller with Gilbert, *Now Pitching,* p. 37.
8. *Washington Post,* June 20, 1947, column by Shirley Povich.
9. Feller with Gilbert, *Now Pitching,* p. 137.
10. *Cincinnati Enquirer,* October 1, 1946.
11. *Chicago Defender,* October 5, 1946.
12. Barthel, *Baseball Barnstorming,* p. 147.
13. Sickels, *Bob Feller,* p. 153–54.
14. Ibid., p. 154.
15. Holway, *Complete Book,* p. 440.
16. Ibid.
17. *Washington Post,* September 11, 1946.
18. Blacks in Wartime/Garybed.co.uk.negro.
19. Vincent, *The Only Game in Town,* p. 49.
20. Sickels, *Bob Feller,* p. 152.
21. *Cleveland News,* September 27, 1946, column by Ed McAuley.
22. Barthel, *Baseball Barnstorming,* p. 148.
23. *Chicago Defender,* September 28, 1946.
24. Ibid.
25. Cole, "Ersatz Octobers," p. 91.
26. *New York Times,* September 30, 1946.
27. *Pittsburgh Courier,* October 4, 1946.
28. Holway, *Complete Book,* p. 441.
29. *Cleveland Call and Post,* October 5, 1946.
30. Cleveland *Plain Dealer,* October 2, 1946.
31. BaseballLibrary.com, Artie Wilson entry.
32. Vincent, *The Only Game in Town,* p. 47.
33. *Chicago Defender,* October 19, 1946, column by Fay Young.
34. Ibid.
35. *Cincinnati Enquirer,* October 3, 1946.
36. Vincent, *The Only Game in Town,* p. 47.
37. *New York Times,* October 5, 1946.
38. *Newark Star-Ledger,* October 6, 1946.
39. *Pittsburgh Courier,* October 12, 1946.
40. Holway, *Complete Book,* p. 441.
41. *New York Times,* October 7, 1946.
42. *Sporting News,* October 16, 1946.
43. *Newark Star-Ledger,* October 5, 1946.
44. *Newark Evening News,* October 7, 1946.
45. Ibid.
46. *Sporting News,* October 16, 1946.
47. E-mail from Richmond librarian Doris Ashbrook, October 2008.
48. *Richmond Palladium-Item,* October 11, 1946.
49. Ibid.
50. Ibid.

51. Ibid.
52. Ibid.
53. Ibid.
54. *Davenport Daily Times,* October 11, 1946.
55. Tye, *Satchel,* p. 172.
56. *New York Times,* October 14, 1946.
57. Holway, *Complete Book,* p. 442.
58. *Baseball Research Journal,* Society for American Baseball Research Archives, interview with Monte Irvin by James Riley.
59. Ibid.
60. Ibid.
61. Barthel, *Baseball Barnstorming,* p. 149.
62. *Long Beach Independent,* October 16, 1946.
63. Ibid.
64. Holway, *Complete Book,* p. 443.
65. *Los Angeles Times,* October 16, 1946.
66. Interview with Mickey Vernon, February 2007.
67. Ibid.
68. Ibid.
69. *Sporting News,* October 30, 1946.
70. *Los Angeles Times,* October 21, 1946.
71. McNeil, *The California Winter League,* p. 231.
72. Ibid.
73. *Sporting News,* November 6, 1946.
74. McNeil, *The California Winter League,* p. 231.
75. *Sporting News,* October 30, 1946.
76. Ibid., November 6, 1946.

CHAPTER TWELVE: BOBBY AND SATCH'S (ALMOST) FAREWELL TOUR

1. *Baltimore Afro-American,* August 16, 1947.
2. *Sporting News,* September 3, 1947.
3. *Los Angeles Times,* September 29, 1947.
4. Ibid.
5. Ibid., October 23, 1947.
6. Interview with Ralph Kiner, November 2006.
7. Barthel, *Baseball Barnstorming,* p. 154.
8. *Chicago Daily Tribune,* November 10, 1947, column by Arch Ward.
9. Interview with Bob Feller, March 2007.
10. *Sporting News,* October 29, 1947.
11. *Los Angeles Times,* October 10, 1947.
12. *New York Times,* October 14, 1947.
13. *Los Angeles Times,* October 15, 1947.
14. Ibid., October 23, 1947.

15. NegroLeagueBaseball.com, Piper Davis entry.
16. PitchBlackBaseball.com, Goose Tatum entry.
17. Baseball-reference.com, Jimmy Newberry entry.
18. *Los Angeles Times,* October 27, 1947.
19. Ibid.
20. Interview with Ralph Kiner, November 2006.
21. Ibid.
22. Paige, *Maybe I'll Pitch Forever,* p. 187.
23. *Los Angeles Times,* October 16, 1947.
24. Ibid.
25. *Sporting News,* October 29, 1947.
26. *Los Angeles Times,* October 20, 1947.
27. Paige, *Maybe I'll Pitch Forever,* p. 188.
28. *Sporting News,* October 29, 1947.
29. Cole, "Ersatz October," p. 91.
30. Interview with Ralph Kiner, November 2006.
31. *Sporting News,* December 12, 1947.
32. *Los Angeles Times,* October 30, 1947.
33. Ibid.
34. Sickels, *Bob Feller,* p. 179.
35. Ibid., p. 178.
36. Paige, *Maybe I'll Pitch Forever,* p. 189.
37. *Los Angeles Times,* November 3, 1947.
38. Ibid.
39. McNeil, *The California Winter League,* p. 233.
40. As quoted in Paige, *Maybe I'll Pitch Forever,* pp. 192–94.
41. *Sporting News,* November 12, 1947.
42. Sickels, p. 179.
43. *Sporting News,* December 12, 1947.

EPILOGUE: SATCH BECOMES A ROOKIE

1. Feller with Gilbert, *Now Pitching,* p. 216.
2. Ibid.
3. Humphrey, *Satchel Paige,* p. 57.
4. Paige, *Maybe I'll Pitch Forever,* p. 197.
5. Ibid.
6. Humphrey, *Satchel Paige,* p. 59.
7. Tye, *Satchel,* p. 206.
8. Paige, *Maybe I'll Pitch Forever,* p. 198.
9. Humphrey, *Satchel Paige,* p. 59.
10. Paige, *Maybe I'll Pitch Forever,* p. 199.
11. As quoted in Tye, *Satchel,* p. 207.
12. Ibid., pp. 207–208.
13. *Cleveland Plain Dealer,* July 10, 1948.

14. Paige, *Maybe I'll Pitch Forever,* pp. 209–10.
15. Feller with Gilbert, *Now Pitching,* p. 116.
16. *Chicago Daily Tribune,* February 7, 1949.
17. Paige, *Maybe I'll Pitch Forever,* p. 212.
18. As quoted in Tye, *Satchel,* p. 211.
19. *Chicago Defender,* February 26, 1949.
20. BaseballHallofFame.org.
21. Tye, *Satchel,* pp. 216–17.
22. Ibid., p. 213.
23. *Sporting News,* February 26, 1949.
24. Feller with Gilbert, *Now Pitching,* p. 150.
25. *Chicago Daily Tribune,* November 3, 1948, column by Arch Ward.
26. *Sporting News,* November 17, 1948.
27. Ibid., November 9, 1949.
28. *Los Angeles Times,* November 1, 1948.
29. *Sporting News,* November 9, 1949.
30. Ibid.
31. *Los Angeles Times,* October 27, 1949.
32. *Sporting News,* November 9, 1949.
33. Sickels, pp. 275–78.
34. Baseball-almanac.com, Browns entry.
35. Tye, *Satchel,* pp. 246–47.
36. *Time,* August 23, 1968.
37. Staten, *Ol' Diz,* pp. 245–50.
38. Barthel, *Baseball Barnstorming,* p. 158.
39. Ibid., p. 169.
40. Ibid., p. 170.
41. Cole, "Ersatz Octobers," p. 75.
42. Ibid., p. 76.
43. Ibid.
44. BaseballHallofFame.org, Dean acceptance remarks.
45. Ibid., Williams acceptance remarks.
46. ClevelandIndianssgblogspot.com.
47. *New York Times,* August 10, 1971.
48. Holway, *Complete Book,* p. 383.
49. Posnanski, *The Soul of Baseball,* p. 177.
50. E-mail from Barry Lewis of the *Tulsa World,* March 2009.
51. *Tulsa World,* July 9, 1973.
52. Ibid.
53. *Washington Post,* June 10, 1982.
54. Baseball-almanac.com.
55. *Newsweek,* July 29, 1974.
56. *Birmingham Weekly,* interview with Allen Barra, 198.
57. *Los Angeles Times,* June 10, 1982, column by Jim Murray.
58. Interview with Rich Marons, May 2008.

Bibliography

UNPUBLISHED SOURCES

Armistead, Trey, teacher at Van Meter, Iowa High School. Interviewed by author, November 2007.

Barra, Allen, baseball historian. Interviewed by author, September 2009.

Barthel, Thomas, baseball barnstorming expert. Interviewed by author, January 2007.

Black, Timuel, Chicago Black Belt resident and folklorist. Interviewed by author, November 2007.

Bozeman, Alma, daughter of Paul Dean. Interviewed by author, March 2008.

Bozeman, Gary, grandson of Paul Dean. Interviewed by author, March 2008.

Carreno, Sesar, Los Angeles history scholar. Interviewed by author, March 2007.

Clark, Dick, Negro Leagues scholar. Interviewed by author, December 2006 and January 2007.

Clawsen, Chuck, Warren County, Pa., native and former sandlot catcher. Interviewed by author, February 2009.

Dickson, Paul, baseball author and scholar. Interviewed by author, November 2006 and February 2009.

Duckett, Mahlon, former Negro Leaguer. Interviewed by author, November 2006.

Evelyn, Lionel, former Negro Leaguer. Interviewed by author, October 2006.

Feller, Bob, Hall of Fame pitcher. Interviewed by author, March 2007, Winter Haven, Fla.

Flug, Michael, senior archivist, Chicago Public Library. Interviewed by author, January 2007.

Gates, Jim, Baseball Hall of Fame and Museum. Interviewed by author, June 2008.

Glenn, Stanley "Doc," president, Negro League Baseball Players Association. Interviewed by author, October 2006 and February 2007.

Hartig, Ed, official historian, Chicago Cubs. Interviewed by author, November 2007.

Heaphy, Leslie A., Negro Leagues scholar. Interviewed by author numerous times, 2007–2009.

Hogan, Larry, Negro Leagues scholar. Interviewed by author, October 2006 and January 2007.

Holway, John, Negro Leagues scholar. Interviewed by author numerous times, 2006–2009.

Irvin, Monte, Hall of Famer. Interviewed by author, February and March 2007.

Jones, Ben, Dizzy Dean scholar and interpreter. Interviewed by author numerous times, 2007–2009.

Kelly, David, historian and archivist, Library of Congress. Interviewed by author, October 2006 and March 2009.

Kiner, Ralph, Hall of Famer. Interviewed by author, December 2006.

Lanctot, Neil, Negro Leagues scholar and author. Interviewed by author, November 2006 and January 2007.

Luke, Bob, Negro Leagues scholar. Interviewed by author, October 2006.

McNeil, William, California Winter League scholar. Interviewed by author, March 2007.

Motley, Bob, former Negro Leagues umpire. Interviewed by author, June 2007.

Motley, Byron, son of Bob. Interviewed by author, June 2007.

Paige, Robert, son of Satchel Paige. Interviewed by author, April 2009.

Peterson, Peg, widow of Negro Leagues historian Robert Peterson. Interviewed by author, February 2007.

Peterson, Tom, son of Negro Leagues historian Robert Peterson. Interviewed by author, February 2007 and April 2009.

Ruck, Rob, University of Pittsburgh professor and multicultural scholar. Interviewed by author, December 2006 and January 2007.

Tye, Larry, Satchel Paige biographer. Interviewed by author, May 2007 and March 2009.

Tygiel, Jules, Negro League scholar. Interviewed by author, December 2006.

Vazquez, Armando, former Negro Leaguer. Interviewed by author, October 2006.

Vernon, John, former archivist, National Archives. Interviewed by author, March 2009.

Vernon, Mickey, former major leaguer. Interviewed by author, February 2007.

PUBLISHED SOURCES

Books

Alexander, Charles C. *Breaking the Slump: Baseball in the Depression Era*. New York: Columbia University Press, 2002.

Appel, Martin, and Burt Goldblatt. *Baseball's Best: The Hall of Fame Gallery*. New York: McGraw-Hill, 1977.

Astor, Gerald, ed. *The Baseball Hall of Fame 50th Anniversary Book*. New York: Prentice Hall, 1988.

Barthel, Thomas. *Baseball Barnstorming and Exhibition Games, 1901–1962: A History of Off-Season Major League Play*. Jefferson, N.C.: McFarland, 2007.

Beck, Warren A., and David A. Williams. *California: A History of the Golden State*. Garden City, N.Y.: Doubleday, 1972.

Broeg, Bob. *Superstars of Baseball*. South Bend, Ind.: Diamond, 1994.

Bruce, Janet. *The Kansas City Monarchs: Champions of Black Baseball*. Lawrence: University Press of Kansas, 1985.

Decaneas, Anthony, ed. *Negro League Baseball*. New York: Abrams, 2004.

Dixon, Phil, with Patrick J. Hannigan. *The Negro Baseball Leagues*. Mattituck, N.Y.: Amereon House, 1992.

Eckhouse, Morris. *Baseball Legends: Bob Feller*. New York: Chelsea House, 1990.

Eig, Jonathan. *Opening Day: The Story of Jackie Robinson's First Season*. New York: Simon & Schuster, 2007.

Feller, Bob. *Bob Feller's Little Black Book of Baseball Wisdom*. Chicago: Contemporary, 2001.

———. *Bob Feller's Strikeout Story*. New York: Grosset & Dunlap, 1947.

Feller, Bob, with Bill Gilbert. *Now Pitching, Bob Feller*. New York: HarperCollins, 1990.

Franklin, John Hope. *From Slavery to Freedom: A History of African Americans*. New York: Knopf, 2000.

Gay, Timothy M. *Tris Speaker: The Rough-and-Tumble Life of a Baseball Legend*. Lincoln: University of Nebraska Press, 2005.

Gilbert, Tom. *Baseball and the Color Line*. New York: Franklin Watts, 1995.

Gregory, Robert. *Diz: The Story of Dizzy Dean and Baseball During the Great Depression*. New York: Penguin, 1992.

Heaphy, Leslie A. *The Negro Leagues, 1869–1960*. Jefferson, N.C.: McFarland, 2003.

Heaphy, Leslie A., ed. *Satchel Paige and Company: Essays on the Kansas City Monarchs, Their Greatest Star and the Negro Leagues*. Jefferson, N.C.: McFarland, 2007.

———. *The 10th Annual Jerry Malloy Negro League Conference*. Portsmouth, Va.: Souvenir, 2007.

Hogan, Lawrence D., ed. *Shades of Glory: The Negro Leagues and the Story of African-American Baseball*. Washington, D.C.: National Geographic Society, 2006.

Holway, John. *Blackball Stars: Negro League Pioneers*. Westport, Conn.: Meckler, 1988.

———. *Black Diamonds: Life in the Negro Leagues from the Men Who Lived It*. New York: Stadium, 1991.

———. *The Complete Book of Baseball's Negro Leagues: The Other Half of Baseball History*. Fern Park, Fla.: Hastings House, 2001.

———. *Josh and Satch: The Life and Times of Josh Gibson and Satchel Paige*. New York: Caroll & Graf, 1991.

———. *Voices from the Great Black Baseball Leagues*. New York: Dodd, Mead, 1975.

Humphrey, Kathryn Long. *Satchel Paige.* New York: Franklin Watts, 1988.

Kavanagh, Jack. *Baseball Legends: Dizzy Dean.* New York: Chelsea House, 1991.

Kirkpatrick, Rob. *Cecil Travis of the Washington Senators: The War-Torn Career of an All-Star Shortstop.* Jefferson, N.C.: McFarland, 2005.

Lanctot, Neil. *Negro League Baseball: The Rise and Ruin of a Black Institution.* Philadelphia: University of Pennsylvania Press, 2004.

Loverro, Thom. *Encyclopedia of Negro League Baseball.* New York: Facts on File, 2003.

Maraniss, David. *Clemente: The Passion and Grace of Baseball's Last Hero.* New York: Simon & Schuster, 2006.

McNary, Kyle. *Black Baseball: A History of African-Americans & the National Game.* New York: PRC, 2003.

McNeil, William F. *The California Winter League: America's First Integrated Professional Baseball League.* Jefferson, N.C.: McFarland, 2002.

Metcalfe, Henry. *A Game for All Races: An Illustrated History of the Negro Leagues.* New York: MetroBooks, 2000.

Montville, Leigh. *The Big Bam.* New York: Anchor, 2006.

Motley, Bob. *Ruling Over the Monarchs, Giants & Stars: Umpiring in the Negro Leagues and Beyond.* Champaign, Ill.: Sports Publishing, 2007.

Okrent, Daniel, and Lewine, Harris, eds. *The Ultimate Baseball Book.* Boston: Houghton Mifflin, 1979.

O'Neil, Buck. *I Was Right on Time: My Journey from the Negro Leagues to the Majors.* New York: Simon & Schuster, 1997.

Paige, Leroy (Satchel), with David Lipman. *Maybe I'll Pitch Forever.* Garden City, NY: Doubleday, 1962.

Paige, Leroy (Satchel), with Hal Lebovitz. *Pitchin' Man.* Reprint, Westport, Conn.: Meckler Books, 1992.

Peterson, Robert. *Only the Ball Was White: A History of Legendary Black Players and All-Black Professional Teams.* New York: Oxford University Press, 1970.

Pollock, Alan J. *Barnstorming to Heaven: Syd Pollock and His Great Black Teams.* Tuscaloosa: University of Alabama Press, 2006.

Posnanski, Joe. *The Soul of Baseball: A Road Trip Through Buck O'Neil's America.* New York: HarperCollins, 2007.

Powers, Jimmy. *Baseball Personalities: Vivid Stories of More Than 50 of the Most Colorful Ball Players of All Time.* New York: Rudolph Field, 1949.

Reichler, Joseph L., ed. *The Baseball Encyclopedia.* New York: Macmillan, 1969.

Reisler, Jim, ed. *Black Writers/Black Baseball: An Anthology of Articles from Black Sportswriters Who Covered the Negro Leagues.* Jefferson, N.C.: McFarland, 2007.

Ribowsky, Mark. *A Complete History of the Negro Leagues: 1884–1955.* New York: Citadel, 2002.

———. *Don't Look Back: Satchel Paige in the Shadows of Baseball.* New York: Simon & Schuster, 1994.

Riley, James A. *The Biographical Encyclopedia of the Negro Baseball Leagues.* New York: Carroll & Graf, 1994.

Ritter, Lawrence S. *The Glory of Their Times*. New York: Morrow, 1984.

Robinson, Frazier, with Paul Bauer. *Catching Dreams: My Life in the Negro Baseball Leagues*. Syracuse, N.Y.: Syracuse University Press, 1999.

Rogosin, Donn. *Invisible Men: Life in Baseball's Negro Leagues*. New York: Atheneum, 1983.

Ruck, Rob. *Sandlot Seasons: Sport in Black Pittsburgh*. Urbana: University of Illinois Press, 1993.

Safire, William. *Safire's New Political Dictionary: The Definitive Guide to the New Language of Politics*. New York: Random House, 1993.

Schoor, Gene. *Bob Feller: Hall of Fame Strikeout Star*. Garden City, NY: Doubleday, 1962.

Seymour, Harold. *Baseball: The Golden Age*. New York: Oxford University Press, 1971.

Shapiro, Milton J. *The Dizzy Dean Story*. New York: Messner, 1964.

Shirley, David. *Satchel Paige: Baseball Great*. New York: Chelsea House, 1993.

Sickels, John. *Bob Feller: Ace of the Greatest Generation*. Dulles, Va.: Potomac, 2004.

Smith, Curt. *America's Dizzy Dean*. St. Louis: Bethany, 1978.

Smith, Red. *Red Smith on Baseball: The Game's Greatest Writer on the Game's Greatest Years*. Chicago: Ivan R. Dee, 2000.

Smith, Robert. *Baseball in the Afternoon: Tales from a Bygone Era*. New York: Simon & Schuster, 1993.

Staten, Vince. *Ol' Diz: A Biography of Dizzy Dean*. New York: HarperCollins, 1992.

Stout, Glenn, and Richard Johnson. *Jackie Robinson: Between the Lines*. San Francisco: Woodford, 1997.

Trouppe, Quincy. *20 Years Too Soon: Prelude to Integrated Baseball*. St. Louis: Missouri Historical Society, 1995.

Tye, Larry. *Satchel: The Life and Times of an American Legend*. New York: Random House, 2009.

Tygiel, Jules. *Baseball's Great Experiment: Jackie Robinson and His Legacy*. New York: Vintage, 1983.

———. *Extra Bases: Reflections on Jackie Robinson, Race, & Baseball History*. Lincoln: University of Nebraska Press, 2002.

Vincent, Fay. *The Only Game in Town: Baseball Stars of the 1930s and 1940s Talk About the Game They Loved*. New York: Simon & Schuster, 2006.

———. *We Would Have Played for Nothing: Baseball Stars of the 1950s and 1960s Talk About the Game They Loved*. New York: Simon & Schuster, 2008.

Broadcast

Burns, Ken, director and writer, with Geoffrey C. Ward, writer. *Baseball*. PBS documentary that originally aired in 1994.

Colla, Richard, director, and Ronald Rubin, screenwriter. *Don't Look Back*. Made-for-television movie about Satchel Paige's life that originally aired in 1981.

Jones, Ben, producer, director, and writer. *Ol' Diz*. One-man show on the life of Dizzy Dean, originally performed in 2002.

Jones, Harmon, director, with Herman Mankiewicz, screenwriter. *The Pride of St. Louis*. Twentieth Century-Fox movie about the life of Dizzy Dean released in 1952.

Parrish, Robert, director with Robert Ardrey, screenwriter. *The Wonderful Country*. United Artists movie starring Robert Mitchum and Satchel Paige released in 1960.

Solarz, Ken, producer. *Only the Ball Was White*. Documentary about the Negro Leagues that was released in 1980; inspired by Robert Peterson's book.

Magazines and Journals

Baseball Digest
Baseball History 4
Bill Mazeroski's Baseball
Collier's
Ebony
Harvard Gazette Online
Holiday
Journal of Sport History
Life
Literary Digest
Look
National Review
Newsweek
New Yorker
New York Times Magazine
Nine
Reader's Digest
Saturday Evening Post
Saturday Review of Literature
Society for American Baseball Research: Negro Leagues Committee Newsletter (and other SABR publications)
Sport
Sporting News
Sports Illustrated
Time
U.S. News & World Report

Newspapers

Baltimore Afro-American
Baltimore Sun
Birmingham Weekly
Bismarck (N.D.) Tribune

Boston Globe
Brooklyn Eagle
Buffalo News
California Eagle
Chicago Daily News
Chicago Daily Times
Chicago Daily Tribune
Chicago Defender
Chicago Herald and Examiner
Chicago Sun
Cincinnati Enquirer
Cleveland Call and Post
Cleveland News
Cleveland *Plain Dealer*
Cleveland Press
Columbia (Mo.) Daily Tribune
Columbus Dispatch
Council Bluffs (Iowa) Daily Nonpareil
Daily Worker
Dallas Morning News
Davenport (Iowa) Daily Times
Dayton News
Denver Post
Des Moines Register
Detroit News
Enid (Okla.) Daily News
Enid (Okla.) Morning News
Fort Worth Star-Telegram
Hartford Courant
Houston Chronicle
Houston Post-Dispatch
Joplin (Mo.) Globe
Joplin (Mo.) News-Herald
Kansas City Call
Kansas City Star
Long Beach Independent
Los Angeles Examiner
Los Angeles Herald-Examiner
Los Angeles Herald and Express
Los Angeles Times
Louisville Courier
Manhattan (Kans.) Mercury
Mansfield (Ohio) News-Journal
McPherson (Kans.) Daily Republic

Miami Herald
Milwaukee Journal
Moline (Ill.) Daily Dispatch
Newark Evening News
Newark Star-Ledger
New York Daily Mirror
New York Daily News
New York Herald Tribune
New York Sun
New York Times
New York World-Telegram
Oakland Journal
Oklahoma City Daily Oklahoman
Omaha World-Herald
Oxford (Neb.) Standard
Paterson (N.J.) Evening News
Paterson (N.J.) Morning Call
Philadelphia Bulletin
Philadelphia Inquirer
Philadelphia News-American
Philadelphia Record
Pittsburgh Courier
Pittsburgh Post-Gazette
Pittsburgh Press
Richmond (Ind.) Palladium-Item
San Antonio Light
San Diego Union
San Francisco Chronicle
San Francisco Examiner
Seattle Post-Intelligencer
Seattle Times
Springfield (Mo.) Leader & Press
Stars and Stripes (North African edition, 1943)
St. Joseph's (Mo.) Gazette
St. Louis Globe-Democrat
St. Louis Post-Dispatch
St. Louis Star
Tulsa Daily World
USA Today
Washington Evening Star
Washington Post
Wenatchee (Wash.) World
Wichita Eagle
York (Pa.) Dispatch

Index